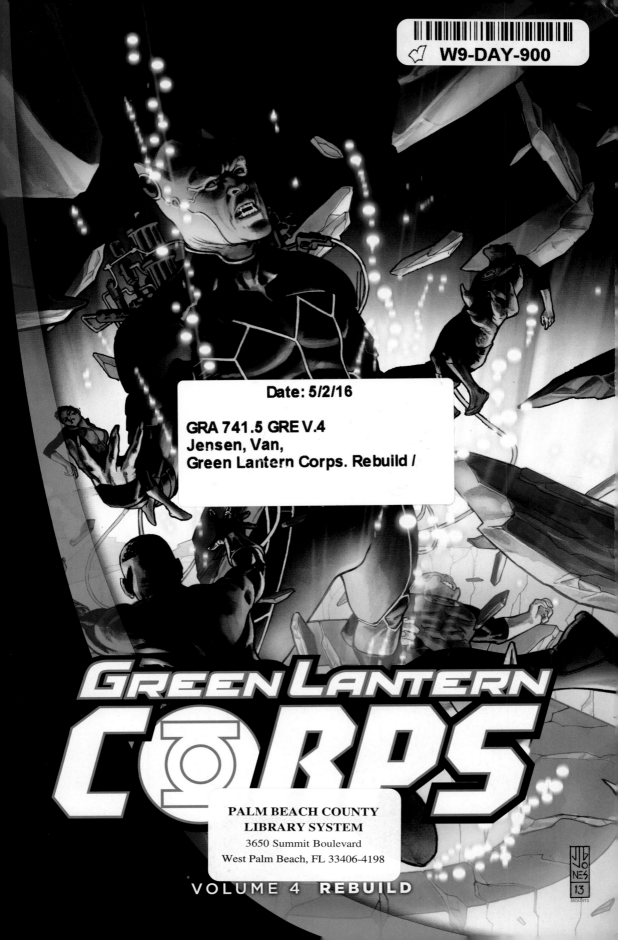

GREEN LANTERN CORPS

VOLUME 4 · REBUILD

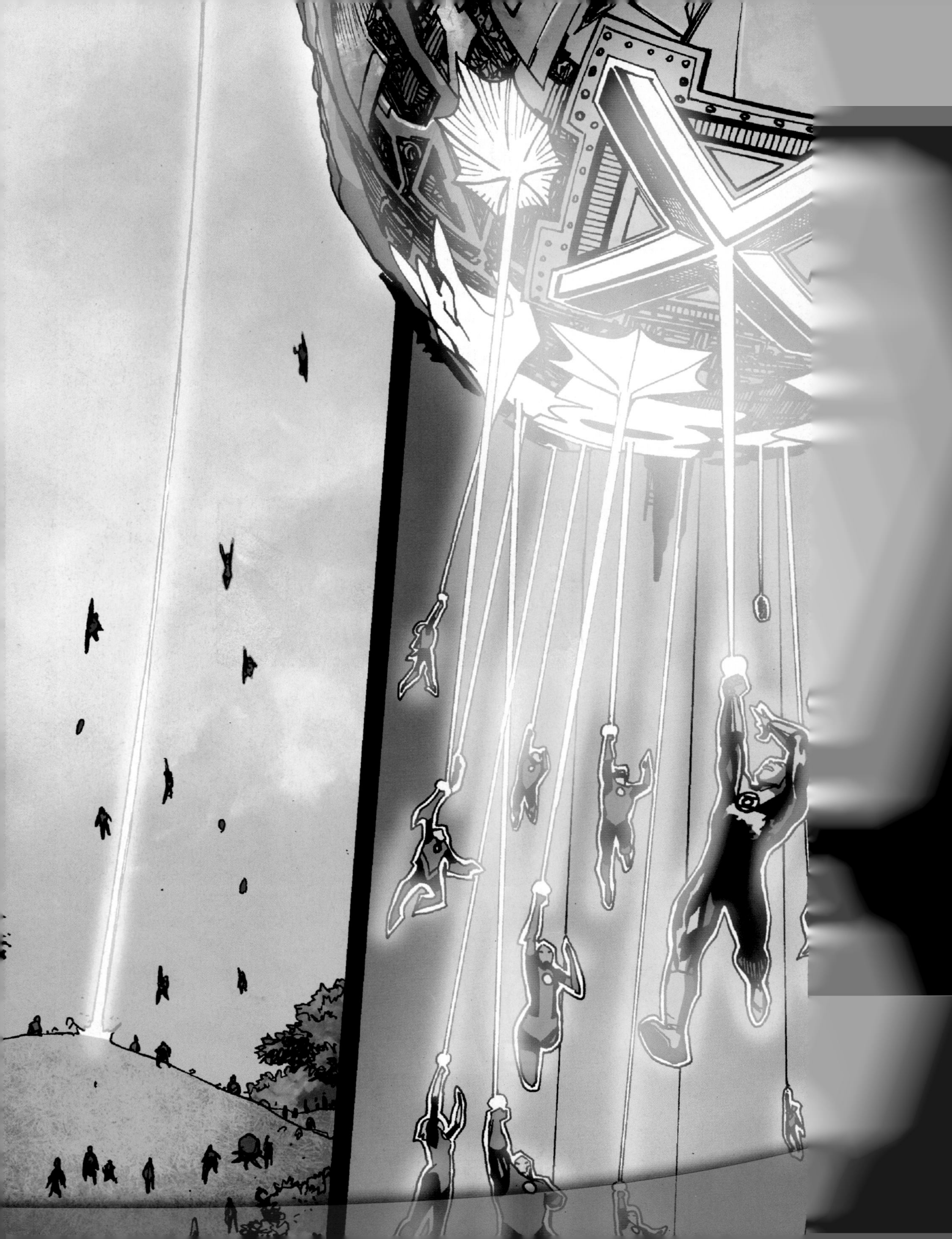

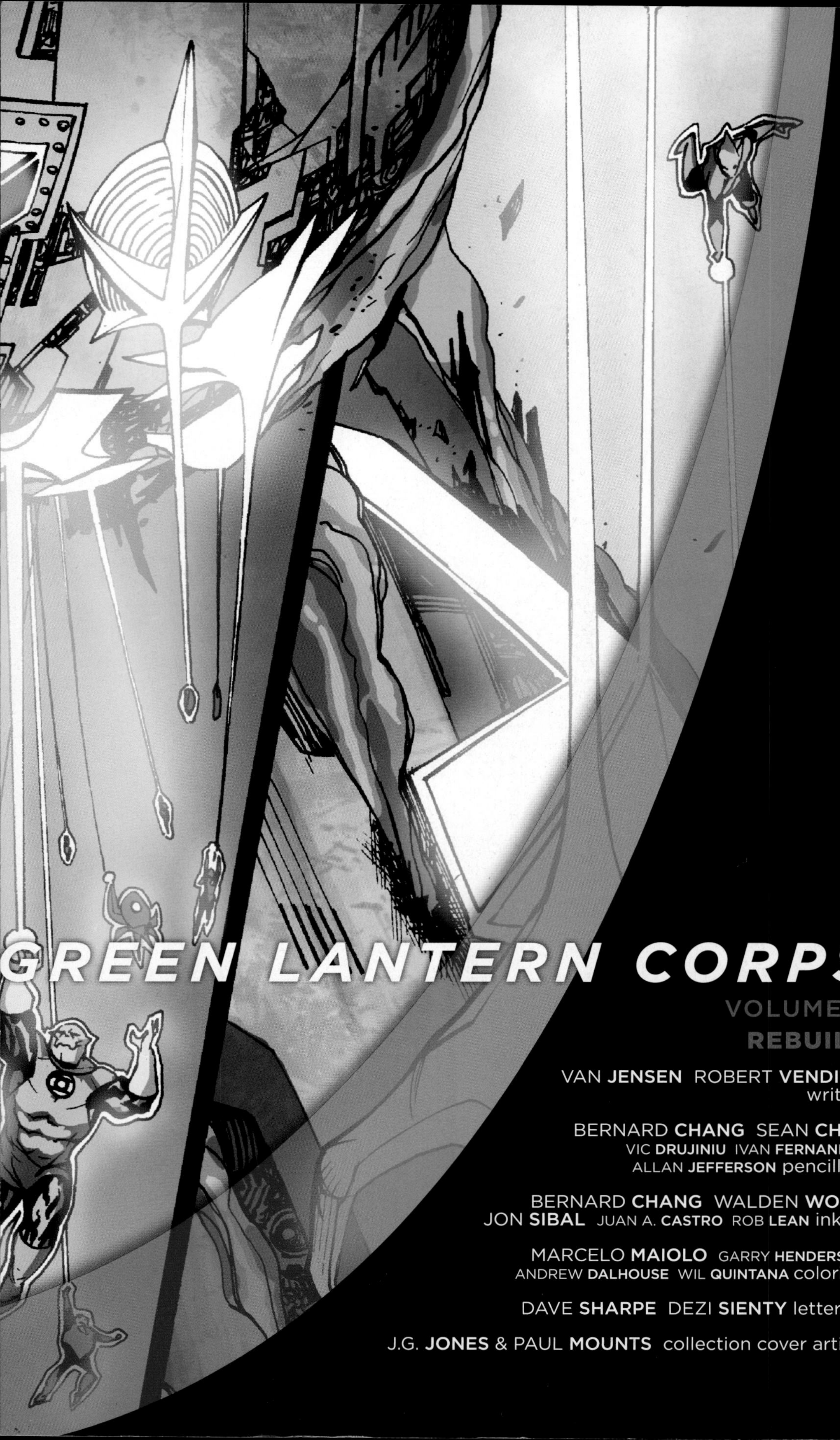

GREEN LANTERN CORPS

VOLUME 4
REBUILD

VAN **JENSEN** ROBERT **VENDITTI**
writers

BERNARD **CHANG** SEAN **CHEN**
VIC **DRUJINIU** IVAN **FERNANDEZ**
ALLAN **JEFFERSON** pencillers

BERNARD **CHANG** WALDEN **WONG**
JON **SIBAL** JUAN A. **CASTRO** ROB **LEAN** inkers

MARCELO **MAIOLO** GARRY **HENDERSON**
ANDREW **DALHOUSE** WIL **QUINTANA** colorists

DAVE **SHARPE** DEZI **SIENTY** letterers

J.G. **JONES** & PAUL **MOUNTS** collection cover artists

MATT IDELSON Editor – Original Series CHRIS CONROY Associate Editor – Original Series RACHEL PINNELAS Editor
ROBBIN BROSTERMAN Design Director – Books ROBBIE BIEDERMAN Publication Design

BOB HARRAS Senior VP – Editor-in-Chief, DC Comics

DIANE NELSON President DAN DIDIO and JIM LEE Co-Publishers GEOFF JOHNS Chief Creative Officer
AMIT DESAI Senior VP – Marketing and Franchise Management
AMY GENKINS Senior VP – Business and Legal Affairs NAIRI GARDINER Senior VP – Finance
JEFF BOISON VP – Publishing Planning MARK CHIARELLO VP – Art Direction and Design
JOHN CUNNINGHAM VP – Marketing TERRI CUNNINGHAM VP – Editorial Administration
LARRY GANEM VP – Talent Relations and Services ALISON GILL Senior VP – Manufacturing and Operations
HANK KANALZ Senior VP – Vertigo and Integrated Publishing JAY KOGAN VP – Business and Legal Affairs, Publishing
JACK MAHAN VP – Business Affairs, Talent NICK NAPOLITANO VP – Manufacturing Administration SUE POHJA VP – Book Sales
FRED RUIZ VP – Manufacturing Operations COURTNEY SIMMONS Senior VP – Publicity BOB WAYNE Senior VP – Sales

GREEN LANTERN CORPS VOLUME 4: REBUILD

DC Comics, 1700 Broadway, New York, NY 10019
A Warner Bros. Entertainment Company.
Printed by RR Donnelley, Salem, VA, USA. 5/30/14. First Printing.

ISBN: 978-1-4012-4745-4

SUSTAINABLE
FORESTRY
INITIATIVE

Certified Chain of Custody
20% Certified Forest Content,
80% Certified Sourcing
www.sfiprogram.org
SFI-01042
APPLIES TO TEXT STOCK ONLY

Library of Congress Cataloging-in-Publication Data

Library of Congress Cataloging-in-Publication Data

Venditti, Robert.
Green Lantern Corps. Volume 4, Rebuild / Robert Venditti, Van Jensen.
pages cm
ISBN 978-1-4012-4745-4 (paperback)
1. Graphic novels. I. Jensen, Van. II. Title. III. Title: Rebuild.
PN6728.G742V46 2014
741.5'973—dc23
2014010272

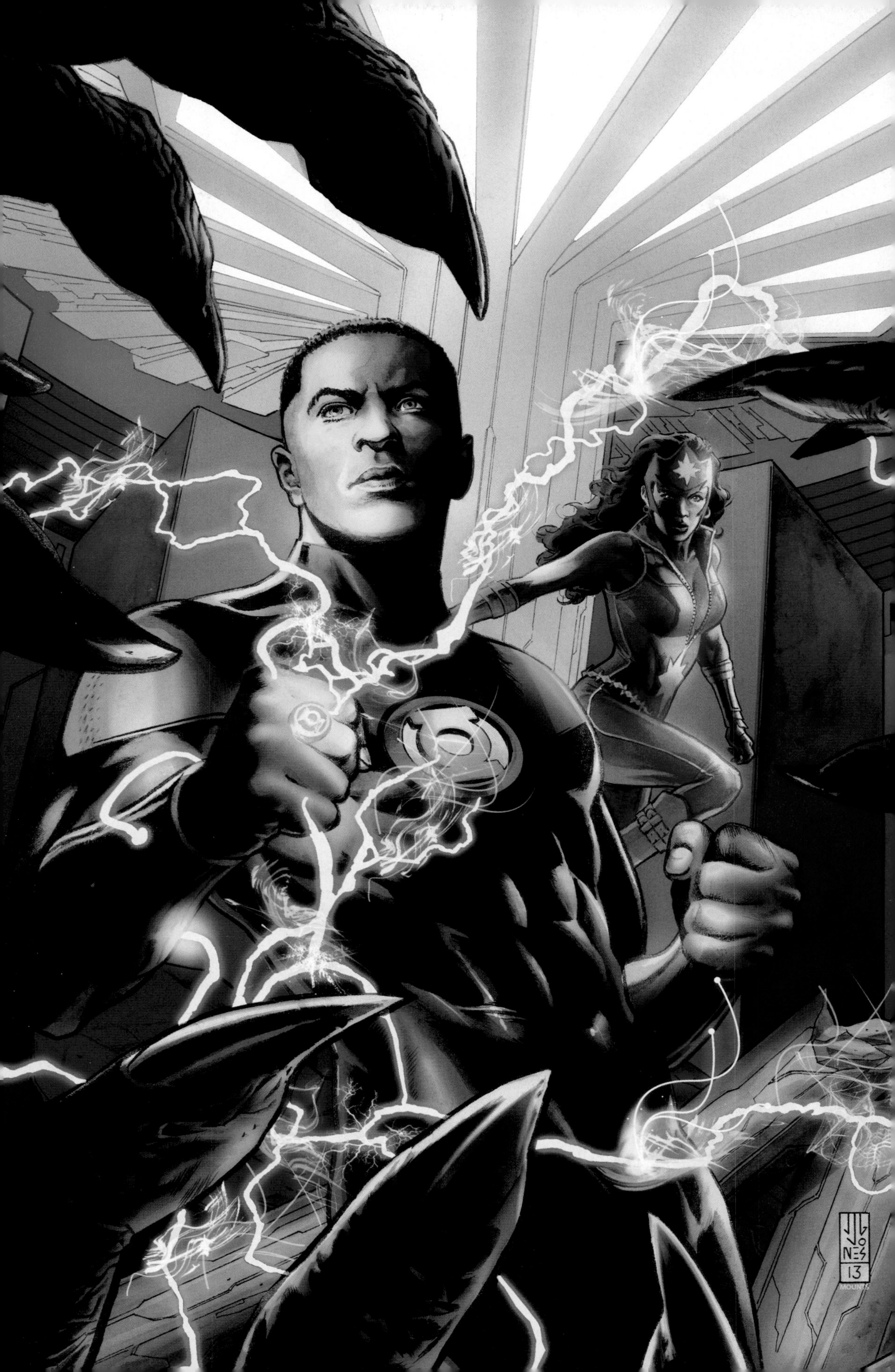

CHAIN REACTION

VAN JENSEN & ROBERT VENDITTI writers **BERNARD CHANG** artist cover art by **J.G. JONES & PAUL MOUNTS**
Relic variant cover pencils by **RAGS MORALES**

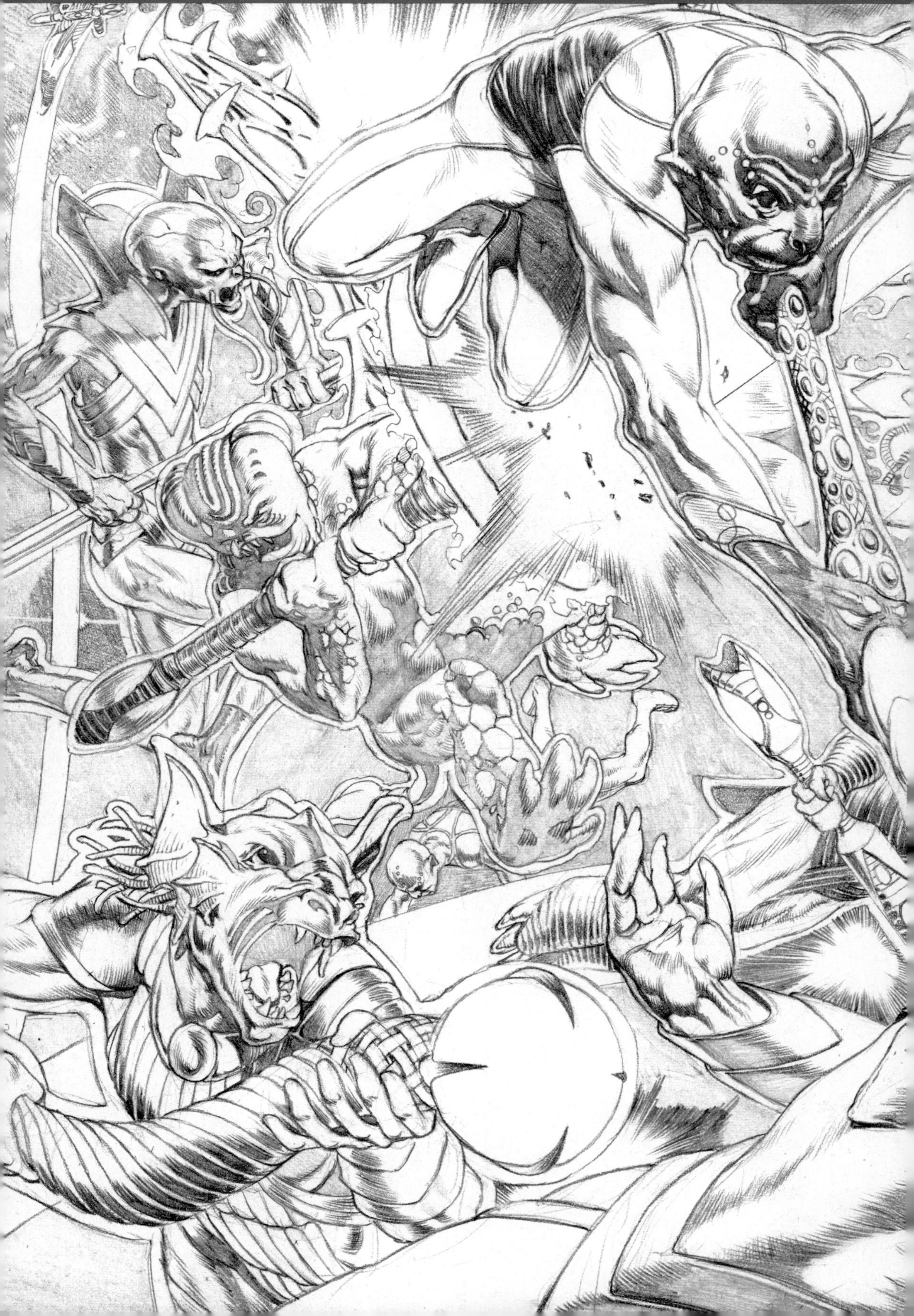

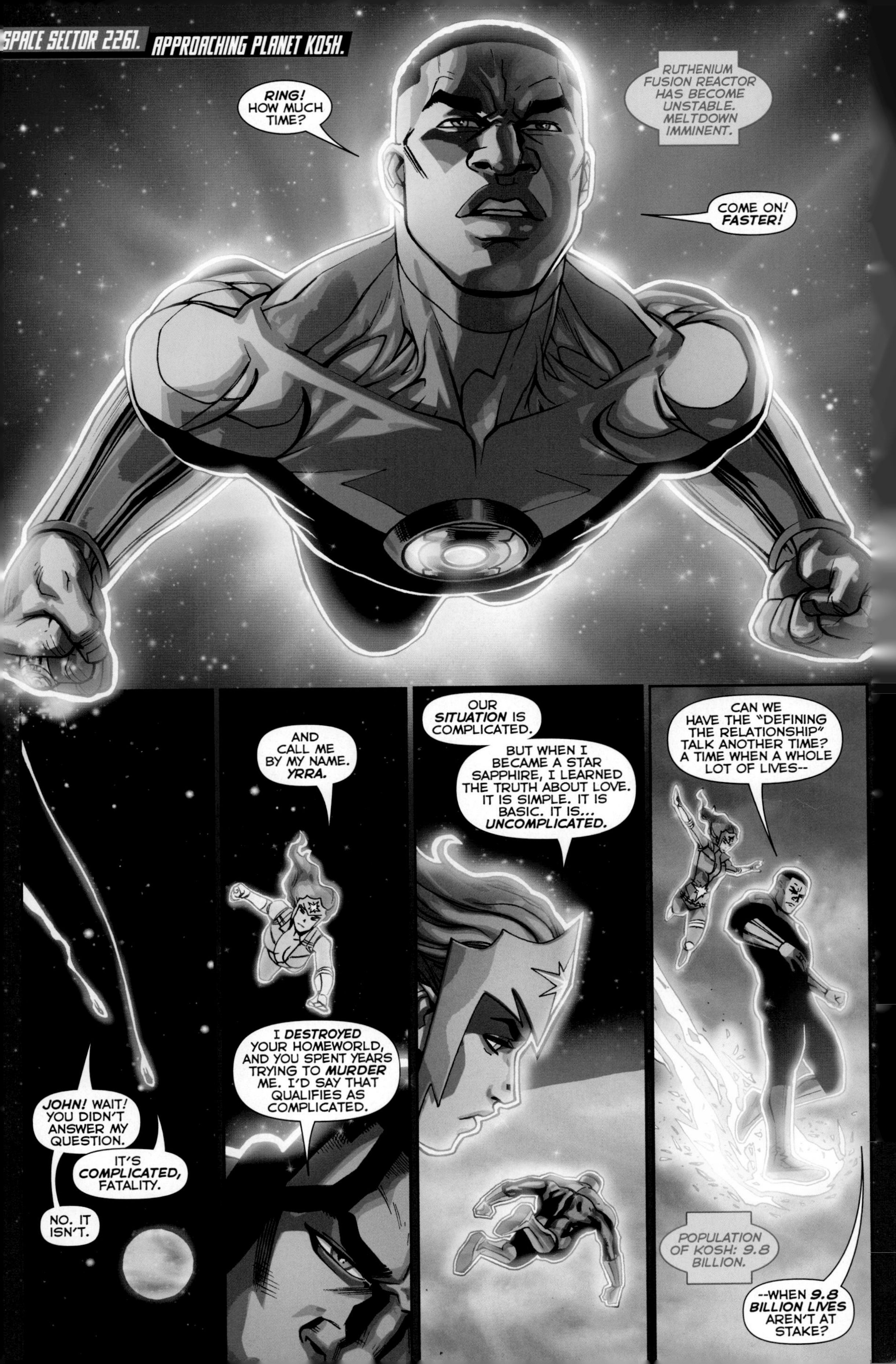
SPACE SECTOR 2261.
APPROACHING PLANET KOSH.
RING! HOW MUCH TIME?
RUTHENIUM FUSION REACTOR HAS BECOME UNSTABLE. MELTDOWN IMMINENT.
COME ON! FASTER!
JOHN! WAIT! YOU DIDN'T ANSWER MY QUESTION.
IT'S COMPLICATED, FATALITY.
NO. IT ISN'T.
AND CALL ME BY MY NAME. YRRA.
I DESTROYED YOUR HOMEWORLD, AND YOU SPENT YEARS TRYING TO MURDER ME. I'D SAY THAT QUALIFIES AS COMPLICATED.
OUR SITUATION IS COMPLICATED.
BUT WHEN I BECAME A STAR SAPPHIRE, I LEARNED THE TRUTH ABOUT LOVE. IT IS SIMPLE. IT IS BASIC. IT IS... UNCOMPLICATED.
CAN WE HAVE THE "DEFINING THE RELATIONSHIP" TALK ANOTHER TIME? A TIME WHEN A WHOLE LOT OF LIVES--
POPULATION OF KOSH: 9.8 BILLION.
--WHEN 9.8 BILLION LIVES AREN'T AT STAKE?

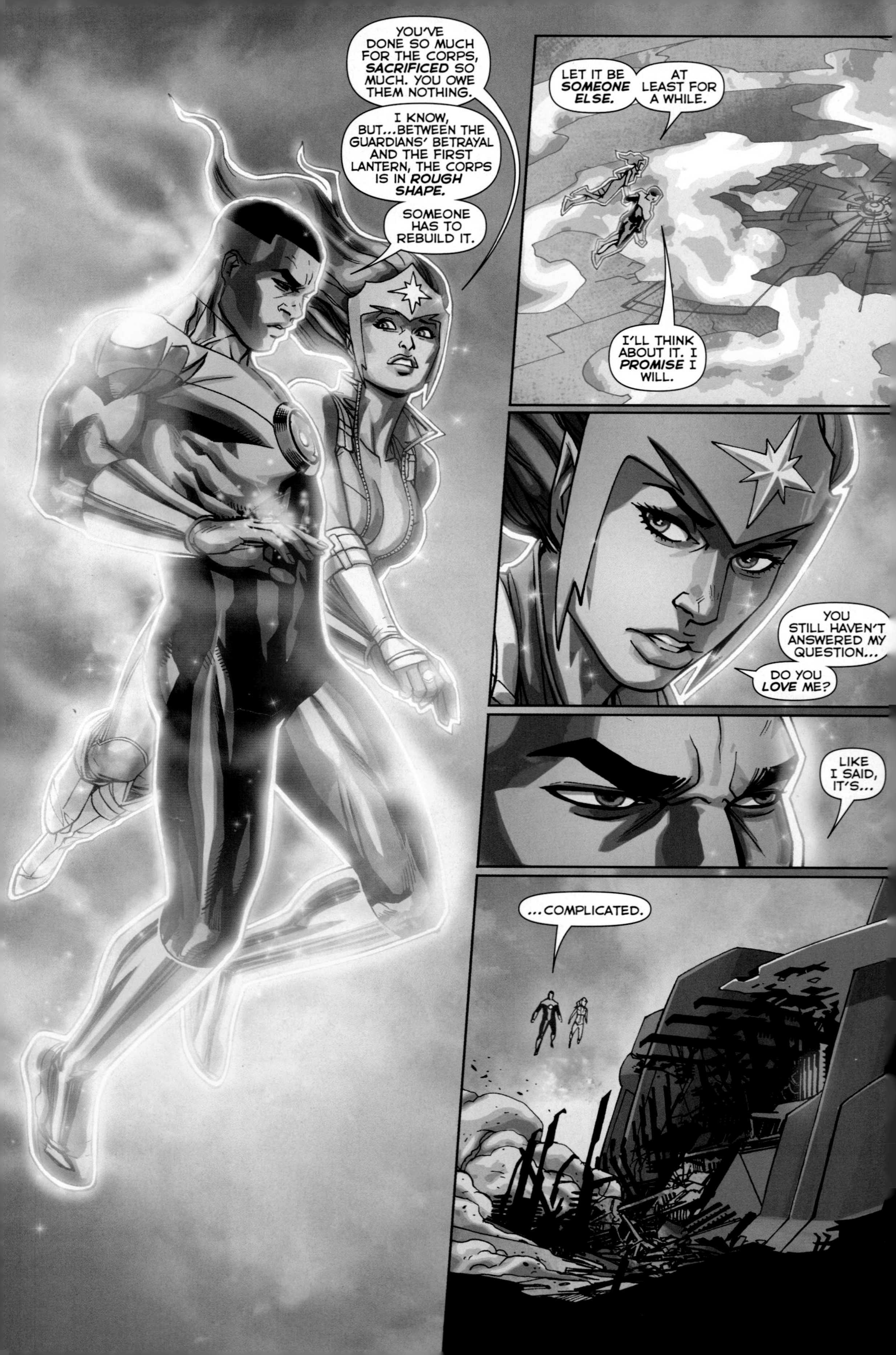
YOU'VE DONE SO MUCH FOR THE CORPS, SACRIFICED SO MUCH. YOU OWE THEM NOTHING.
I KNOW, BUT...BETWEEN THE GUARDIANS' BETRAYAL AND THE FIRST LANTERN, THE CORPS IS IN ROUGH SHAPE.
SOMEONE HAS TO REBUILD IT.
LET IT BE SOMEONE ELSE.
AT LEAST FOR A WHILE.
I'LL THINK ABOUT IT. I PROMISE I WILL.
YOU STILL HAVEN'T ANSWERED MY QUESTION...
DO YOU LOVE ME?
LIKE I SAID, IT'S...
...COMPLICATED.

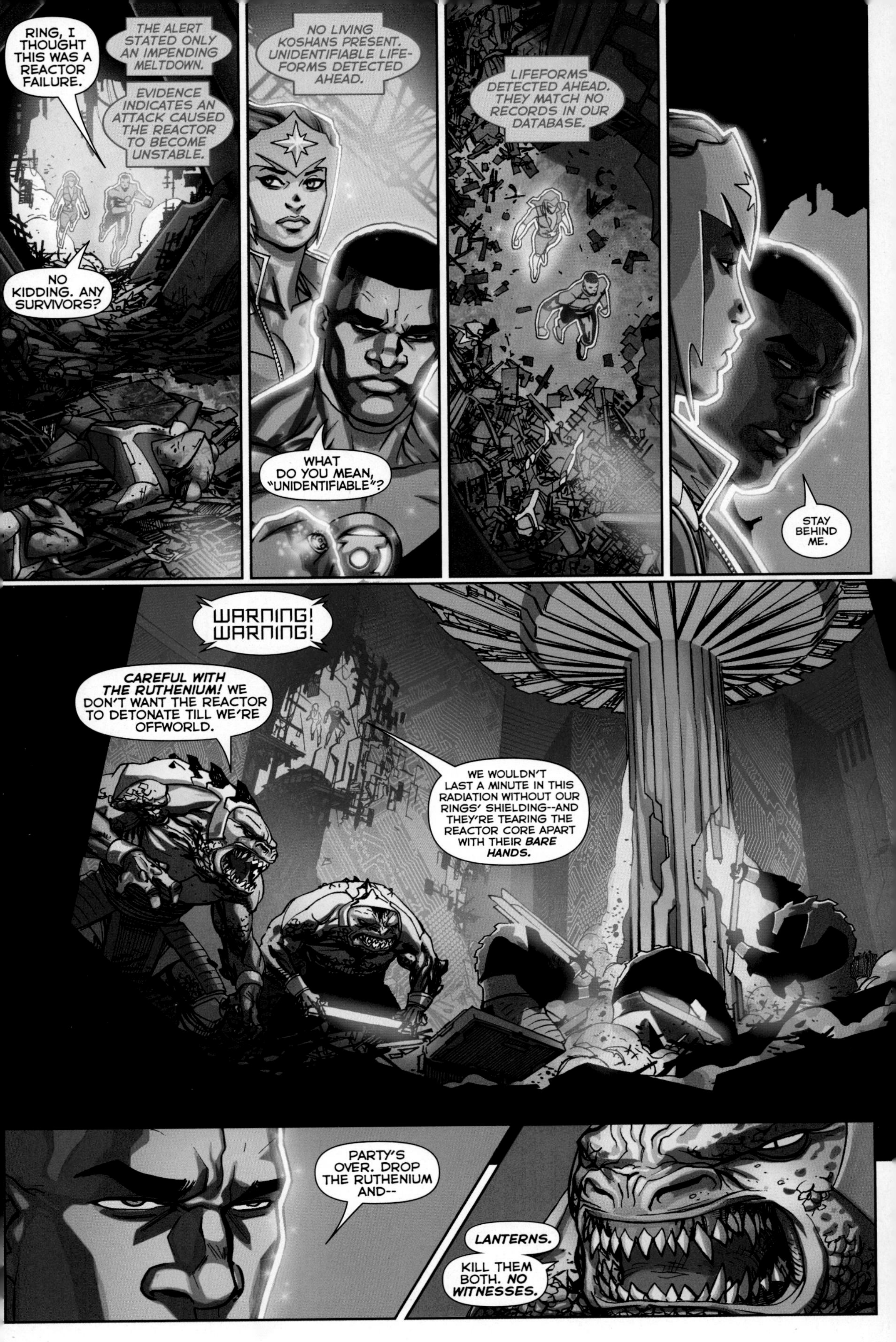
RING, I THOUGHT THIS WAS A REACTOR FAILURE.
THE ALERT STATED ONLY AN IMPENDING MELTDOWN.
EVIDENCE INDICATES AN ATTACK CAUSED THE REACTOR TO BECOME UNSTABLE.
NO KIDDING. ANY SURVIVORS?
NO LIVING KOSHANS PRESENT. UNIDENTIFIABLE LIFE-FORMS DETECTED AHEAD.
WHAT DO YOU MEAN, "UNIDENTIFIABLE"?
LIFEFORMS DETECTED AHEAD. THEY MATCH NO RECORDS IN OUR DATABASE.
STAY BEHIND ME.
WARNING! WARNING!
CAREFUL WITH THE RUTHENIUM! WE DON'T WANT THE REACTOR TO DETONATE TILL WE'RE OFFWORLD.
WE WOULDN'T LAST A MINUTE IN THIS RADIATION WITHOUT OUR RINGS' SHIELDING--AND THEY'RE TEARING THE REACTOR CORE APART WITH THEIR BARE HANDS.
PARTY'S OVER. DROP THE RUTHENIUM AND--
LANTERNS.
KILL THEM BOTH. NO WITNESSES.

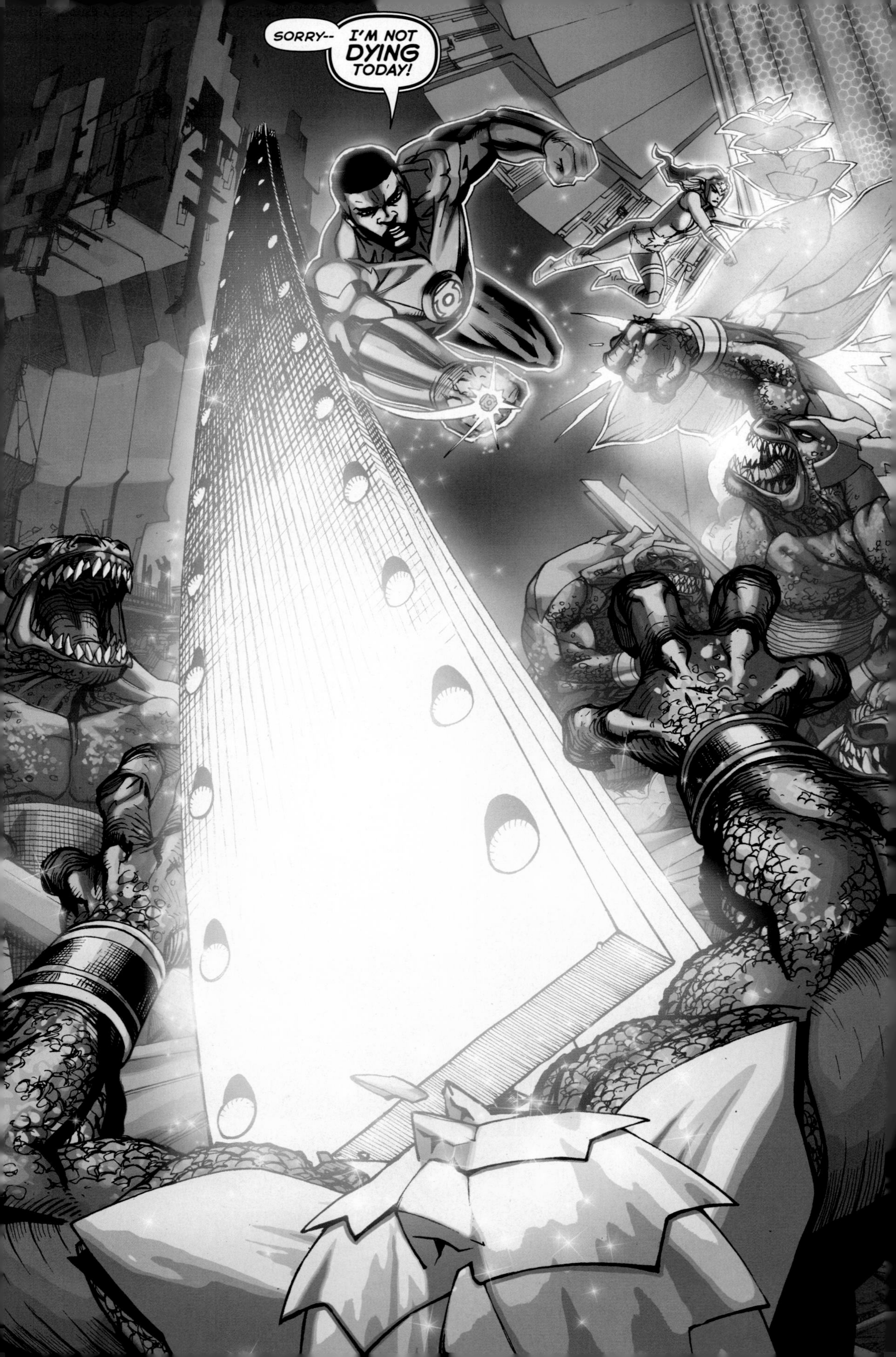
SORRY-- I'M NOT DYING TODAY!

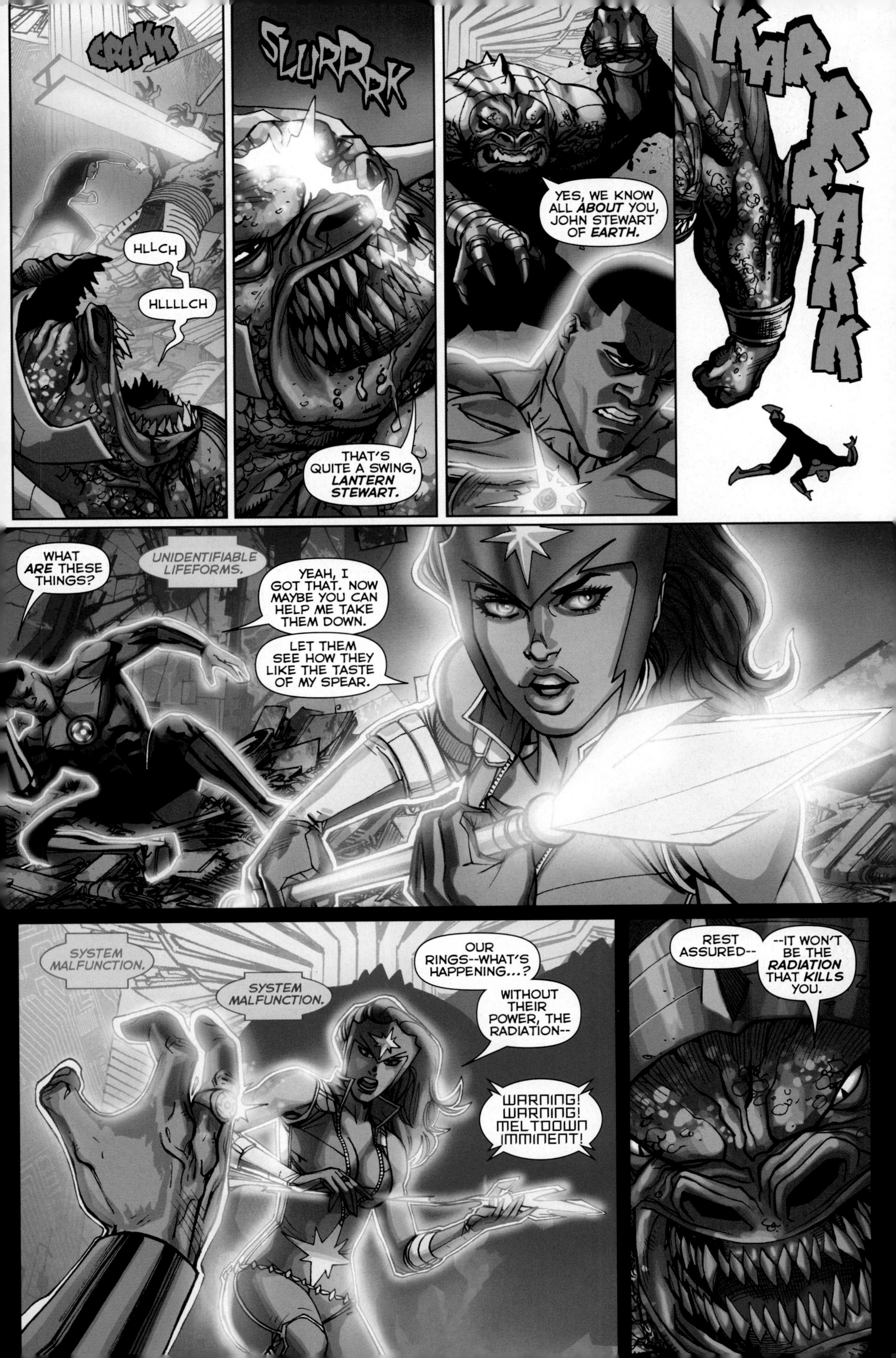

CRAKK
HLLCH
HLLLLCH
SLURRRK
THAT'S QUITE A SWING, LANTERN STEWART.
YES, WE KNOW ALL ABOUT YOU, JOHN STEWART OF EARTH.
KARRRAKK
WHAT ARE THESE THINGS?
UNIDENTIFIABLE LIFEFORMS.
YEAH, I GOT THAT. NOW MAYBE YOU CAN HELP ME TAKE THEM DOWN.
LET THEM SEE HOW THEY LIKE THE TASTE OF MY SPEAR.
SYSTEM MALFUNCTION.
SYSTEM MALFUNCTION.
OUR RINGS--WHAT'S HAPPENING...?
WITHOUT THEIR POWER, THE RADIATION--
WARNING! WARNING! MELTDOWN IMMINENT!
REST ASSURED--
--IT WON'T BE THE RADIATION THAT KILLS YOU.

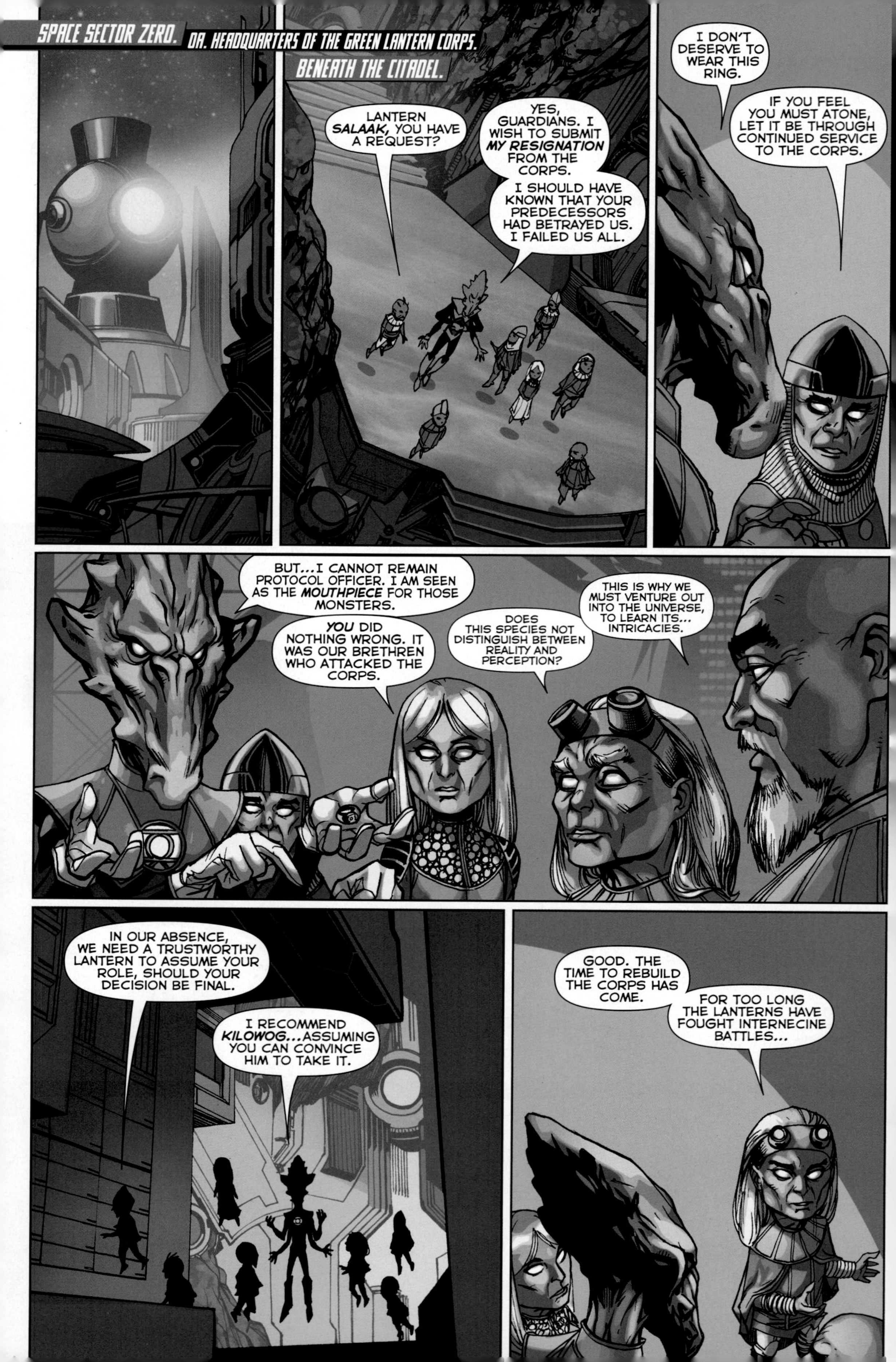
SPACE SECTOR ZERO.
OA. HEADQUARTERS OF THE GREEN LANTERN CORPS.
BENEATH THE CITADEL.
LANTERN SALAAK, YOU HAVE A REQUEST?
YES, GUARDIANS. I WISH TO SUBMIT MY RESIGNATION FROM THE CORPS.
I SHOULD HAVE KNOWN THAT YOUR PREDECESSORS HAD BETRAYED US. I FAILED US ALL.
I DON'T DESERVE TO WEAR THIS RING.
IF YOU FEEL YOU MUST ATONE, LET IT BE THROUGH CONTINUED SERVICE TO THE CORPS.
BUT...I CANNOT REMAIN PROTOCOL OFFICER. I AM SEEN AS THE MOUTHPIECE FOR THOSE MONSTERS.
YOU DID NOTHING WRONG. IT WAS OUR BRETHREN WHO ATTACKED THE CORPS.
DOES THIS SPECIES NOT DISTINGUISH BETWEEN REALITY AND PERCEPTION?
THIS IS WHY WE MUST VENTURE OUT INTO THE UNIVERSE, TO LEARN ITS... INTRICACIES.
IN OUR ABSENCE, WE NEED A TRUSTWORTHY LANTERN TO ASSUME YOUR ROLE, SHOULD YOUR DECISION BE FINAL.
I RECOMMEND KILOWOG...ASSUMING YOU CAN CONVINCE HIM TO TAKE IT.
GOOD. THE TIME TO REBUILD THE CORPS HAS COME.
FOR TOO LONG THE LANTERNS HAVE FOUGHT INTERNECINE BATTLES...

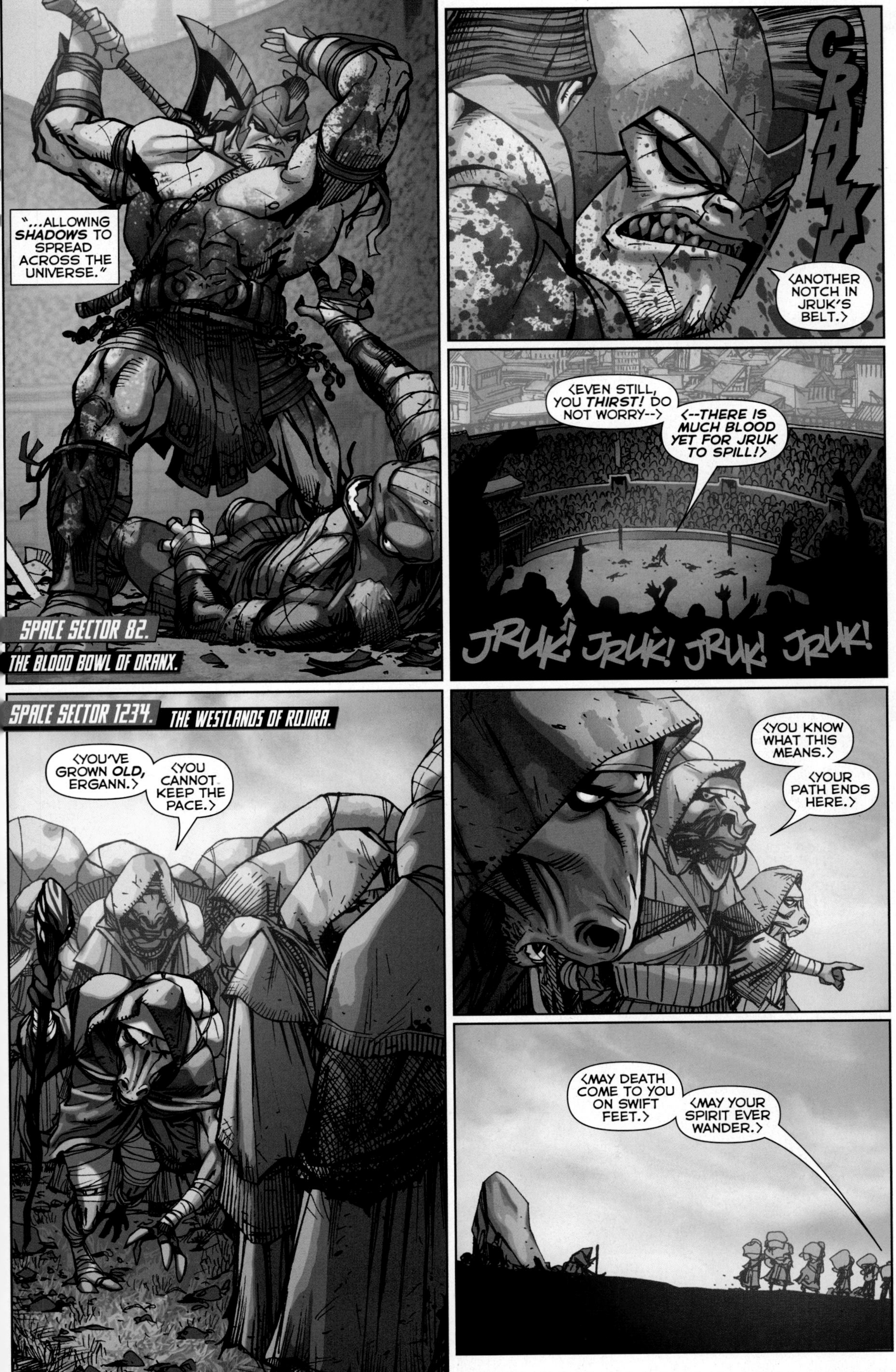
"...ALLOWING SHADOWS TO SPREAD ACROSS THE UNIVERSE."
SPACE SECTOR 82.
THE BLOOD BOWL OF ORANX.
CRAKK
<ANOTHER NOTCH IN JRUK'S BELT.>
<EVEN STILL, YOU THIRST! DO NOT WORRY-->
<--THERE IS MUCH BLOOD YET FOR JRUK TO SPILL!>
JRUK! JRUK! JRUK! JRUK!
SPACE SECTOR 1234.
THE WESTLANDS OF ROJIRA.
<YOU'VE GROWN OLD, ERGANN.>
<YOU CANNOT KEEP THE PACE.>
<YOU KNOW WHAT THIS MEANS.>
<YOUR PATH ENDS HERE.>
<MAY DEATH COME TO YOU ON SWIFT FEET.>
<MAY YOUR SPIRIT EVER WANDER.>

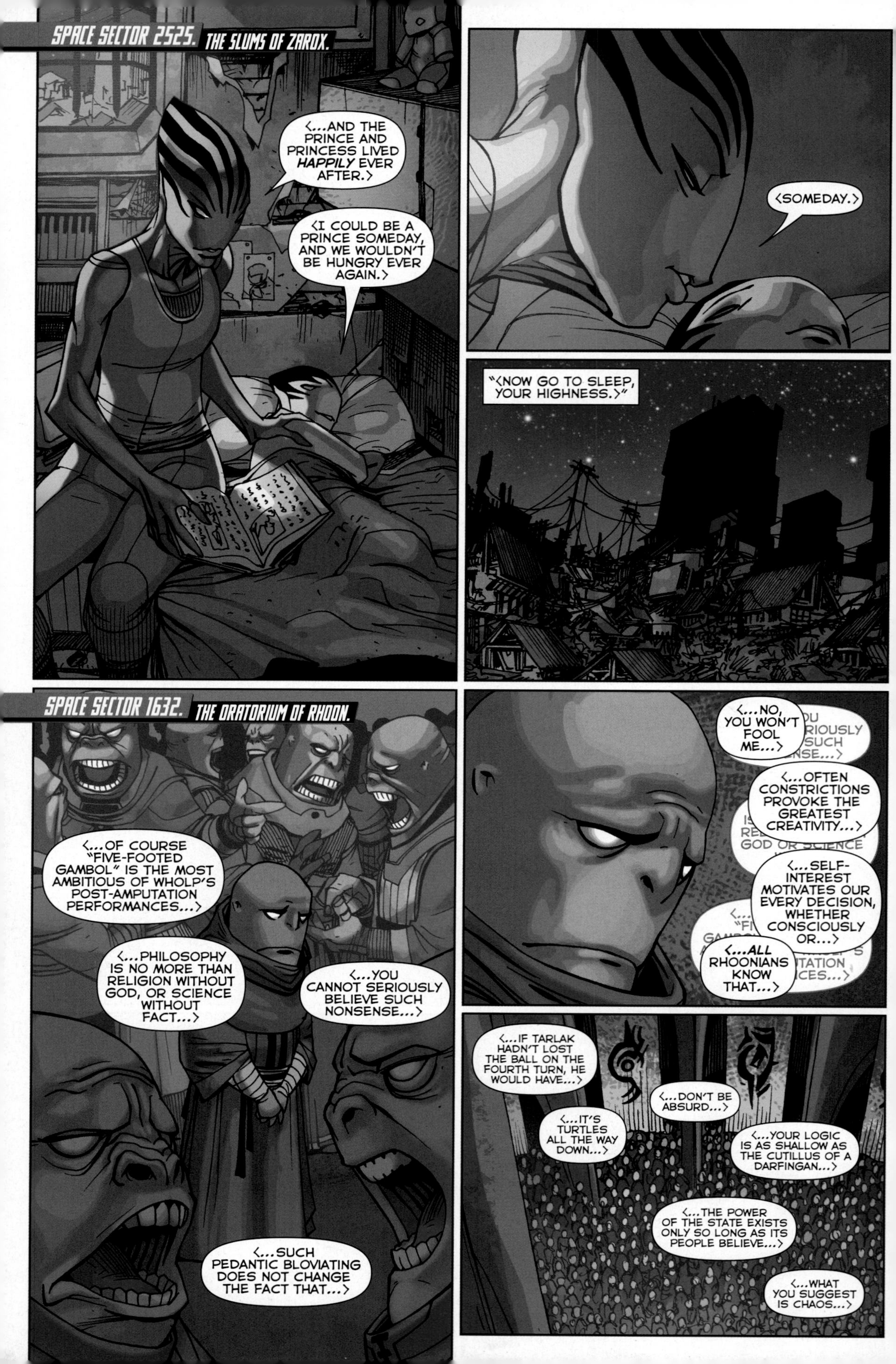
SPACE SECTOR 2525. THE SLUMS OF ZAROX.
<...AND THE PRINCE AND PRINCESS LIVED HAPPILY EVER AFTER.>
<I COULD BE A PRINCE SOMEDAY, AND WE WOULDN'T BE HUNGRY EVER AGAIN.>
<SOMEDAY.>
"<NOW GO TO SLEEP, YOUR HIGHNESS.>"
SPACE SECTOR 1632. THE ORATORIUM OF RHOON.
<...OF COURSE "FIVE-FOOTED GAMBOL" IS THE MOST AMBITIOUS OF WHOLP'S POST-AMPUTATION PERFORMANCES...>
<...PHILOSOPHY IS NO MORE THAN RELIGION WITHOUT GOD, OR SCIENCE WITHOUT FACT...>
<...YOU CANNOT SERIOUSLY BELIEVE SUCH NONSENSE...>
<...SUCH PEDANTIC BLOVIATING DOES NOT CHANGE THE FACT THAT...>
<...NO, YOU WON'T FOOL ME...>
<...OFTEN CONSTRICTIONS PROVOKE THE GREATEST CREATIVITY...>
<...SELF-INTEREST MOTIVATES OUR EVERY DECISION, WHETHER CONSCIOUSLY OR...>
<...ALL RHOONIANS KNOW THAT...>
<...IF TARLAK HADN'T LOST THE BALL ON THE FOURTH TURN, HE WOULD HAVE...>
<...DON'T BE ABSURD...>
<...IT'S TURTLES ALL THE WAY DOWN...>
<...YOUR LOGIC IS AS SHALLOW AS THE CUTILLUS OF A DARFINGAN...>
<...THE POWER OF THE STATE EXISTS ONLY SO LONG AS ITS PEOPLE BELIEVE...>
<...WHAT YOU SUGGEST IS CHAOS...>

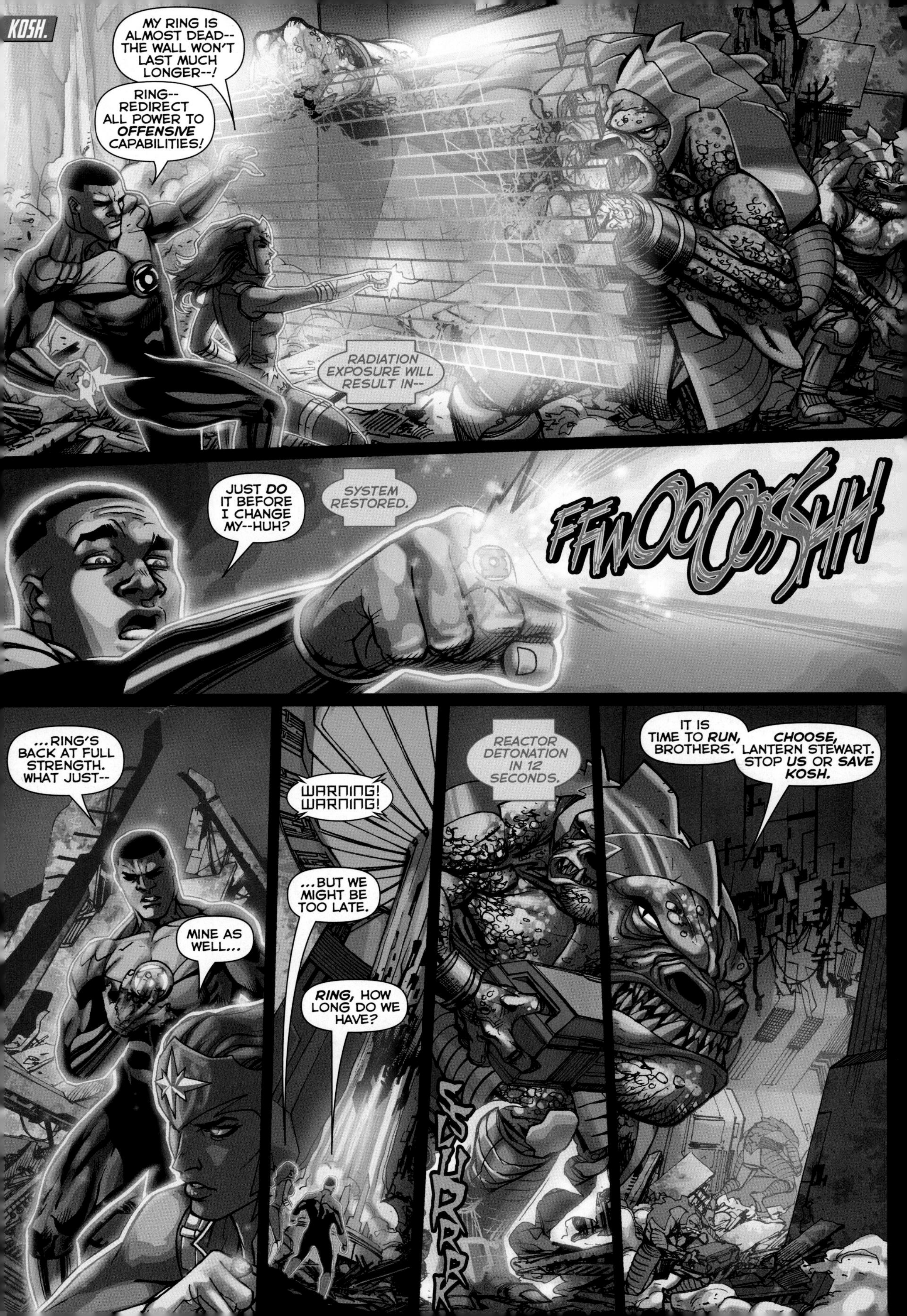
KOSH.
MY RING IS ALMOST DEAD-- THE WALL WON'T LAST MUCH LONGER--!
RING-- REDIRECT ALL POWER TO OFFENSIVE CAPABILITIES!
RADIATION EXPOSURE WILL RESULT IN--
JUST DO IT BEFORE I CHANGE MY--HUH?
SYSTEM RESTORED.
FFWOOOOSHH
...RING'S BACK AT FULL STRENGTH. WHAT JUST--
MINE AS WELL...
WARNING! WARNING!
...BUT WE MIGHT BE TOO LATE.
RING, HOW LONG DO WE HAVE?
REACTOR DETONATION IN 12 SECONDS.
SHRRRK
IT IS TIME TO RUN, BROTHERS.
CHOOSE, LANTERN STEWART. STOP US OR SAVE KOSH.

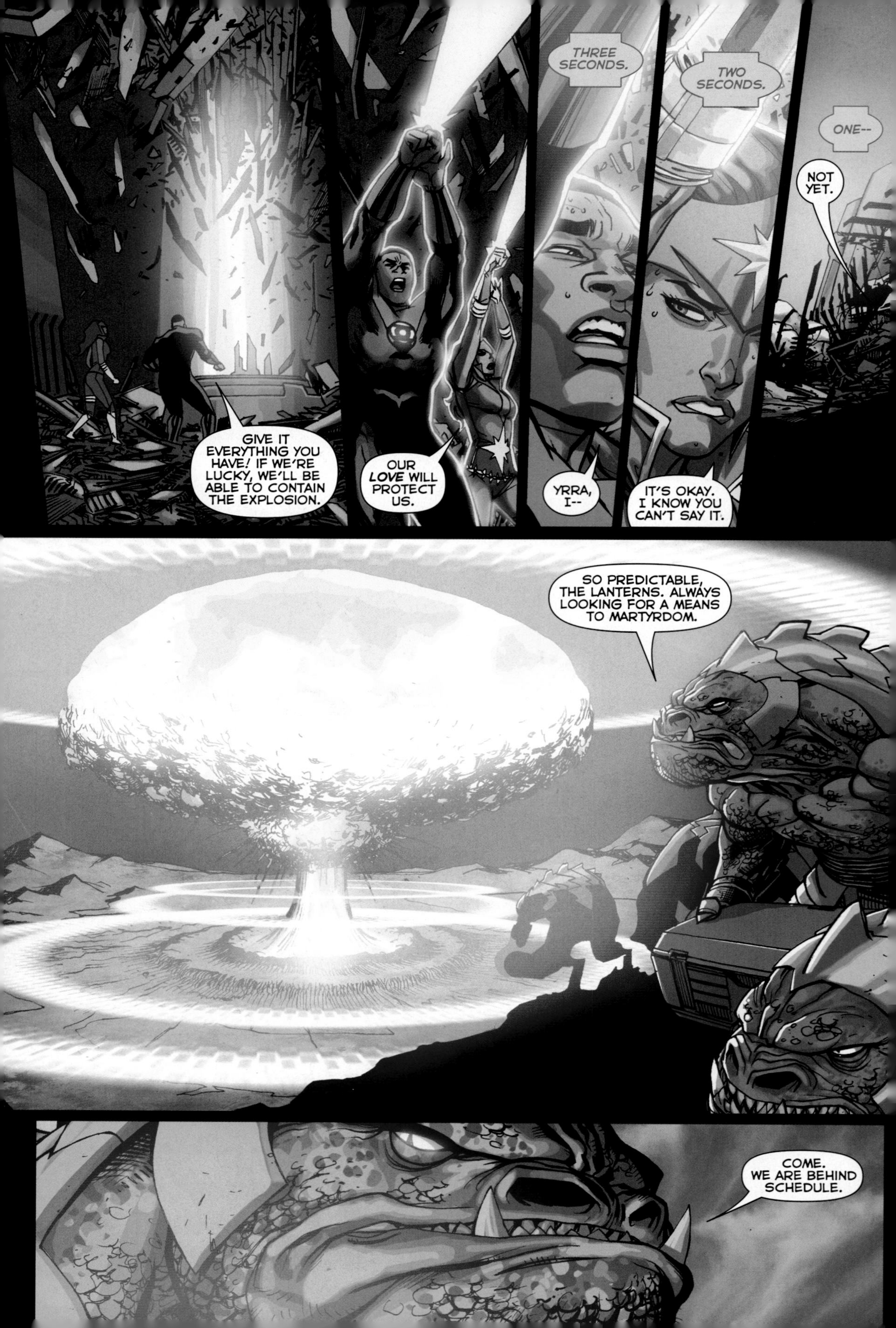
GIVE IT EVERYTHING YOU HAVE! IF WE'RE LUCKY, WE'LL BE ABLE TO CONTAIN THE EXPLOSION.
OUR LOVE WILL PROTECT US.
THREE SECONDS.
YRRA, I--
TWO SECONDS.
IT'S OKAY. I KNOW YOU CAN'T SAY IT.
ONE--
NOT YET.
SO PREDICTABLE, THE LANTERNS. ALWAYS LOOKING FOR A MEANS TO MARTYRDOM.
COME. WE ARE BEHIND SCHEDULE.

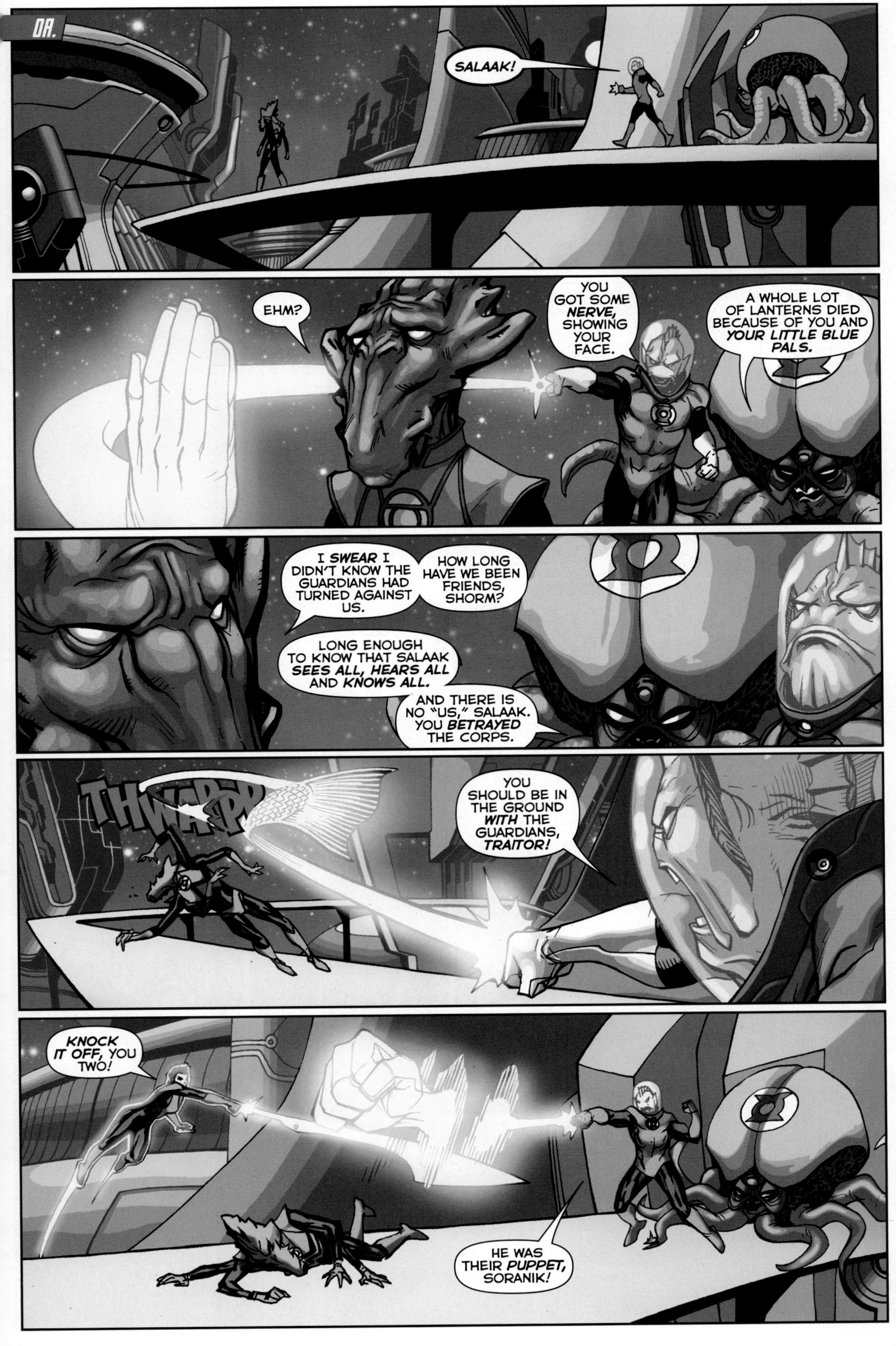
SALAAK!
EHM?
YOU GOT SOME NERVE, SHOWING YOUR FACE.
A WHOLE LOT OF LANTERNS DIED BECAUSE OF YOU AND YOUR LITTLE BLUE PALS.
I SWEAR I DIDN'T KNOW THE GUARDIANS HAD TURNED AGAINST US.
HOW LONG HAVE WE BEEN FRIENDS, SHORM?
LONG ENOUGH TO KNOW THAT SALAAK SEES ALL, HEARS ALL AND KNOWS ALL.
AND THERE IS NO "US," SALAAK. YOU BETRAYED THE CORPS.
THWARPP
YOU SHOULD BE IN THE GROUND WITH THE GUARDIANS, TRAITOR!
KNOCK IT OFF, YOU TWO!
HE WAS THEIR PUPPET, SORANIK!

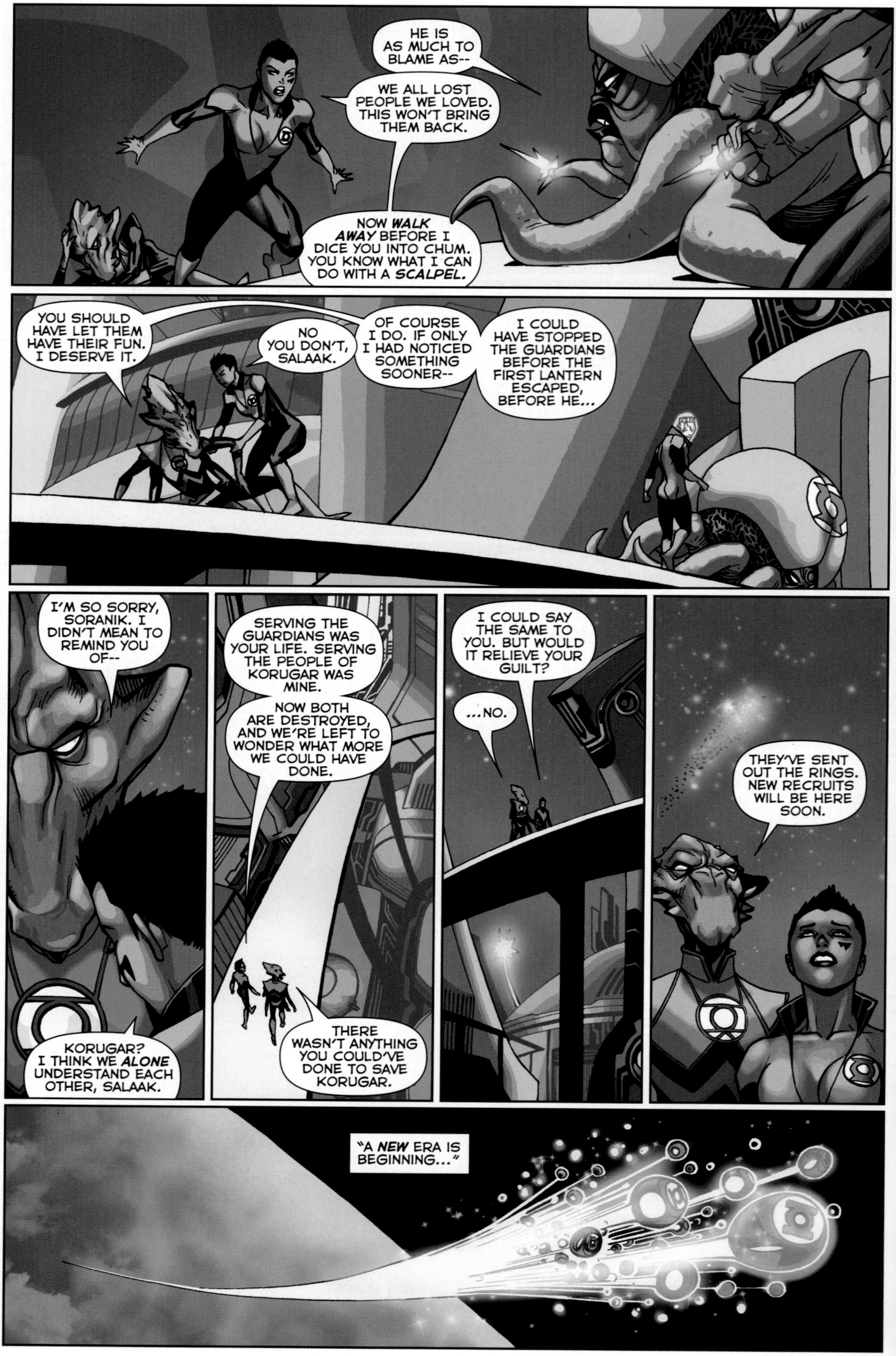
HE IS AS MUCH TO BLAME AS--
WE ALL LOST PEOPLE WE LOVED. THIS WON'T BRING THEM BACK.
NOW WALK AWAY BEFORE I DICE YOU INTO CHUM. YOU KNOW WHAT I CAN DO WITH A SCALPEL.
YOU SHOULD HAVE LET THEM HAVE THEIR FUN. I DESERVE IT.
NO YOU DON'T, SALAAK.
OF COURSE I DO. IF ONLY I HAD NOTICED SOMETHING SOONER--
I COULD HAVE STOPPED THE GUARDIANS BEFORE THE FIRST LANTERN ESCAPED, BEFORE HE...
I'M SO SORRY, SORANIK. I DIDN'T MEAN TO REMIND YOU OF--
KORUGAR? I THINK WE ALONE UNDERSTAND EACH OTHER, SALAAK.
SERVING THE GUARDIANS WAS YOUR LIFE. SERVING THE PEOPLE OF KORUGAR WAS MINE.
NOW BOTH ARE DESTROYED, AND WE'RE LEFT TO WONDER WHAT MORE WE COULD HAVE DONE.
THERE WASN'T ANYTHING YOU COULD'VE DONE TO SAVE KORUGAR.
I COULD SAY THE SAME TO YOU. BUT WOULD IT RELIEVE YOUR GUILT?
...NO.
THEY'VE SENT OUT THE RINGS. NEW RECRUITS WILL BE HERE SOON.
"A NEW ERA IS BEGINNING..."

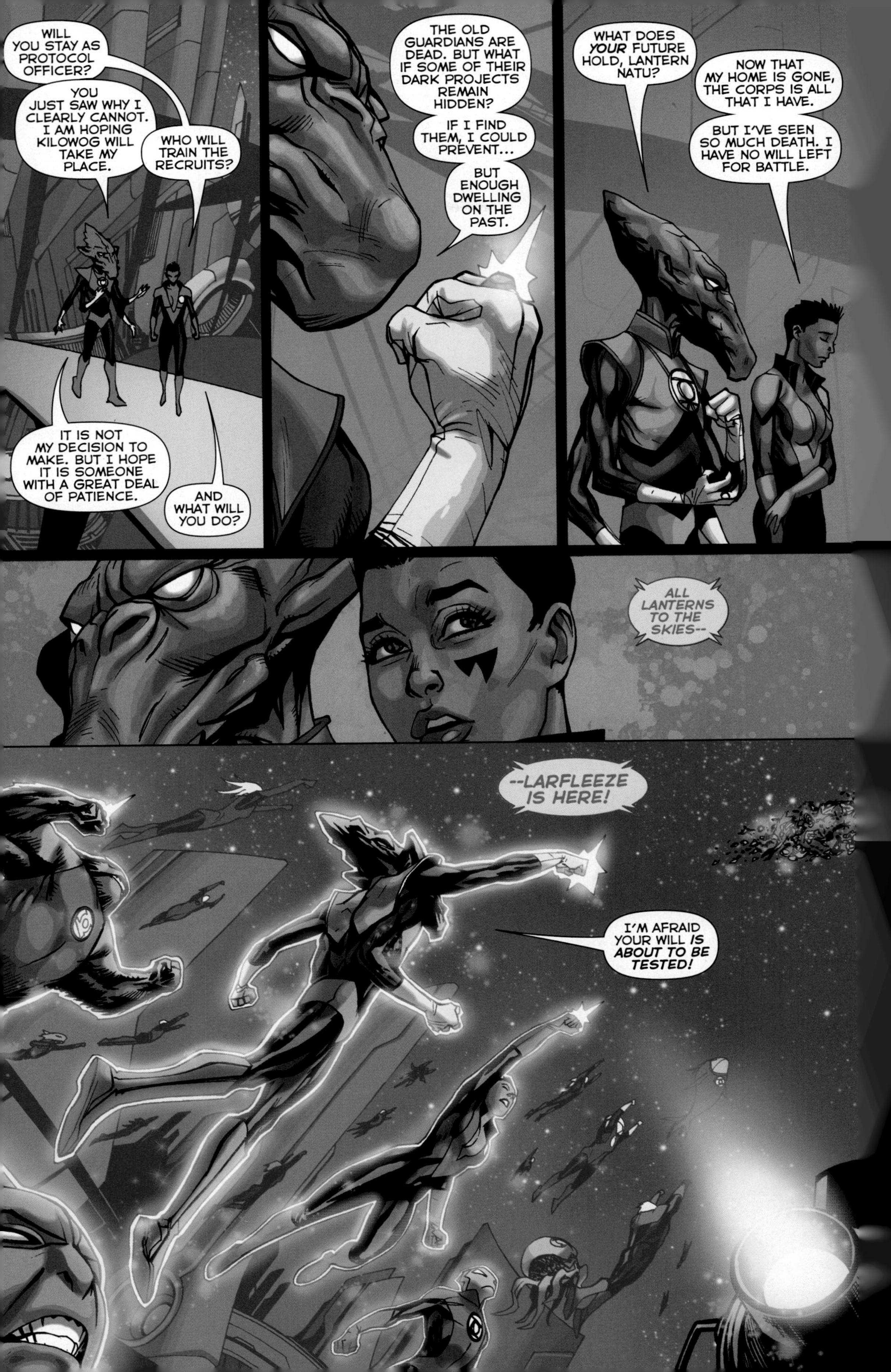

WILL YOU STAY AS PROTOCOL OFFICER?
YOU JUST SAW WHY I CLEARLY CANNOT. I AM HOPING KILOWOG WILL TAKE MY PLACE.
WHO WILL TRAIN THE RECRUITS?
IT IS NOT MY DECISION TO MAKE. BUT I HOPE IT IS SOMEONE WITH A GREAT DEAL OF PATIENCE.
AND WHAT WILL YOU DO?
THE OLD GUARDIANS ARE DEAD. BUT WHAT IF SOME OF THEIR DARK PROJECTS REMAIN HIDDEN?
IF I FIND THEM, I COULD PREVENT...
BUT ENOUGH DWELLING ON THE PAST.
WHAT DOES *YOUR* FUTURE HOLD, LANTERN NATU?
NOW THAT MY HOME IS GONE, THE CORPS IS ALL THAT I HAVE.
BUT I'VE SEEN SO MUCH DEATH. I HAVE NO WILL LEFT FOR BATTLE.
ALL LANTERNS TO THE SKIES--
--LARFLEEZE IS HERE!
I'M AFRAID YOUR WILL *IS ABOUT TO BE TESTED!*

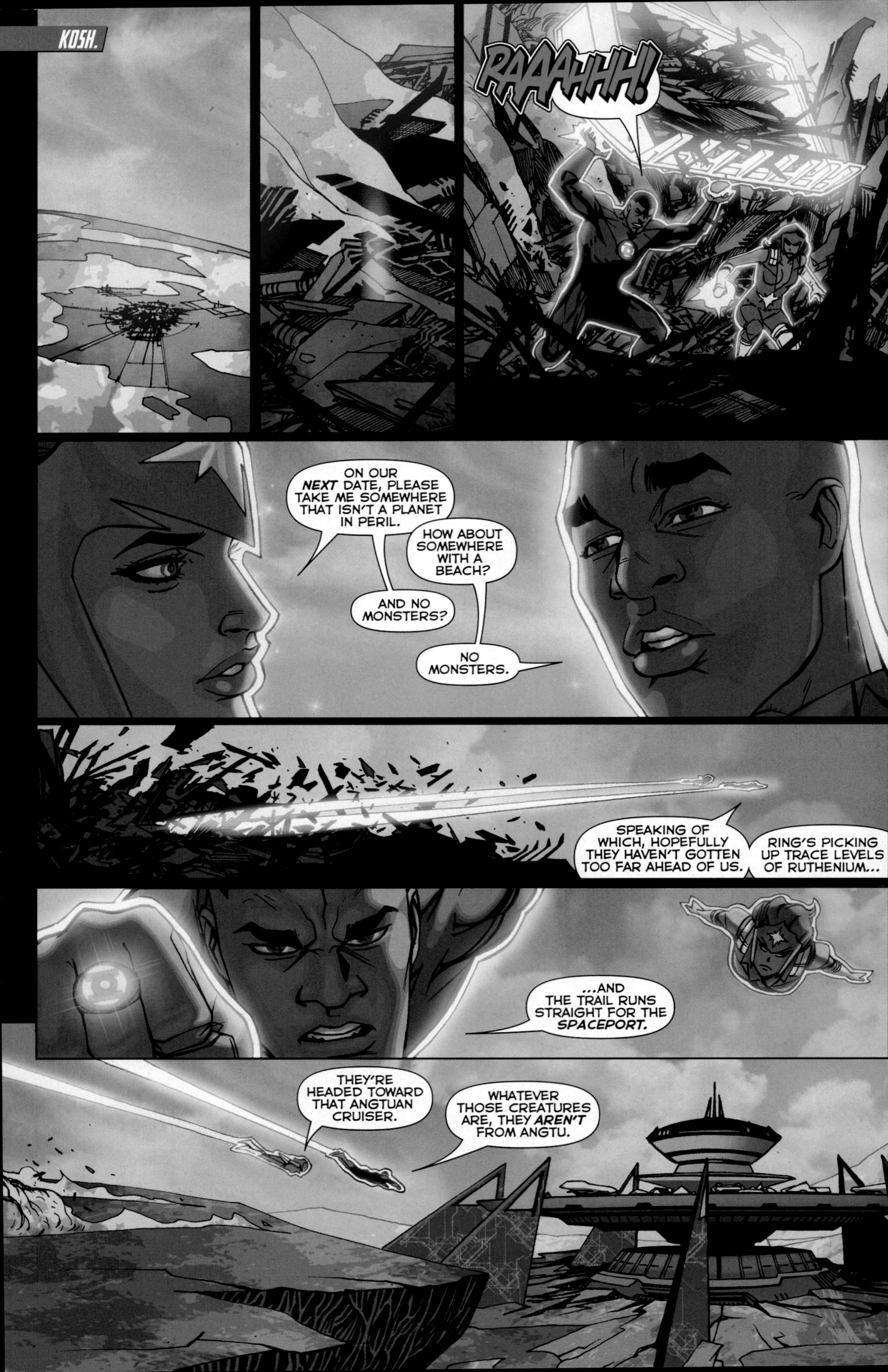
KOSH.
RAAAHHH!
ON OUR NEXT DATE, PLEASE TAKE ME SOMEWHERE THAT ISN'T A PLANET IN PERIL.
HOW ABOUT SOMEWHERE WITH A BEACH?
AND NO MONSTERS?
NO MONSTERS.
SPEAKING OF WHICH, HOPEFULLY THEY HAVEN'T GOTTEN TOO FAR AHEAD OF US.
RING'S PICKING UP TRACE LEVELS OF RUTHENIUM...
...AND THE TRAIL RUNS STRAIGHT FOR THE SPACEPORT.
THEY'RE HEADED TOWARD THAT ANGTUAN CRUISER.
WHATEVER THOSE CREATURES ARE, THEY AREN'T FROM ANGTU.

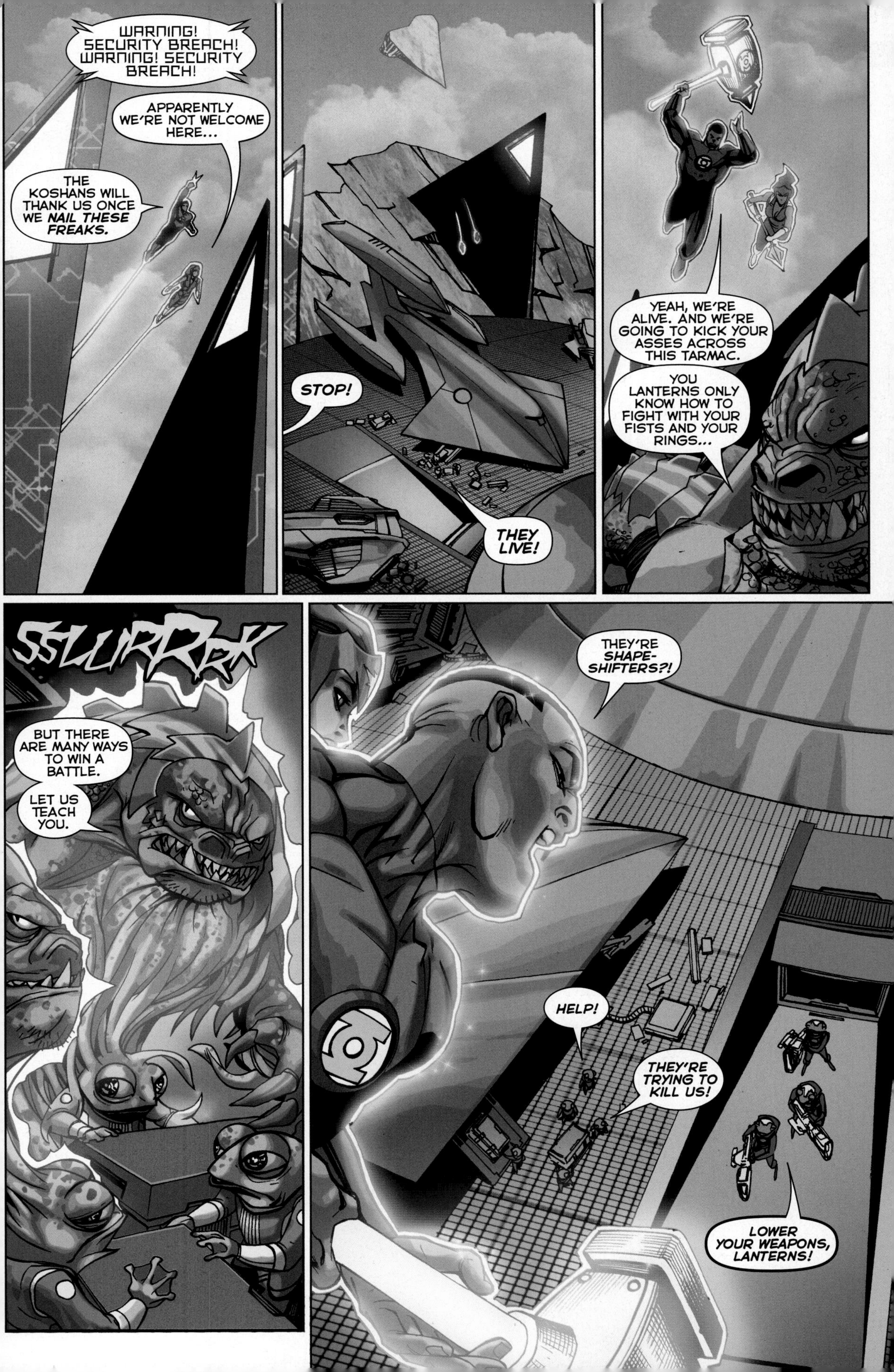

WARNING! SECURITY BREACH! WARNING! SECURITY BREACH!
APPARENTLY WE'RE NOT WELCOME HERE...
THE KOSHANS WILL THANK US ONCE WE *NAIL THESE FREAKS.*
STOP!
THEY LIVE!
YEAH, WE'RE ALIVE. AND WE'RE GOING TO KICK YOUR ASSES ACROSS THIS TARMAC.
YOU LANTERNS ONLY KNOW HOW TO FIGHT WITH YOUR FISTS AND YOUR RINGS...
SSLURRRK
BUT THERE ARE MANY WAYS TO WIN A BATTLE.
LET US TEACH YOU.
THEY'RE *SHAPE-SHIFTERS?!*
HELP!
THEY'RE TRYING TO KILL US!
LOWER YOUR WEAPONS, LANTERNS!

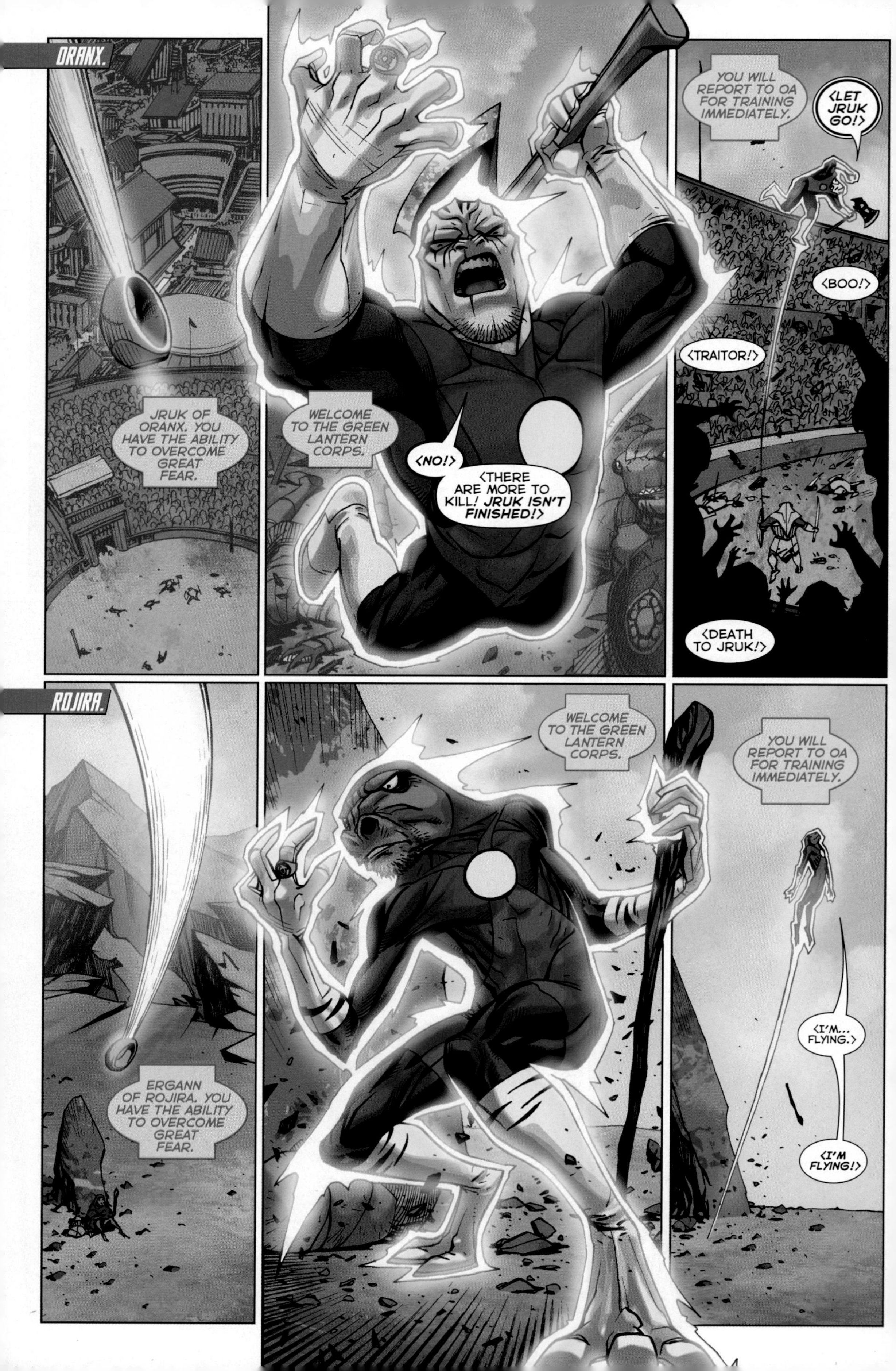
ORANX.
JRUK OF ORANX. YOU HAVE THE ABILITY TO OVERCOME GREAT FEAR.
WELCOME TO THE GREEN LANTERN CORPS.
<NO!>
<THERE ARE MORE TO KILL! JRUK ISN'T FINISHED!>
YOU WILL REPORT TO OA FOR TRAINING IMMEDIATELY.
<LET JRUK GO!>
<BOO!>
<TRAITOR!>
<DEATH TO JRUK!>
ROJIRA.
ERGANN OF ROJIRA. YOU HAVE THE ABILITY TO OVERCOME GREAT FEAR.
WELCOME TO THE GREEN LANTERN CORPS.
YOU WILL REPORT TO OA FOR TRAINING IMMEDIATELY.
<I'M... FLYING.>
<I'M FLYING!>

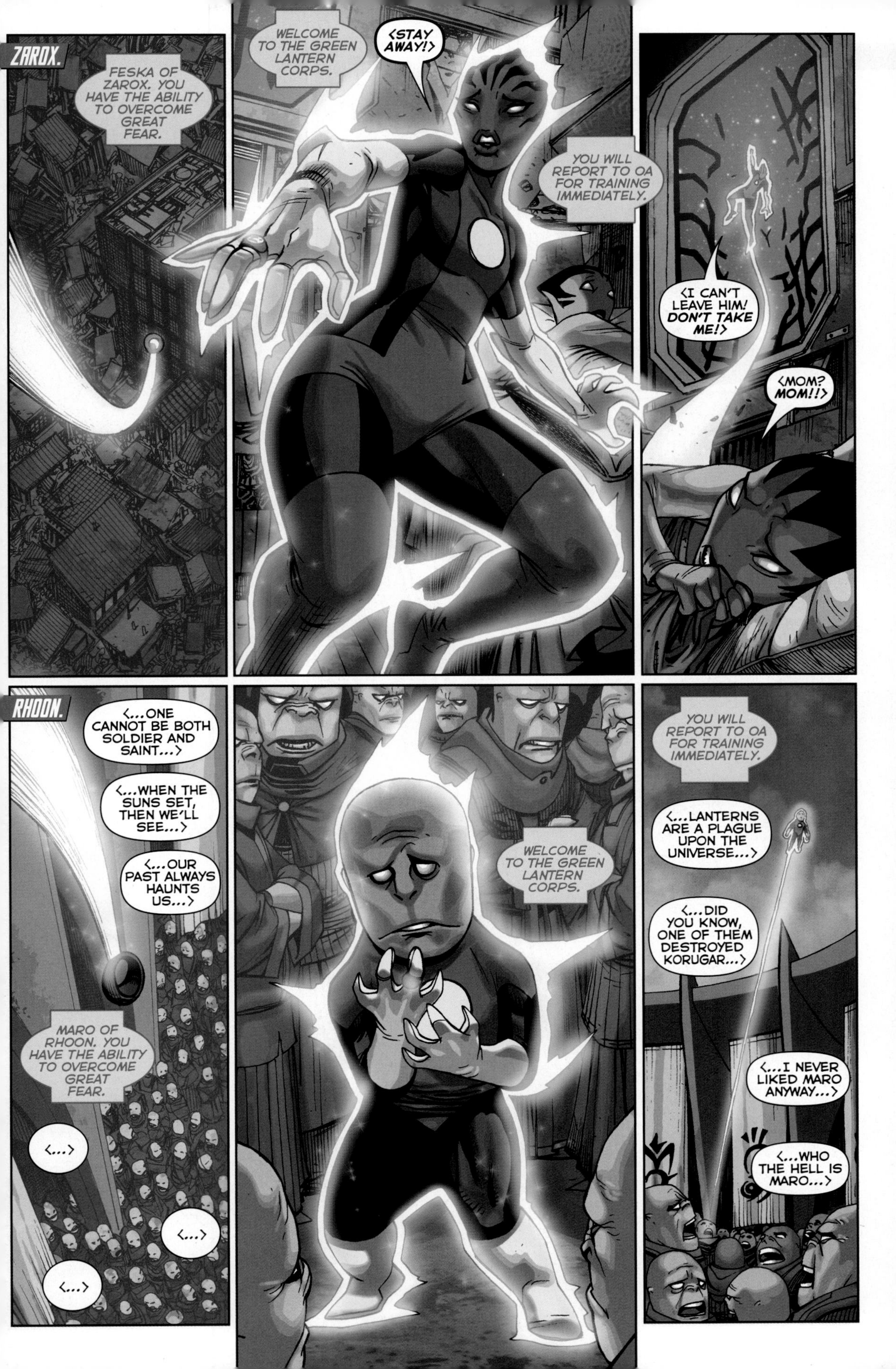
ZAROX.
FESKA OF ZAROX. YOU HAVE THE ABILITY TO OVERCOME GREAT FEAR.
WELCOME TO THE GREEN LANTERN CORPS.
<STAY AWAY!>
YOU WILL REPORT TO OA FOR TRAINING IMMEDIATELY.
<I CAN'T LEAVE HIM! DON'T TAKE ME!>
<MOM? MOM!!>
RHOON.
<...ONE CANNOT BE BOTH SOLDIER AND SAINT...>
<...WHEN THE SUNS SET, THEN WE'LL SEE...>
<...OUR PAST ALWAYS HAUNTS US...>
MARO OF RHOON. YOU HAVE THE ABILITY TO OVERCOME GREAT FEAR.
<...>
<...>
<...>
WELCOME TO THE GREEN LANTERN CORPS.
YOU WILL REPORT TO OA FOR TRAINING IMMEDIATELY.
<...LANTERNS ARE A PLAGUE UPON THE UNIVERSE...>
<...DID YOU KNOW, ONE OF THEM DESTROYED KORUGAR...>
<...I NEVER LIKED MARO ANYWAY...>
<...WHO THE HELL IS MARO...>

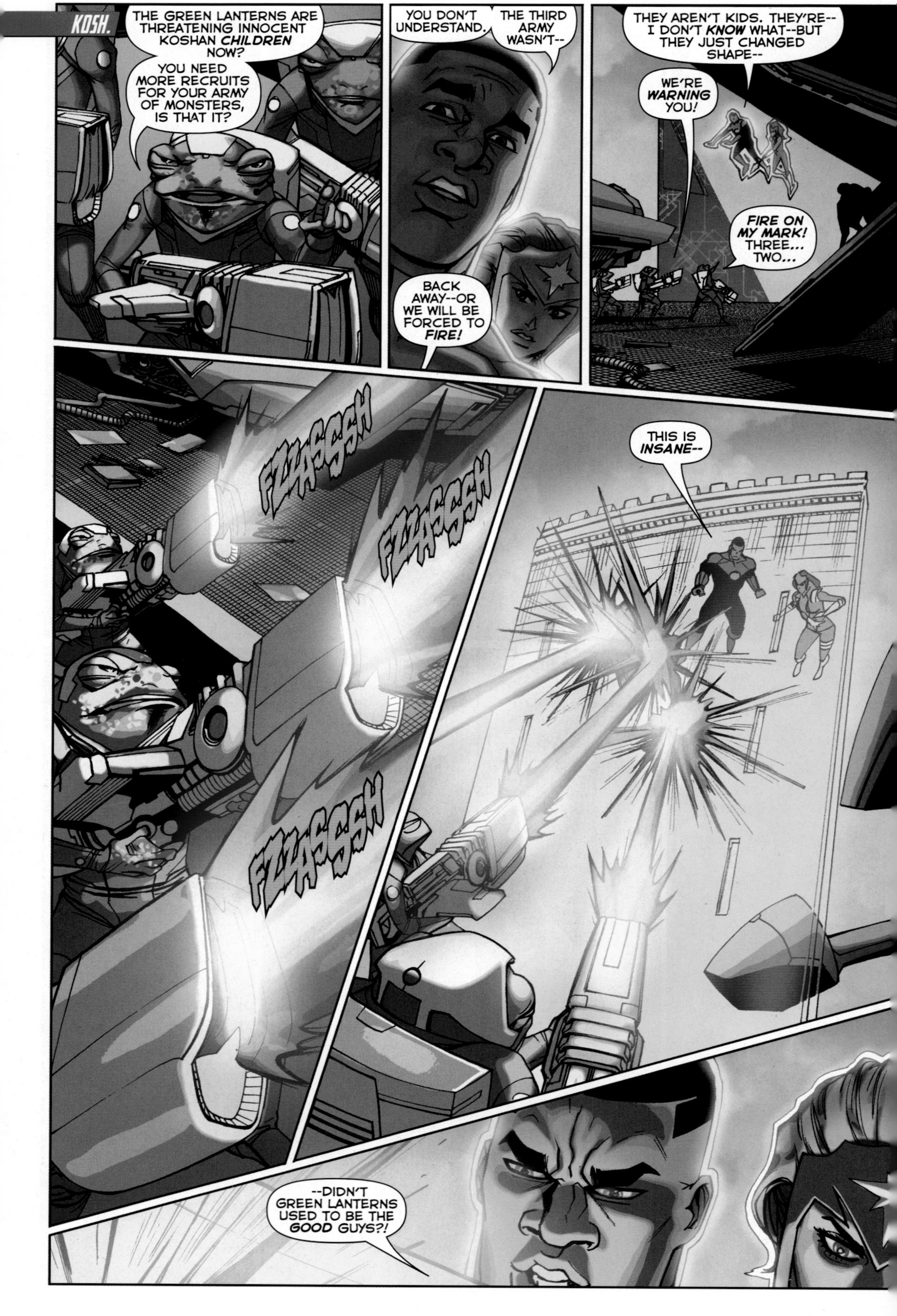
KOSH.
THE GREEN LANTERNS ARE THREATENING INNOCENT KOSHAN CHILDREN NOW?
YOU NEED MORE RECRUITS FOR YOUR ARMY OF MONSTERS, IS THAT IT?
YOU DON'T UNDERSTAND.
THE THIRD ARMY WASN'T--
BACK AWAY--OR WE WILL BE FORCED TO FIRE!
THEY AREN'T KIDS. THEY'RE-- I DON'T KNOW WHAT--BUT THEY JUST CHANGED SHAPE--
WE'RE WARNING YOU!
FIRE ON MY MARK! THREE... TWO...
FZZASSSH
FZZASSSH
FZZASSSH
THIS IS INSANE--
--DIDN'T GREEN LANTERNS USED TO BE THE GOOD GUYS?!

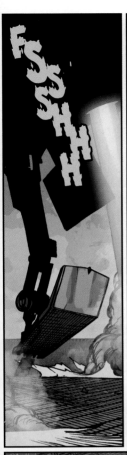

FSSSHHH

RRRRmmmmBBBLL

GET DOWN!

GKKKOOMM

WHERE ARE THE CHILDREN?

THE LANTERNS MUST HAVE ABDUCTED THEM!

DON'T YOU GET IT?! THERE NEVER WERE ANY CHILDREN!

ALL LANTERNS TO OA! CITADEL IS UNDER ATTACK FROM LARFLEEZE!

NOT NOW...

GO. I'LL FOLLOW THE SHIP.

I CAN'T LEAVE YOU--

YOU HAVE TO. I UNDERSTAND. BUT REMEMBER YOUR PROMISE. PLEASE...

CONSIDER A LIFE AWAY FROM THE CORPS.

I WILL...

BE SAFE, YRRA.

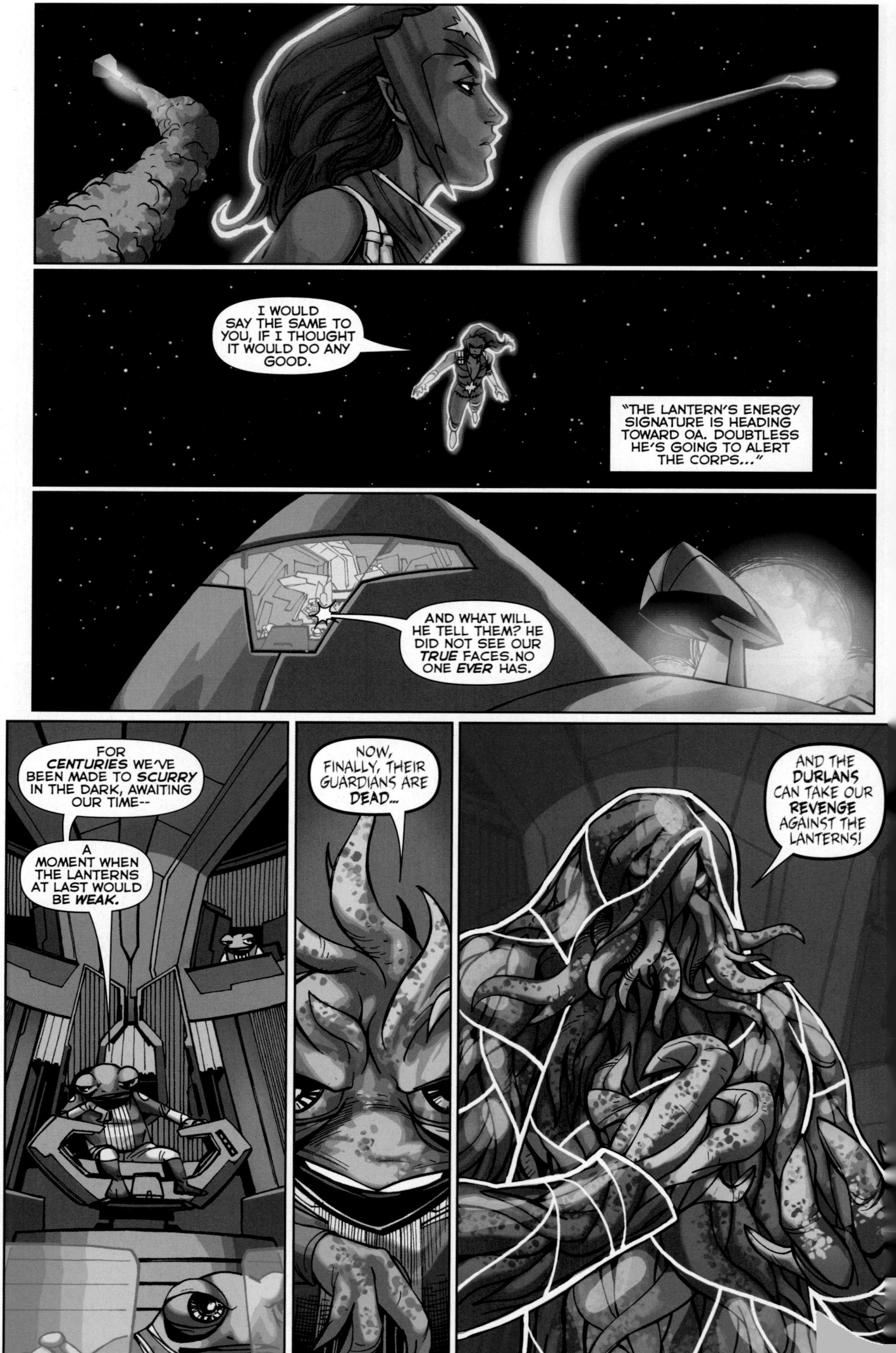
I WOULD SAY THE SAME TO YOU, IF I THOUGHT IT WOULD DO ANY GOOD.
"THE LANTERN'S ENERGY SIGNATURE IS HEADING TOWARD OA. DOUBTLESS HE'S GOING TO ALERT THE CORPS..."
AND WHAT WILL HE TELL THEM? HE DID NOT SEE OUR TRUE FACES. NO ONE EVER HAS.
FOR CENTURIES WE'VE BEEN MADE TO SCURRY IN THE DARK, AWAITING OUR TIME--
A MOMENT WHEN THE LANTERNS AT LAST WOULD BE WEAK.
NOW, FINALLY, THEIR GUARDIANS ARE DEAD...
AND THE DURLANS CAN TAKE OUR REVENGE AGAINST THE LANTERNS!

MELTDOWN

VAN JENSEN & ROBERT VENDITTI writers **BERNARD CHANG** artist cover art by **J.G. JONES & PAUL MOUNTS**

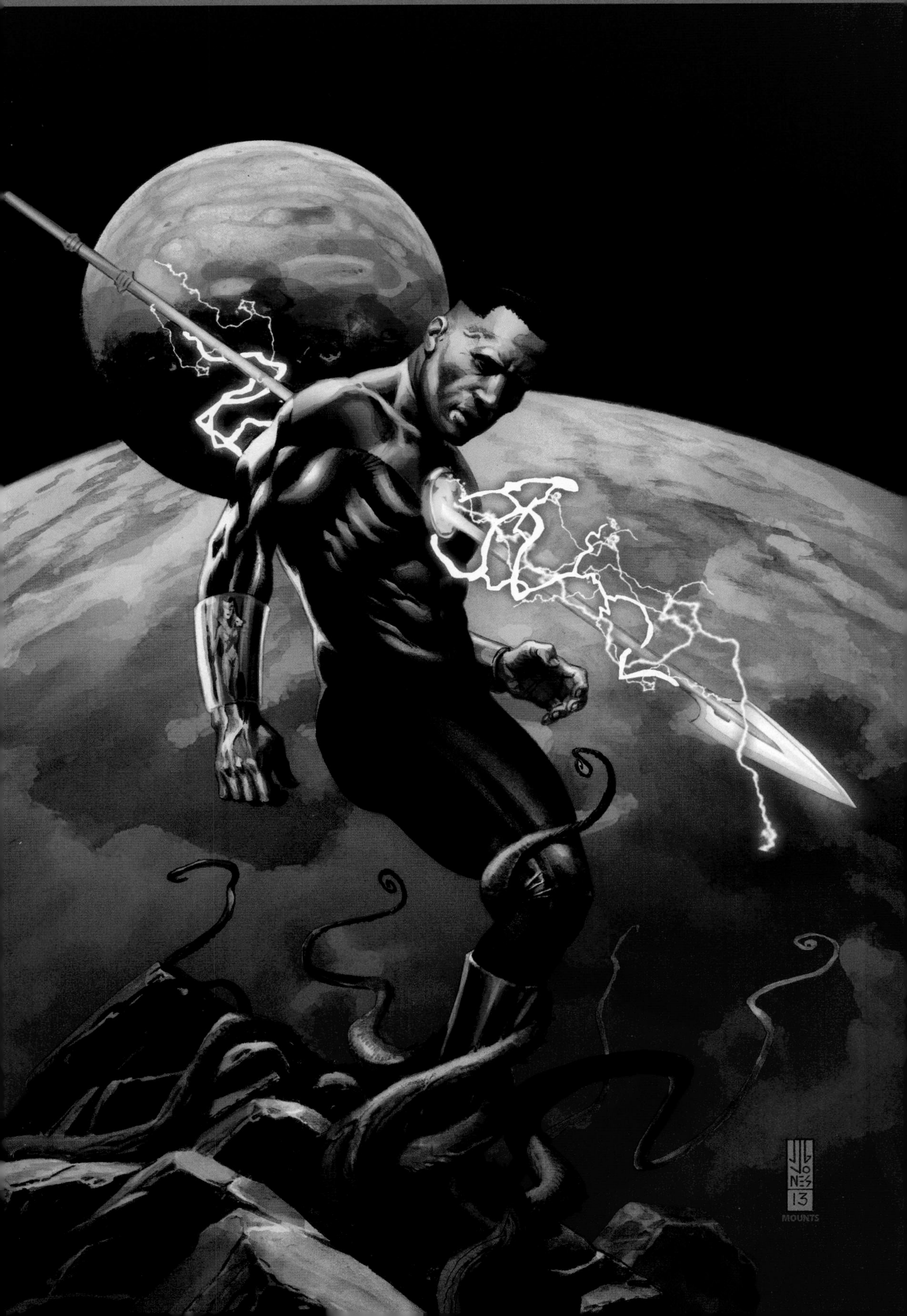
MOUNTS

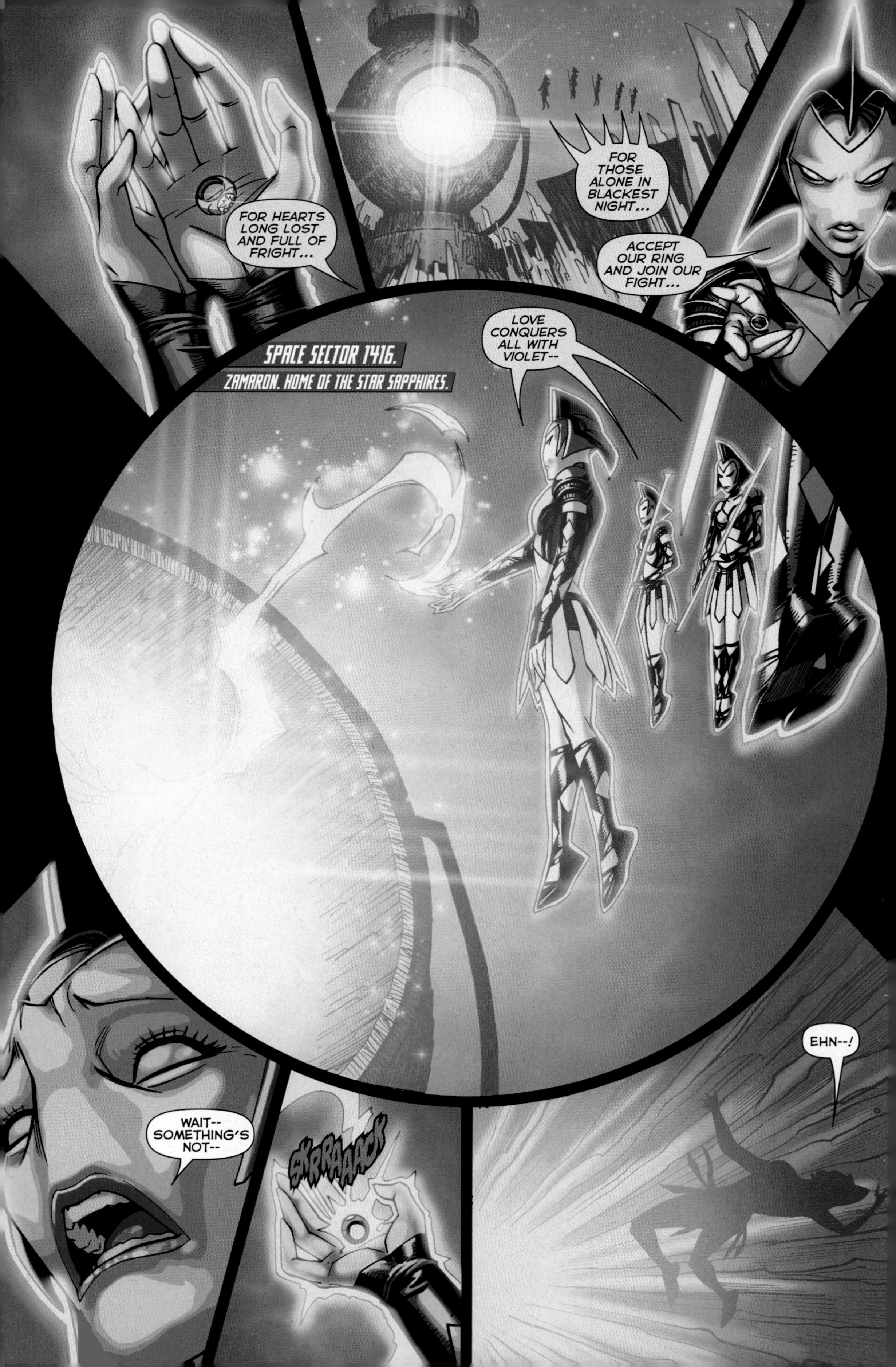
FOR HEARTS LONG LOST AND FULL OF FRIGHT...
FOR THOSE ALONE IN BLACKEST NIGHT...
ACCEPT OUR RING AND JOIN OUR FIGHT...
SPACE SECTOR 1416.
ZAMARON. HOME OF THE STAR SAPPHIRES.
LOVE CONQUERS ALL WITH VIOLET--
WAIT-- SOMETHING'S NOT--
SKRAAACK
EHN--!

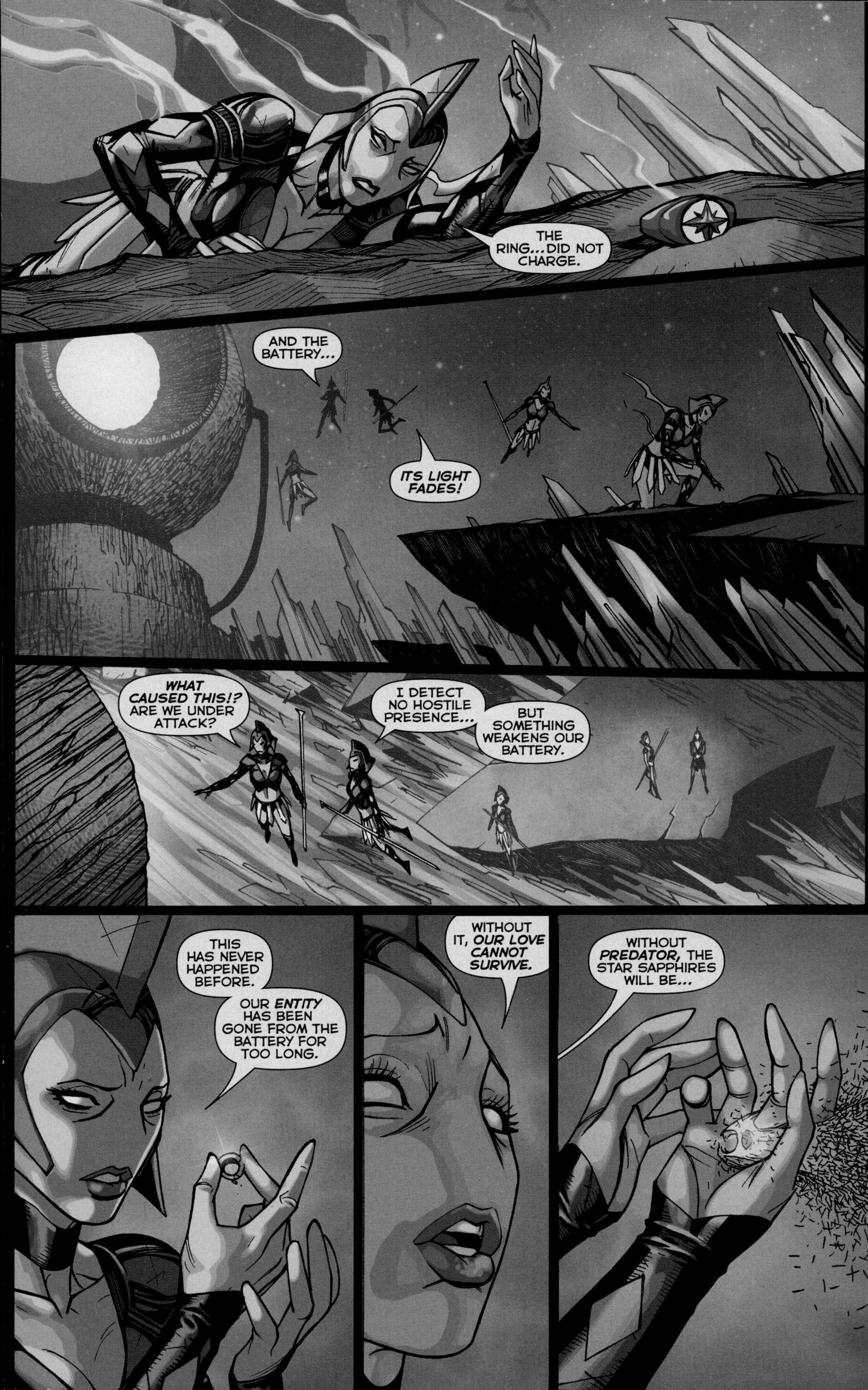
THE RING...DID NOT CHARGE.
AND THE BATTERY...
ITS LIGHT FADES!
WHAT CAUSED THIS!? ARE WE UNDER ATTACK?
I DETECT NO HOSTILE PRESENCE...
BUT SOMETHING WEAKENS OUR BATTERY.
THIS HAS NEVER HAPPENED BEFORE.
OUR ENTITY HAS BEEN GONE FROM THE BATTERY FOR TOO LONG.
WITHOUT IT, OUR LOVE CANNOT SURVIVE.
WITHOUT PREDATOR, THE STAR SAPPHIRES WILL BE...

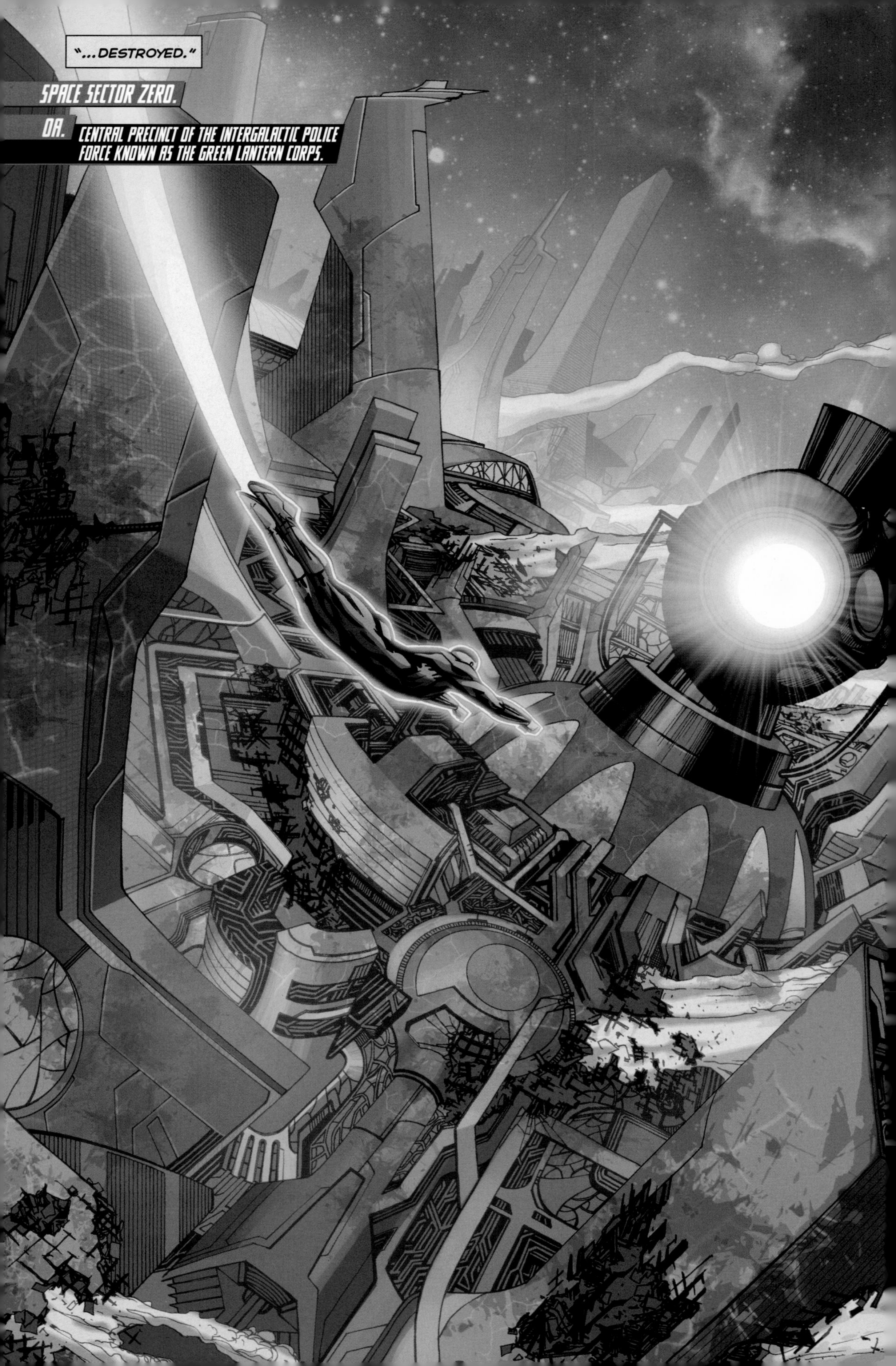
"...DESTROYED."
SPACE SECTOR ZERO.
OA.
CENTRAL PRECINCT OF THE INTERGALACTIC POLICE FORCE KNOWN AS THE GREEN LANTERN CORPS.

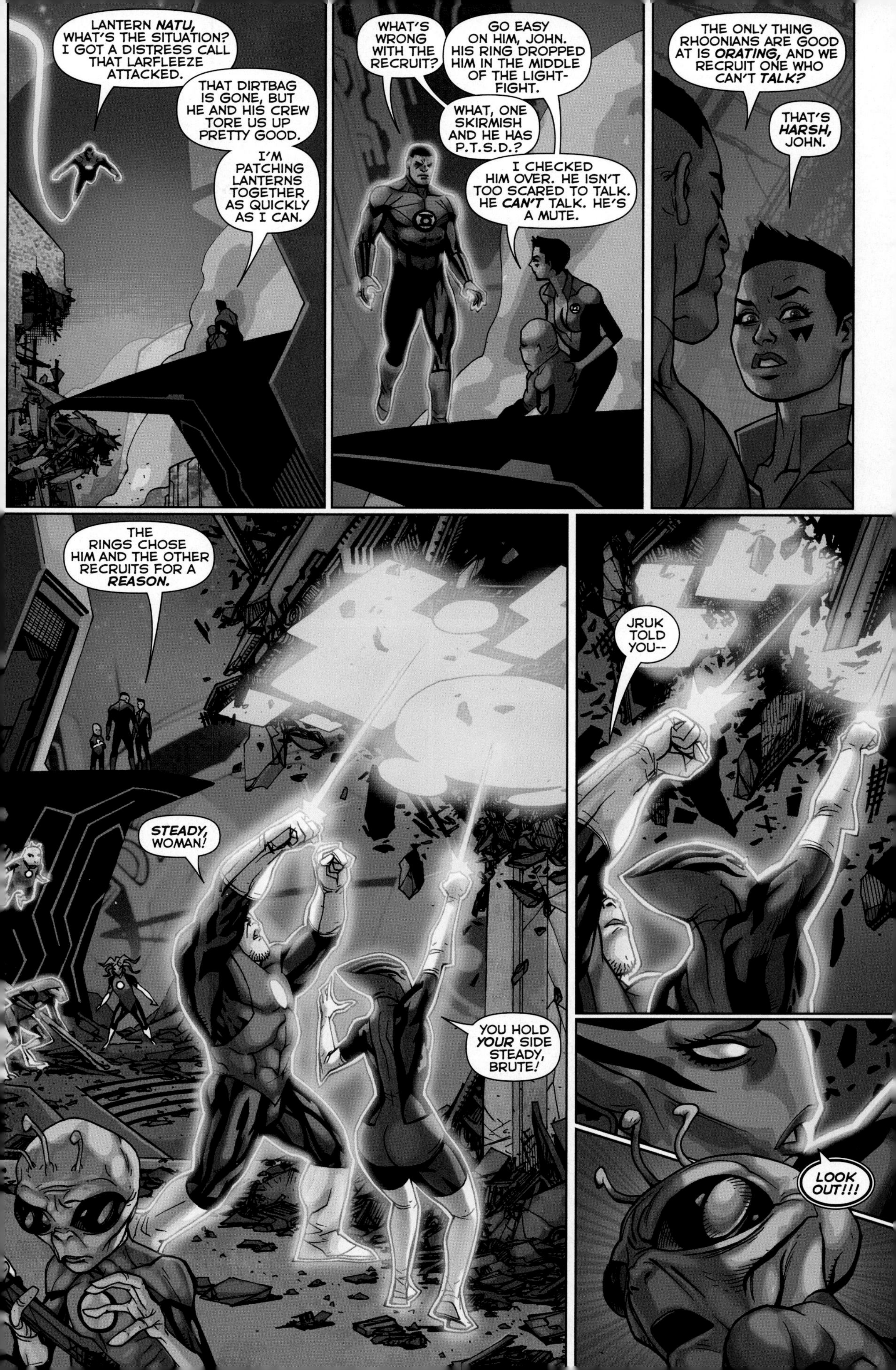

LANTERN NATU, WHAT'S THE SITUATION? I GOT A DISTRESS CALL THAT LARFLEEZE ATTACKED.
THAT DIRTBAG IS GONE, BUT HE AND HIS CREW TORE US UP PRETTY GOOD.
I'M PATCHING LANTERNS TOGETHER AS QUICKLY AS I CAN.
WHAT'S WRONG WITH THE RECRUIT?
GO EASY ON HIM, JOHN. HIS RING DROPPED HIM IN THE MIDDLE OF THE LIGHT-FIGHT.
WHAT, ONE SKIRMISH AND HE HAS P.T.S.D.?
I CHECKED HIM OVER. HE ISN'T TOO SCARED TO TALK. HE CAN'T TALK. HE'S A MUTE.
THE ONLY THING RHOONIANS ARE GOOD AT IS ORATING, AND WE RECRUIT ONE WHO CAN'T TALK?
THAT'S HARSH, JOHN.
THE RINGS CHOSE HIM AND THE OTHER RECRUITS FOR A REASON.
STEADY, WOMAN!
YOU HOLD YOUR SIDE STEADY, BRUTE!
JRUK TOLD YOU--
LOOK OUT!!!

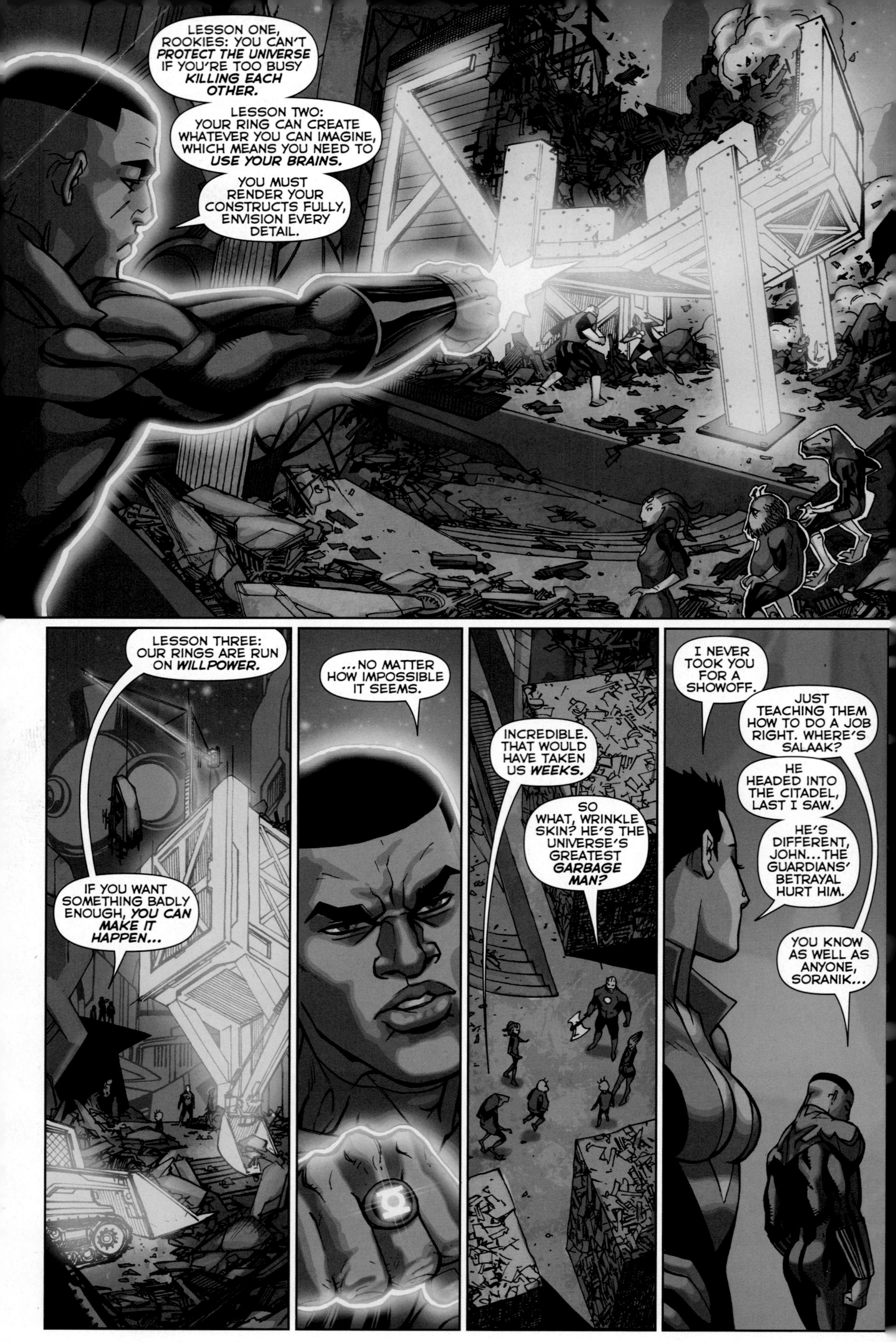
LESSON ONE, ROOKIES: YOU CAN'T PROTECT THE UNIVERSE IF YOU'RE TOO BUSY KILLING EACH OTHER.
LESSON TWO: YOUR RING CAN CREATE WHATEVER YOU CAN IMAGINE, WHICH MEANS YOU NEED TO USE YOUR BRAINS.
YOU MUST RENDER YOUR CONSTRUCTS FULLY, ENVISION EVERY DETAIL.
LESSON THREE: OUR RINGS ARE RUN ON WILLPOWER.
IF YOU WANT SOMETHING BADLY ENOUGH, YOU CAN MAKE IT HAPPEN...
...NO MATTER HOW IMPOSSIBLE IT SEEMS.
INCREDIBLE. THAT WOULD HAVE TAKEN US WEEKS.
SO WHAT, WRINKLE SKIN? HE'S THE UNIVERSE'S GREATEST GARBAGE MAN?
I NEVER TOOK YOU FOR A SHOWOFF.
JUST TEACHING THEM HOW TO DO A JOB RIGHT. WHERE'S SALAAK?
HE HEADED INTO THE CITADEL, LAST I SAW.
HE'S DIFFERENT, JOHN...THE GUARDIANS' BETRAYAL HURT HIM.
YOU KNOW AS WELL AS ANYONE, SORANIK...

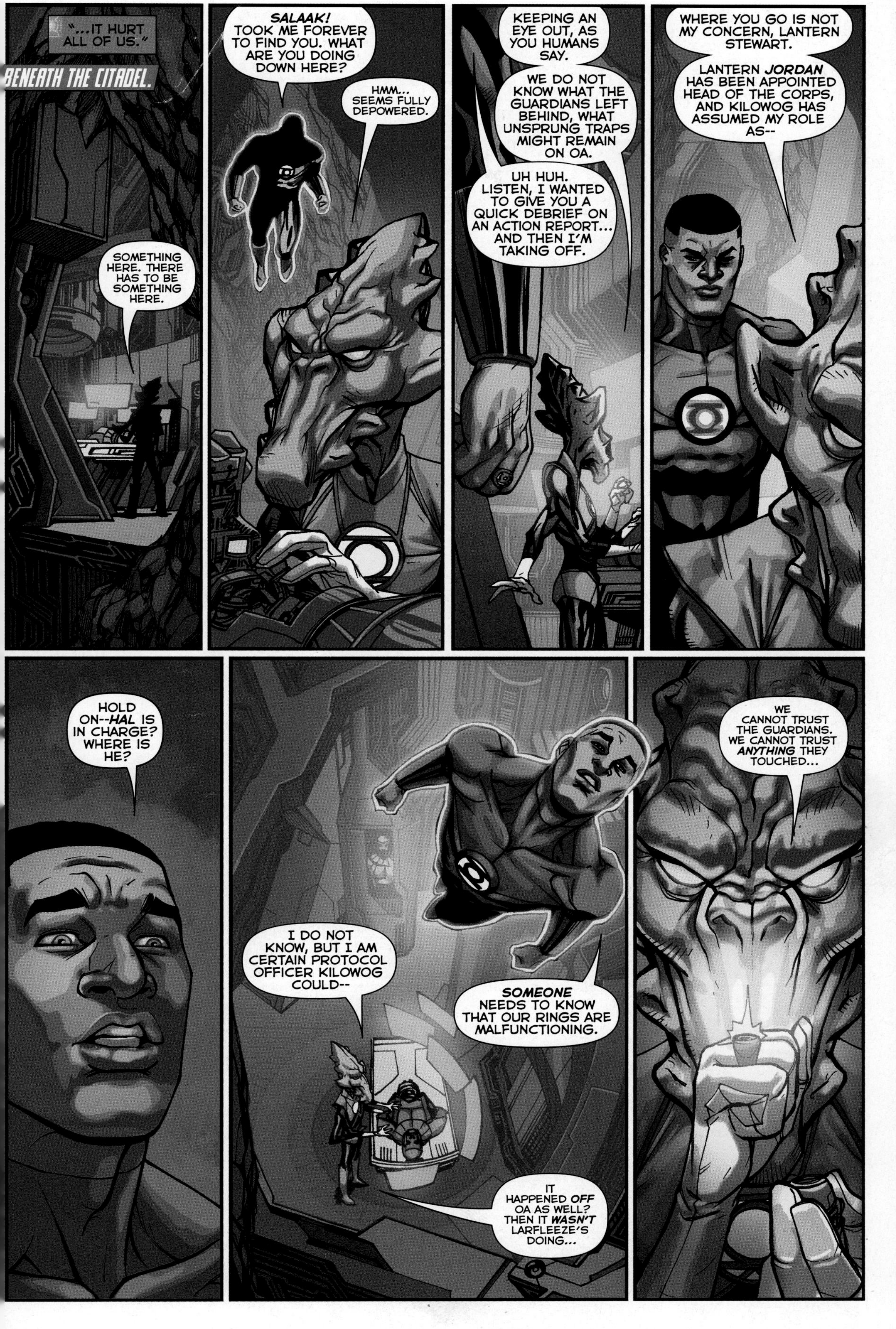
"...IT HURT ALL OF US."
BENEATH THE CITADEL.
SOMETHING HERE. THERE HAS TO BE SOMETHING HERE.
SALAAK! TOOK ME FOREVER TO FIND YOU. WHAT ARE YOU DOING DOWN HERE?
HMM... SEEMS FULLY DEPOWERED.
KEEPING AN EYE OUT, AS YOU HUMANS SAY.
WE DO NOT KNOW WHAT THE GUARDIANS LEFT BEHIND, WHAT UNSPRUNG TRAPS MIGHT REMAIN ON OA.
UH HUH. LISTEN, I WANTED TO GIVE YOU A QUICK DEBRIEF ON AN ACTION REPORT... AND THEN I'M TAKING OFF.
WHERE YOU GO IS NOT MY CONCERN, LANTERN STEWART.
LANTERN JORDAN HAS BEEN APPOINTED HEAD OF THE CORPS, AND KILOWOG HAS ASSUMED MY ROLE AS--
HOLD ON--HAL IS IN CHARGE? WHERE IS HE?
I DO NOT KNOW, BUT I AM CERTAIN PROTOCOL OFFICER KILOWOG COULD--
SOMEONE NEEDS TO KNOW THAT OUR RINGS ARE MALFUNCTIONING.
IT HAPPENED OFF OA AS WELL? THEN IT WASN'T LARFLEEZE'S DOING...
WE CANNOT TRUST THE GUARDIANS. WE CANNOT TRUST ANYTHING THEY TOUCHED...

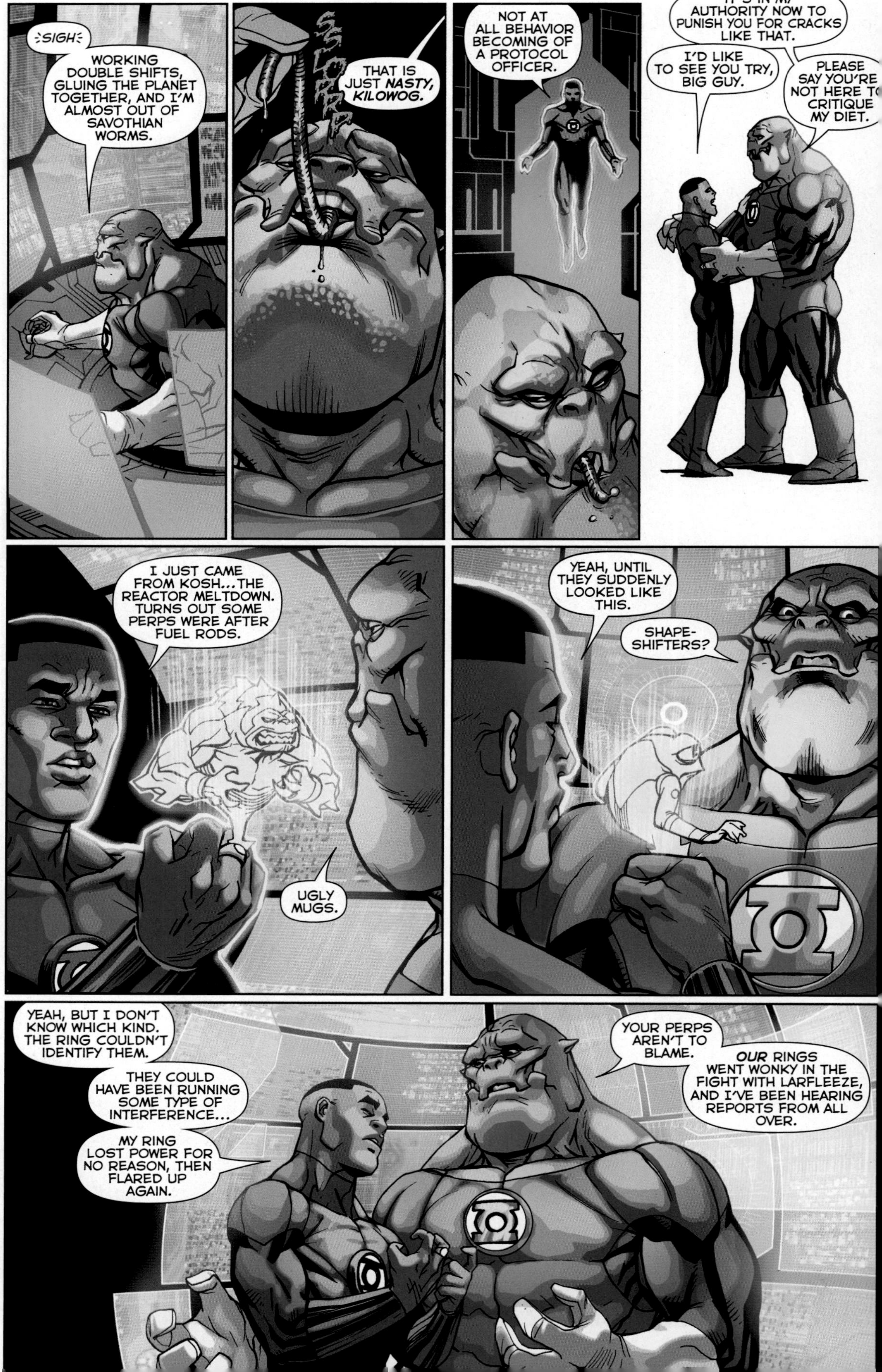
SIGH
WORKING DOUBLE SHIFTS, GLUING THE PLANET TOGETHER, AND I'M ALMOST OUT OF SAVOTHIAN WORMS.
SSLORRP
THAT IS JUST NASTY, KILOWOG.
NOT AT ALL BEHAVIOR BECOMING OF A PROTOCOL OFFICER.
IT'S IN MY AUTHORITY NOW TO PUNISH YOU FOR CRACKS LIKE THAT.
I'D LIKE TO SEE YOU TRY, BIG GUY.
PLEASE SAY YOU'RE NOT HERE TO CRITIQUE MY DIET.
I JUST CAME FROM KOSH...THE REACTOR MELTDOWN. TURNS OUT SOME PERPS WERE AFTER FUEL RODS.
UGLY MUGS.
YEAH, UNTIL THEY SUDDENLY LOOKED LIKE THIS.
SHAPE-SHIFTERS?
YEAH, BUT I DON'T KNOW WHICH KIND. THE RING COULDN'T IDENTIFY THEM.
THEY COULD HAVE BEEN RUNNING SOME TYPE OF INTERFERENCE...
MY RING LOST POWER FOR NO REASON, THEN FLARED UP AGAIN.
YOUR PERPS AREN'T TO BLAME.
OUR RINGS WENT WONKY IN THE FIGHT WITH LARFLEEZE, AND I'VE BEEN HEARING REPORTS FROM ALL OVER.

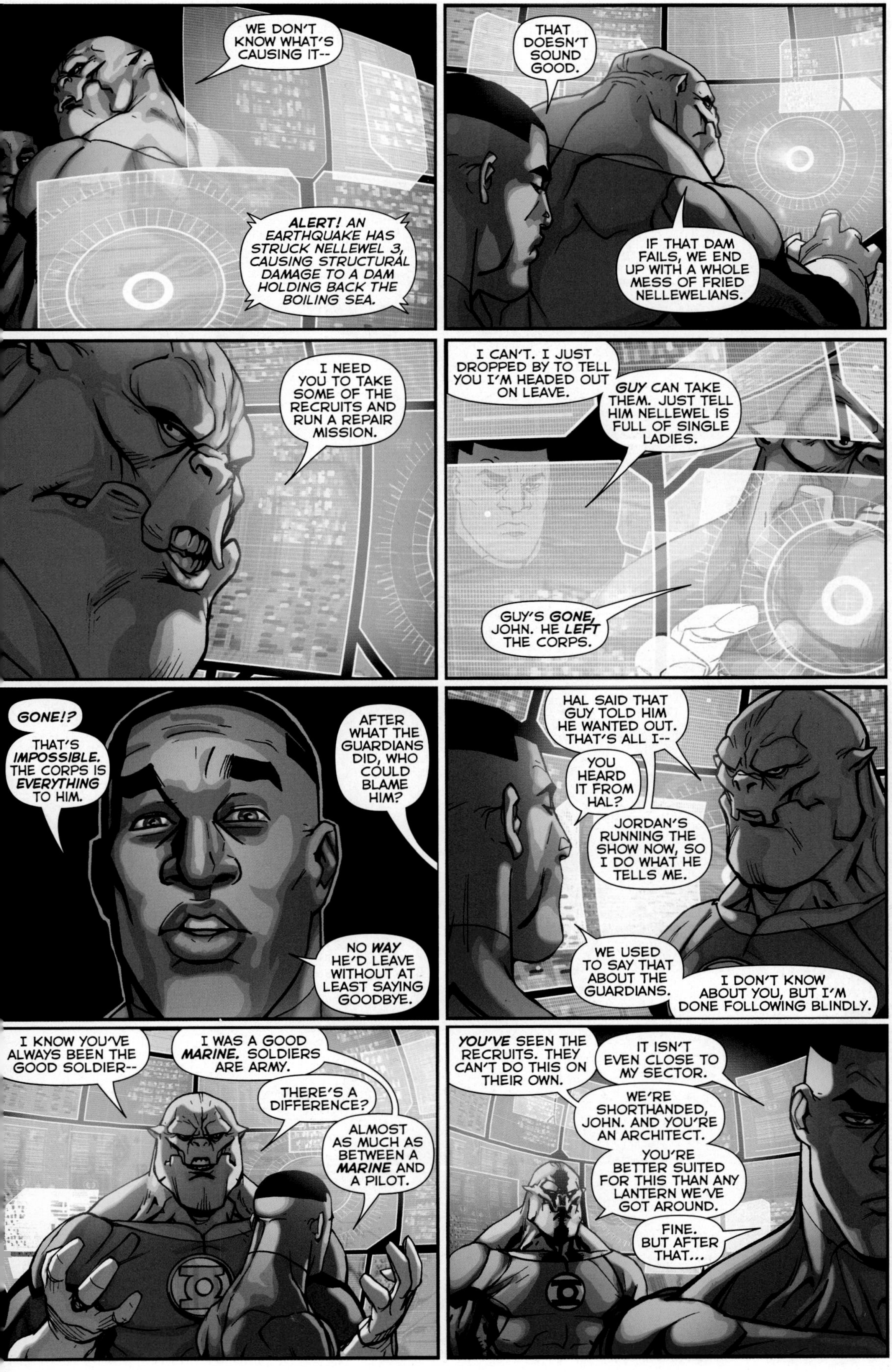
WE DON'T KNOW WHAT'S CAUSING IT--
ALERT! AN EARTHQUAKE HAS STRUCK NELLEWEL 3, CAUSING STRUCTURAL DAMAGE TO A DAM HOLDING BACK THE BOILING SEA.
THAT DOESN'T SOUND GOOD.
IF THAT DAM FAILS, WE END UP WITH A WHOLE MESS OF FRIED NELLEWELIANS.
I NEED YOU TO TAKE SOME OF THE RECRUITS AND RUN A REPAIR MISSION.
I CAN'T. I JUST DROPPED BY TO TELL YOU I'M HEADED OUT ON LEAVE.
GUY CAN TAKE THEM. JUST TELL HIM NELLEWEL IS FULL OF SINGLE LADIES.
GUY'S GONE, JOHN. HE LEFT THE CORPS.
GONE!?
THAT'S IMPOSSIBLE. THE CORPS IS EVERYTHING TO HIM.
AFTER WHAT THE GUARDIANS DID, WHO COULD BLAME HIM?
NO WAY HE'D LEAVE WITHOUT AT LEAST SAYING GOODBYE.
HAL SAID THAT GUY TOLD HIM HE WANTED OUT. THAT'S ALL I--
YOU HEARD IT FROM HAL?
JORDAN'S RUNNING THE SHOW NOW, SO I DO WHAT HE TELLS ME.
WE USED TO SAY THAT ABOUT THE GUARDIANS.
I DON'T KNOW ABOUT YOU, BUT I'M DONE FOLLOWING BLINDLY.
I KNOW YOU'VE ALWAYS BEEN THE GOOD SOLDIER--
I WAS A GOOD MARINE. SOLDIERS ARE ARMY.
THERE'S A DIFFERENCE?
ALMOST AS MUCH AS BETWEEN A MARINE AND A PILOT.
YOU'VE SEEN THE RECRUITS. THEY CAN'T DO THIS ON THEIR OWN.
IT ISN'T EVEN CLOSE TO MY SECTOR.
WE'RE SHORTHANDED, JOHN. AND YOU'RE AN ARCHITECT.
YOU'RE BETTER SUITED FOR THIS THAN ANY LANTERN WE'VE GOT AROUND.
FINE. BUT AFTER THAT...

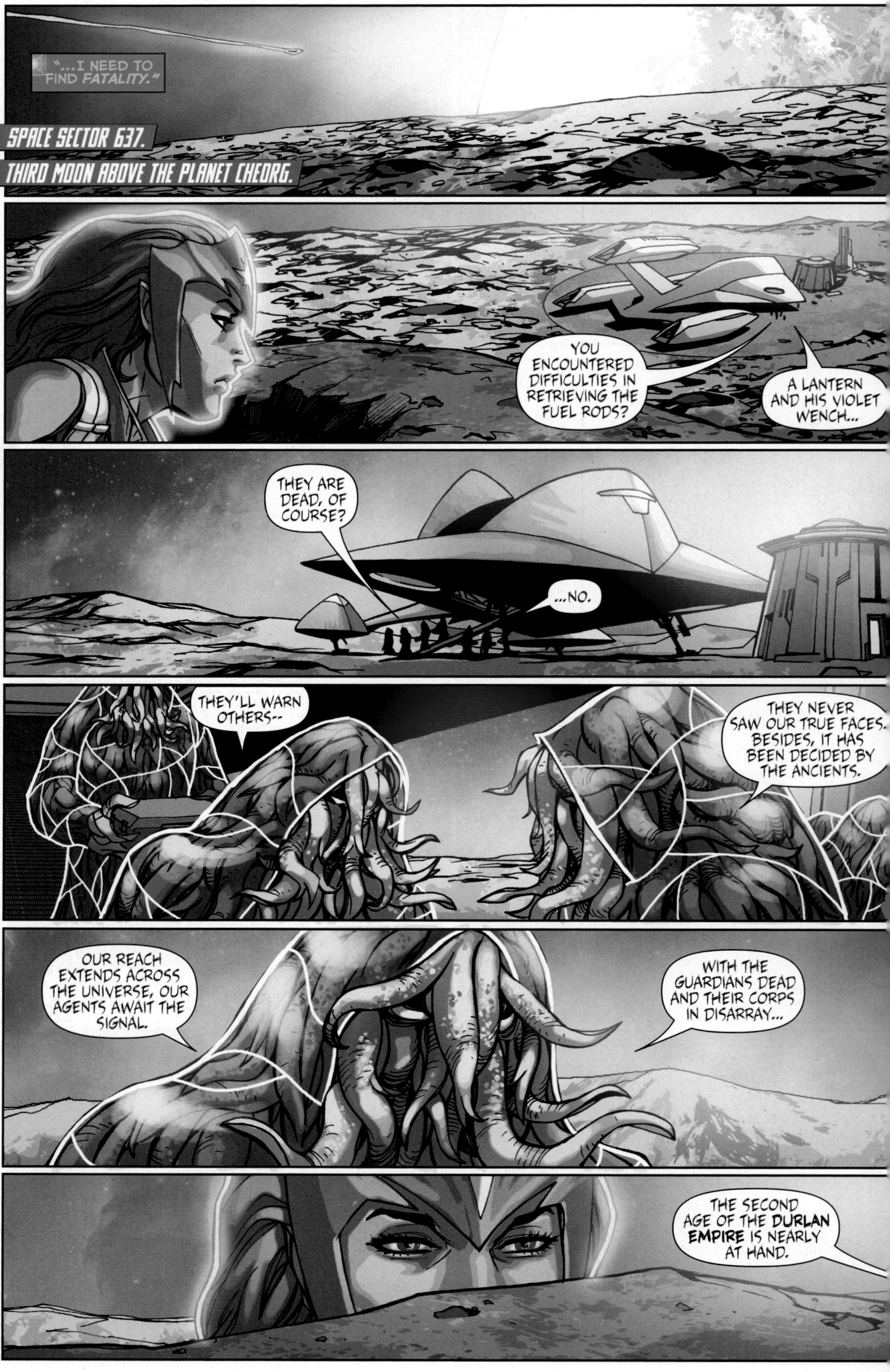
"...I NEED TO FIND FATALITY."
SPACE SECTOR 637.
THIRD MOON ABOVE THE PLANET CHEORG.
YOU ENCOUNTERED DIFFICULTIES IN RETRIEVING THE FUEL RODS?
A LANTERN AND HIS VIOLET WENCH...
THEY ARE DEAD, OF COURSE?
...NO.
THEY'LL WARN OTHERS--
THEY NEVER SAW OUR TRUE FACES. BESIDES, IT HAS BEEN DECIDED BY THE ANCIENTS.
OUR REACH EXTENDS ACROSS THE UNIVERSE, OUR AGENTS AWAIT THE SIGNAL.
WITH THE GUARDIANS DEAD AND THEIR CORPS IN DISARRAY...
THE SECOND AGE OF THE DURLAN EMPIRE IS NEARLY AT HAND.

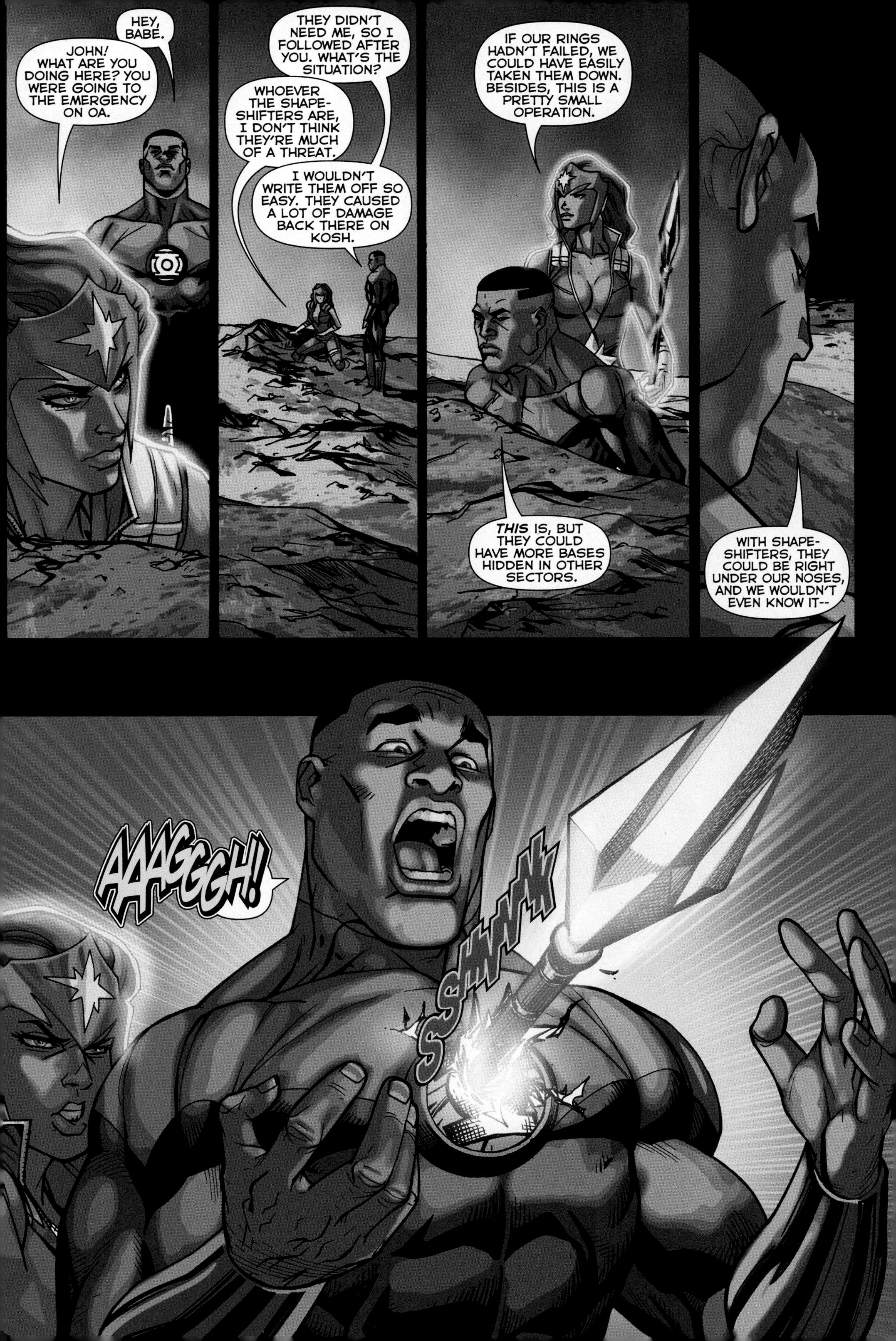
HEY, BABE.
JOHN! WHAT ARE YOU DOING HERE? YOU WERE GOING TO THE EMERGENCY ON OA.
THEY DIDN'T NEED ME, SO I FOLLOWED AFTER YOU. WHAT'S THE SITUATION?
WHOEVER THE SHAPE-SHIFTERS ARE, I DON'T THINK THEY'RE MUCH OF A THREAT.
I WOULDN'T WRITE THEM OFF SO EASY. THEY CAUSED A LOT OF DAMAGE BACK THERE ON KOSH.
IF OUR RINGS HADN'T FAILED, WE COULD HAVE EASILY TAKEN THEM DOWN. BESIDES, THIS IS A PRETTY SMALL OPERATION.
THIS IS, BUT THEY COULD HAVE MORE BASES HIDDEN IN OTHER SECTORS.
WITH SHAPE-SHIFTERS, THEY COULD BE RIGHT UNDER OUR NOSES, AND WE WOULDN'T EVEN KNOW IT--
AAAGGGH!
SSHHNNK

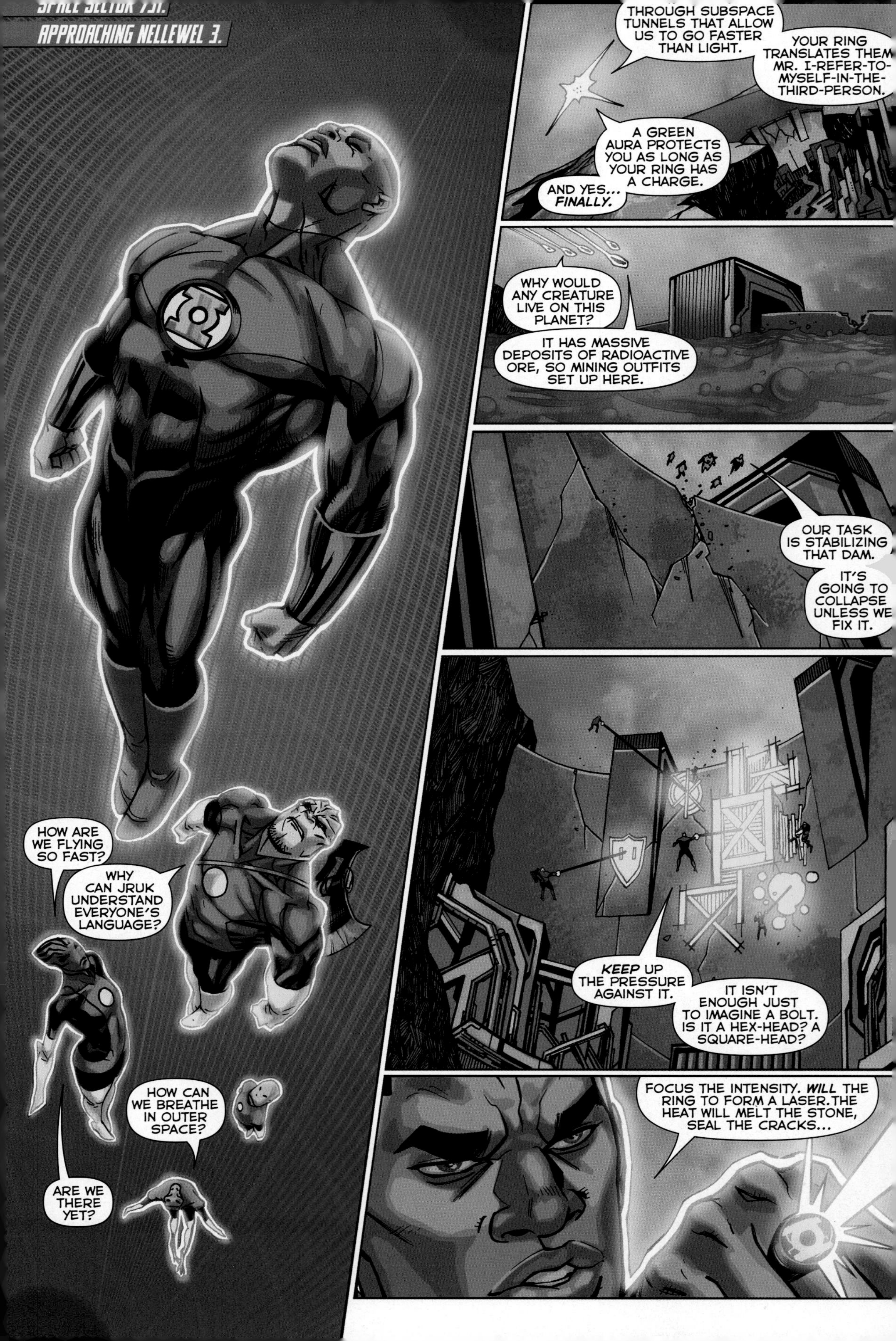

APPROACHING NELLEWEL 3.
HOW ARE WE FLYING SO FAST?
WHY CAN JRUK UNDERSTAND EVERYONE'S LANGUAGE?
HOW CAN WE BREATHE IN OUTER SPACE?
ARE WE THERE YET?
THROUGH SUBSPACE TUNNELS THAT ALLOW US TO GO FASTER THAN LIGHT.
YOUR RING TRANSLATES THEM MR. I-REFER-TO-MYSELF-IN-THE-THIRD-PERSON.
A GREEN AURA PROTECTS YOU AS LONG AS YOUR RING HAS A CHARGE.
AND YES... *FINALLY.*
WHY WOULD ANY CREATURE LIVE ON THIS PLANET?
IT HAS MASSIVE DEPOSITS OF RADIOACTIVE ORE, SO MINING OUTFITS SET UP HERE.
OUR TASK IS STABILIZING THAT DAM.
IT'S GOING TO COLLAPSE UNLESS WE FIX IT.
KEEP UP THE PRESSURE AGAINST IT.
IT ISN'T ENOUGH JUST TO IMAGINE A BOLT. IS IT A HEX-HEAD? A SQUARE-HEAD?
FOCUS THE INTENSITY. *WILL* THE RING TO FORM A LASER. THE HEAT WILL MELT THE STONE, SEAL THE CRACKS...

SYSTEM MALFUNCTION.

NOT AGAIN!

GRAB ON TO SOMETHING!

AHHH!

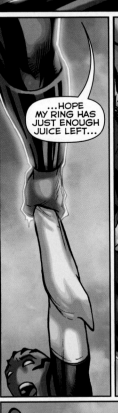

...HOPE MY RING HAS JUST ENOUGH JUICE LEFT...

...TO GET EVERYONE...

...TO THE GROUND.

JRUK'S RING IS THE ONLY *GOOD* PART ABOUT BEING A LANTERN, AND NOW IT DOESN'T EVEN *WORK?*

UM, WE HAVE SOMETHING MUCH BIGGER TO WORRY ABOUT...

CRRAAKKK

RUN! THE DAM IS GIVING WAY!

THE LANTERNS HAVE FAILED-- AGAIN!

COME ON, *POWER UP!*

NEGATIVE. SYSTEM MALFUNCTION.

WE'RE GOING TO *DIE* HERE!

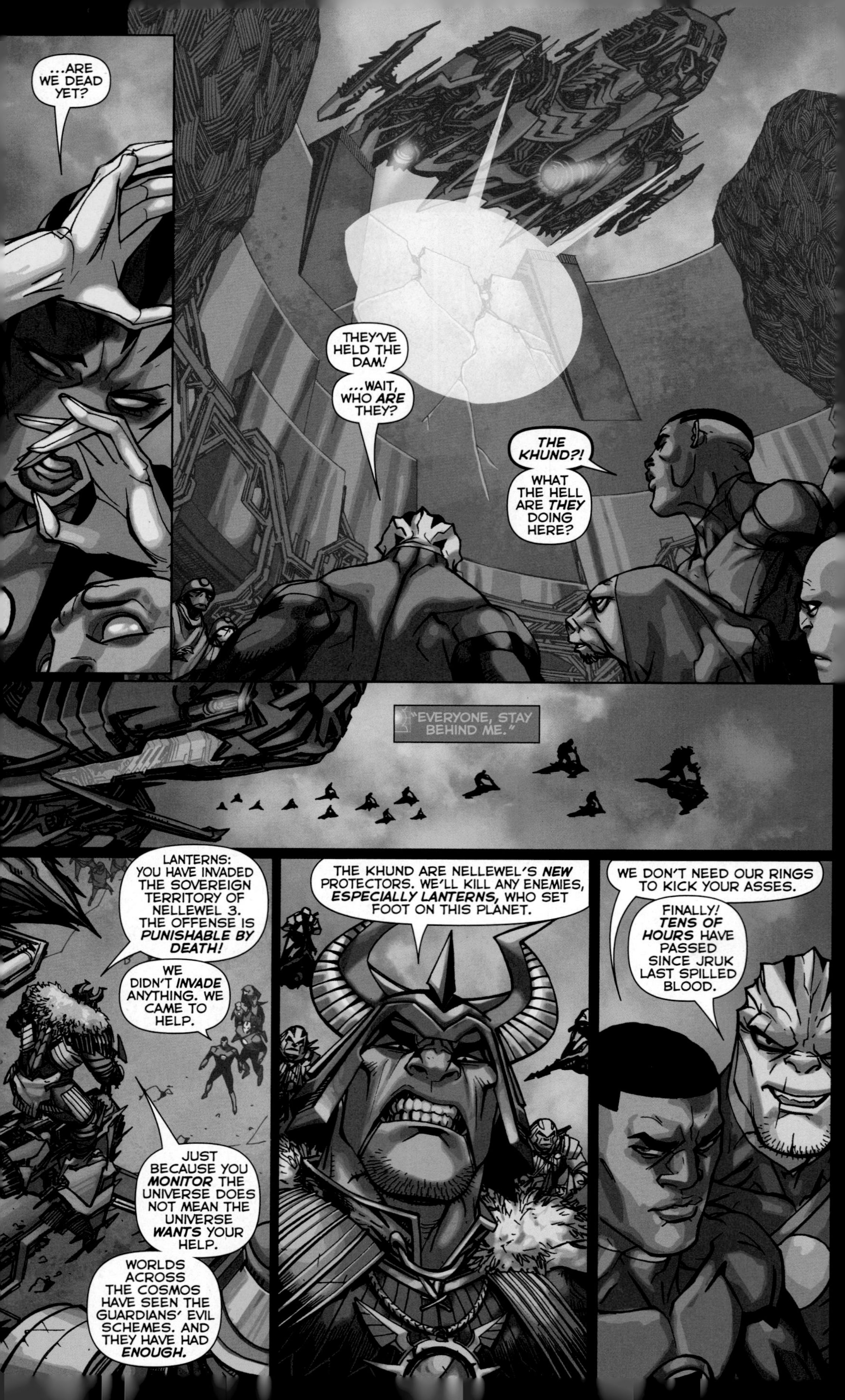

...ARE WE DEAD YET?
THEY'VE HELD THE DAM!
...WAIT, WHO ARE THEY?
THE KHUND?!
WHAT THE HELL ARE THEY DOING HERE?
"EVERYONE, STAY BEHIND ME."
LANTERNS: YOU HAVE INVADED THE SOVEREIGN TERRITORY OF NELLEWEL 3. THE OFFENSE IS PUNISHABLE BY DEATH!
WE DIDN'T INVADE ANYTHING. WE CAME TO HELP.
JUST BECAUSE YOU MONITOR THE UNIVERSE DOES NOT MEAN THE UNIVERSE WANTS YOUR HELP.
WORLDS ACROSS THE COSMOS HAVE SEEN THE GUARDIANS' EVIL SCHEMES. AND THEY HAVE HAD ENOUGH.
THE KHUND ARE NELLEWEL'S NEW PROTECTORS. WE'LL KILL ANY ENEMIES, ESPECIALLY LANTERNS, WHO SET FOOT ON THIS PLANET.
WE DON'T NEED OUR RINGS TO KICK YOUR ASSES.
FINALLY! TENS OF HOURS HAVE PASSED SINCE JRUK LAST SPILLED BLOOD.

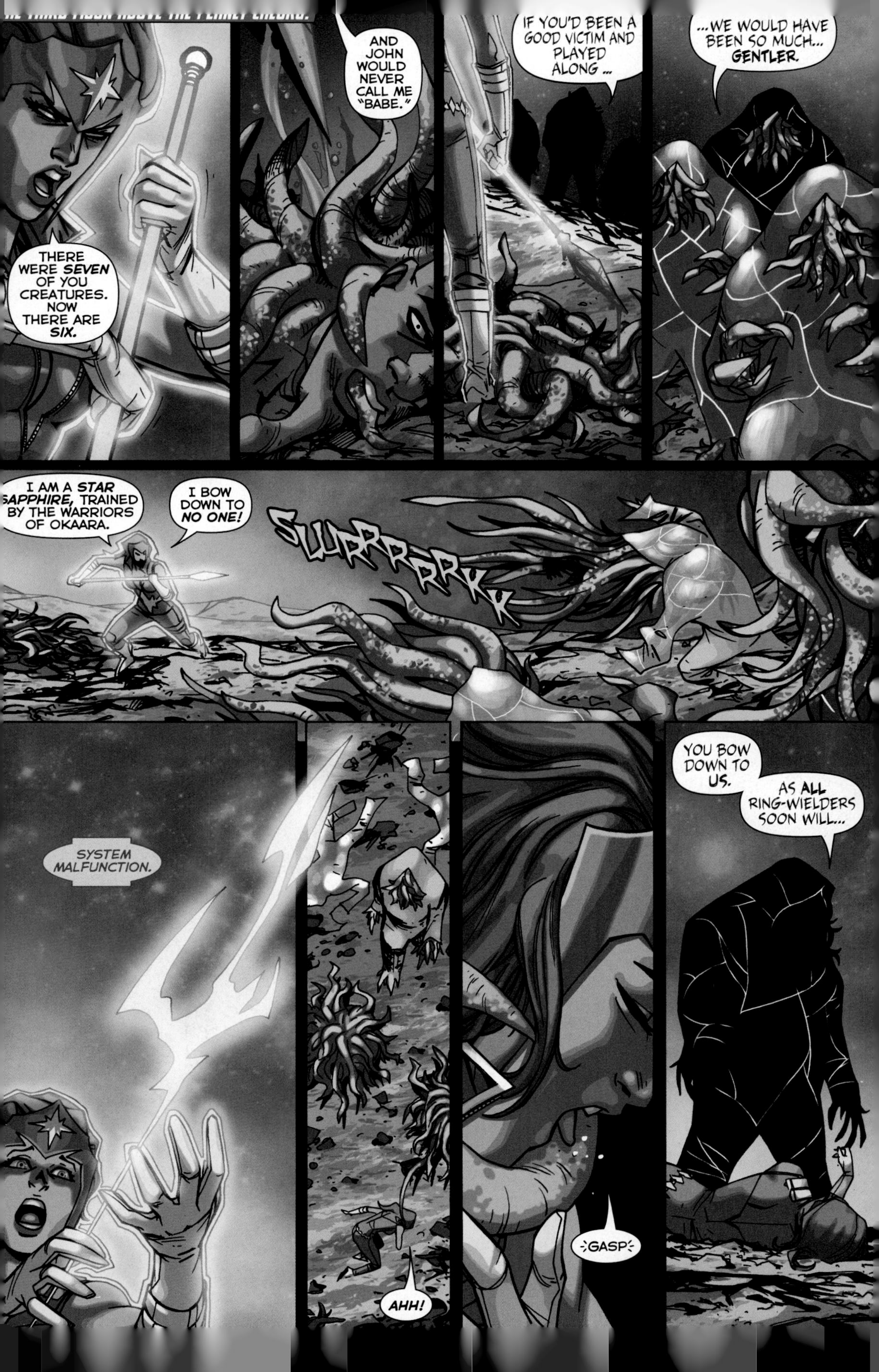
THERE WERE SEVEN OF YOU CREATURES. NOW THERE ARE SIX.
AND JOHN WOULD NEVER CALL ME "BABE."
IF YOU'D BEEN A GOOD VICTIM AND PLAYED ALONG ...
...WE WOULD HAVE BEEN SO MUCH... GENTLER.
I AM A STAR SAPPHIRE, TRAINED BY THE WARRIORS OF OKAARA.
I BOW DOWN TO NO ONE!
SLURRRRRKK
SYSTEM MALFUNCTION.
AHH!
GASP
YOU BOW DOWN TO US.
AS ALL RING-WIELDERS SOON WILL...

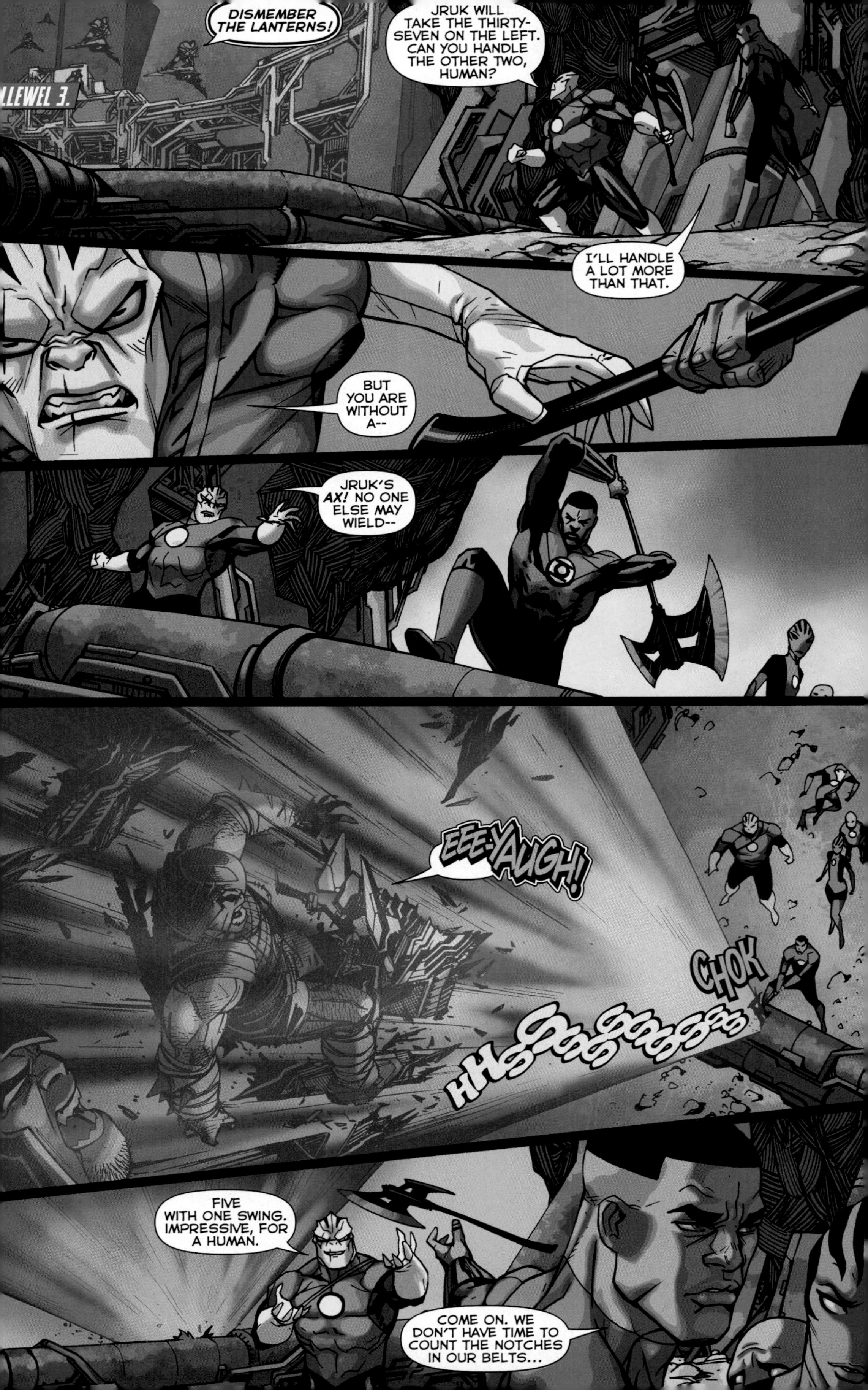
DISMEMBER THE LANTERNS!
JRUK WILL TAKE THE THIRTY-SEVEN ON THE LEFT. CAN YOU HANDLE THE OTHER TWO, HUMAN?
LLEWEL 3.
I'LL HANDLE A LOT MORE THAN THAT.
BUT YOU ARE WITHOUT A--
JRUK'S AX! NO ONE ELSE MAY WIELD--
EEE-YAUGH!
CHOK
HHOOOOOOOOOOOO
FIVE WITH ONE SWING. IMPRESSIVE, FOR A HUMAN.
COME ON. WE DON'T HAVE TIME TO COUNT THE NOTCHES IN OUR BELTS...

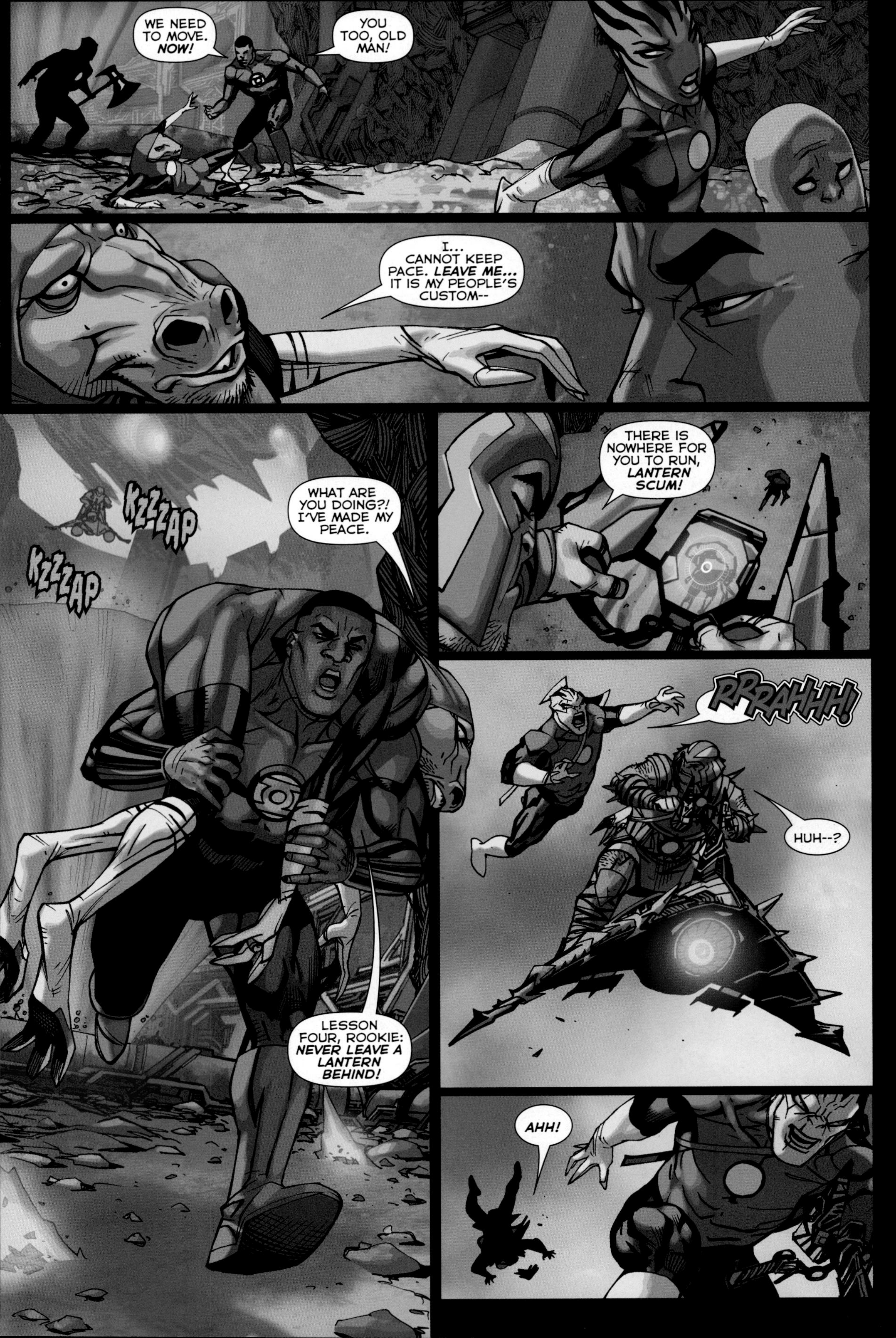
WE NEED TO MOVE. NOW!
YOU TOO, OLD MAN!
I... CANNOT KEEP PACE. LEAVE ME... IT IS MY PEOPLE'S CUSTOM--
KZZZAP
KZZZAP
WHAT ARE YOU DOING?! I'VE MADE MY PEACE.
LESSON FOUR, ROOKIE: NEVER LEAVE A LANTERN BEHIND!
THERE IS NOWHERE FOR YOU TO RUN, LANTERN SCUM!
RRRAHHH!
HUH--?
AHH!

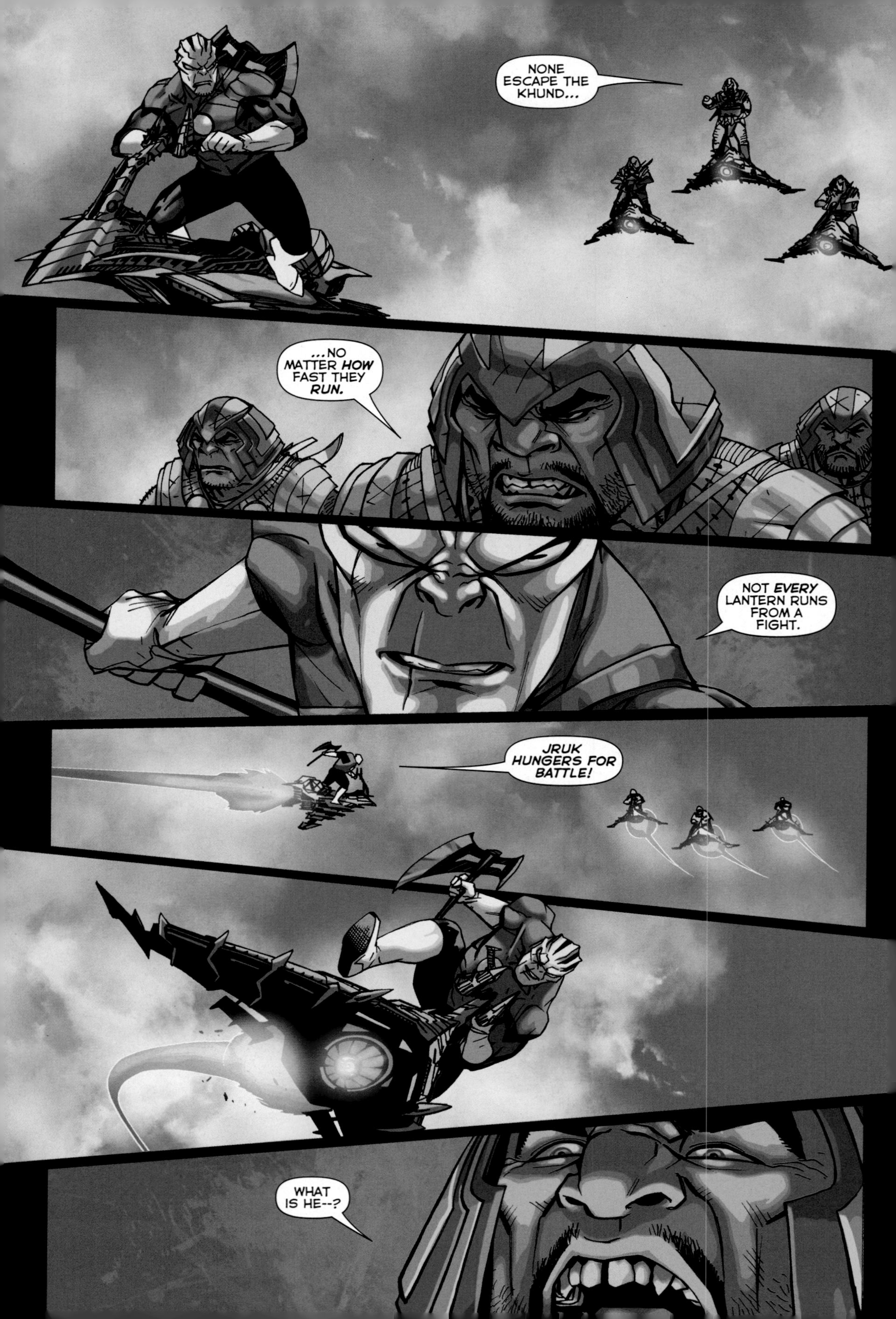
NONE ESCAPE THE KHUND...
...NO MATTER HOW FAST THEY RUN.
NOT EVERY LANTERN RUNS FROM A FIGHT.
JRUK HUNGERS FOR BATTLE!
WHAT IS HE--?

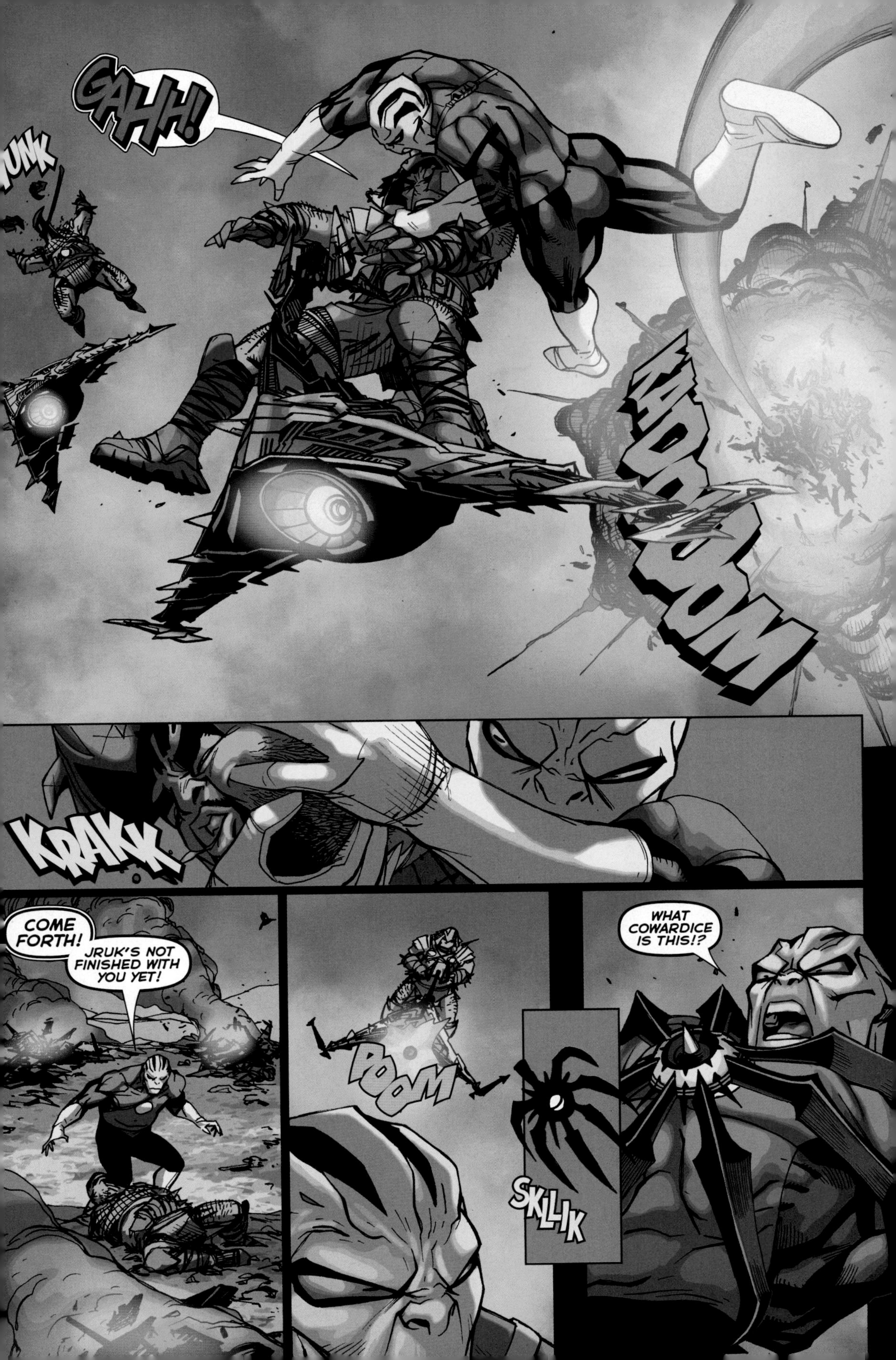

GAHH!
THUNK
KADOOOOM
KRAKK
COME FORTH!
JRUK'S NOT FINISHED WITH YOU YET!
POOM
WHAT COWARDICE IS THIS!?
SKLLIK

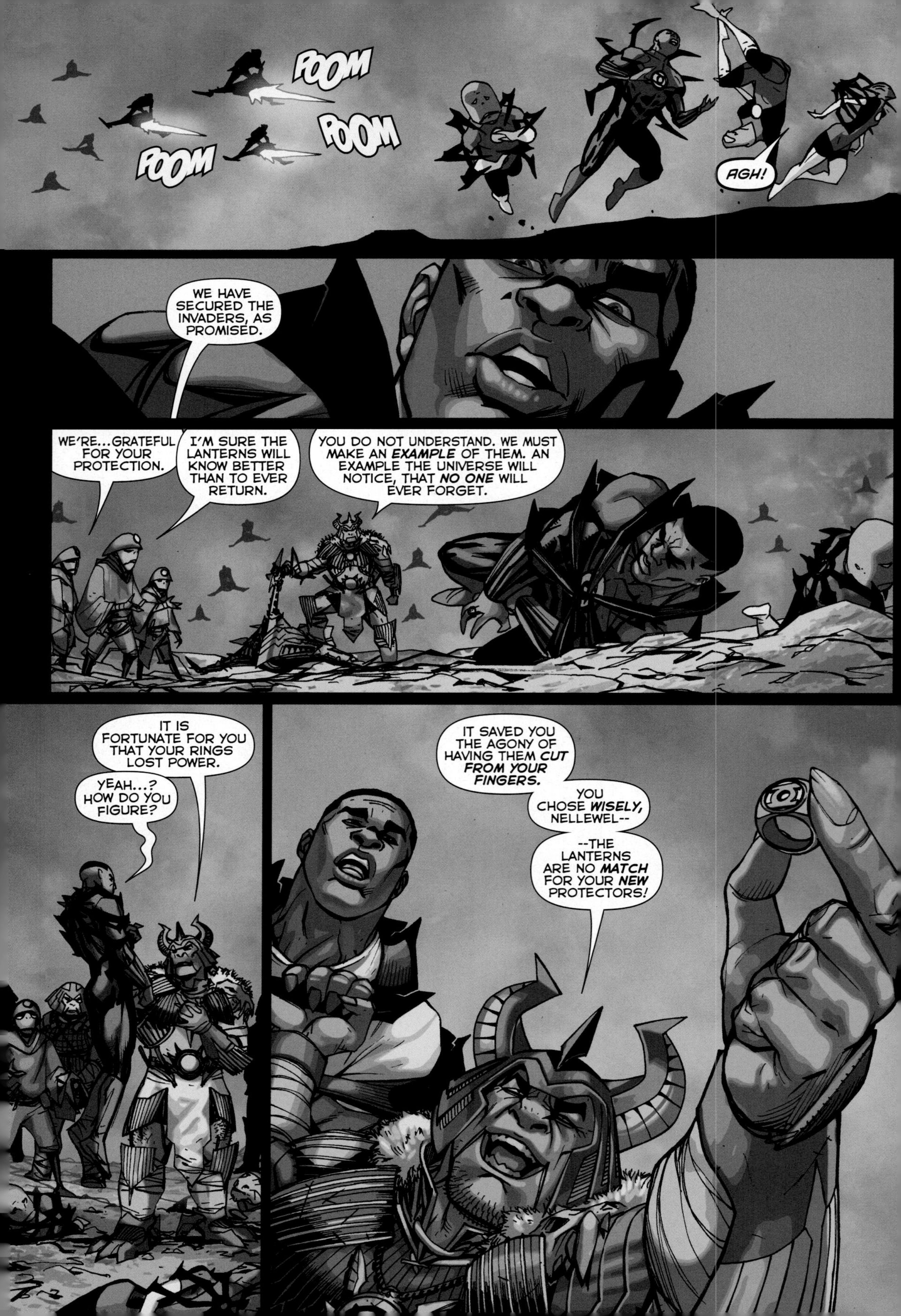
POOM
POOM
POOM
AGH!
WE HAVE SECURED THE INVADERS, AS PROMISED.
WE'RE...GRATEFUL FOR YOUR PROTECTION.
I'M SURE THE LANTERNS WILL KNOW BETTER THAN TO EVER RETURN.
YOU DO NOT UNDERSTAND. WE MUST MAKE AN *EXAMPLE* OF THEM. AN EXAMPLE THE UNIVERSE WILL NOTICE, THAT *NO ONE* WILL EVER FORGET.
IT IS FORTUNATE FOR YOU THAT YOUR RINGS LOST POWER.
YEAH...? HOW DO YOU FIGURE?
IT SAVED YOU THE AGONY OF HAVING THEM *CUT FROM YOUR FINGERS.*
YOU CHOSE *WISELY,* NELLEWEL--
--THE LANTERNS ARE NO *MATCH* FOR YOUR *NEW* PROTECTORS!

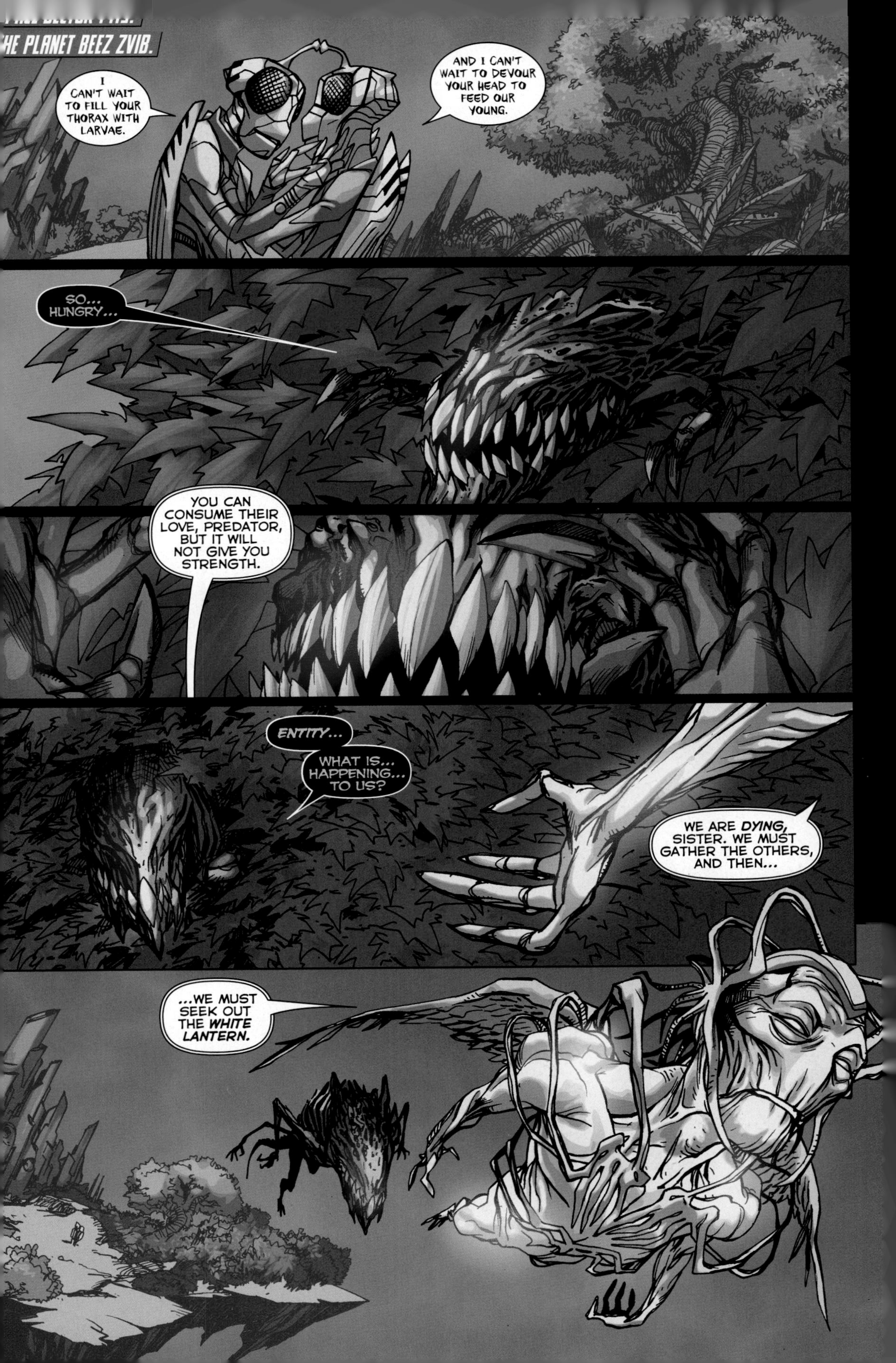
HE PLANET BEEZ ZVIB.
I CAN'T WAIT TO FILL YOUR THORAX WITH LARVAE.
AND I CAN'T WAIT TO DEVOUR YOUR HEAD TO FEED OUR YOUNG.
SO... HUNGRY...
YOU CAN CONSUME THEIR LOVE, PREDATOR, BUT IT WILL NOT GIVE YOU STRENGTH.
ENTITY...
WHAT IS... HAPPENING... TO US?
WE ARE DYING, SISTER. WE MUST GATHER THE OTHERS, AND THEN...
...WE MUST SEEK OUT THE WHITE LANTERN.

A DATE WITH THE EXECUTIONER

VAN JENSEN & ROBERT VENDITTI writers **BERNARD CHANG** artist cover art by **BERNARD CHANG & MARCELO MAIOLO**

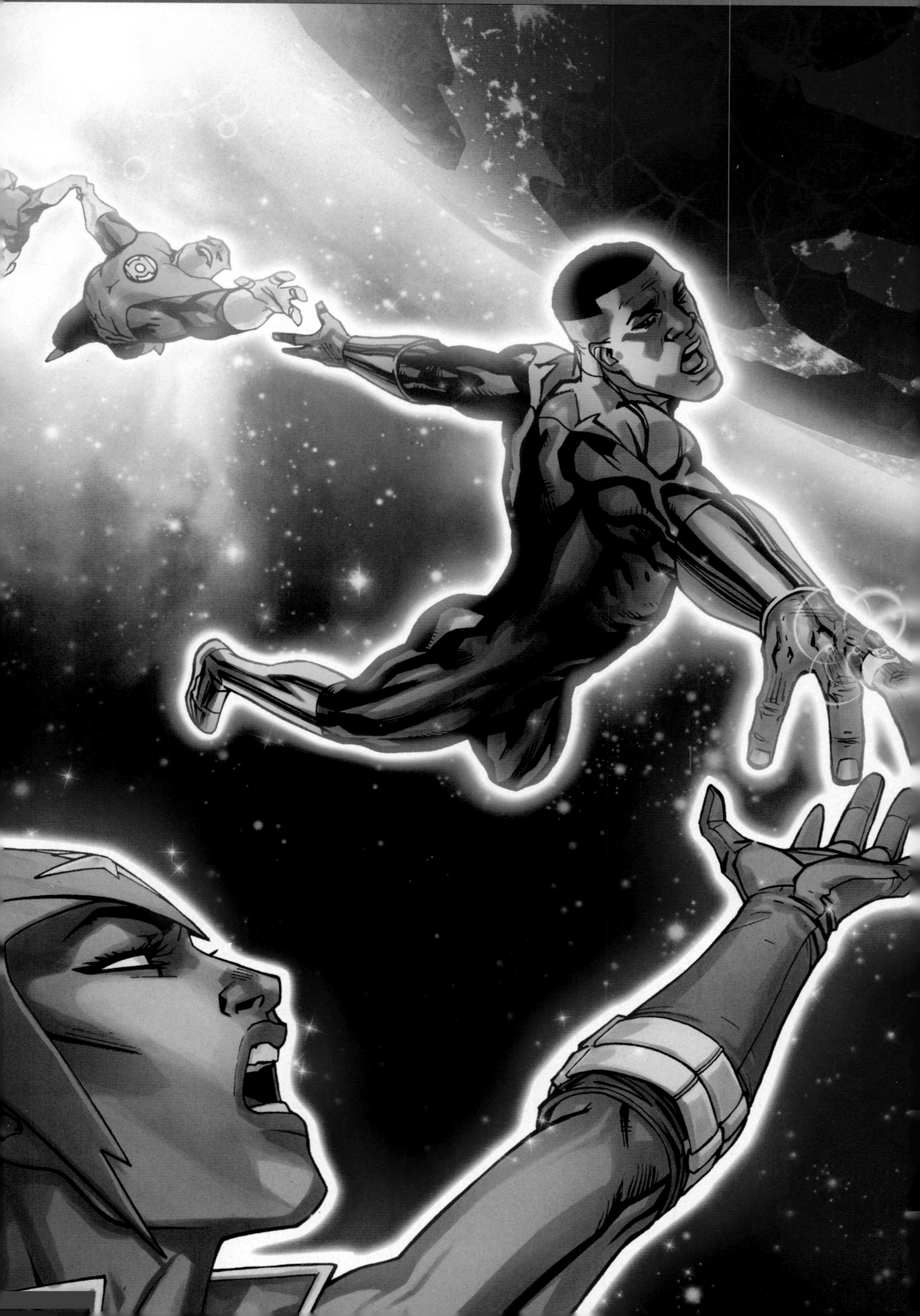

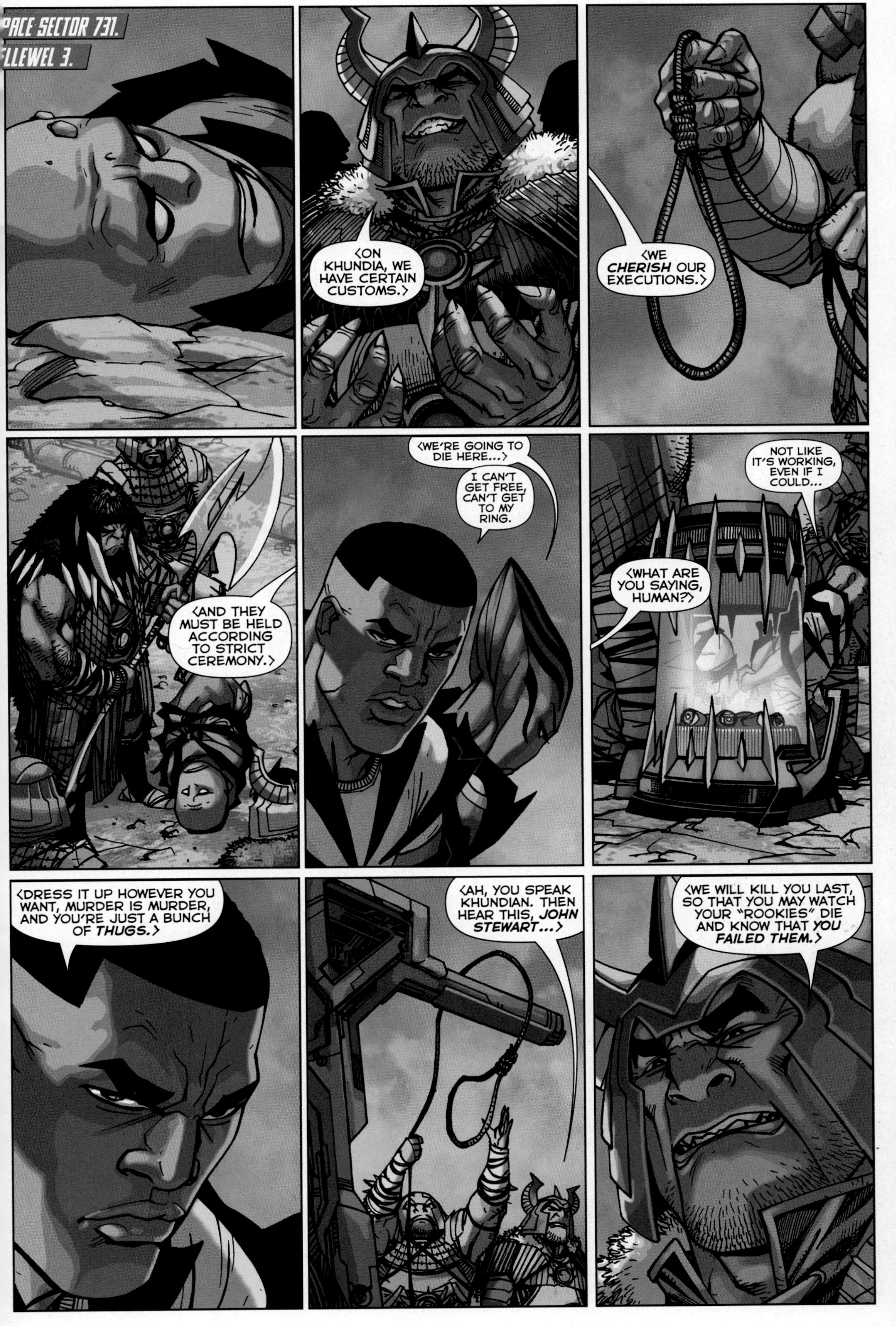
PACE SECTOR 731.
LLEWEL 3.
<ON KHUNDIA, WE HAVE CERTAIN CUSTOMS.>
<WE CHERISH OUR EXECUTIONS.>
<AND THEY MUST BE HELD ACCORDING TO STRICT CEREMONY.>
<WE'RE GOING TO DIE HERE...>
I CAN'T GET FREE, CAN'T GET TO MY RING.
NOT LIKE IT'S WORKING, EVEN IF I COULD...
<WHAT ARE YOU SAYING, HUMAN?>
<DRESS IT UP HOWEVER YOU WANT, MURDER IS MURDER, AND YOU'RE JUST A BUNCH OF THUGS.>
<AH, YOU SPEAK KHUNDIAN. THEN HEAR THIS, JOHN STEWART...>
<WE WILL KILL YOU LAST, SO THAT YOU MAY WATCH YOUR "ROOKIES" DIE AND KNOW THAT YOU FAILED THEM.>

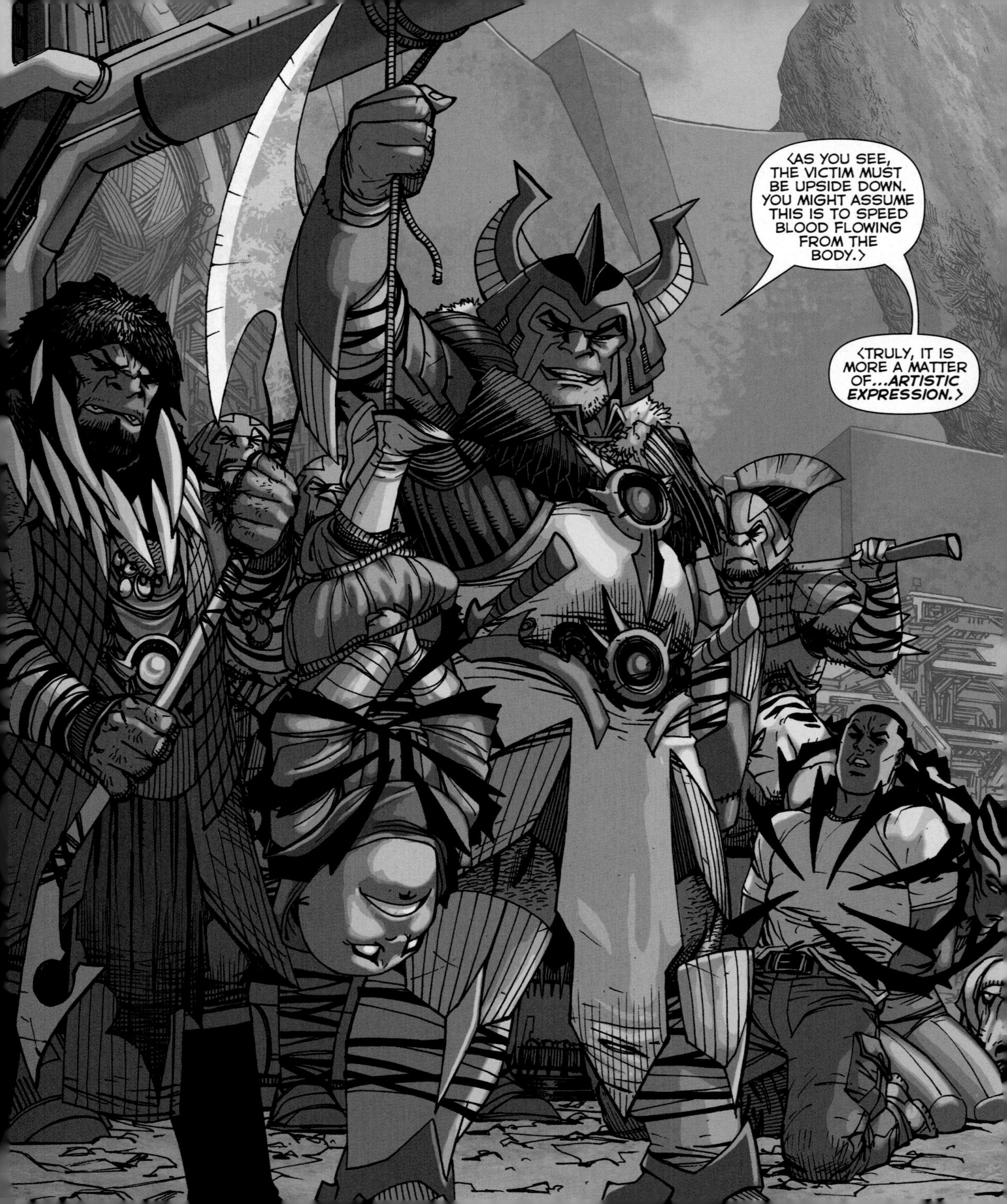

<AS YOU SEE, THE VICTIM MUST BE UPSIDE DOWN. YOU MIGHT ASSUME THIS IS TO SPEED BLOOD FLOWING FROM THE BODY.>
<TRULY, IT IS MORE A MATTER OF...ARTISTIC EXPRESSION.>

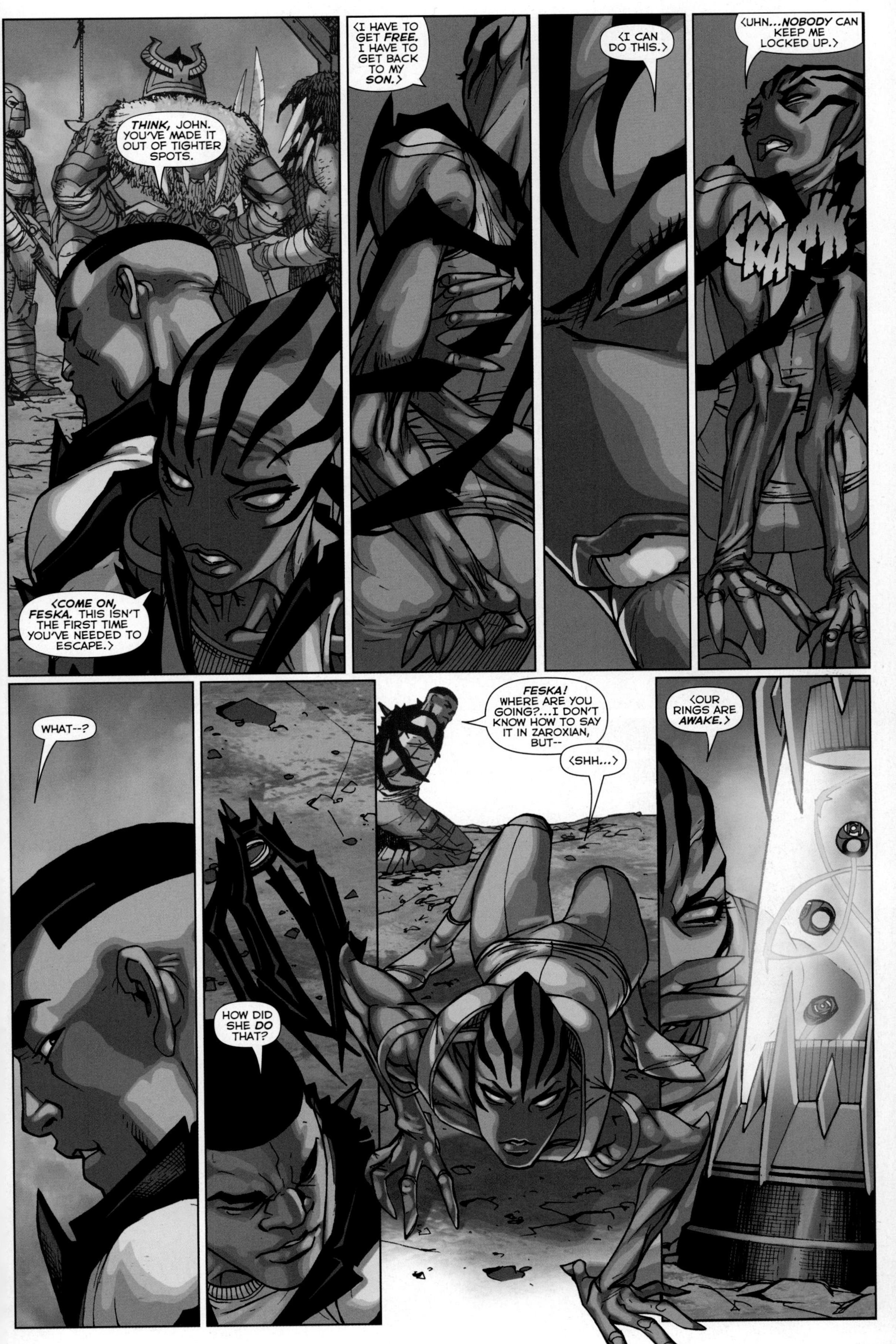

THINK, JOHN. YOU'VE MADE IT OUT OF TIGHTER SPOTS.
<COME ON, FESKA. THIS ISN'T THE FIRST TIME YOU'VE NEEDED TO ESCAPE.>
<I HAVE TO GET FREE. I HAVE TO GET BACK TO MY SON.>
<I CAN DO THIS.>
<UHN...NOBODY CAN KEEP ME LOCKED UP.>
CRACK
WHAT--?
HOW DID SHE DO THAT?
FESKA! WHERE ARE YOU GOING?...I DON'T KNOW HOW TO SAY IT IN ZAROXIAN, BUT--
<SHH...>
<OUR RINGS ARE AWAKE.>

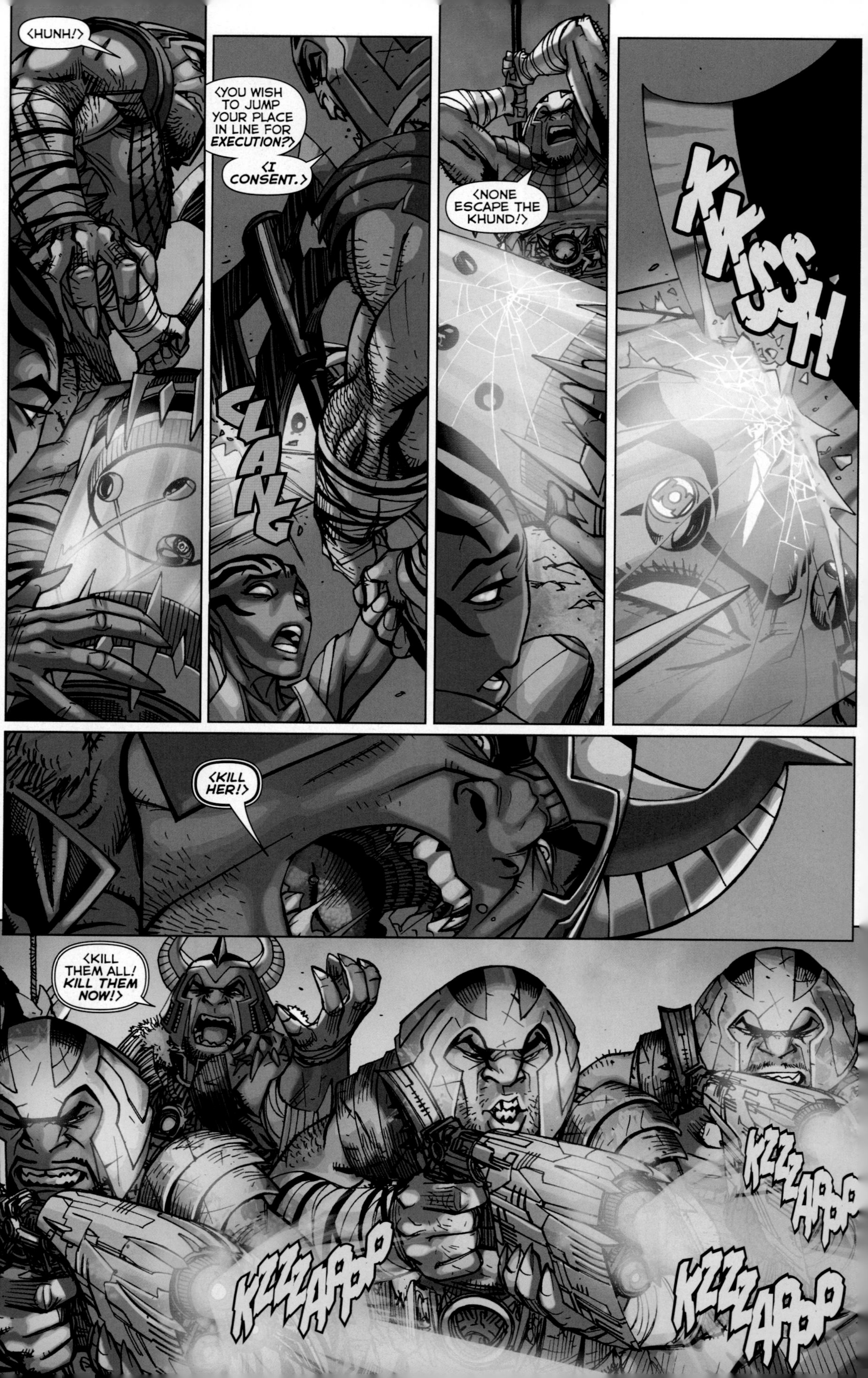
<HUNH!>
<YOU WISH TO JUMP YOUR PLACE IN LINE FOR EXECUTION?>
<I CONSENT.>
CLANG
<NONE ESCAPE THE KHUND!>
KKISSH!
<KILL HER!>
<KILL THEM ALL! KILL THEM NOW!>
KZZZAPP
KZZZAPP
KZZZAPP

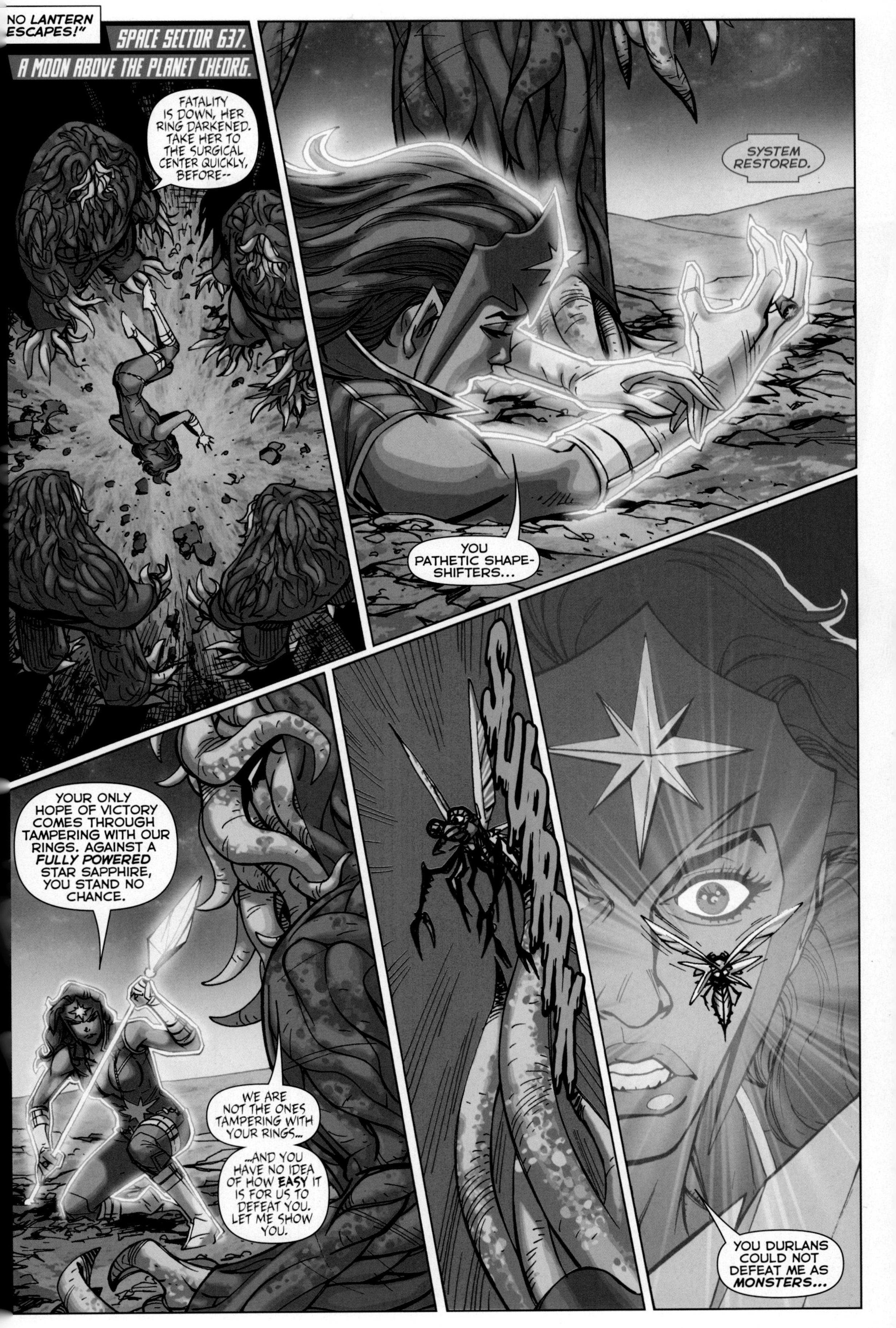
NO LANTERN ESCAPES!"
SPACE SECTOR 637.
A MOON ABOVE THE PLANET CHEORG.
FATALITY IS DOWN, HER RING DARKENED. TAKE HER TO THE SURGICAL CENTER QUICKLY, BEFORE--
SYSTEM RESTORED.
YOU PATHETIC SHAPE-SHIFTERS...
YOUR ONLY HOPE OF VICTORY COMES THROUGH TAMPERING WITH OUR RINGS. AGAINST A FULLY POWERED STAR SAPPHIRE, YOU STAND NO CHANCE.
WE ARE NOT THE ONES TAMPERING WITH YOUR RINGS...
...AND YOU HAVE NO IDEA OF HOW EASY IT IS FOR US TO DEFEAT YOU. LET ME SHOW YOU.
YOU DURLANS COULD NOT DEFEAT ME AS MONSTERS...

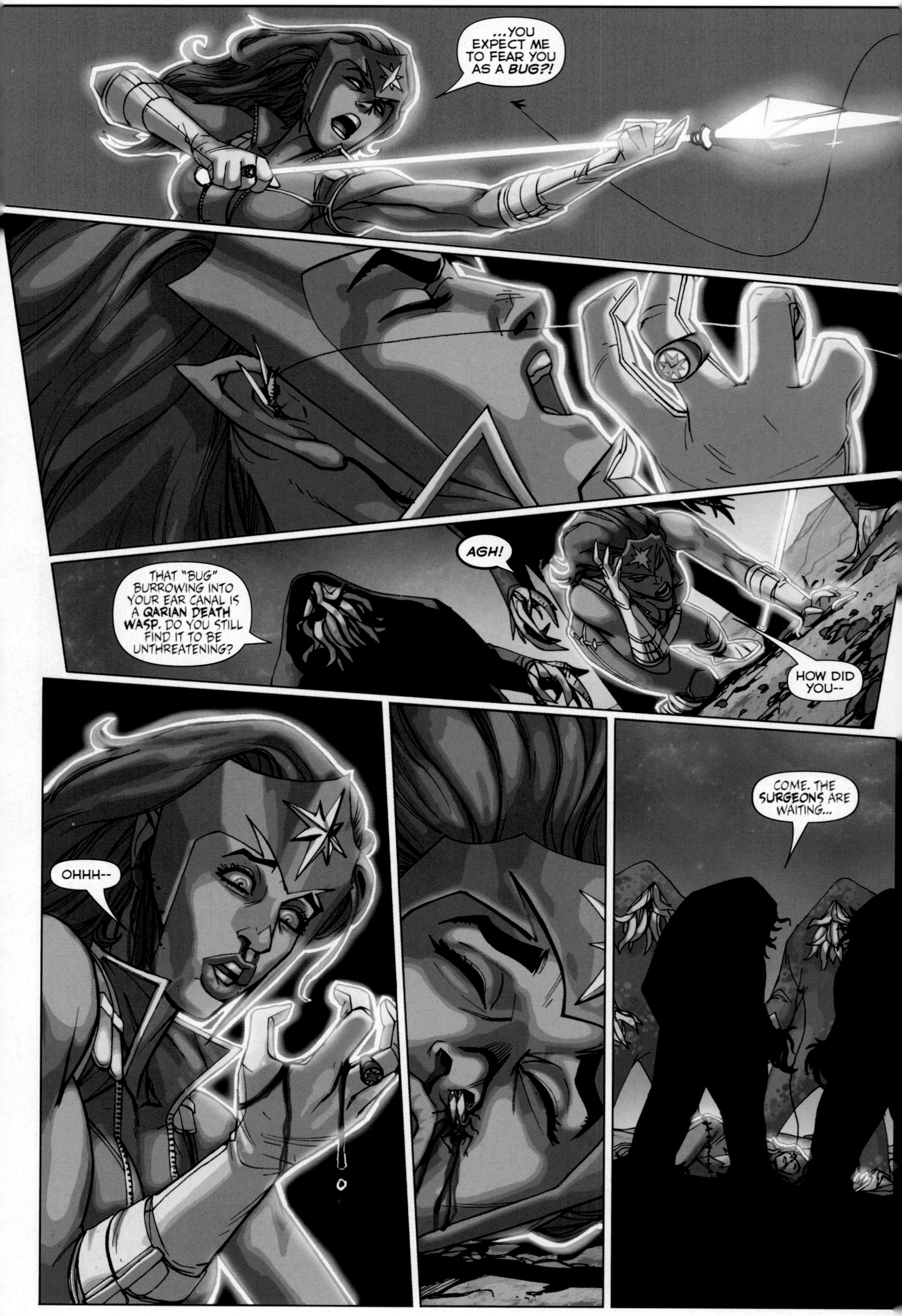
...YOU EXPECT ME TO FEAR YOU AS A BUG?!
THAT "BUG" BURROWING INTO YOUR EAR CANAL IS A QARIAN DEATH WASP. DO YOU STILL FIND IT TO BE UNTHREATENING?
AGH!
HOW DID YOU--
OHHH--
COME. THE SURGEONS ARE WAITING...

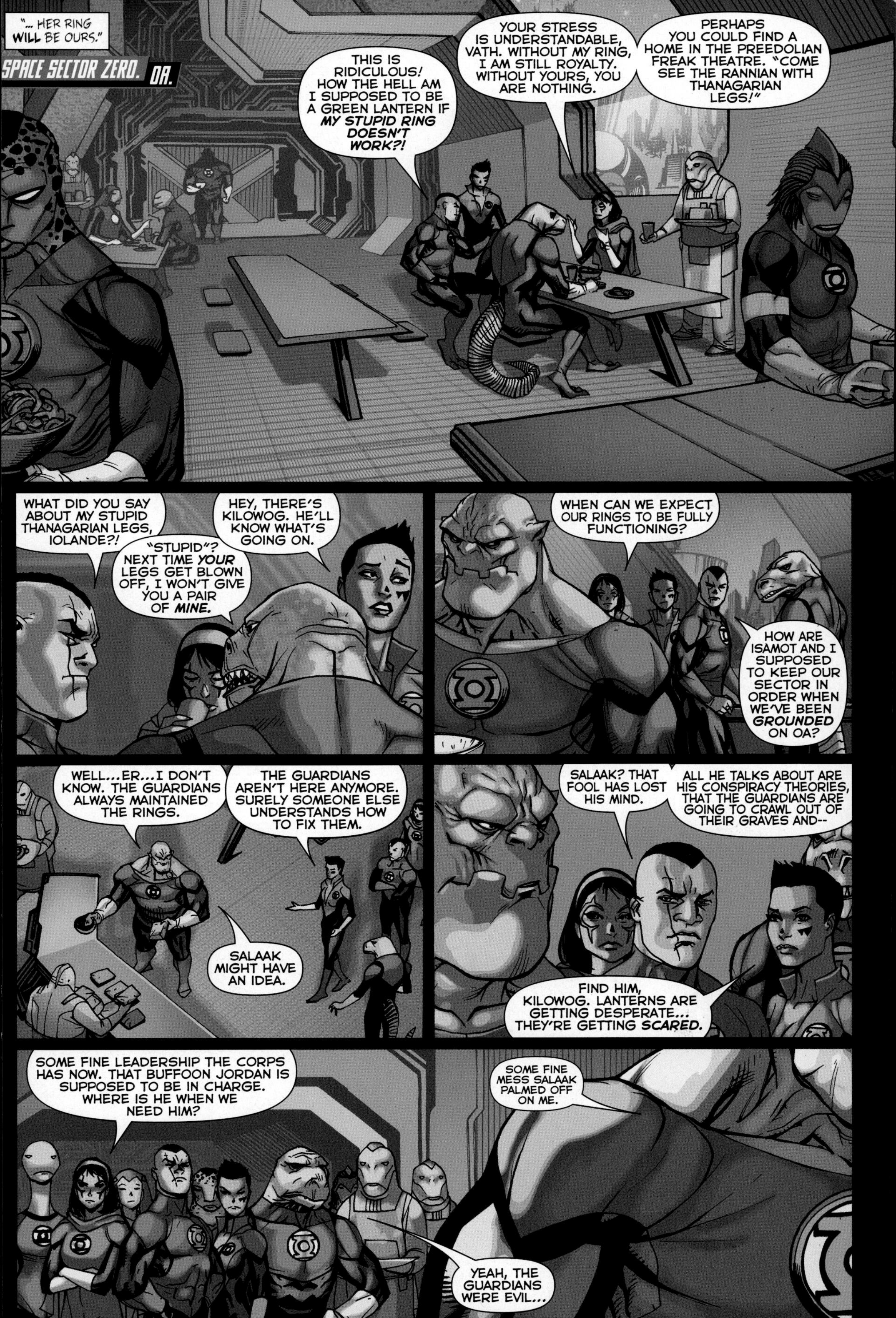
"... HER RING WILL BE OURS."
SPACE SECTOR ZERO. OA.
THIS IS RIDICULOUS! HOW THE HELL AM I SUPPOSED TO BE A GREEN LANTERN IF MY STUPID RING DOESN'T WORK?!
YOUR STRESS IS UNDERSTANDABLE, VATH. WITHOUT MY RING, I AM STILL ROYALTY. WITHOUT YOURS, YOU ARE NOTHING.
PERHAPS YOU COULD FIND A HOME IN THE PREEDOLIAN FREAK THEATRE. "COME SEE THE RANNIAN WITH THANAGARIAN LEGS!"
WHAT DID YOU SAY ABOUT MY STUPID THANAGARIAN LEGS, IOLANDE?!
"STUPID"? NEXT TIME YOUR LEGS GET BLOWN OFF, I WON'T GIVE YOU A PAIR OF MINE.
HEY, THERE'S KILOWOG. HE'LL KNOW WHAT'S GOING ON.
WHEN CAN WE EXPECT OUR RINGS TO BE FULLY FUNCTIONING?
HOW ARE ISAMOT AND I SUPPOSED TO KEEP OUR SECTOR IN ORDER WHEN WE'VE BEEN GROUNDED ON OA?
WELL...ER...I DON'T KNOW. THE GUARDIANS ALWAYS MAINTAINED THE RINGS.
THE GUARDIANS AREN'T HERE ANYMORE. SURELY SOMEONE ELSE UNDERSTANDS HOW TO FIX THEM.
SALAAK MIGHT HAVE AN IDEA.
SALAAK? THAT FOOL HAS LOST HIS MIND.
ALL HE TALKS ABOUT ARE HIS CONSPIRACY THEORIES, THAT THE GUARDIANS ARE GOING TO CRAWL OUT OF THEIR GRAVES AND--
FIND HIM, KILOWOG. LANTERNS ARE GETTING DESPERATE... THEY'RE GETTING SCARED.
SOME FINE LEADERSHIP THE CORPS HAS NOW. THAT BUFFOON JORDAN IS SUPPOSED TO BE IN CHARGE. WHERE IS HE WHEN WE NEED HIM?
SOME FINE MESS SALAAK PALMED OFF ON ME.
YEAH, THE GUARDIANS WERE EVIL...

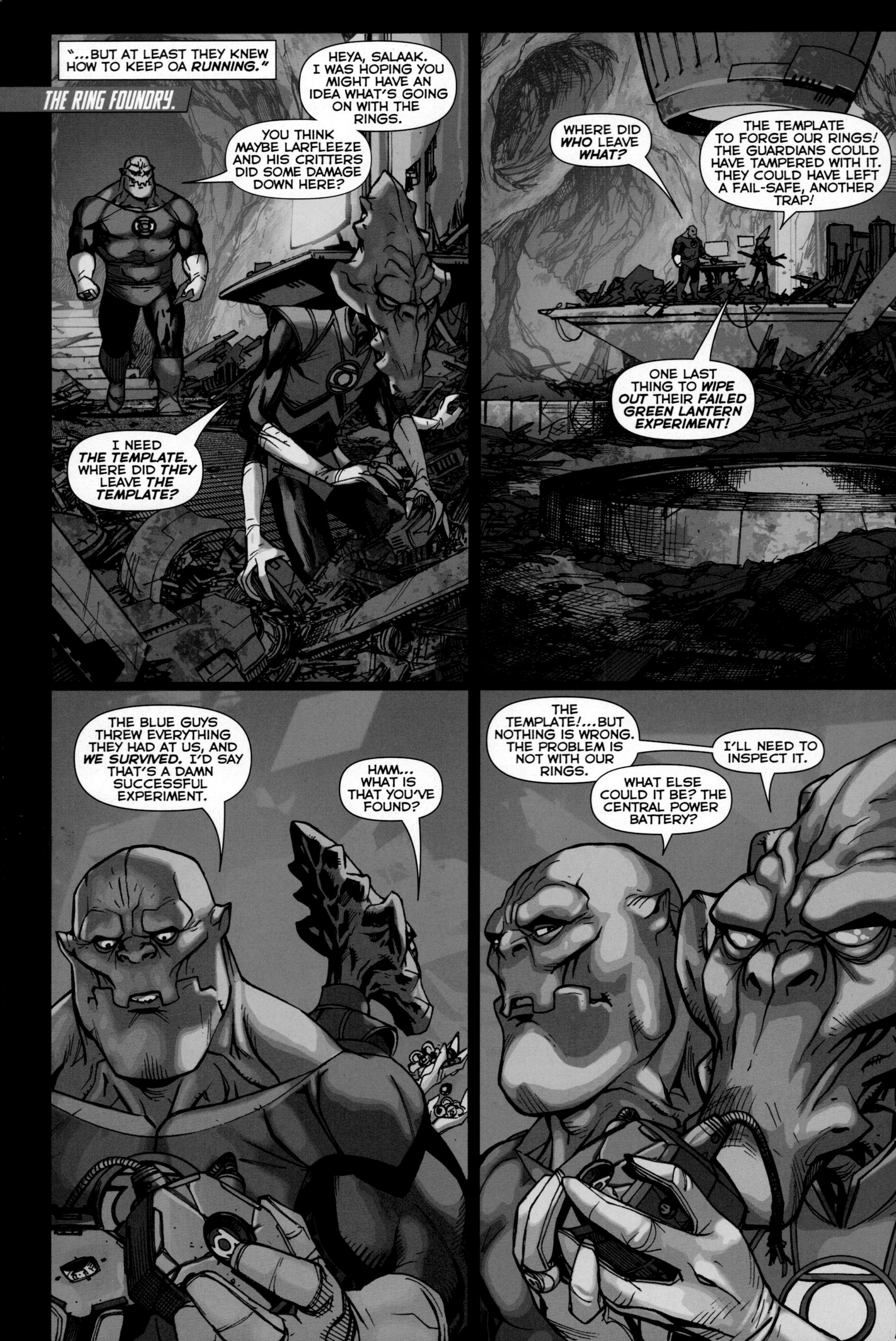
"...BUT AT LEAST THEY KNEW HOW TO KEEP OA RUNNING."
THE RING FOUNDRY.
HEYA, SALAAK. I WAS HOPING YOU MIGHT HAVE AN IDEA WHAT'S GOING ON WITH THE RINGS.
YOU THINK MAYBE LARFLEEZE AND HIS CRITTERS DID SOME DAMAGE DOWN HERE?
I NEED THE TEMPLATE. WHERE DID THEY LEAVE THE TEMPLATE?
WHERE DID WHO LEAVE WHAT?
THE TEMPLATE TO FORGE OUR RINGS! THE GUARDIANS COULD HAVE TAMPERED WITH IT. THEY COULD HAVE LEFT A FAIL-SAFE, ANOTHER TRAP!
ONE LAST THING TO WIPE OUT THEIR FAILED GREEN LANTERN EXPERIMENT!
THE BLUE GUYS THREW EVERYTHING THEY HAD AT US, AND WE SURVIVED. I'D SAY THAT'S A DAMN SUCCESSFUL EXPERIMENT.
HMM... WHAT IS THAT YOU'VE FOUND?
THE TEMPLATE!...BUT NOTHING IS WRONG. THE PROBLEM IS NOT WITH OUR RINGS.
I'LL NEED TO INSPECT IT.
WHAT ELSE COULD IT BE? THE CENTRAL POWER BATTERY?

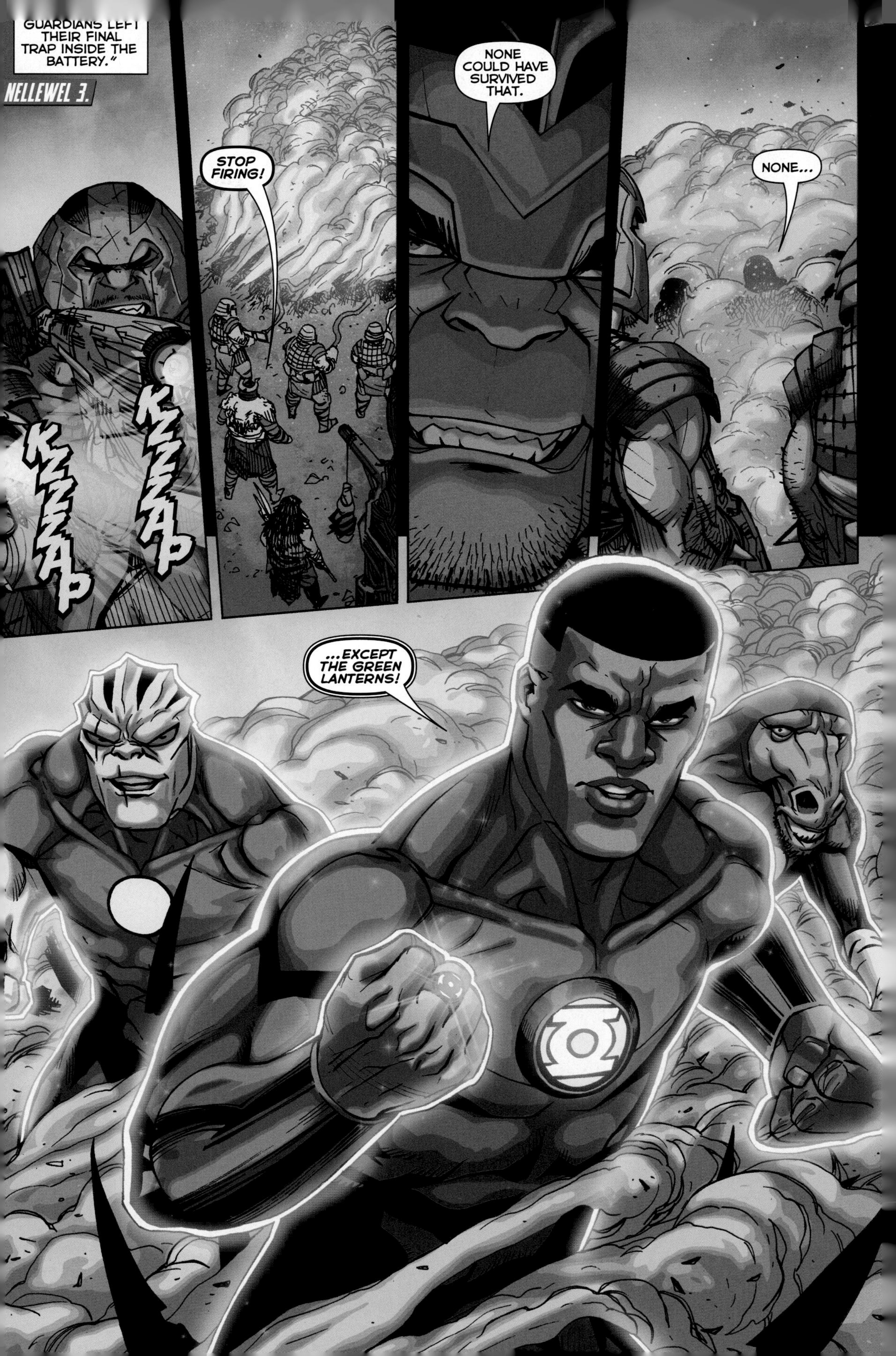
GUARDIANS LEFT THEIR FINAL TRAP INSIDE THE BATTERY."
NELLEWEL 3.
KZZZAP
KZZZAP
STOP FIRING!
NONE COULD HAVE SURVIVED THAT.
NONE...
...EXCEPT THE GREEN LANTERNS!

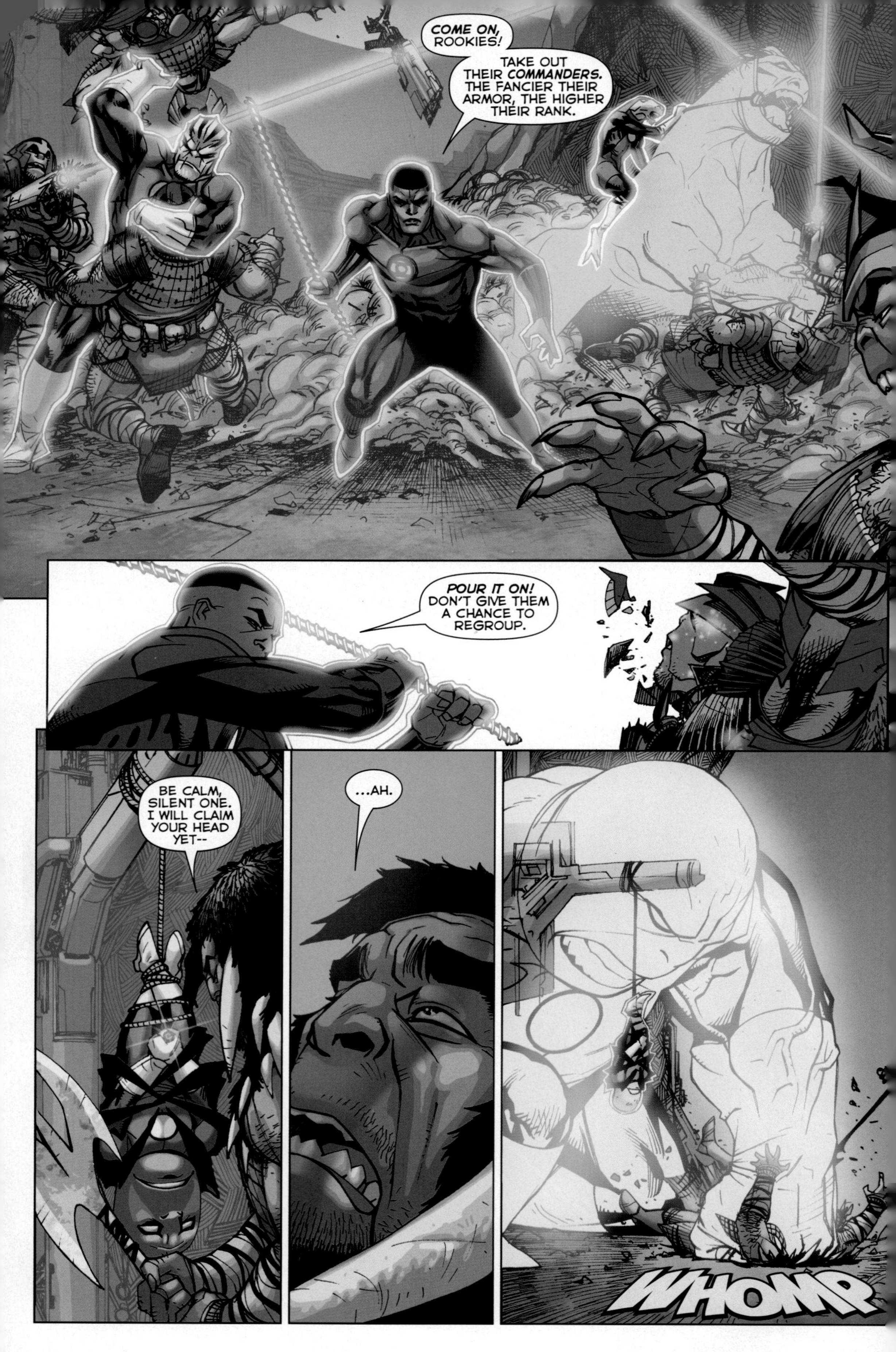
COME ON, ROOKIES!
TAKE OUT THEIR COMMANDERS. THE FANCIER THEIR ARMOR, THE HIGHER THEIR RANK.
POUR IT ON! DON'T GIVE THEM A CHANCE TO REGROUP.
BE CALM, SILENT ONE. I WILL CLAIM YOUR HEAD YET--
...AH.
WHOMP

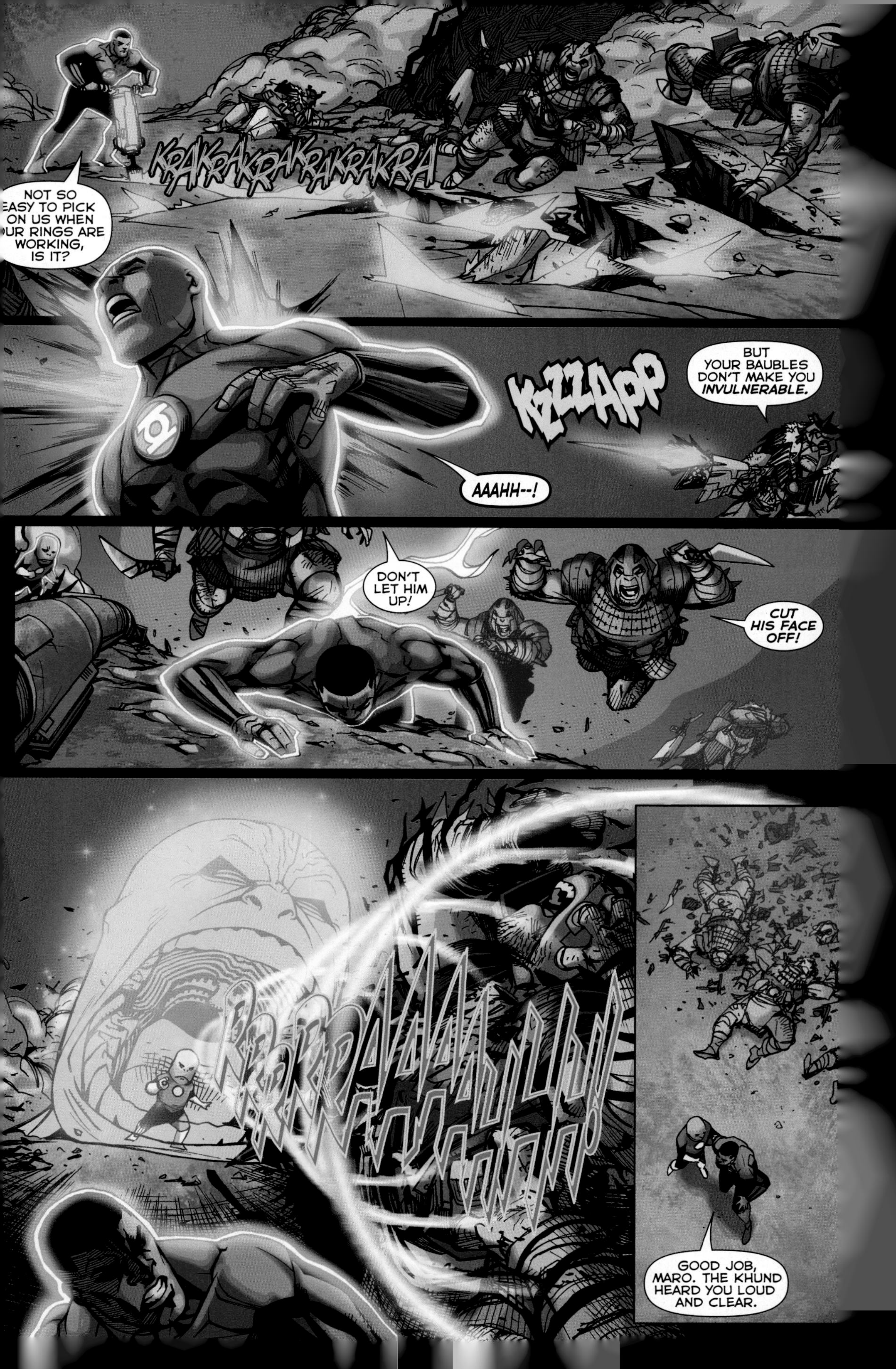
KRAKRAKRAKRAKRAKRAKRA
NOT SO EASY TO PICK ON US WHEN OUR RINGS ARE WORKING, IS IT?
KZZZAPP
BUT YOUR BAUBLES DON'T MAKE YOU *INVULNERABLE.*
AAAHH--!
DON'T LET HIM UP!
CUT HIS FACE OFF!
GOOD JOB, MARO. THE KHUND HEARD YOU LOUD AND CLEAR.

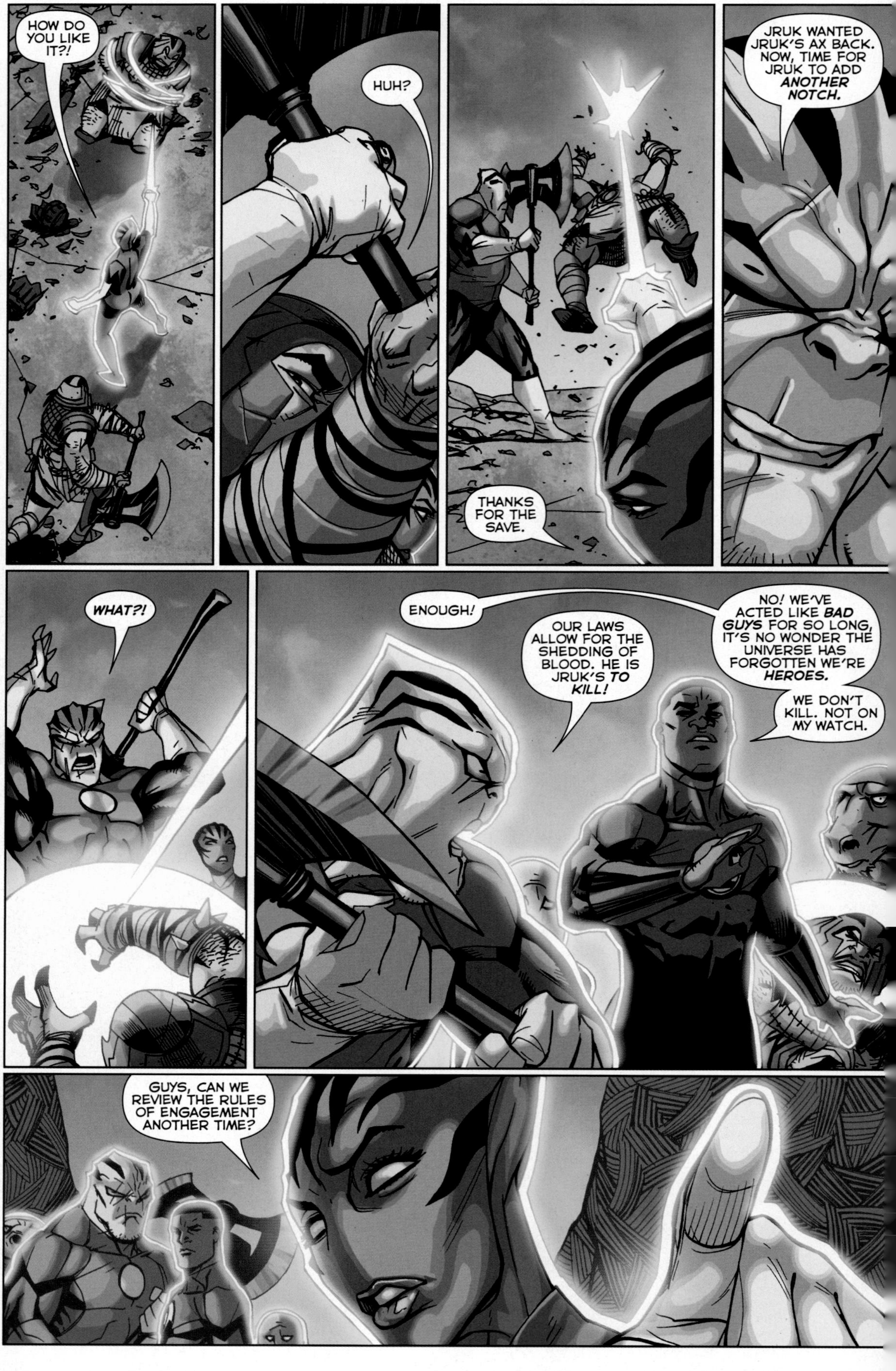
HOW DO YOU LIKE IT?!
HUH?
THANKS FOR THE SAVE.
JRUK WANTED JRUK'S AX BACK. NOW, TIME FOR JRUK TO ADD ANOTHER NOTCH.
WHAT?!
ENOUGH!
OUR LAWS ALLOW FOR THE SHEDDING OF BLOOD. HE IS JRUK'S TO KILL!
NO! WE'VE ACTED LIKE BAD GUYS FOR SO LONG, IT'S NO WONDER THE UNIVERSE HAS FORGOTTEN WE'RE HEROES.
WE DON'T KILL. NOT ON MY WATCH.
GUYS, CAN WE REVIEW THE RULES OF ENGAGEMENT ANOTHER TIME?

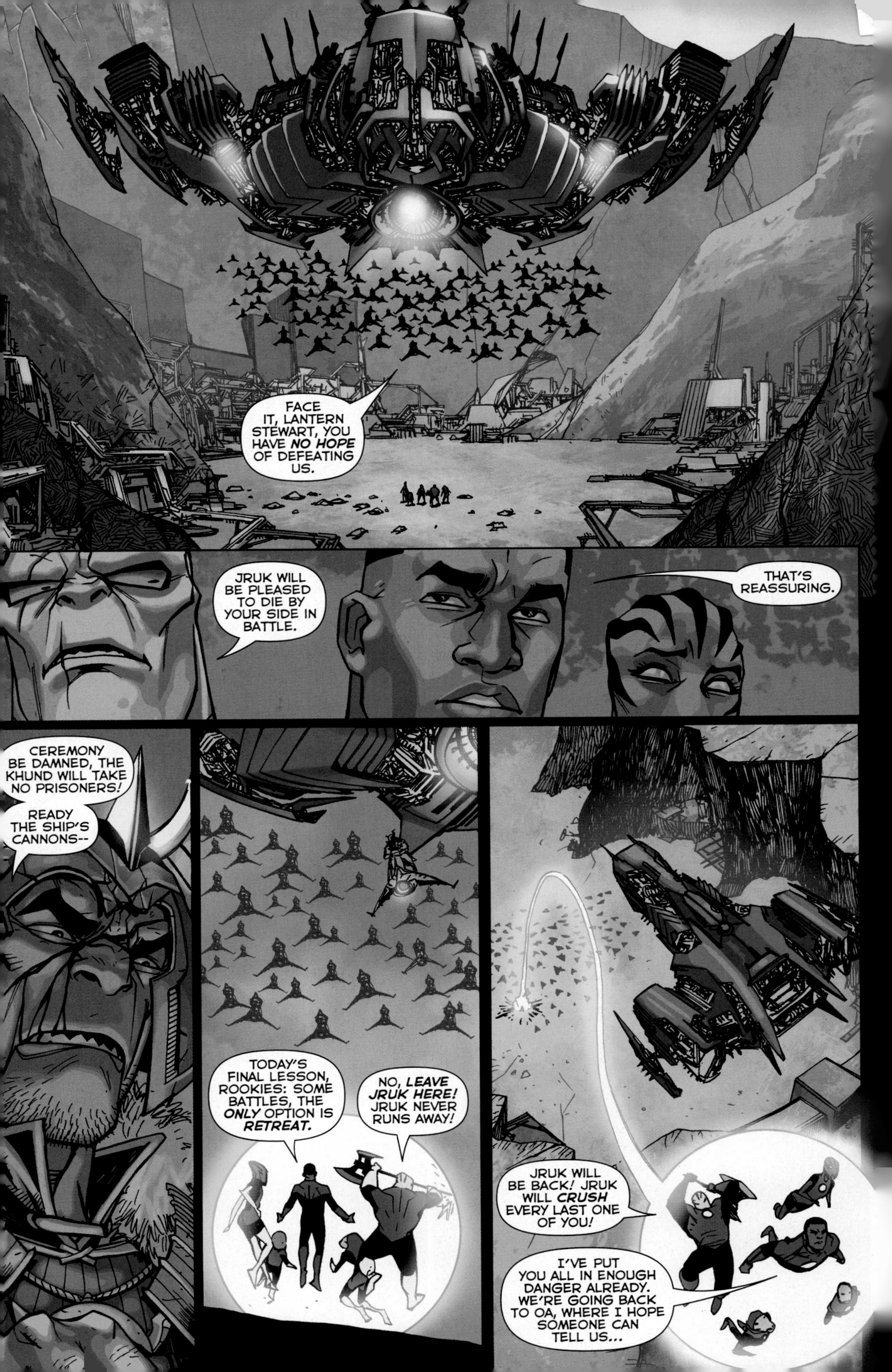
FACE IT, LANTERN STEWART, YOU HAVE *NO HOPE* OF DEFEATING US.
JRUK WILL BE PLEASED TO DIE BY YOUR SIDE IN BATTLE.
THAT'S REASSURING.
CEREMONY BE DAMNED, THE KHUND WILL TAKE NO PRISONERS!
READY THE SHIP'S CANNONS--
TODAY'S FINAL LESSON, ROOKIES: SOME BATTLES, THE *ONLY* OPTION IS *RETREAT.*
NO, *LEAVE JRUK HERE!* JRUK NEVER RUNS AWAY!
JRUK WILL BE BACK! JRUK WILL *CRUSH* EVERY LAST ONE OF YOU!
I'VE PUT YOU ALL IN ENOUGH DANGER ALREADY. WE'RE GOING BACK TO OA, WHERE I HOPE SOMEONE CAN TELL US...

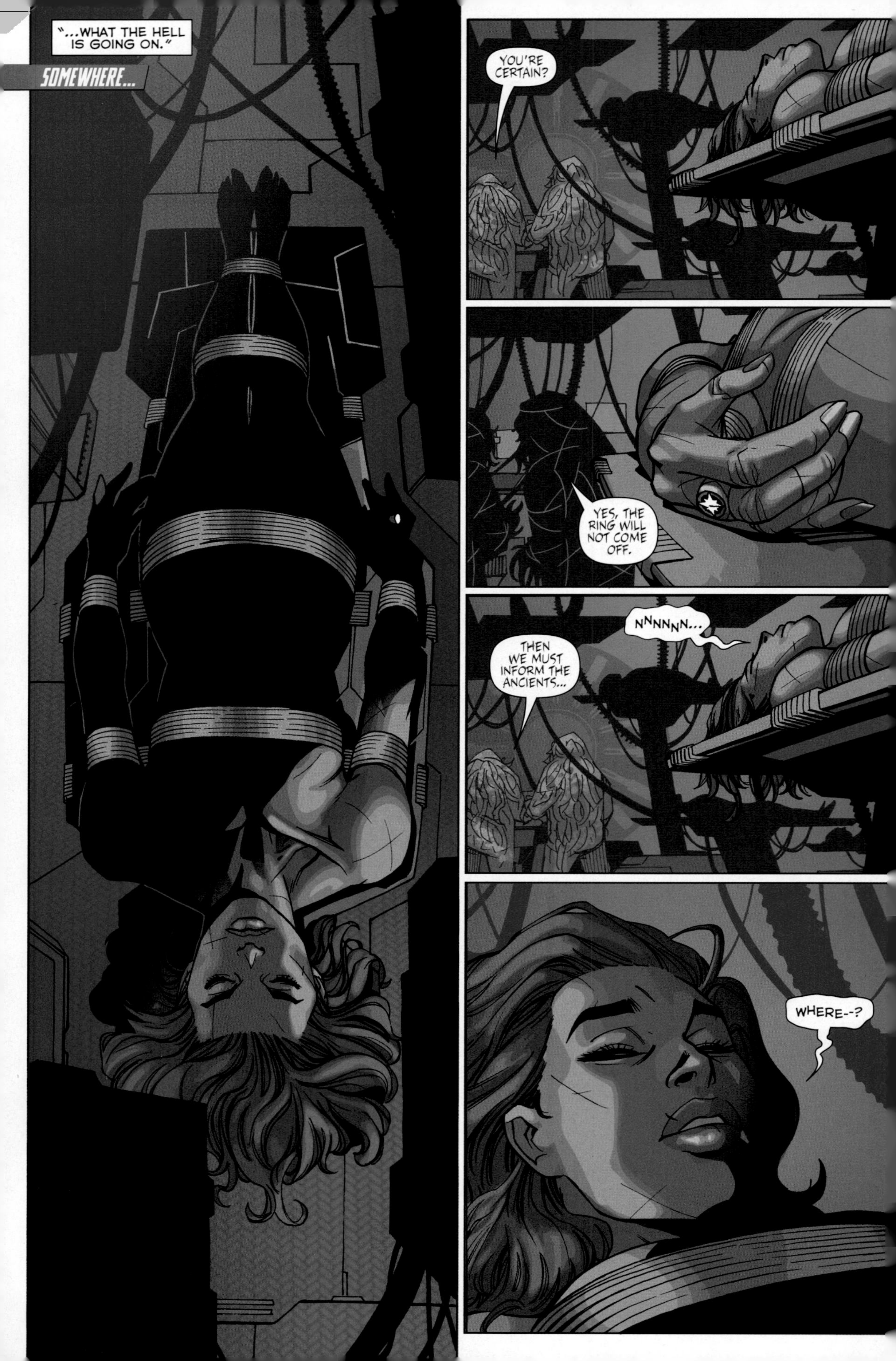
"...WHAT THE HELL IS GOING ON."
SOMEWHERE...
YOU'RE CERTAIN?
YES, THE RING WILL NOT COME OFF.
NNNNNN...
THEN WE MUST INFORM THE ANCIENTS...
WHERE--?

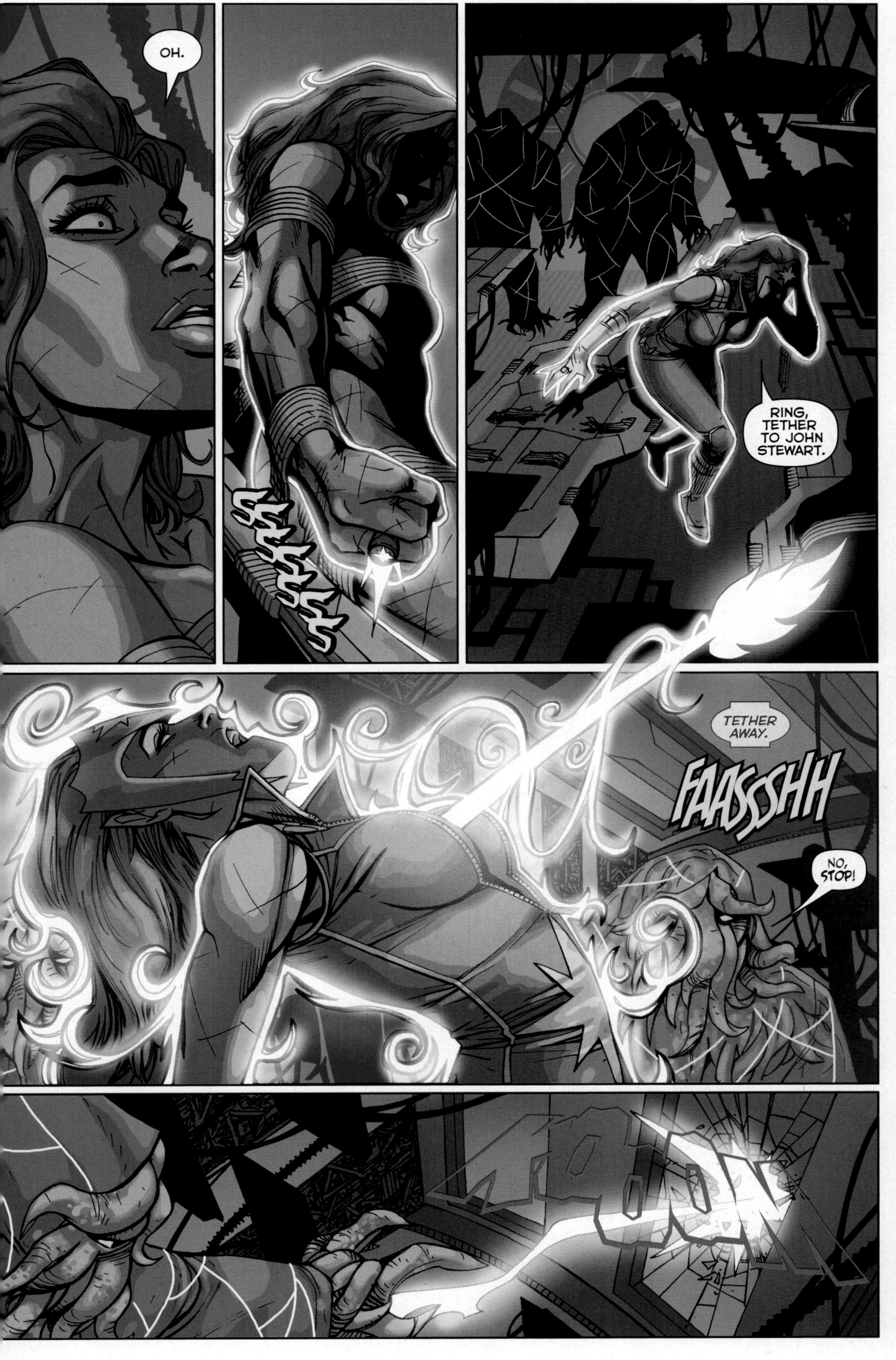
OH.
SSSSSS
RING, TETHER TO JOHN STEWART.
TETHER AWAY.
FAASSSHH
NO, STOP!

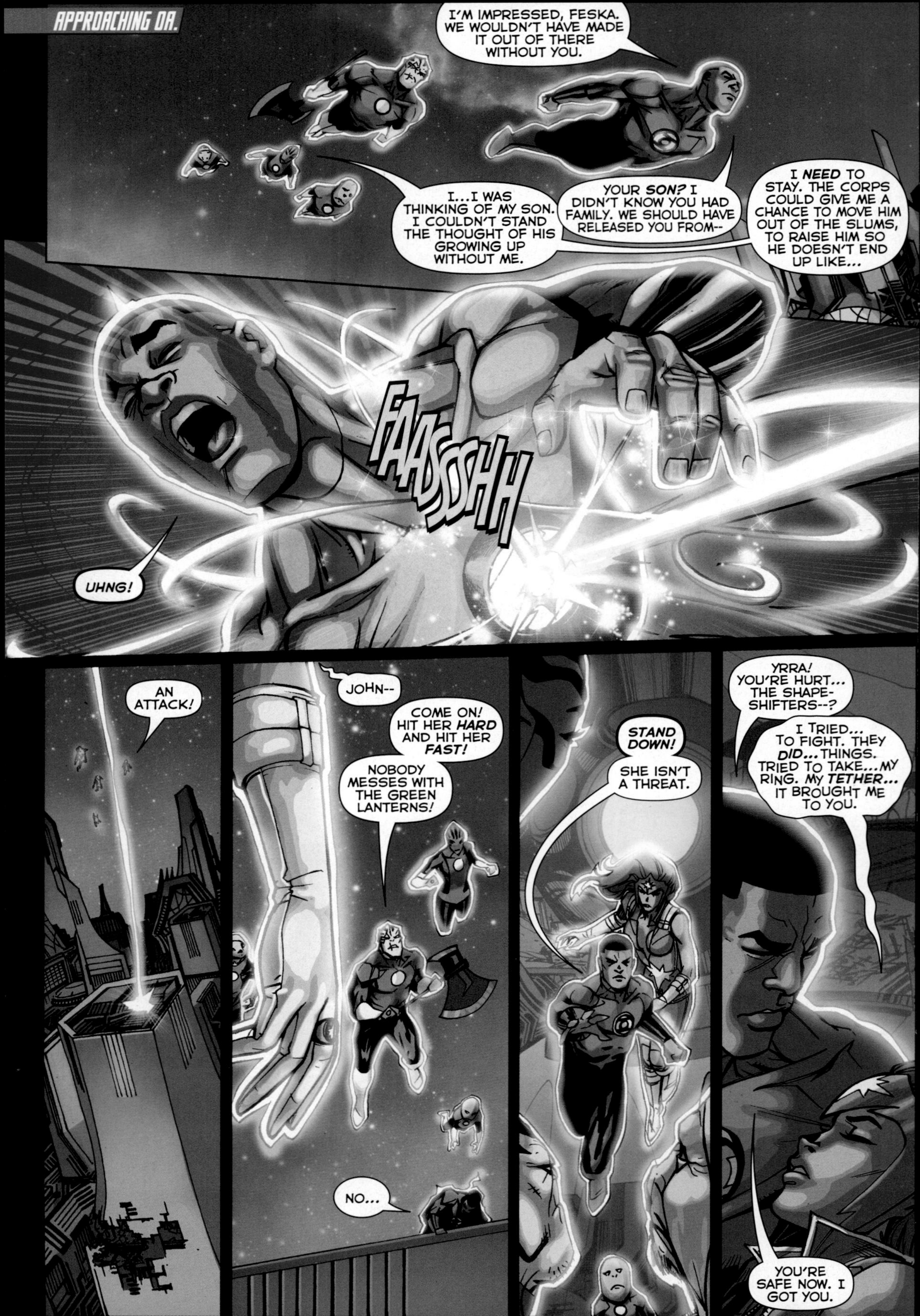
APPROACHING OA.
I'M IMPRESSED, FESKA. WE WOULDN'T HAVE MADE IT OUT OF THERE WITHOUT YOU.
I...I WAS THINKING OF MY SON. I COULDN'T STAND THE THOUGHT OF HIS GROWING UP WITHOUT ME.
YOUR SON? I DIDN'T KNOW YOU HAD FAMILY. WE SHOULD HAVE RELEASED YOU FROM--
I NEED TO STAY. THE CORPS COULD GIVE ME A CHANCE TO MOVE HIM OUT OF THE SLUMS, TO RAISE HIM SO HE DOESN'T END UP LIKE...
FAASSSHH
UHNG!
AN ATTACK!
JOHN--
COME ON! HIT HER HARD AND HIT HER FAST!
NOBODY MESSES WITH THE GREEN LANTERNS!
NO...
STAND DOWN!
SHE ISN'T A THREAT.
YRRA! YOU'RE HURT... THE SHAPE-SHIFTERS--?
I TRIED... TO FIGHT. THEY DID... THINGS. TRIED TO TAKE... MY RING. MY TETHER... IT BROUGHT ME TO YOU.
YOU'RE SAFE NOW. I GOT YOU.

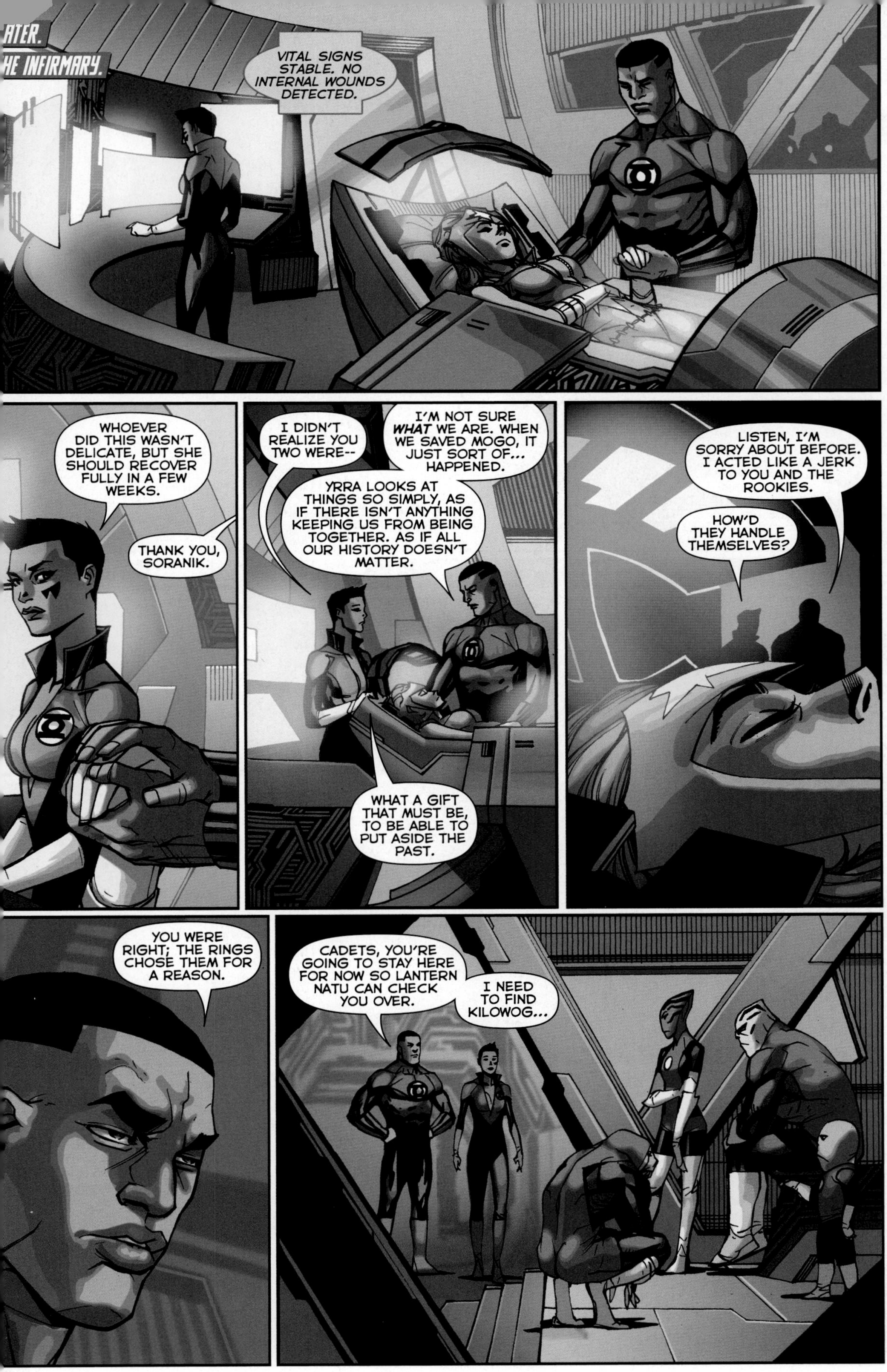
ATER.
HE INFIRMARY.
VITAL SIGNS STABLE. NO INTERNAL WOUNDS DETECTED.
WHOEVER DID THIS WASN'T DELICATE, BUT SHE SHOULD RECOVER FULLY IN A FEW WEEKS.
THANK YOU, SORANIK.
I DIDN'T REALIZE YOU TWO WERE--
I'M NOT SURE *WHAT* WE ARE. WHEN WE SAVED MOGO, IT JUST SORT OF... HAPPENED.
YRRA LOOKS AT THINGS SO SIMPLY, AS IF THERE ISN'T ANYTHING KEEPING US FROM BEING TOGETHER. AS IF ALL OUR HISTORY DOESN'T MATTER.
WHAT A GIFT THAT MUST BE, TO BE ABLE TO PUT ASIDE THE PAST.
LISTEN, I'M SORRY ABOUT BEFORE. I ACTED LIKE A JERK TO YOU AND THE ROOKIES.
HOW'D THEY HANDLE THEMSELVES?
YOU WERE RIGHT; THE RINGS CHOSE THEM FOR A REASON.
CADETS, YOU'RE GOING TO STAY HERE FOR NOW SO LANTERN NATU CAN CHECK YOU OVER.
I NEED TO FIND KILOWOG...

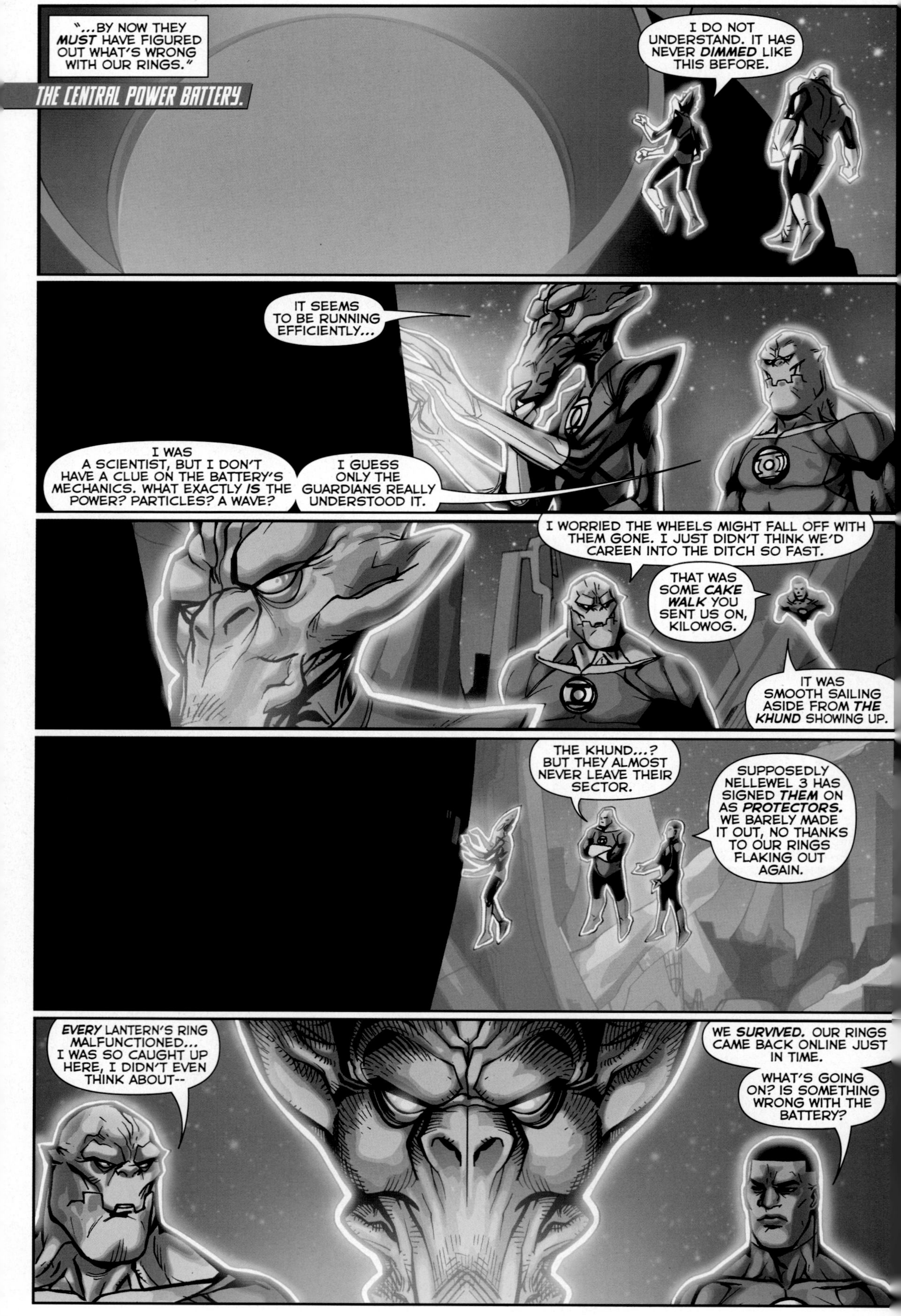
"...BY NOW THEY MUST HAVE FIGURED OUT WHAT'S WRONG WITH OUR RINGS."
THE CENTRAL POWER BATTERY.
I DO NOT UNDERSTAND. IT HAS NEVER DIMMED LIKE THIS BEFORE.
IT SEEMS TO BE RUNNING EFFICIENTLY...
I WAS A SCIENTIST, BUT I DON'T HAVE A CLUE ON THE BATTERY'S MECHANICS. WHAT EXACTLY IS THE POWER? PARTICLES? A WAVE?
I GUESS ONLY THE GUARDIANS REALLY UNDERSTOOD IT.
I WORRIED THE WHEELS MIGHT FALL OFF WITH THEM GONE. I JUST DIDN'T THINK WE'D CAREEN INTO THE DITCH SO FAST.
THAT WAS SOME CAKE WALK YOU SENT US ON, KILOWOG.
IT WAS SMOOTH SAILING ASIDE FROM THE KHUND SHOWING UP.
THE KHUND...? BUT THEY ALMOST NEVER LEAVE THEIR SECTOR.
SUPPOSEDLY NELLEWEL 3 HAS SIGNED THEM ON AS PROTECTORS. WE BARELY MADE IT OUT, NO THANKS TO OUR RINGS FLAKING OUT AGAIN.
EVERY LANTERN'S RING MALFUNCTIONED... I WAS SO CAUGHT UP HERE, I DIDN'T EVEN THINK ABOUT--
WE SURVIVED. OUR RINGS CAME BACK ONLINE JUST IN TIME.
WHAT'S GOING ON? IS SOMETHING WRONG WITH THE BATTERY?

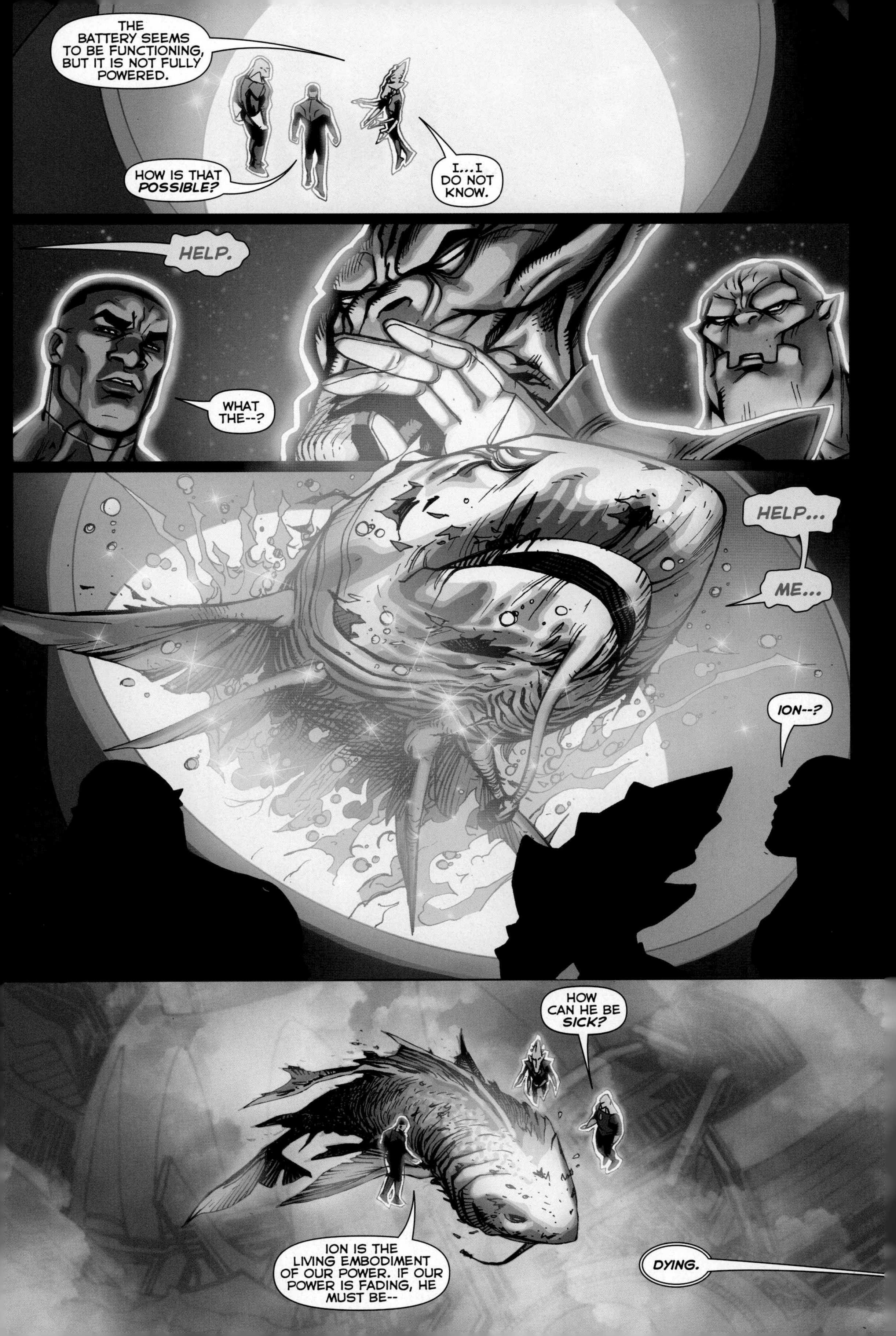
THE BATTERY SEEMS TO BE FUNCTIONING, BUT IT IS NOT FULLY POWERED.
HOW IS THAT POSSIBLE?
I...I DO NOT KNOW.
HELP.
WHAT THE--?
HELP...
ME...
ION--?
HOW CAN HE BE SICK?
ION IS THE LIVING EMBODIMENT OF OUR POWER. IF OUR POWER IS FADING, HE MUST BE--
DYING.

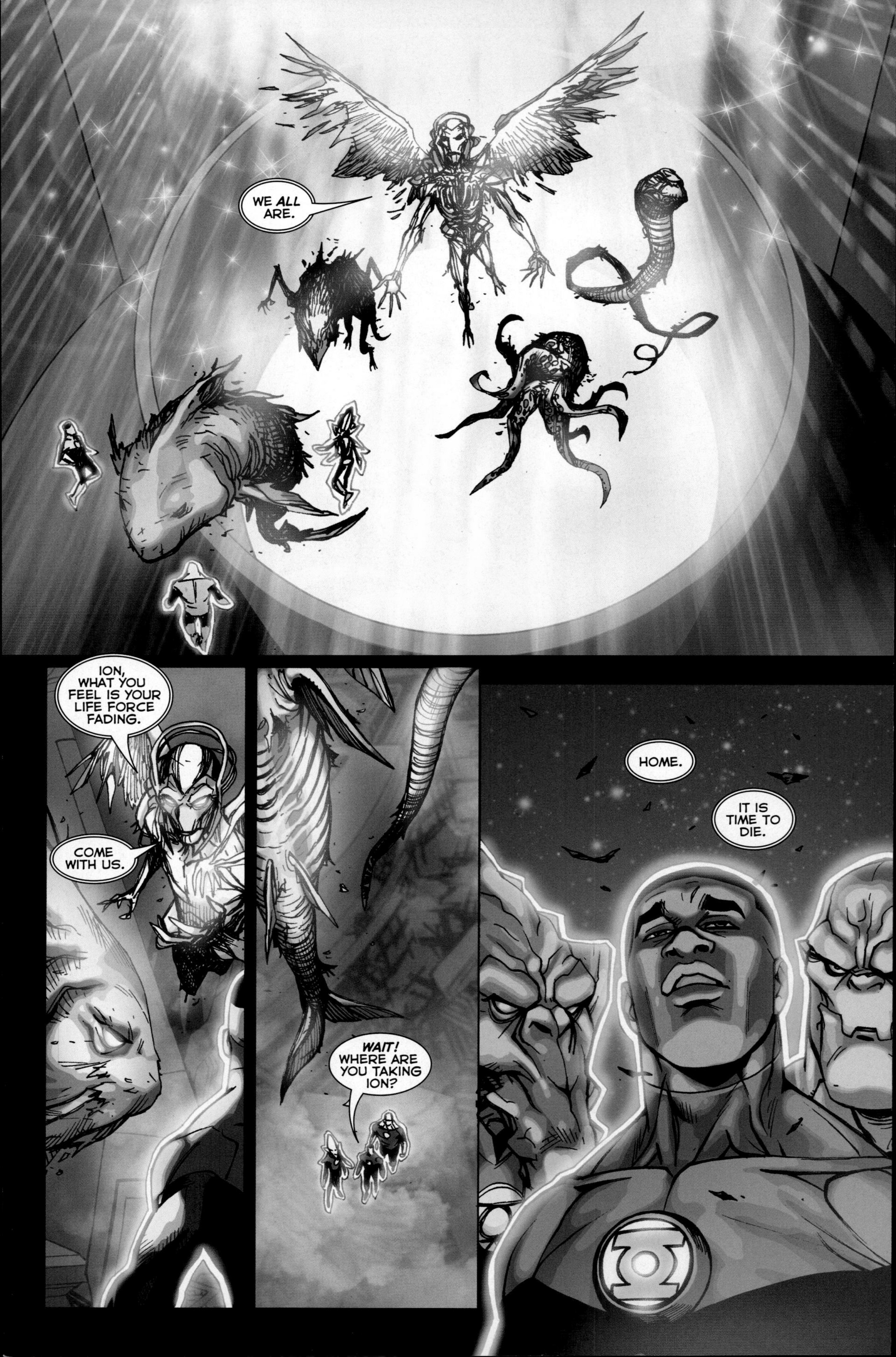
WE ALL ARE.
ION, WHAT YOU FEEL IS YOUR LIFE FORCE FADING.
COME WITH US.
WAIT! WHERE ARE YOU TAKING ION?
HOME.
IT IS TIME TO DIE.

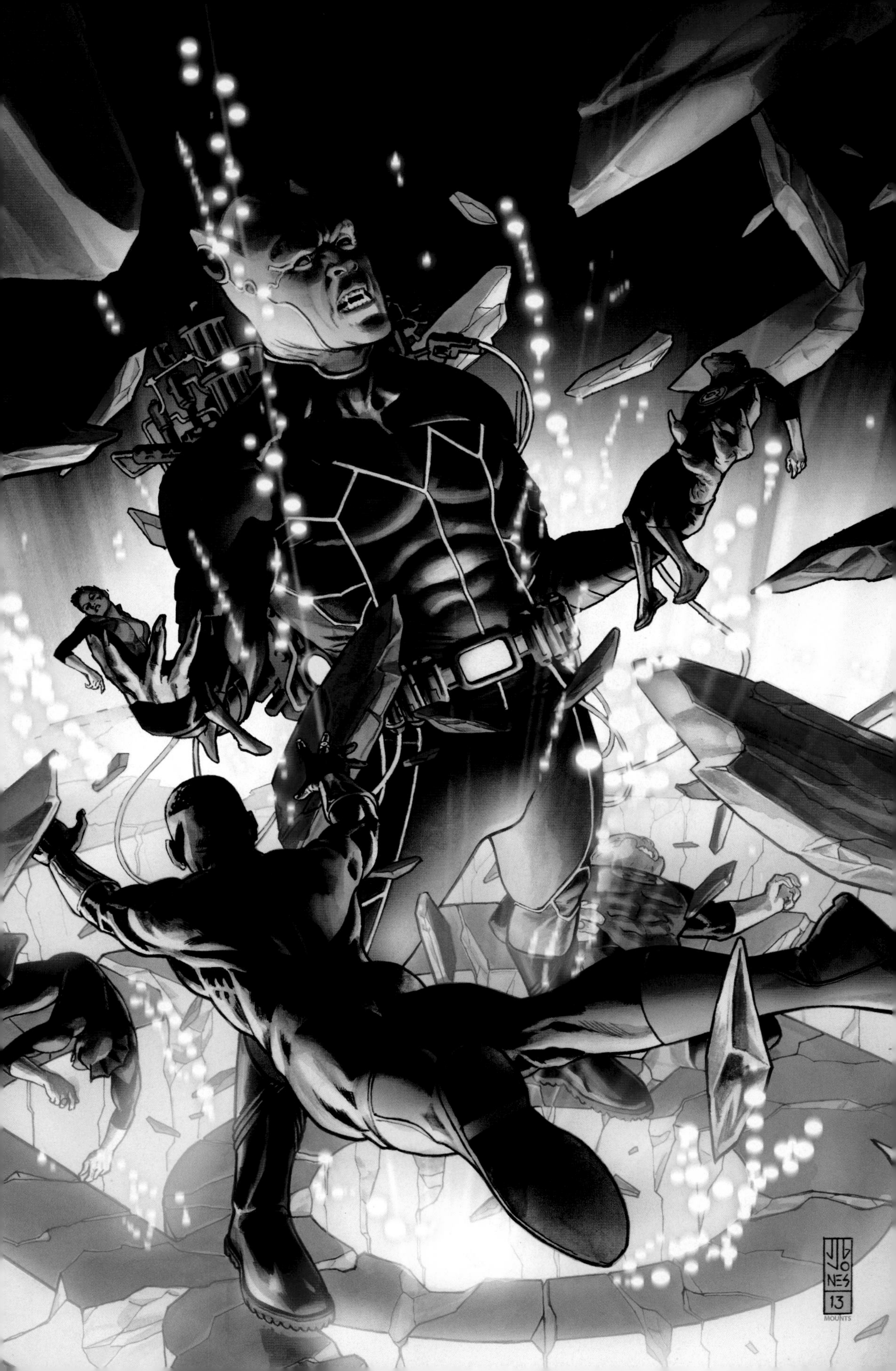
JG JONES
13
MOUNTS

OA'S LAST STAND

VAN JENSEN & ROBERT VENDITTI writers **BERNARD CHANG** artist cover art by **J.G. JONES & PAUL MOUNTS**

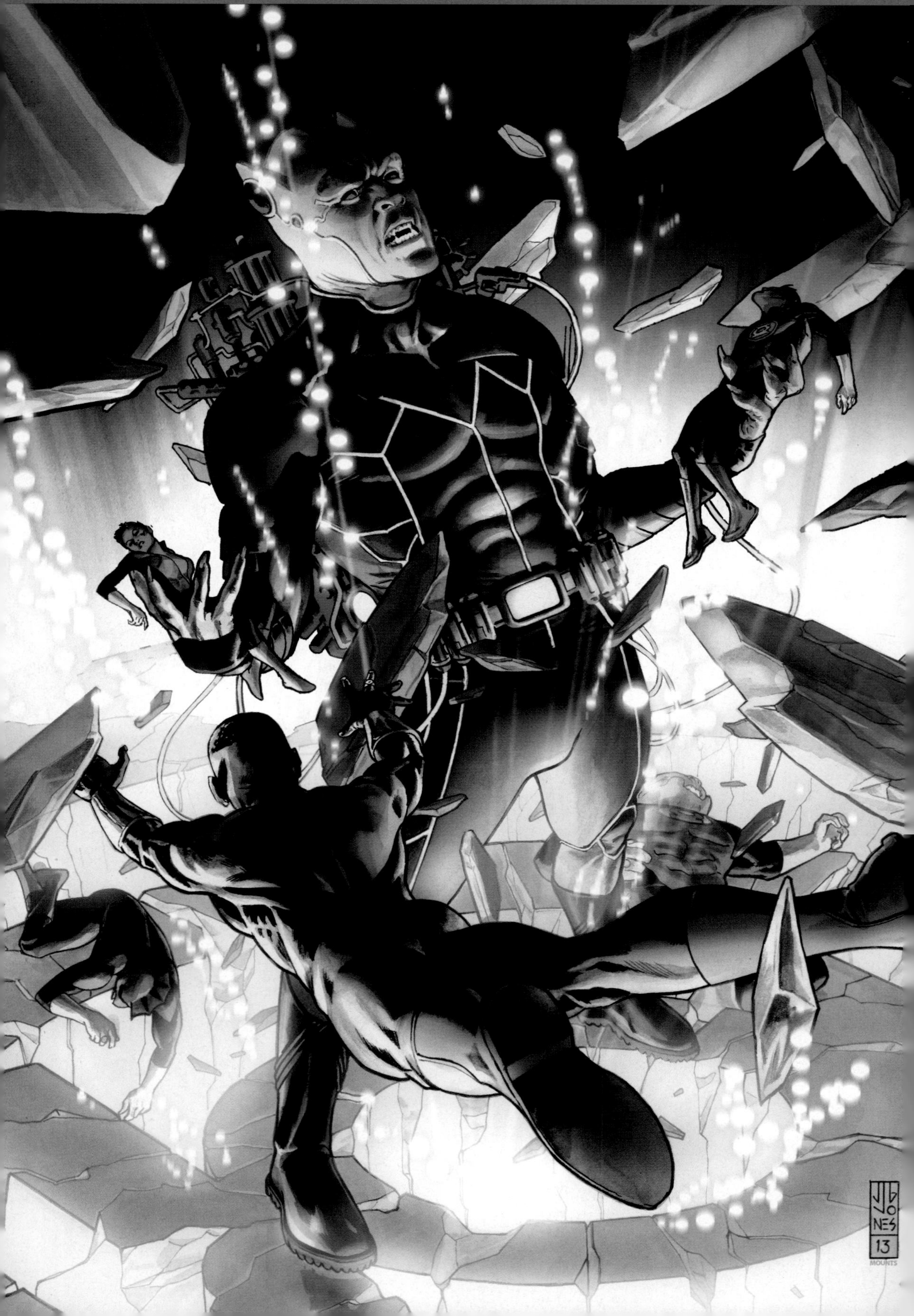

JG JONES 13
MOUNTS

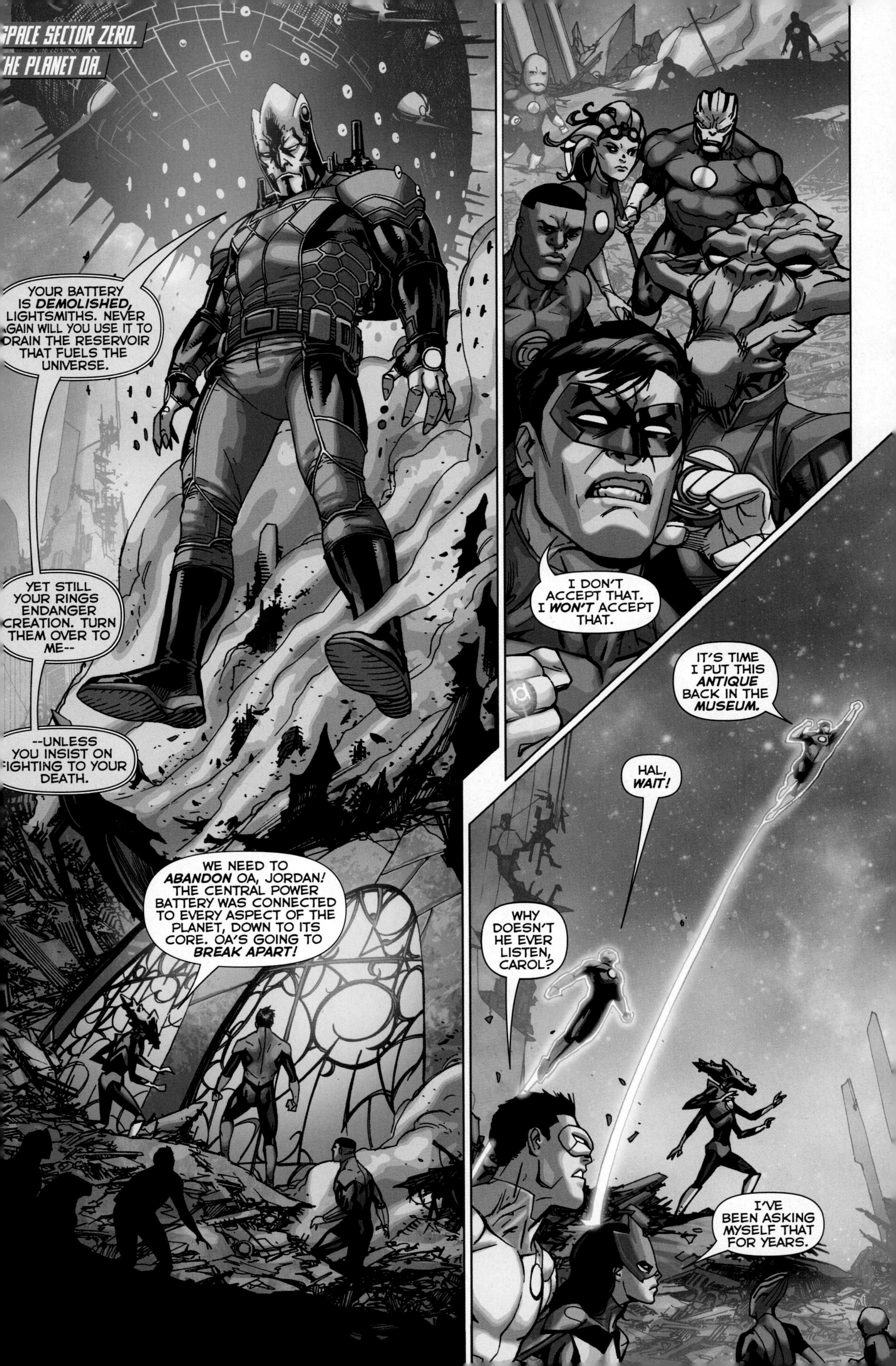
SPACE SECTOR ZERO.
THE PLANET OA.
YOUR BATTERY IS DEMOLISHED, LIGHTSMITHS. NEVER AGAIN WILL YOU USE IT TO DRAIN THE RESERVOIR THAT FUELS THE UNIVERSE.
YET STILL YOUR RINGS ENDANGER CREATION. TURN THEM OVER TO ME--
--UNLESS YOU INSIST ON FIGHTING TO YOUR DEATH.
I DON'T ACCEPT THAT. I WON'T ACCEPT THAT.
IT'S TIME I PUT THIS ANTIQUE BACK IN THE MUSEUM.
HAL, WAIT!
WE NEED TO ABANDON OA, JORDAN! THE CENTRAL POWER BATTERY WAS CONNECTED TO EVERY ASPECT OF THE PLANET, DOWN TO ITS CORE. OA'S GOING TO BREAK APART!
WHY DOESN'T HE EVER LISTEN, CAROL?
I'VE BEEN ASKING MYSELF THAT FOR YEARS.

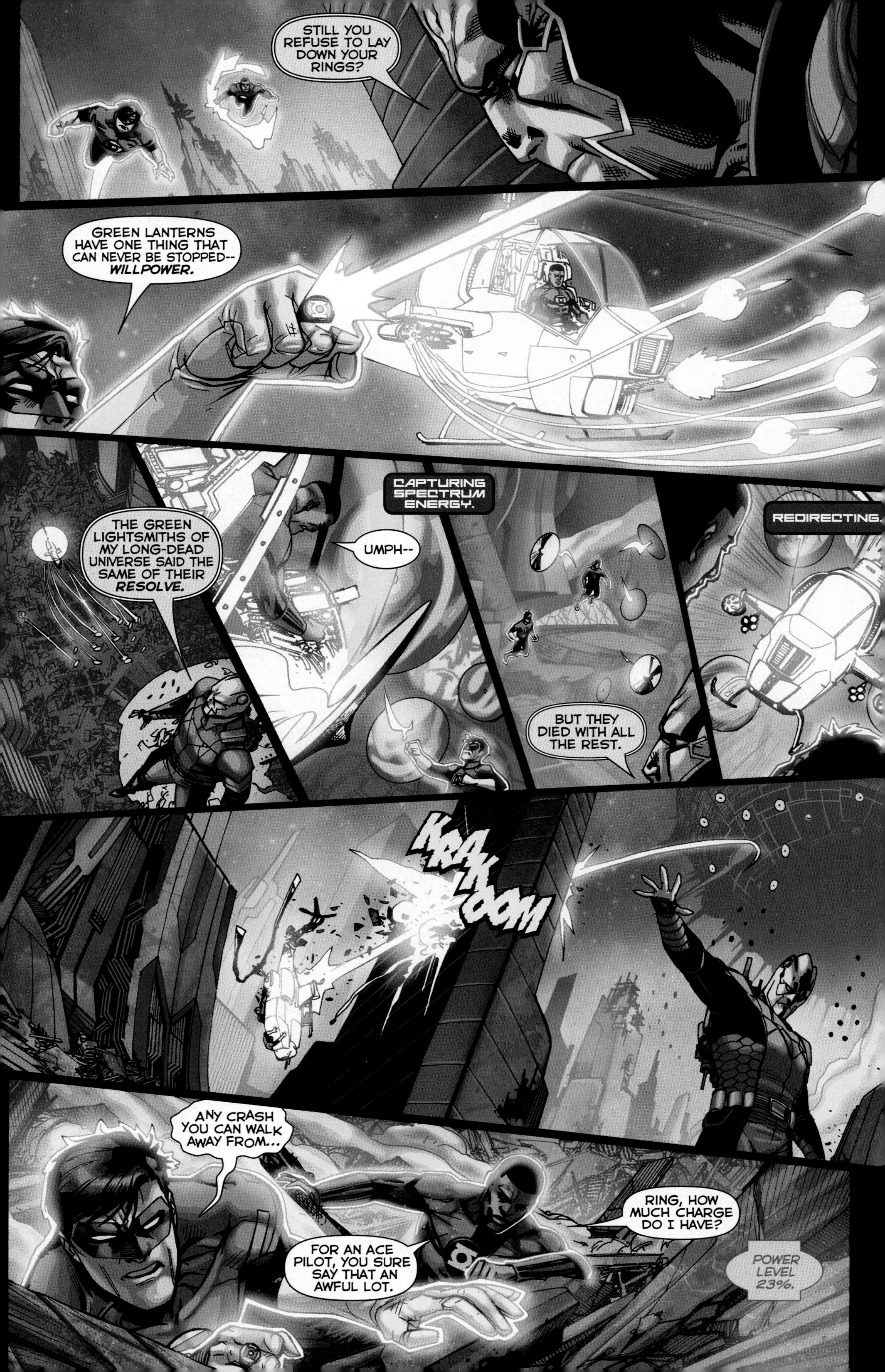
STILL YOU REFUSE TO LAY DOWN YOUR RINGS?
GREEN LANTERNS HAVE ONE THING THAT CAN NEVER BE STOPPED-- WILLPOWER.
THE GREEN LIGHTSMITHS OF MY LONG-DEAD UNIVERSE SAID THE SAME OF THEIR RESOLVE.
UMPH--
CAPTURING SPECTRUM ENERGY.
BUT THEY DIED WITH ALL THE REST.
REDIRECTING.
KRAKOOM
ANY CRASH YOU CAN WALK AWAY FROM...
FOR AN ACE PILOT, YOU SURE SAY THAT AN AWFUL LOT.
RING, HOW MUCH CHARGE DO I HAVE?
POWER LEVEL 23%.

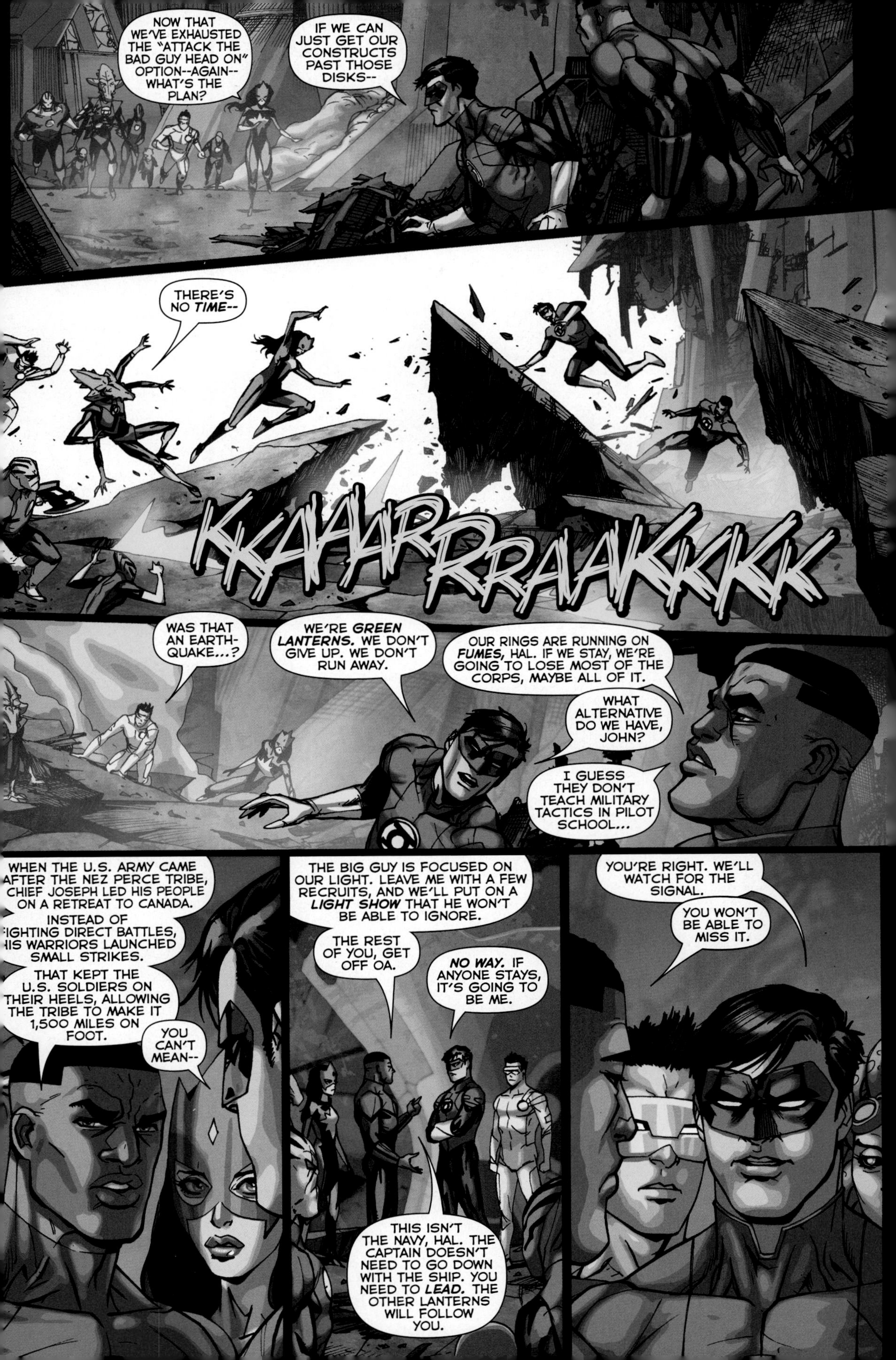
NOW THAT WE'VE EXHAUSTED THE "ATTACK THE BAD GUY HEAD ON" OPTION--AGAIN--WHAT'S THE PLAN?
IF WE CAN JUST GET OUR CONSTRUCTS PAST THOSE DISKS--
THERE'S NO *TIME*--
KKAAARRRAAKKKK
WAS THAT AN EARTH-QUAKE...?
WE'RE *GREEN LANTERNS.* WE DON'T GIVE UP. WE DON'T RUN AWAY.
OUR RINGS ARE RUNNING ON *FUMES,* HAL. IF WE STAY, WE'RE GOING TO LOSE MOST OF THE CORPS, MAYBE ALL OF IT.
WHAT ALTERNATIVE DO WE HAVE, JOHN?
I GUESS THEY DON'T TEACH MILITARY TACTICS IN PILOT SCHOOL...
WHEN THE U.S. ARMY CAME AFTER THE NEZ PERCE TRIBE, CHIEF JOSEPH LED HIS PEOPLE ON A RETREAT TO CANADA.
INSTEAD OF FIGHTING DIRECT BATTLES, HIS WARRIORS LAUNCHED SMALL STRIKES.
THAT KEPT THE U.S. SOLDIERS ON THEIR HEELS, ALLOWING THE TRIBE TO MAKE IT 1,500 MILES ON FOOT.
YOU CAN'T MEAN--
THE BIG GUY IS FOCUSED ON OUR LIGHT. LEAVE ME WITH A FEW RECRUITS, AND WE'LL PUT ON A *LIGHT SHOW* THAT HE WON'T BE ABLE TO IGNORE.
THE REST OF YOU, GET OFF OA.
NO WAY. IF ANYONE STAYS, IT'S GOING TO BE ME.
THIS ISN'T THE NAVY, HAL. THE CAPTAIN DOESN'T NEED TO GO DOWN WITH THE SHIP. YOU NEED TO *LEAD.* THE OTHER LANTERNS WILL FOLLOW YOU.
YOU'RE RIGHT. WE'LL WATCH FOR THE SIGNAL.
YOU WON'T BE ABLE TO MISS IT.

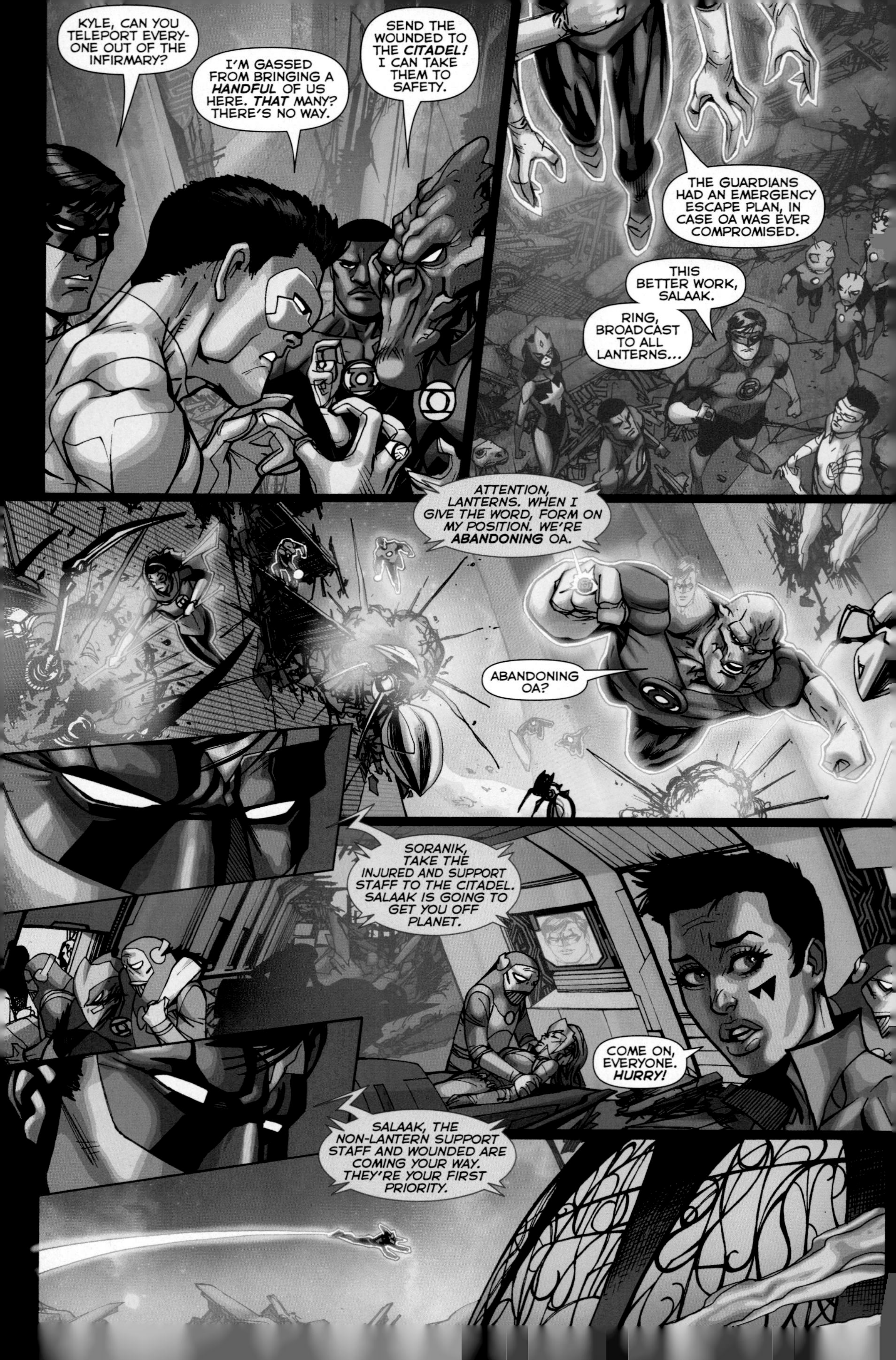
KYLE, CAN YOU TELEPORT EVERY-ONE OUT OF THE INFIRMARY?
I'M GASSED FROM BRINGING A HANDFUL OF US HERE. THAT MANY? THERE'S NO WAY.
SEND THE WOUNDED TO THE CITADEL! I CAN TAKE THEM TO SAFETY.
THE GUARDIANS HAD AN EMERGENCY ESCAPE PLAN, IN CASE OA WAS EVER COMPROMISED.
THIS BETTER WORK, SALAAK.
RING, BROADCAST TO ALL LANTERNS...
ATTENTION, LANTERNS. WHEN I GIVE THE WORD, FORM ON MY POSITION. WE'RE ABANDONING OA.
ABANDONING OA?
SORANIK, TAKE THE INJURED AND SUPPORT STAFF TO THE CITADEL. SALAAK IS GOING TO GET YOU OFF PLANET.
COME ON, EVERYONE. HURRY!
SALAAK, THE NON-LANTERN SUPPORT STAFF AND WOUNDED ARE COMING YOUR WAY. THEY'RE YOUR FIRST PRIORITY.

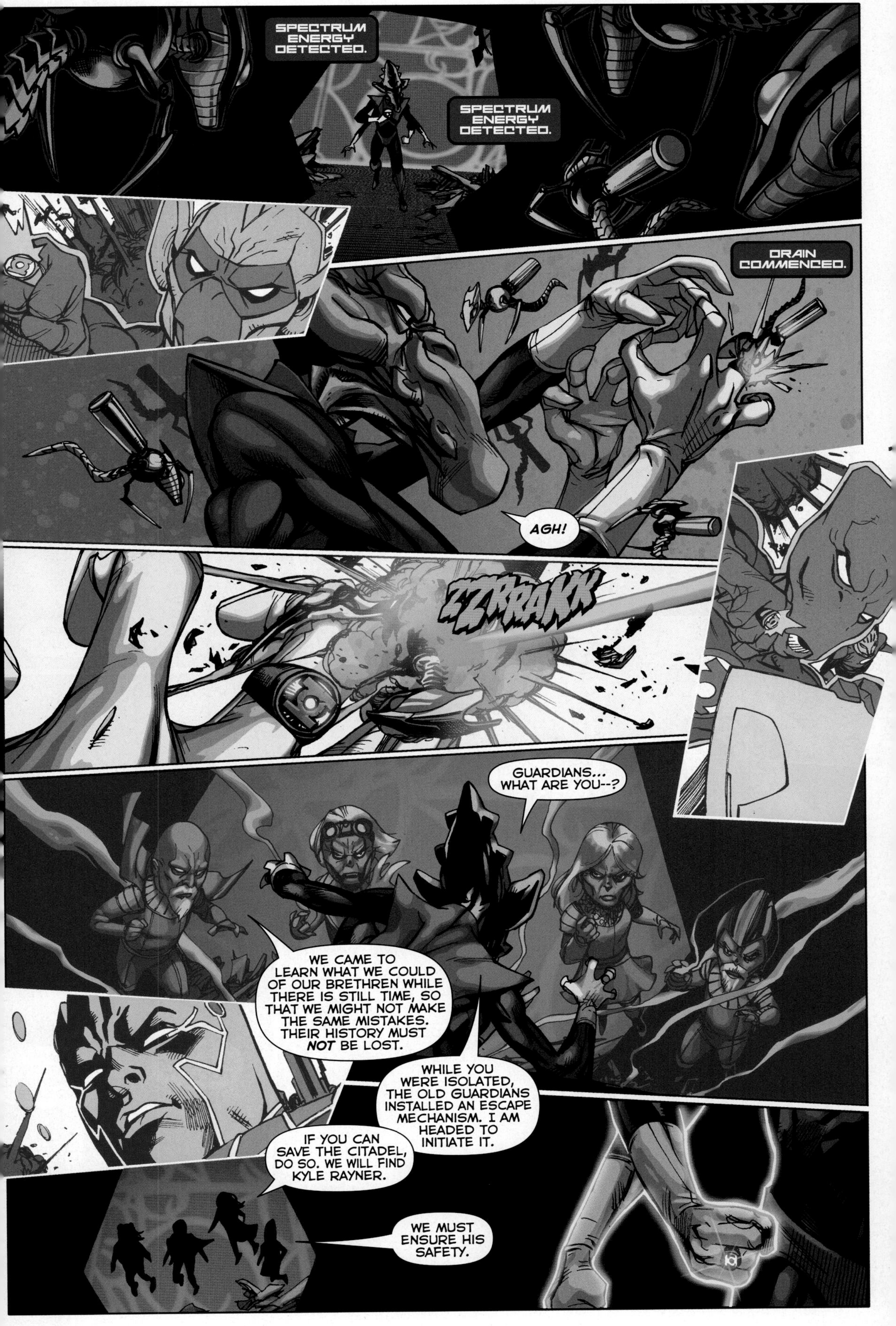
SPECTRUM ENERGY DETECTED.
SPECTRUM ENERGY DETECTED.
DRAIN COMMENCED.
AGH!
ZZRRAKK
GUARDIANS... WHAT ARE YOU--?
WE CAME TO LEARN WHAT WE COULD OF OUR BRETHREN WHILE THERE IS STILL TIME, SO THAT WE MIGHT NOT MAKE THE SAME MISTAKES. THEIR HISTORY MUST NOT BE LOST.
WHILE YOU WERE ISOLATED, THE OLD GUARDIANS INSTALLED AN ESCAPE MECHANISM. I AM HEADED TO INITIATE IT.
IF YOU CAN SAVE THE CITADEL, DO SO. WE WILL FIND KYLE RAYNER.
WE MUST ENSURE HIS SAFETY.

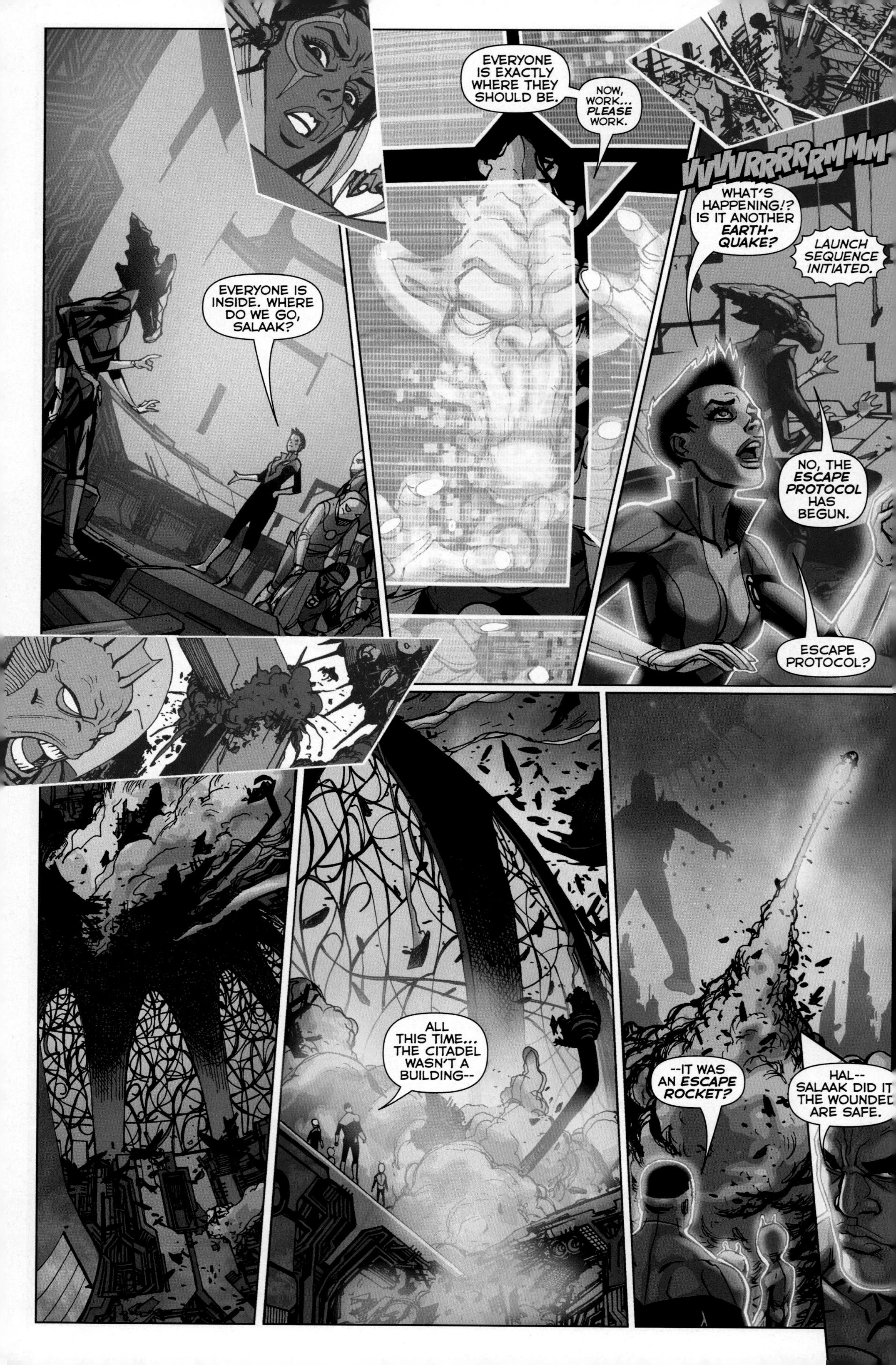
EVERYONE IS INSIDE. WHERE DO WE GO, SALAAK?
EVERYONE IS EXACTLY WHERE THEY SHOULD BE.
NOW, WORK... PLEASE WORK.
VVVWRRRRRMMMM
WHAT'S HAPPENING!? IS IT ANOTHER EARTH-QUAKE?
LAUNCH SEQUENCE INITIATED.
NO, THE ESCAPE PROTOCOL HAS BEGUN.
ESCAPE PROTOCOL?
ALL THIS TIME... THE CITADEL WASN'T A BUILDING--
--IT WAS AN ESCAPE ROCKET?
HAL-- SALAAK DID IT THE WOUNDED ARE SAFE.

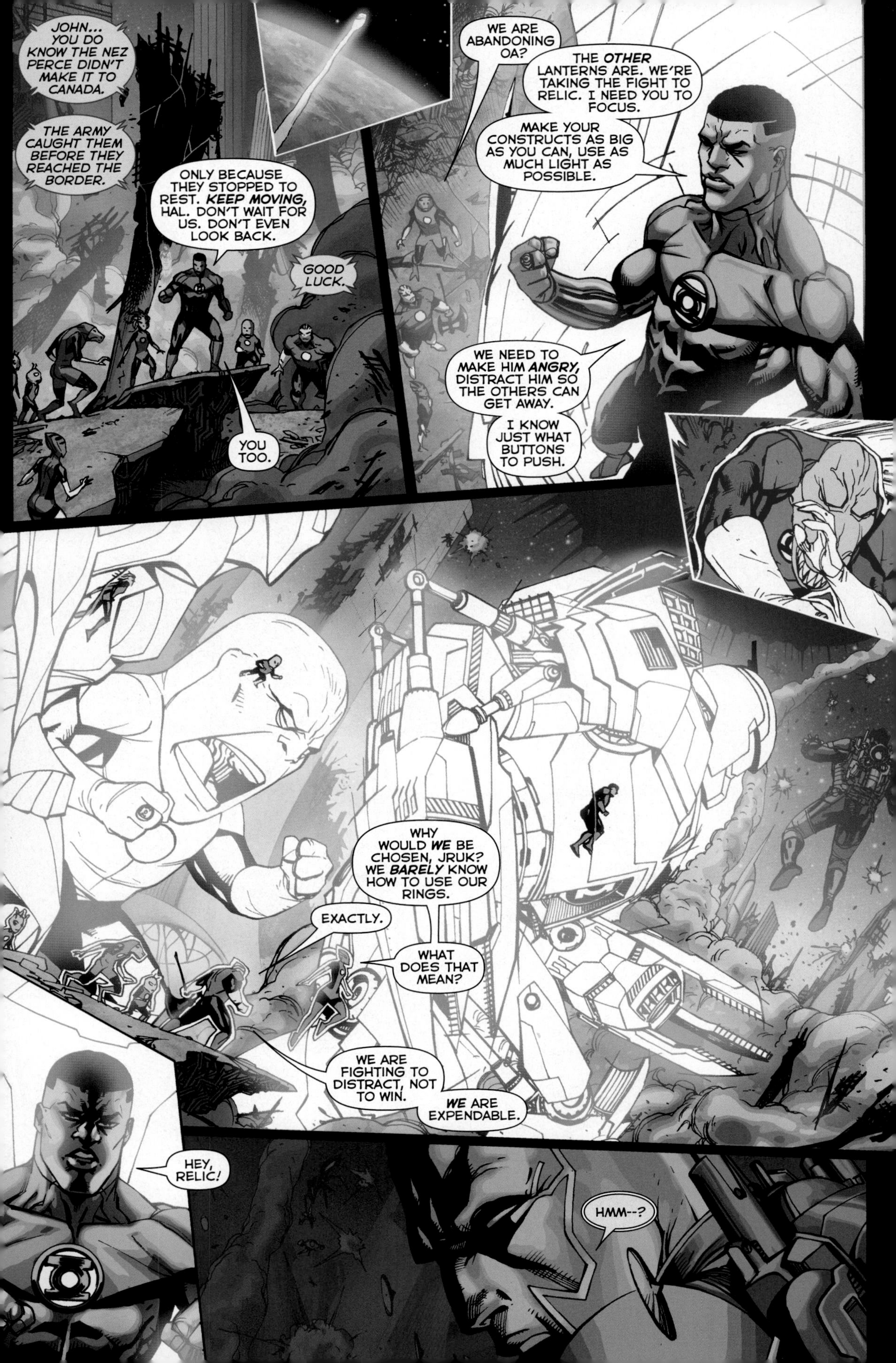
JOHN... YOU DO KNOW THE NEZ PERCE DIDN'T MAKE IT TO CANADA.
THE ARMY CAUGHT THEM BEFORE THEY REACHED THE BORDER.
ONLY BECAUSE THEY STOPPED TO REST. KEEP MOVING, HAL. DON'T WAIT FOR US. DON'T EVEN LOOK BACK.
GOOD LUCK.
YOU TOO.
WE ARE ABANDONING OA?
THE OTHER LANTERNS ARE. WE'RE TAKING THE FIGHT TO RELIC. I NEED YOU TO FOCUS.
MAKE YOUR CONSTRUCTS AS BIG AS YOU CAN, USE AS MUCH LIGHT AS POSSIBLE.
WE NEED TO MAKE HIM ANGRY, DISTRACT HIM SO THE OTHERS CAN GET AWAY.
I KNOW JUST WHAT BUTTONS TO PUSH.
WHY WOULD WE BE CHOSEN, JRUK? WE BARELY KNOW HOW TO USE OUR RINGS.
EXACTLY.
WHAT DOES THAT MEAN?
WE ARE FIGHTING TO DISTRACT, NOT TO WIN.
WE ARE EXPENDABLE.
HEY, RELIC!
HMM--?

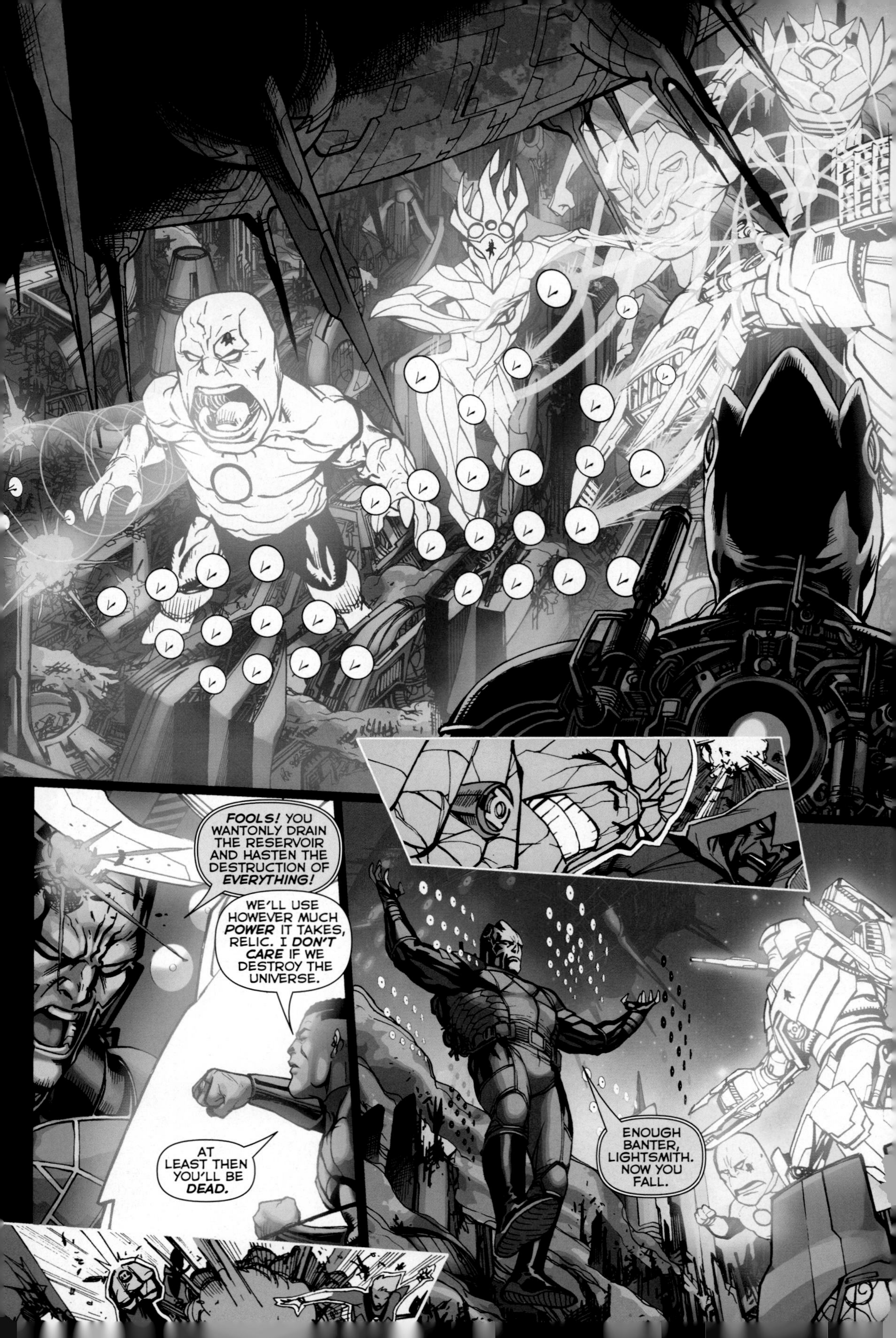

FOOLS! YOU WANTONLY DRAIN THE RESERVOIR AND HASTEN THE DESTRUCTION OF EVERYTHING!
WE'LL USE HOWEVER MUCH POWER IT TAKES, RELIC. I DON'T CARE IF WE DESTROY THE UNIVERSE.
AT LEAST THEN YOU'LL BE DEAD.
ENOUGH BANTER, LIGHTSMITH. NOW YOU FALL.

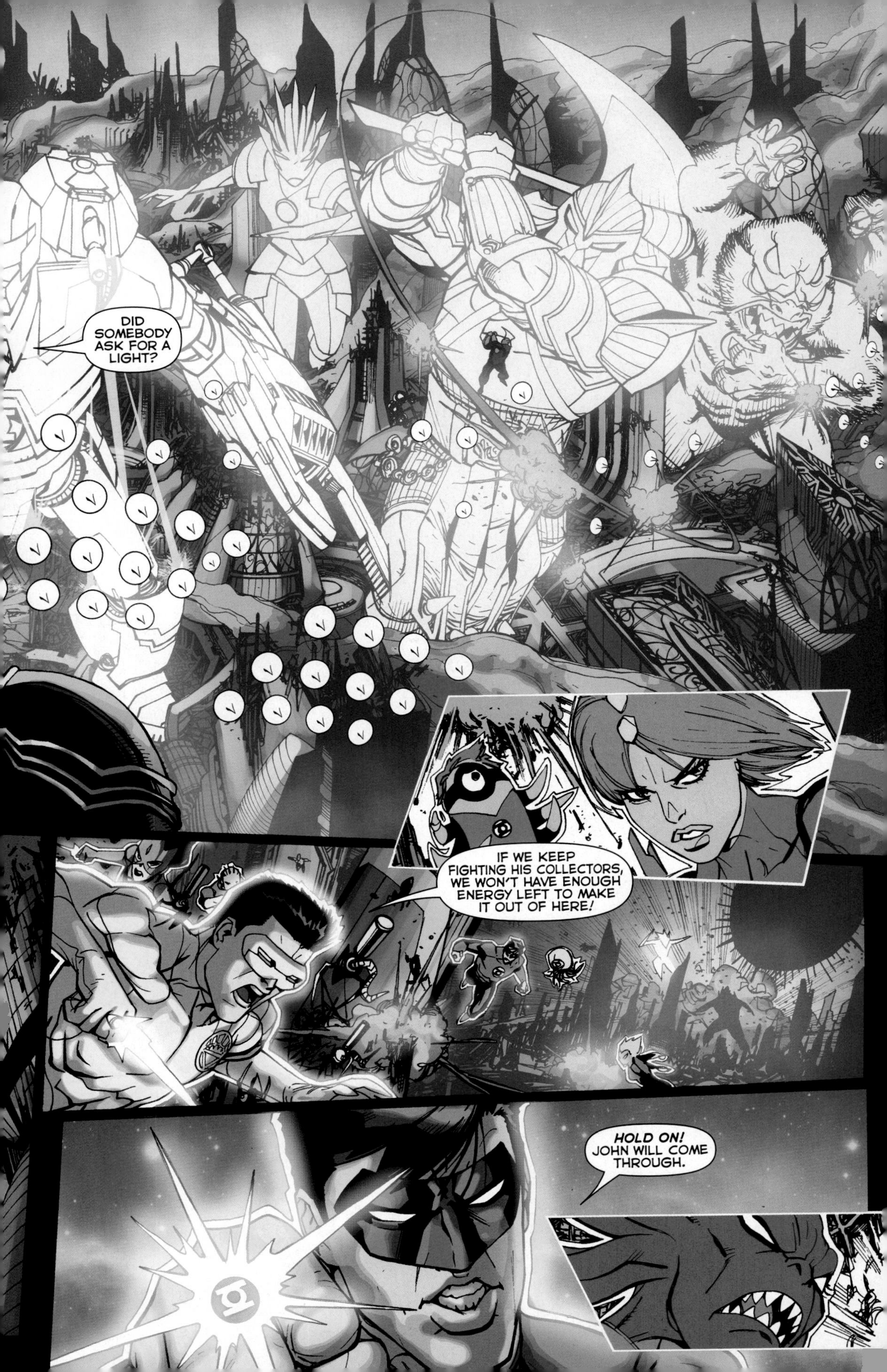
DID SOMEBODY ASK FOR A LIGHT?
IF WE KEEP FIGHTING HIS COLLECTORS, WE WON'T HAVE ENOUGH ENERGY LEFT TO MAKE IT OUT OF HERE!
HOLD ON! JOHN WILL COME THROUGH.

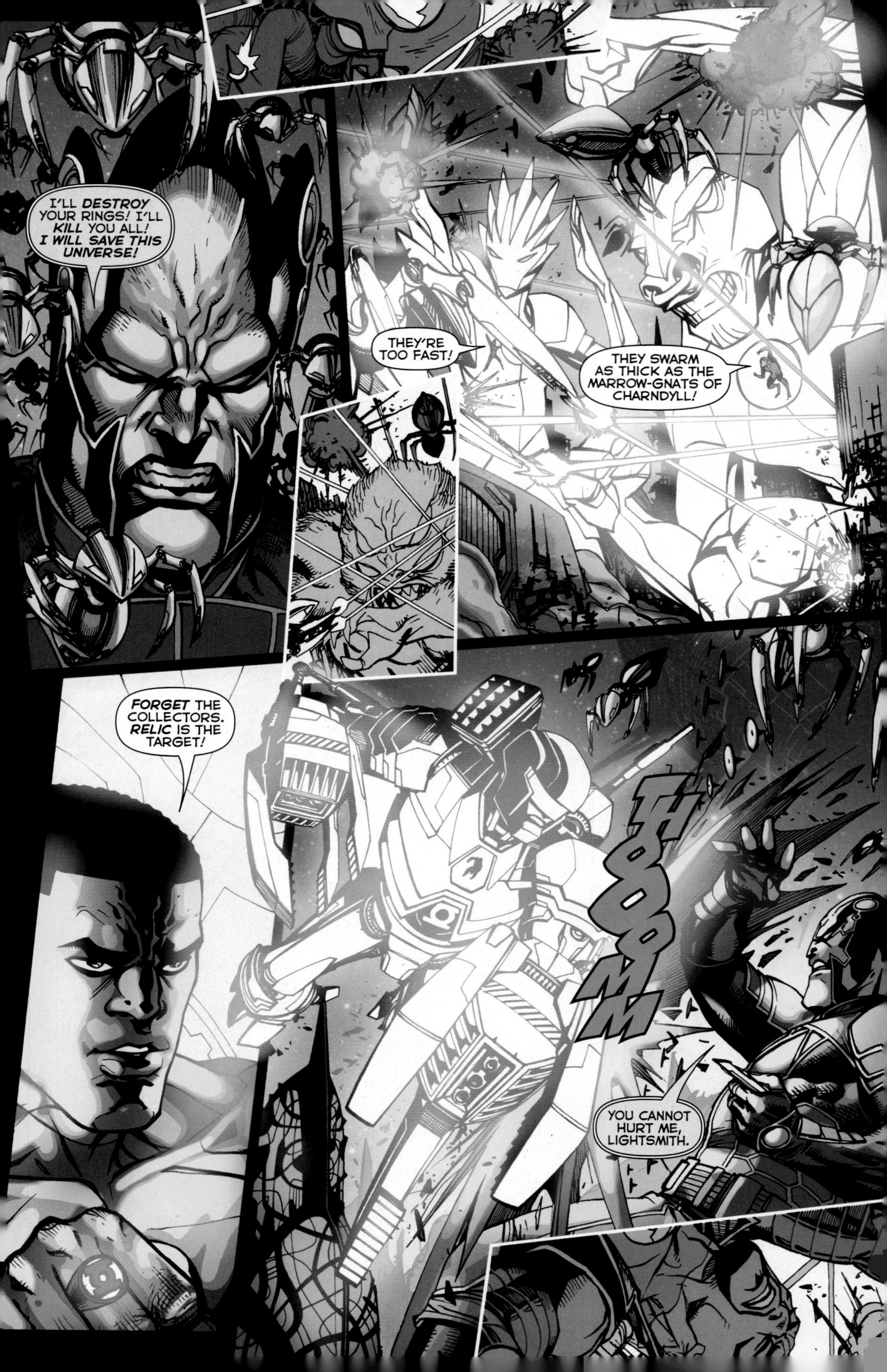
I'LL DESTROY YOUR RINGS! I'LL KILL YOU ALL! I WILL SAVE THIS UNIVERSE!
THEY'RE TOO FAST!
THEY SWARM AS THICK AS THE MARROW-GNATS OF CHARNDYLL!
FORGET THE COLLECTORS. RELIC IS THE TARGET!
THOOOOMM
YOU CANNOT HURT ME, LIGHTSMITH.

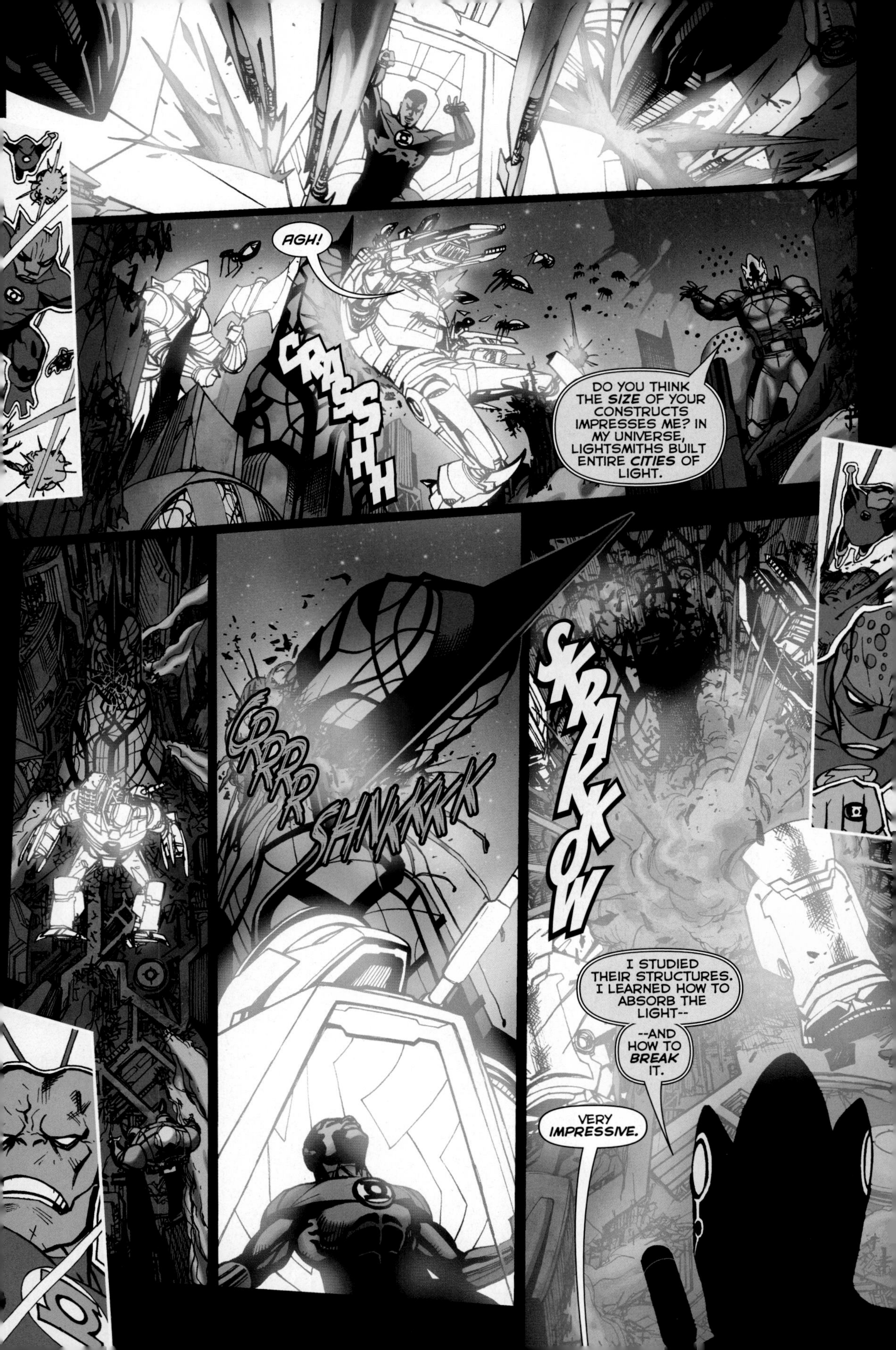

AGH!
CRASSHHH
DO YOU THINK THE SIZE OF YOUR CONSTRUCTS IMPRESSES ME? IN MY UNIVERSE, LIGHTSMITHS BUILT ENTIRE CITIES OF LIGHT.
CRRRR
SHNKKKKK
SKRAKOW
I STUDIED THEIR STRUCTURES. I LEARNED HOW TO ABSORB THE LIGHT--
--AND HOW TO BREAK IT.
VERY IMPRESSIVE.

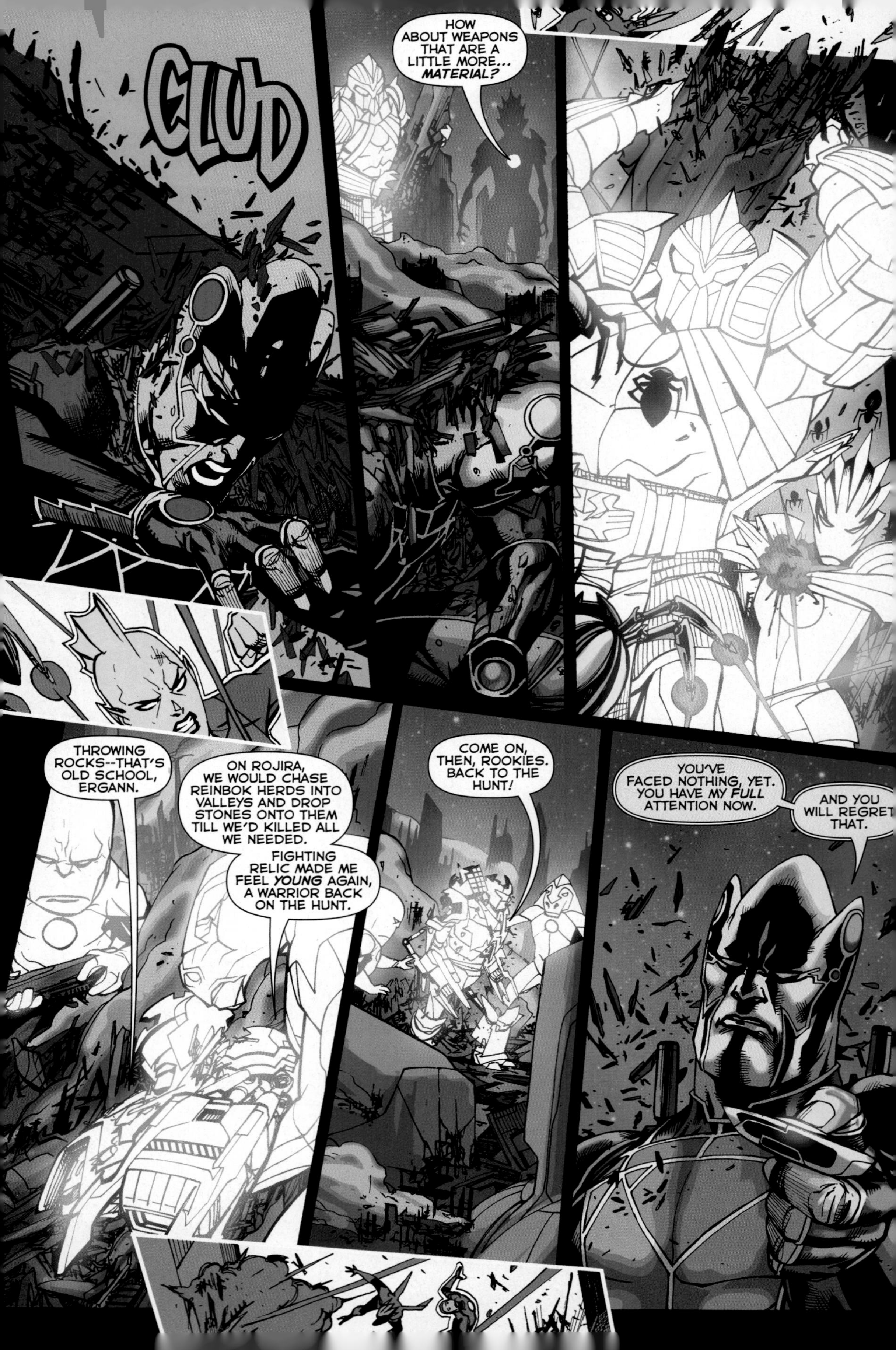
CLUD
HOW ABOUT WEAPONS THAT ARE A LITTLE MORE... MATERIAL?
THROWING ROCKS--THAT'S OLD SCHOOL, ERGANN.
ON ROJIRA, WE WOULD CHASE REINBOK HERDS INTO VALLEYS AND DROP STONES ONTO THEM TILL WE'D KILLED ALL WE NEEDED.
FIGHTING RELIC MADE ME FEEL YOUNG AGAIN, A WARRIOR BACK ON THE HUNT.
COME ON, THEN, ROOKIES. BACK TO THE HUNT!
YOU'VE FACED NOTHING, YET. YOU HAVE MY FULL ATTENTION NOW.
AND YOU WILL REGRET THAT.

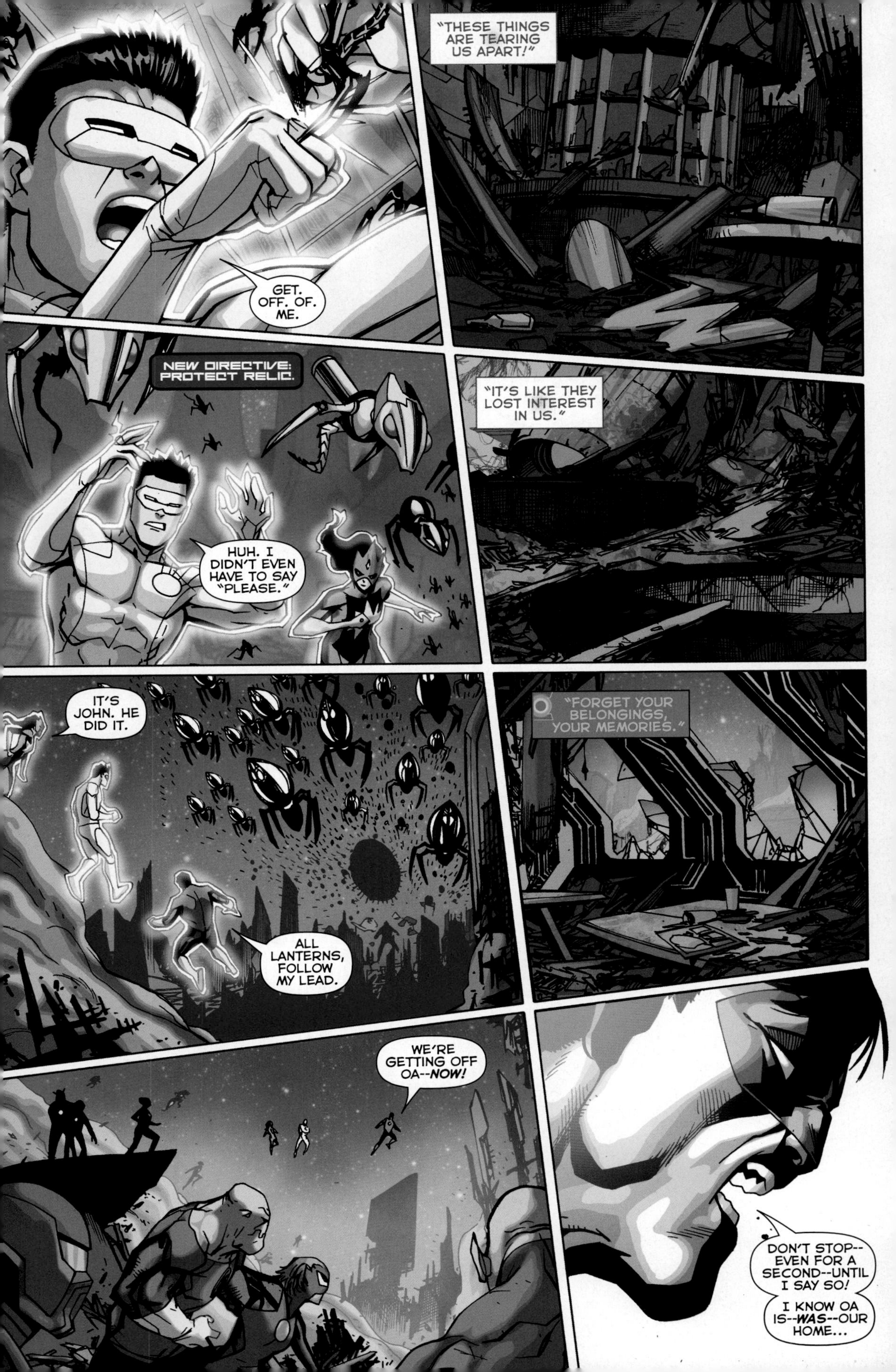
GET. OFF. OF. ME.
"THESE THINGS ARE TEARING US APART!"
NEW DIRECTIVE: PROTECT RELIC.
HUH. I DIDN'T EVEN HAVE TO SAY "PLEASE."
"IT'S LIKE THEY LOST INTEREST IN US."
IT'S JOHN. HE DID IT.
ALL LANTERNS, FOLLOW MY LEAD.
"FORGET YOUR BELONGINGS, YOUR MEMORIES."
WE'RE GETTING OFF OA--*NOW!*
DON'T STOP-- EVEN FOR A SECOND--UNTIL I SAY SO!
I KNOW OA IS--*WAS*--OUR HOME...

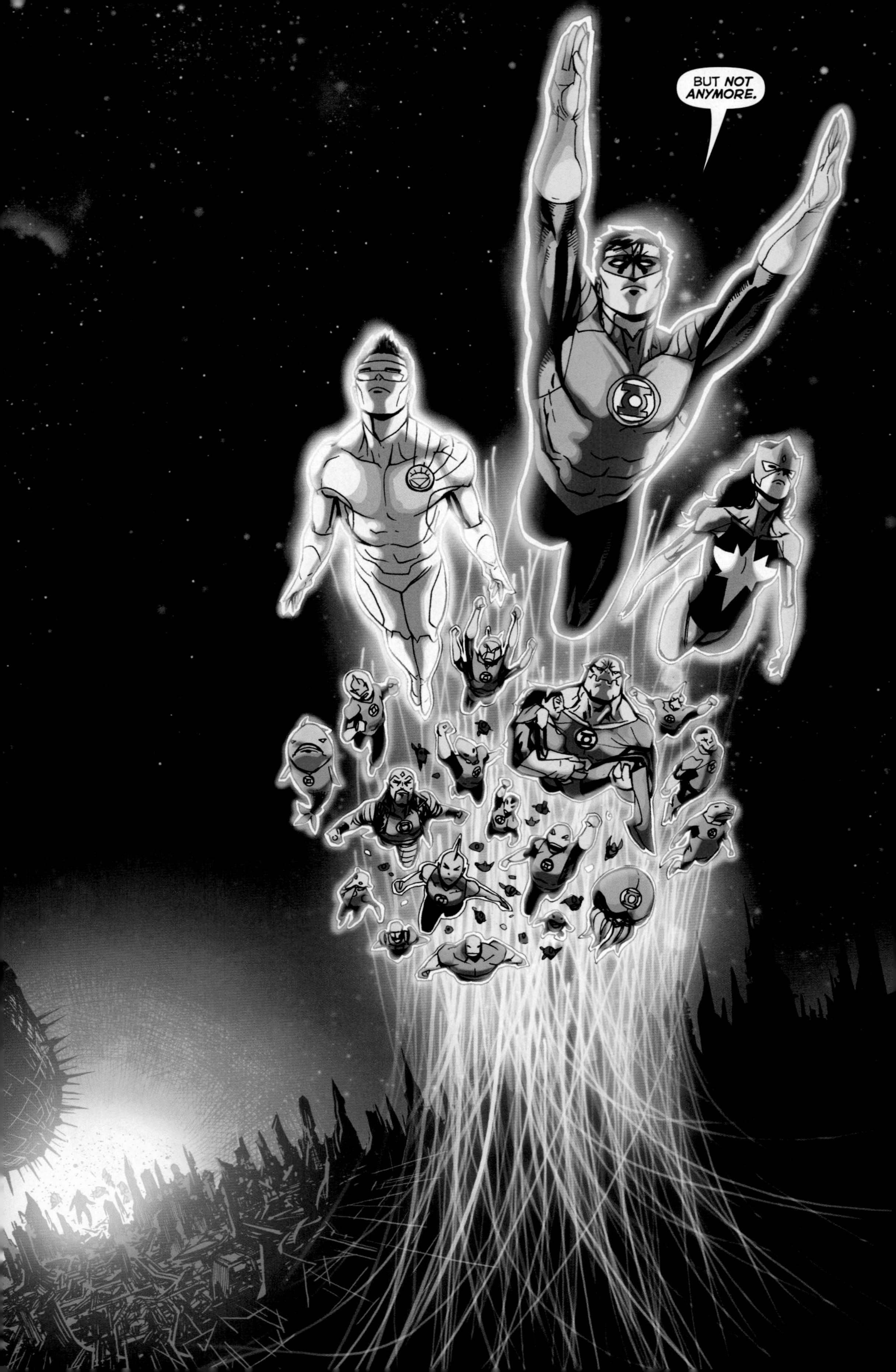
BUT NOT ANYMORE.

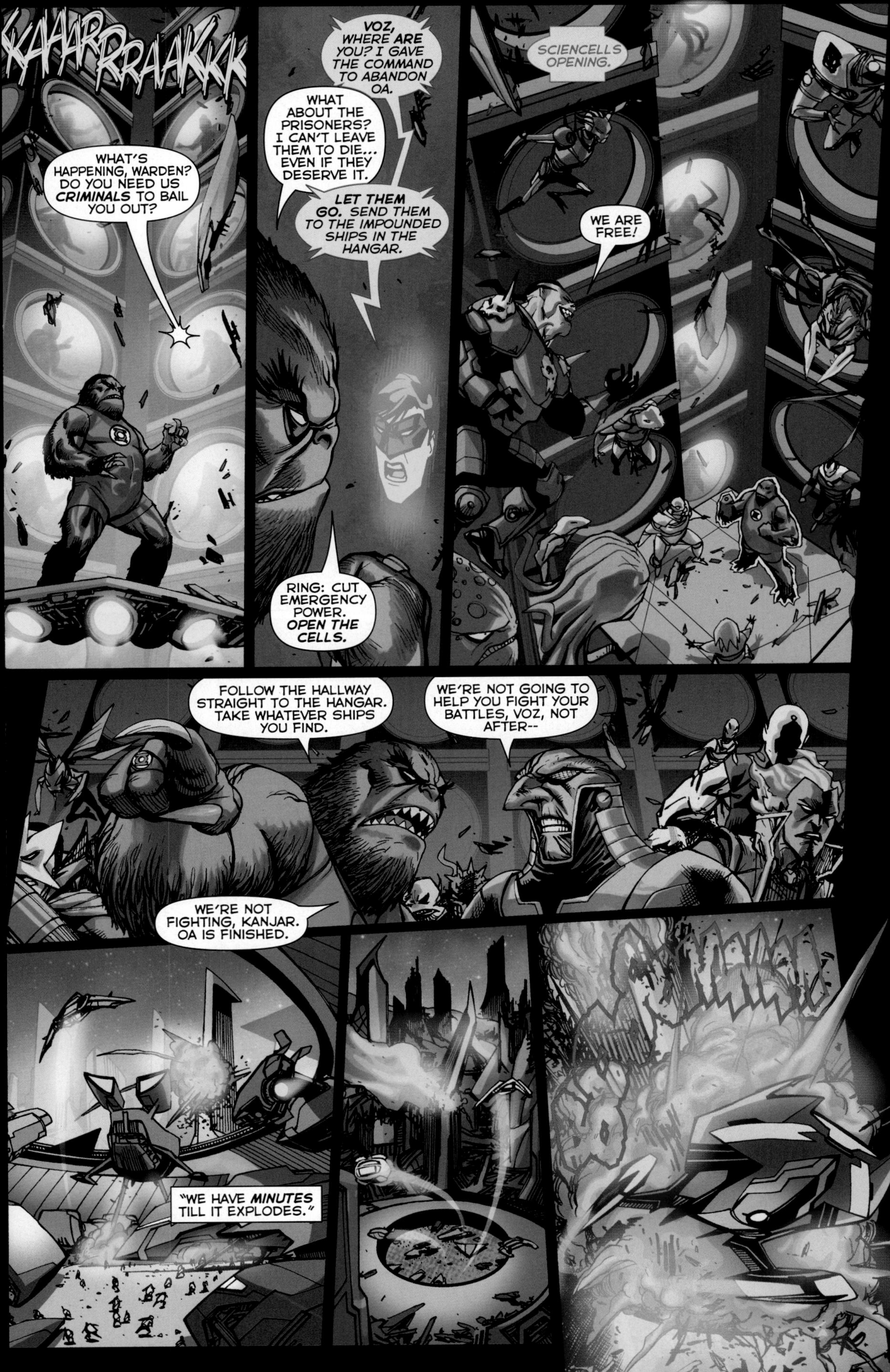
KAAAR RRAAKKK
WHAT'S HAPPENING, WARDEN? DO YOU NEED US CRIMINALS TO BAIL YOU OUT?
VOZ, WHERE ARE YOU? I GAVE THE COMMAND TO ABANDON OA.
WHAT ABOUT THE PRISONERS? I CAN'T LEAVE THEM TO DIE... EVEN IF THEY DESERVE IT.
LET THEM GO. SEND THEM TO THE IMPOUNDED SHIPS IN THE HANGAR.
RING: CUT EMERGENCY POWER. OPEN THE CELLS.
SCIENCELLS OPENING.
WE ARE FREE!
FOLLOW THE HALLWAY STRAIGHT TO THE HANGAR. TAKE WHATEVER SHIPS YOU FIND.
WE'RE NOT GOING TO HELP YOU FIGHT YOUR BATTLES, VOZ, NOT AFTER--
WE'RE NOT FIGHTING, KANJAR. OA IS FINISHED.
"WE HAVE MINUTES TILL IT EXPLODES."

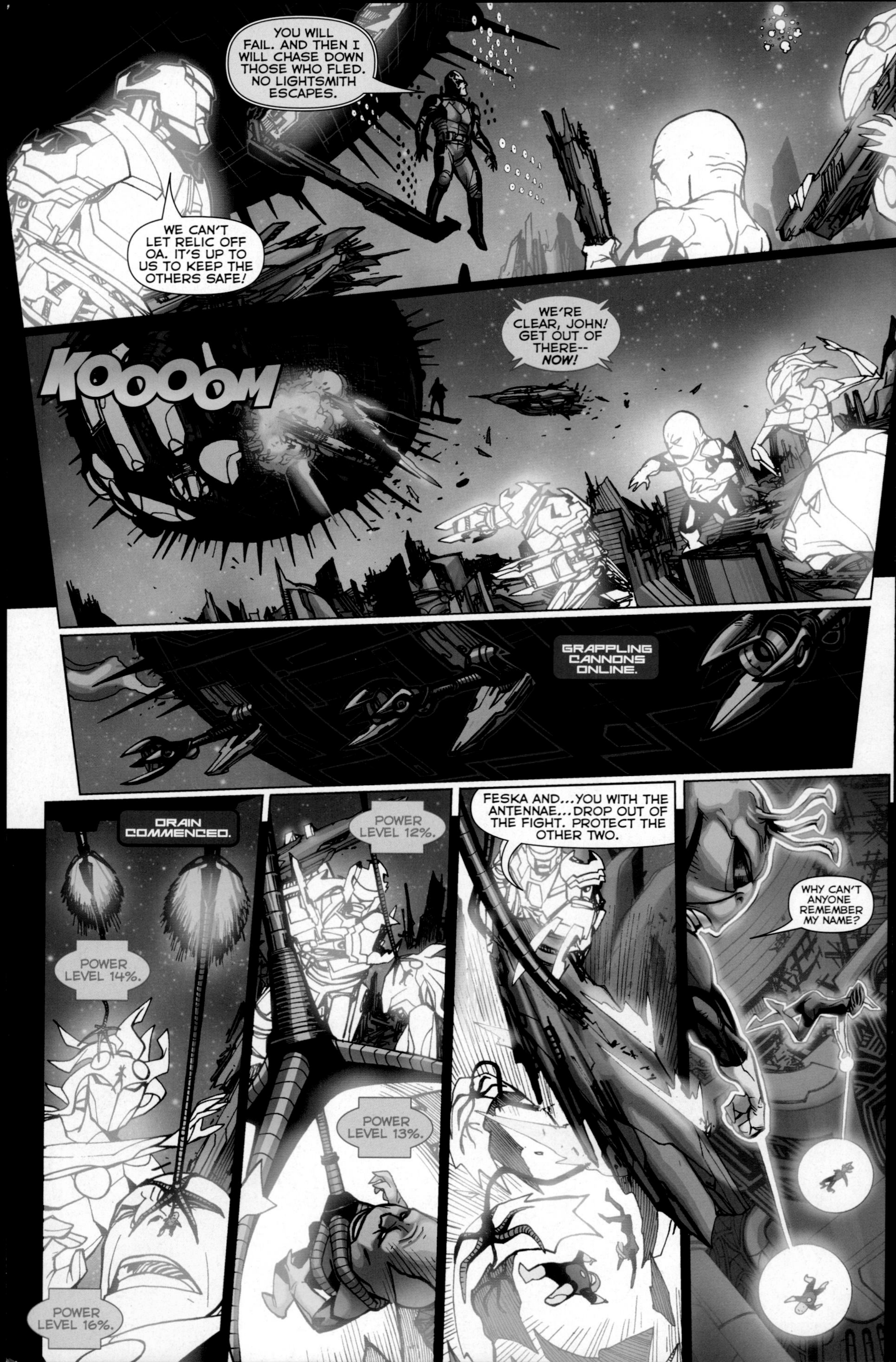
YOU WILL FAIL. AND THEN I WILL CHASE DOWN THOSE WHO FLED. NO LIGHTSMITH ESCAPES.
WE CAN'T LET RELIC OFF OA. IT'S UP TO US TO KEEP THE OTHERS SAFE!
KOOOOM
WE'RE CLEAR, JOHN! GET OUT OF THERE-- NOW!
GRAPPLING CANNONS ONLINE.
DRAIN COMMENCED.
POWER LEVEL 14%.
POWER LEVEL 16%.
POWER LEVEL 12%.
POWER LEVEL 13%.
FESKA AND...YOU WITH THE ANTENNAE...DROP OUT OF THE FIGHT. PROTECT THE OTHER TWO.
WHY CAN'T ANYONE REMEMBER MY NAME?

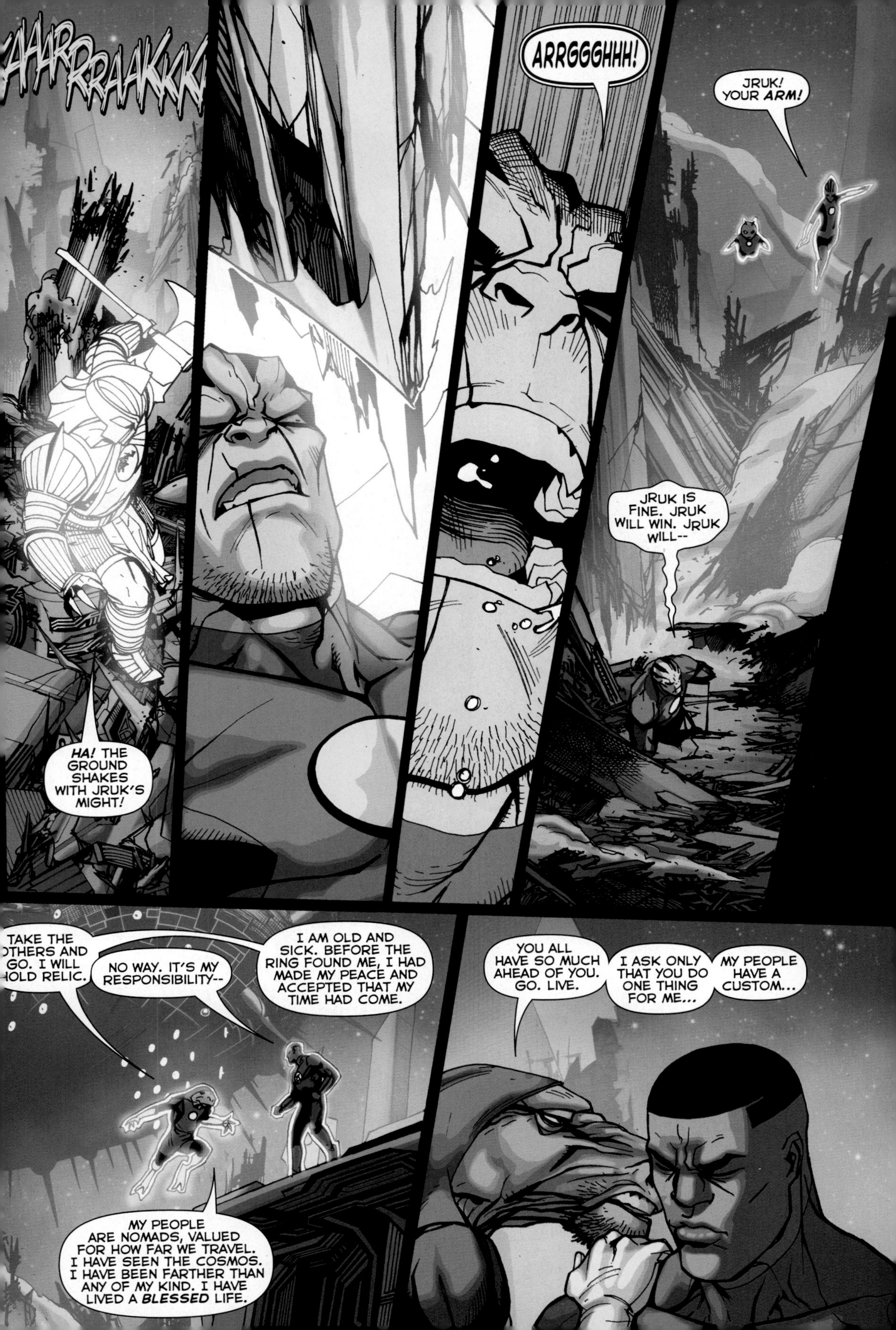
AAARRRAAKKKK
HA! THE GROUND SHAKES WITH JRUK'S MIGHT!
ARRGGGHHH!
JRUK! YOUR ARM!
JRUK IS FINE. JRUK WILL WIN. JRUK WILL--
TAKE THE OTHERS AND GO. I WILL HOLD RELIC.
NO WAY. IT'S MY RESPONSIBILITY--
I AM OLD AND SICK. BEFORE THE RING FOUND ME, I HAD MADE MY PEACE AND ACCEPTED THAT MY TIME HAD COME.
MY PEOPLE ARE NOMADS, VALUED FOR HOW FAR WE TRAVEL. I HAVE SEEN THE COSMOS. I HAVE BEEN FARTHER THAN ANY OF MY KIND. I HAVE LIVED A BLESSED LIFE.
YOU ALL HAVE SO MUCH AHEAD OF YOU. GO. LIVE.
I ASK ONLY THAT YOU DO ONE THING FOR ME...
MY PEOPLE HAVE A CUSTOM...

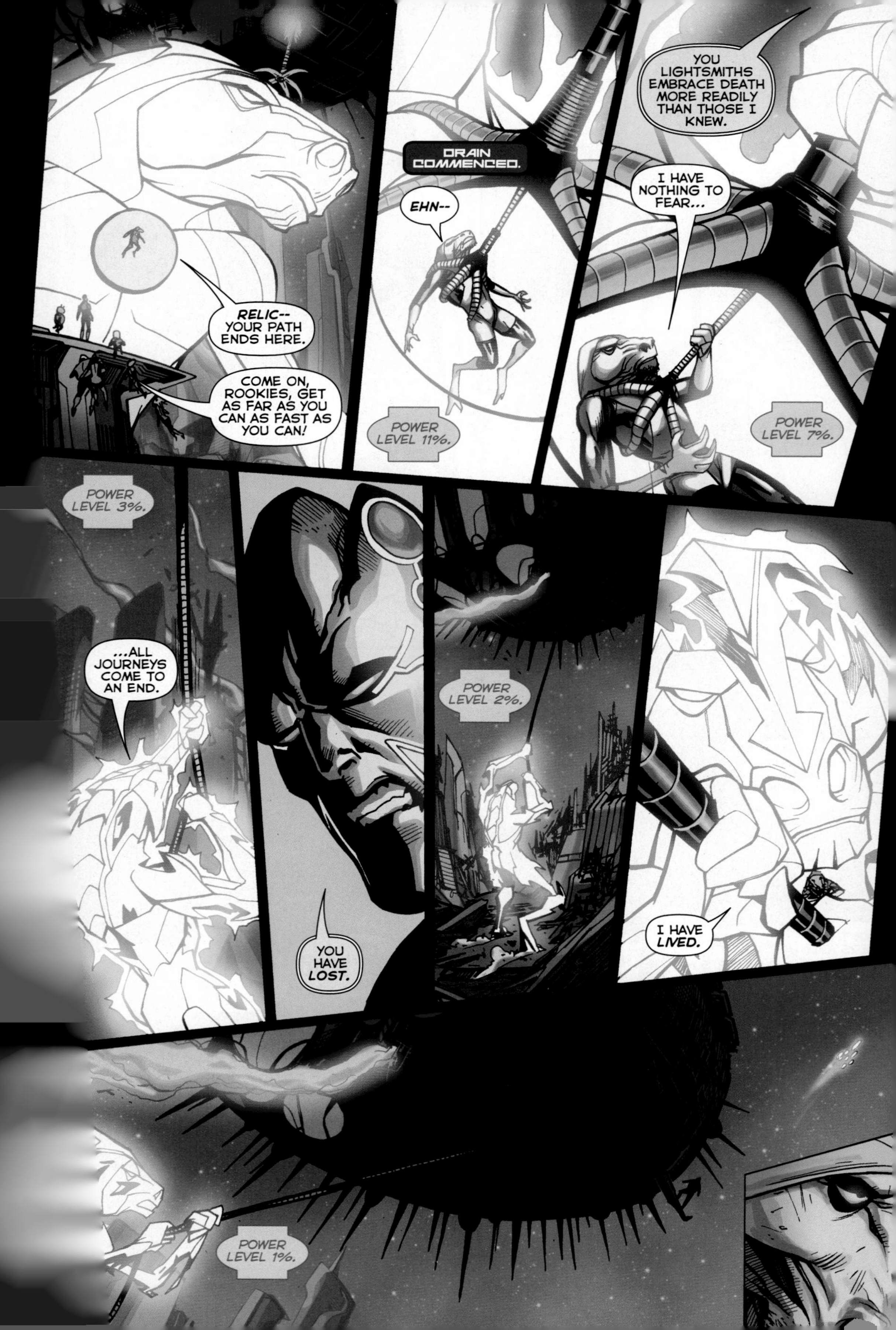
RELIC-- YOUR PATH ENDS HERE.
COME ON, ROOKIES, GET AS FAR AS YOU CAN AS FAST AS YOU CAN!
DRAIN COMMENCED.
EHN--
POWER LEVEL 11%.
YOU LIGHTSMITHS EMBRACE DEATH MORE READILY THAN THOSE I KNEW.
I HAVE NOTHING TO FEAR...
POWER LEVEL 7%.
POWER LEVEL 3%.
...ALL JOURNEYS COME TO AN END.
YOU HAVE LOST.
POWER LEVEL 2%.
I HAVE LIVED.
POWER LEVEL 1%.

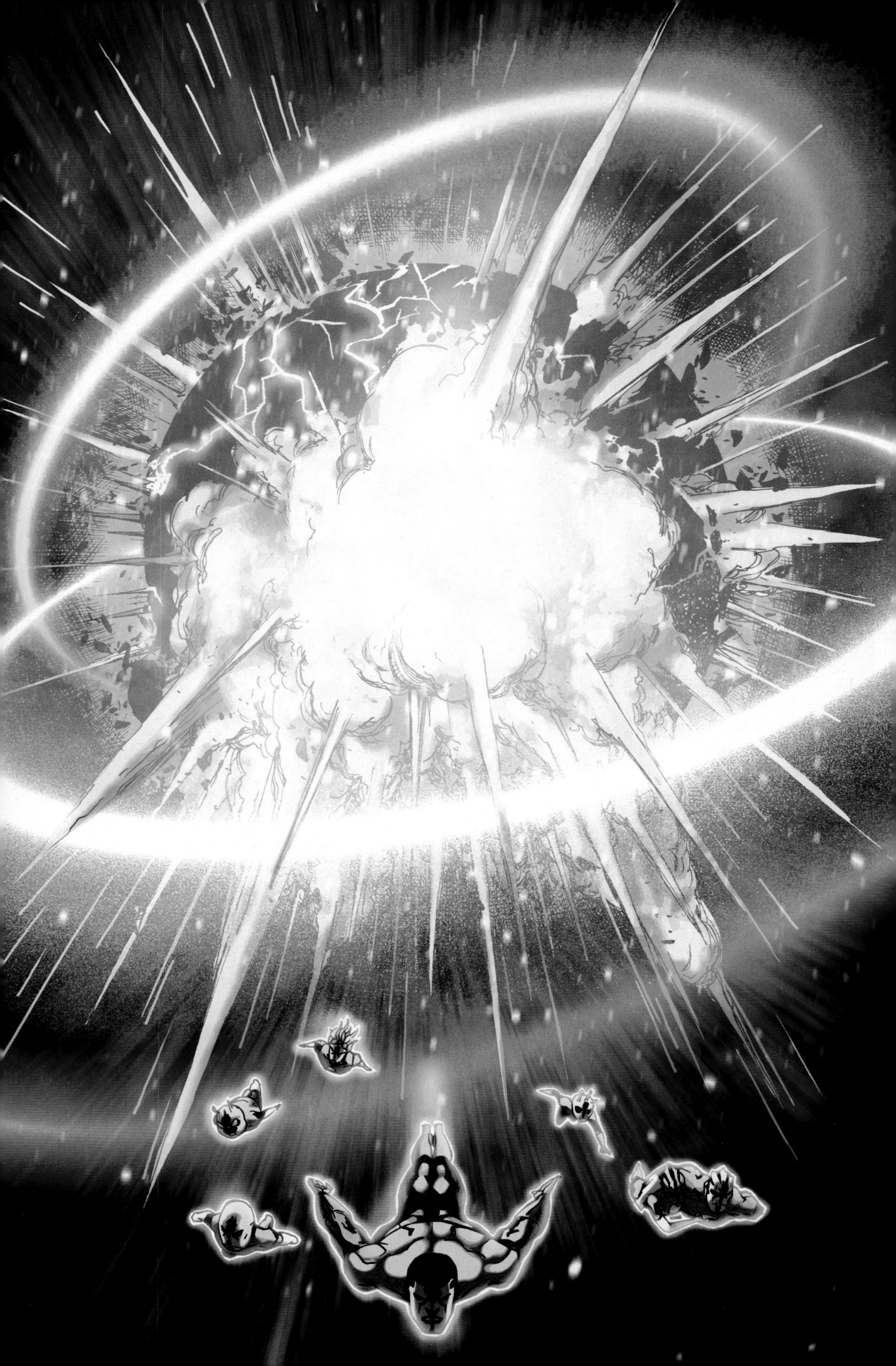

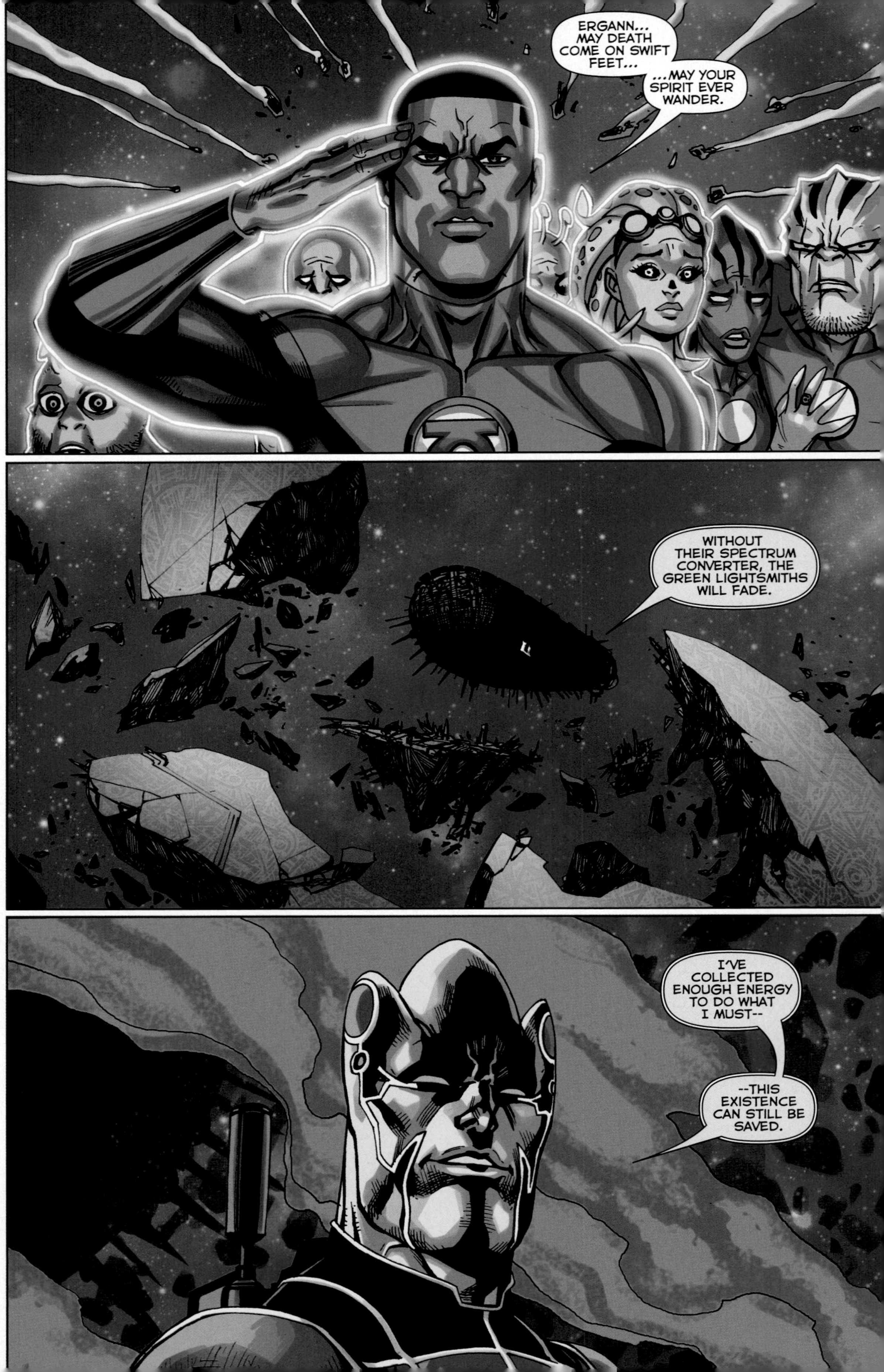
ERGANN... MAY DEATH COME ON SWIFT FEET...
...MAY YOUR SPIRIT EVER WANDER.
WITHOUT THEIR SPECTRUM CONVERTER, THE GREEN LIGHTSMITHS WILL FADE.
I'VE COLLECTED ENOUGH ENERGY TO DO WHAT I MUST--
--THIS EXISTENCE CAN STILL BE SAVED.

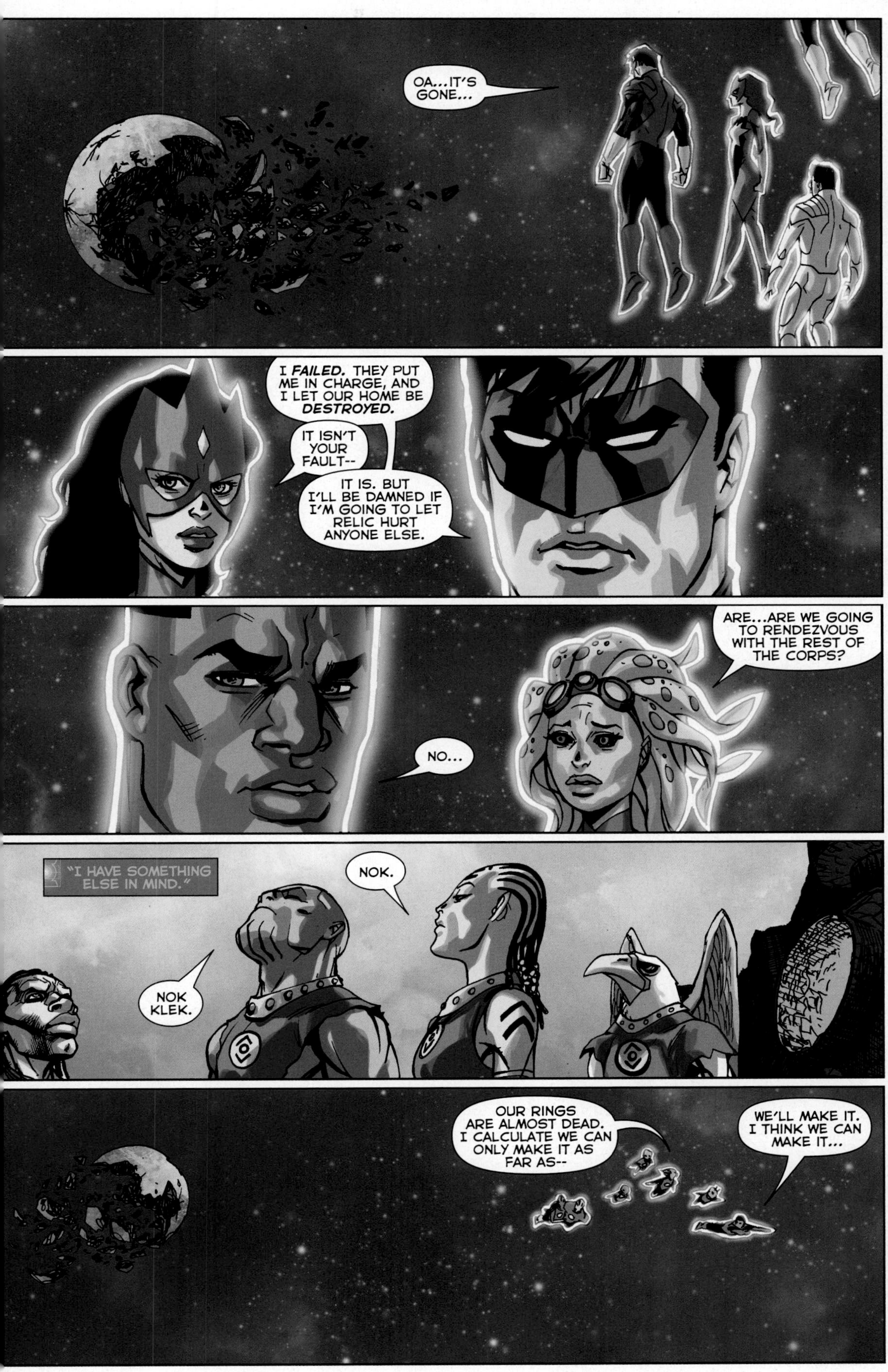
OA...IT'S GONE...
I **FAILED.** THEY PUT ME IN CHARGE, AND I LET OUR HOME BE **DESTROYED.**
IT ISN'T YOUR FAULT--
IT IS. BUT I'LL BE DAMNED IF I'M GOING TO LET RELIC HURT ANYONE ELSE.
ARE...ARE WE GOING TO RENDEZVOUS WITH THE REST OF THE CORPS?
NO...
"I HAVE SOMETHING ELSE IN MIND."
NOK.
NOK KLEK.
OUR RINGS ARE ALMOST DEAD. I CALCULATE WE CAN ONLY MAKE IT AS FAR AS--
WE'LL MAKE IT. I THINK WE CAN MAKE IT...

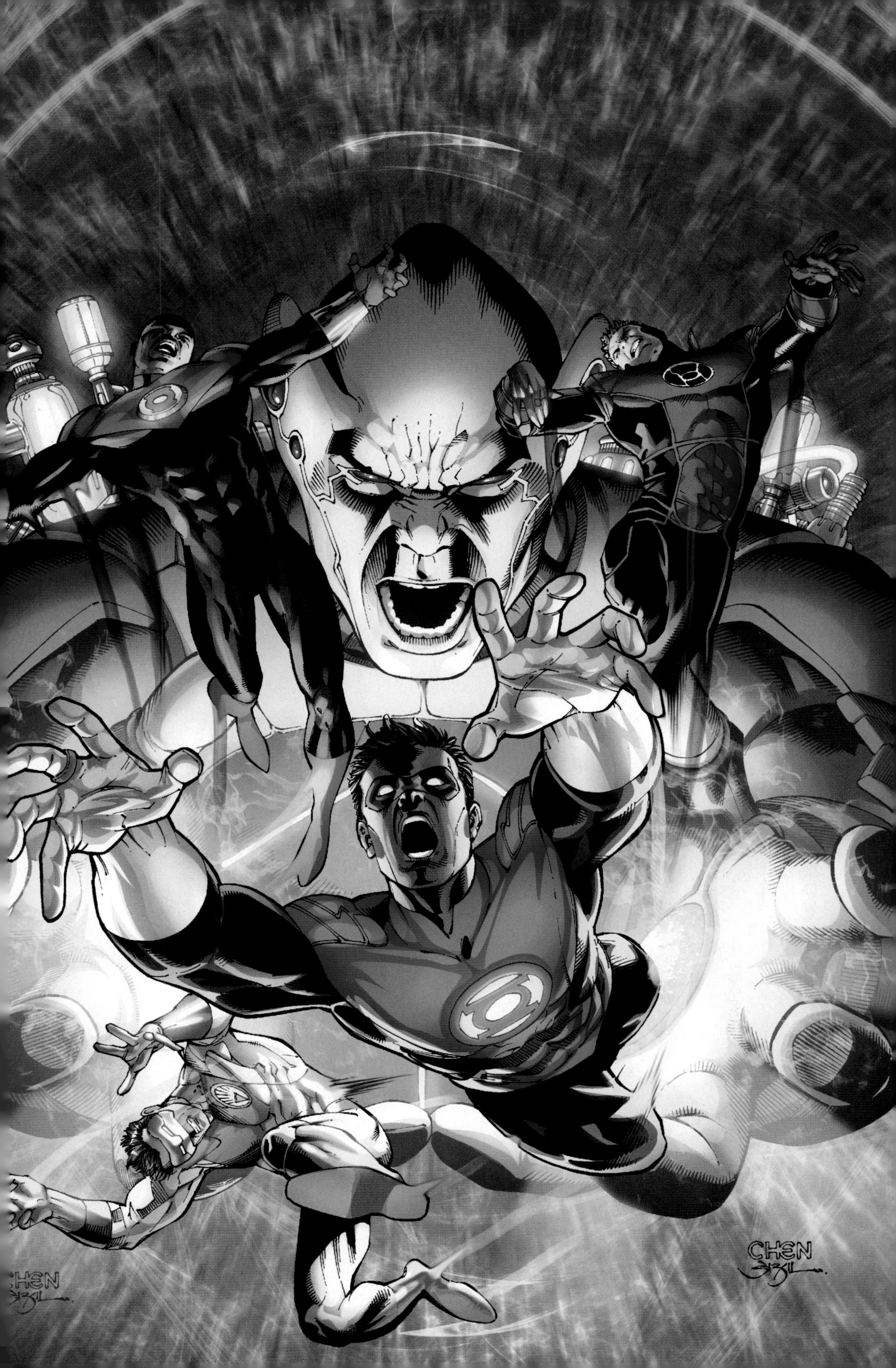
CHEN

THE SOURCE

ROBERT VENDITTI writer SEAN CHEN penciller JON SIBAL & WALDEN WONG inkers
cover art by SEAN CHEN, JON SIBAL & ALEX SINCLAIR

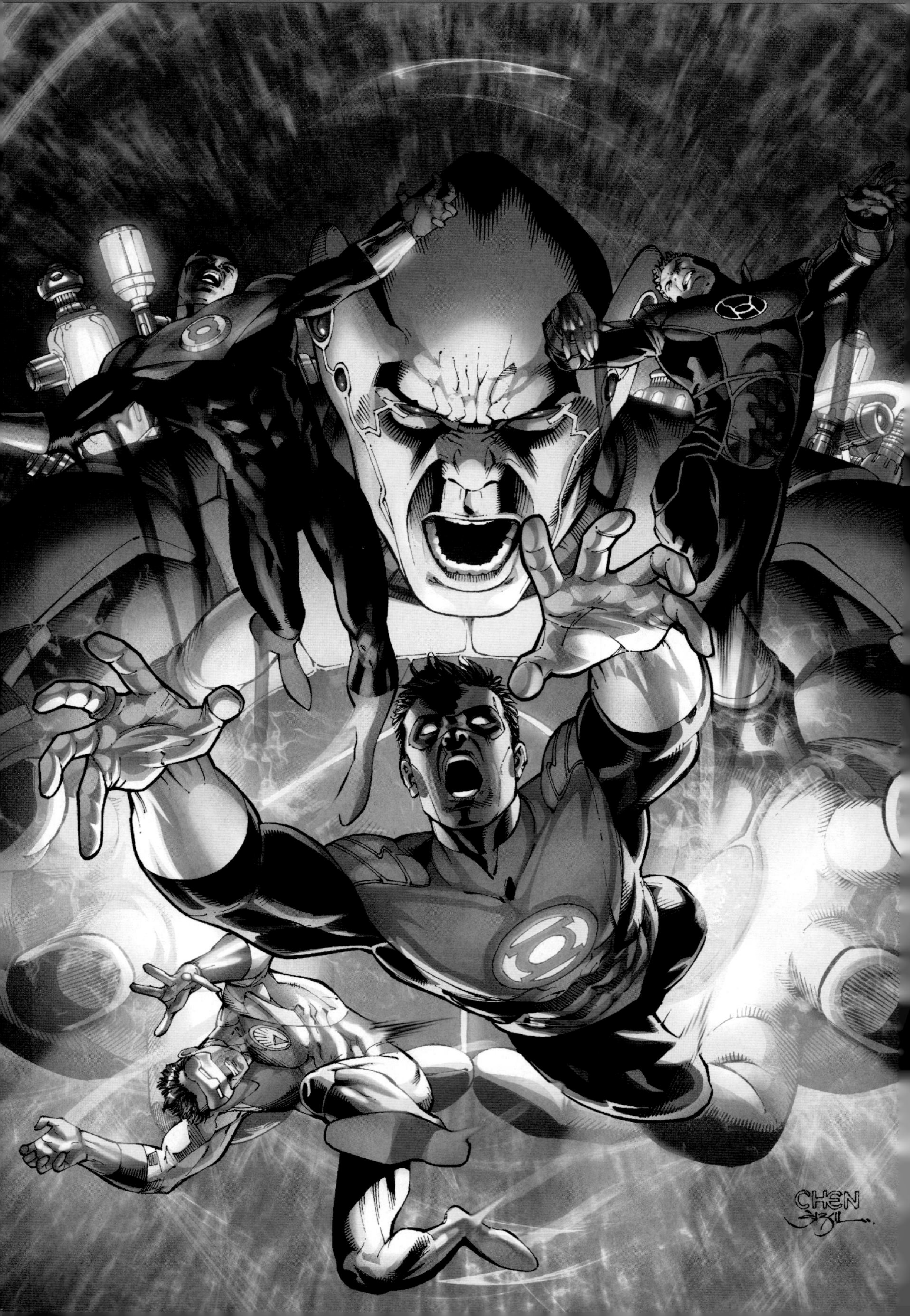
CHEN
SIBAL

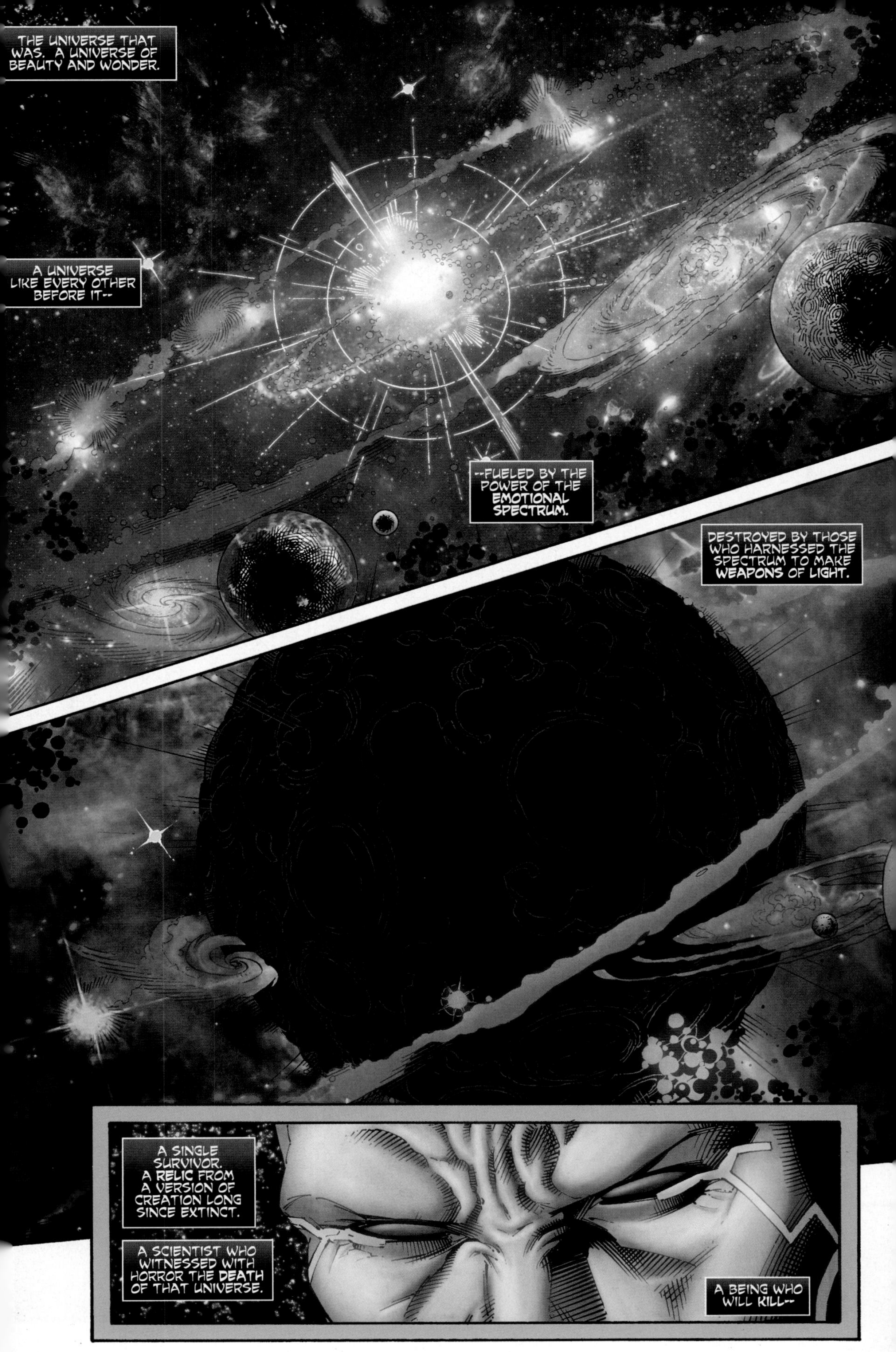
THE UNIVERSE THAT WAS. A UNIVERSE OF BEAUTY AND WONDER.
A UNIVERSE LIKE EVERY OTHER BEFORE IT--
--FUELED BY THE POWER OF THE EMOTIONAL SPECTRUM.
DESTROYED BY THOSE WHO HARNESSED THE SPECTRUM TO MAKE WEAPONS OF LIGHT.
A SINGLE SURVIVOR. A RELIC FROM A VERSION OF CREATION LONG SINCE EXTINCT.
A SCIENTIST WHO WITNESSED WITH HORROR THE DEATH OF THAT UNIVERSE.
A BEING WHO WILL KILL--

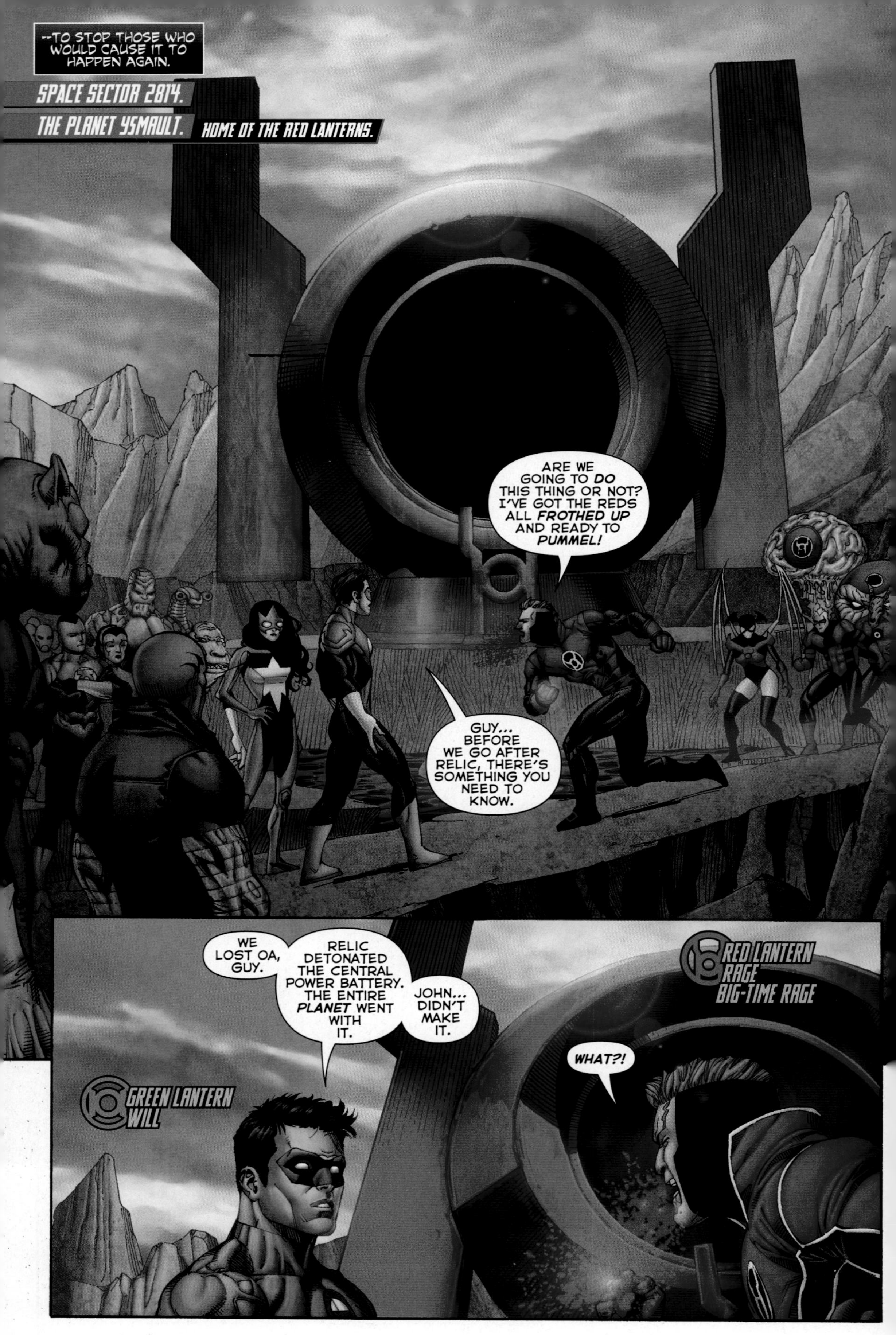
--TO STOP THOSE WHO WOULD CAUSE IT TO HAPPEN AGAIN.
SPACE SECTOR 2814.
THE PLANET YSMAULT.
HOME OF THE RED LANTERNS.
ARE WE GOING TO DO THIS THING OR NOT? I'VE GOT THE REDS ALL FROTHED UP AND READY TO PUMMEL!
GUY... BEFORE WE GO AFTER RELIC, THERE'S SOMETHING YOU NEED TO KNOW.
WE LOST OA, GUY.
RELIC DETONATED THE CENTRAL POWER BATTERY. THE ENTIRE PLANET WENT WITH IT.
JOHN... DIDN'T MAKE IT.
RED LANTERN RAGE BIG-TIME RAGE
WHAT?!
GREEN LANTERN WILL

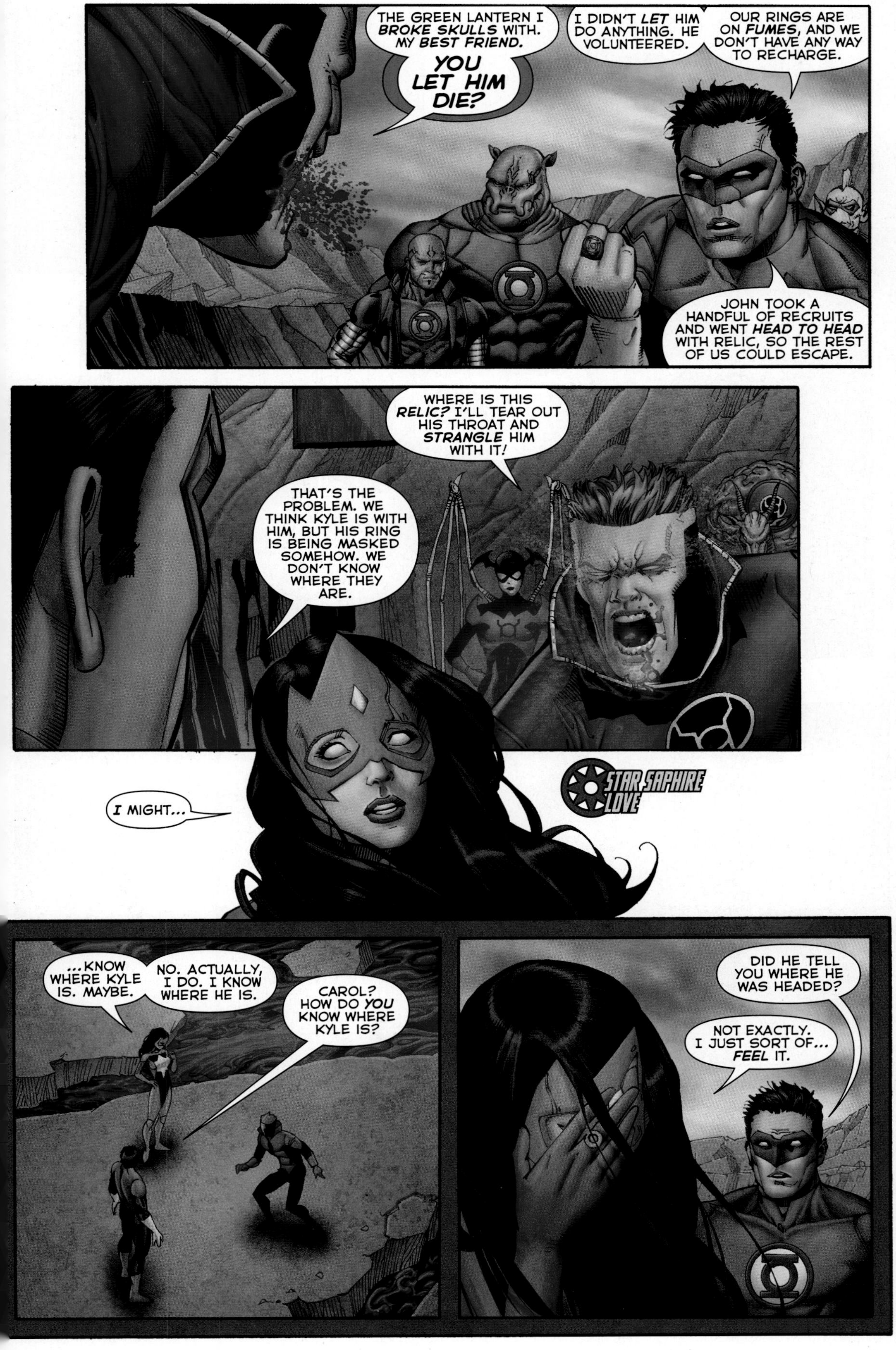

THE GREEN LANTERN I BROKE SKULLS WITH. MY BEST FRIEND.
YOU LET HIM DIE?
I DIDN'T LET HIM DO ANYTHING. HE VOLUNTEERED.
OUR RINGS ARE ON FUMES, AND WE DON'T HAVE ANY WAY TO RECHARGE.
JOHN TOOK A HANDFUL OF RECRUITS AND WENT HEAD TO HEAD WITH RELIC, SO THE REST OF US COULD ESCAPE.
WHERE IS THIS RELIC? I'LL TEAR OUT HIS THROAT AND STRANGLE HIM WITH IT!
THAT'S THE PROBLEM. WE THINK KYLE IS WITH HIM, BUT HIS RING IS BEING MASKED SOMEHOW. WE DON'T KNOW WHERE THEY ARE.
STAR SAPHIRE LOVE
I MIGHT...
...KNOW WHERE KYLE IS. MAYBE.
NO. ACTUALLY, I DO. I KNOW WHERE HE IS.
CAROL? HOW DO YOU KNOW WHERE KYLE IS?
DID HE TELL YOU WHERE HE WAS HEADED?
NOT EXACTLY. I JUST SORT OF... FEEL IT.

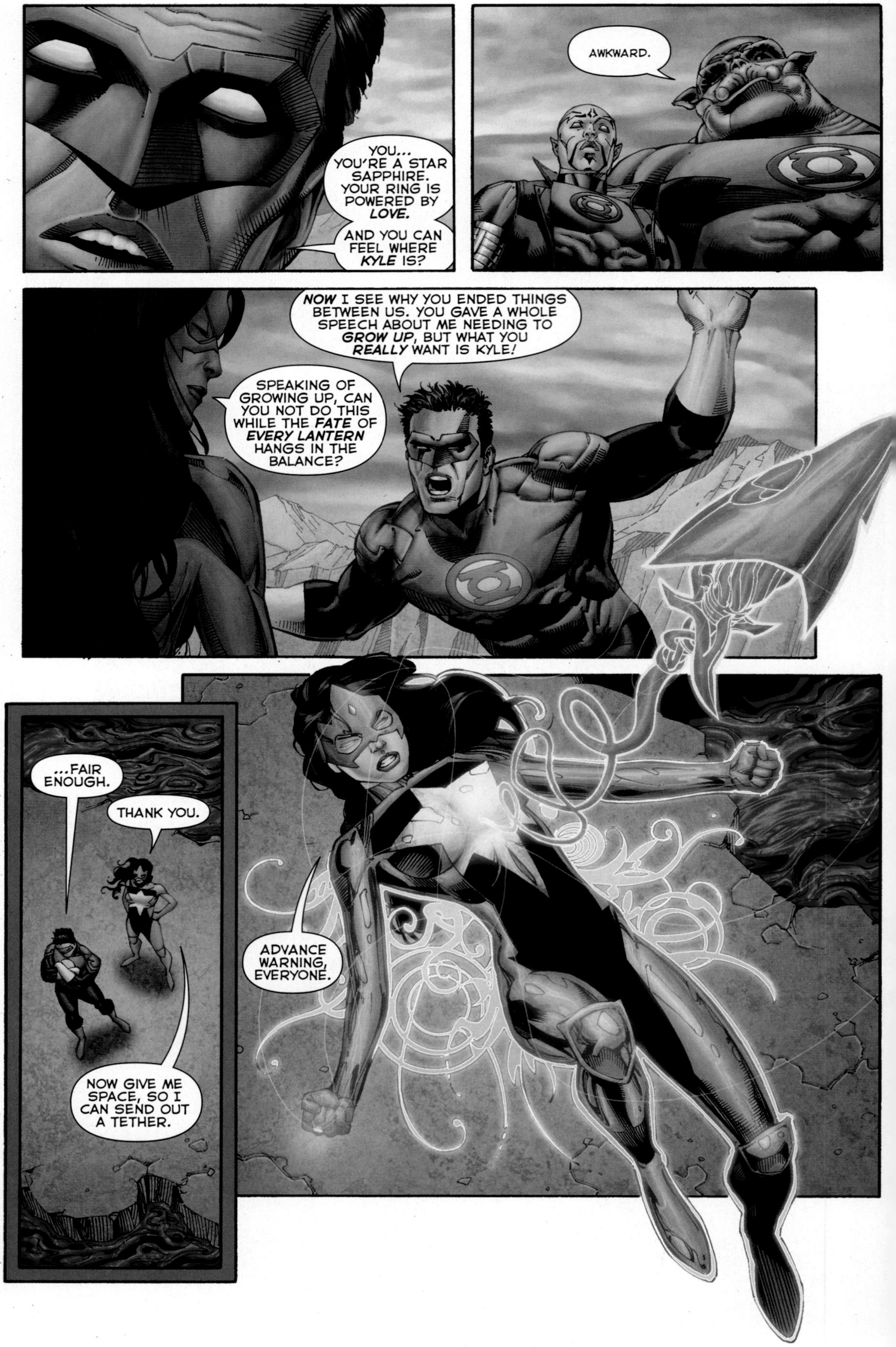
YOU... YOU'RE A STAR SAPPHIRE. YOUR RING IS POWERED BY LOVE.
AND YOU CAN FEEL WHERE KYLE IS?
AWKWARD.
NOW I SEE WHY YOU ENDED THINGS BETWEEN US. YOU GAVE A WHOLE SPEECH ABOUT ME NEEDING TO GROW UP, BUT WHAT YOU REALLY WANT IS KYLE!
SPEAKING OF GROWING UP, CAN YOU NOT DO THIS WHILE THE FATE OF EVERY LANTERN HANGS IN THE BALANCE?
...FAIR ENOUGH.
THANK YOU.
NOW GIVE ME SPACE, SO I CAN SEND OUT A TETHER.
ADVANCE WARNING, EVERYONE.

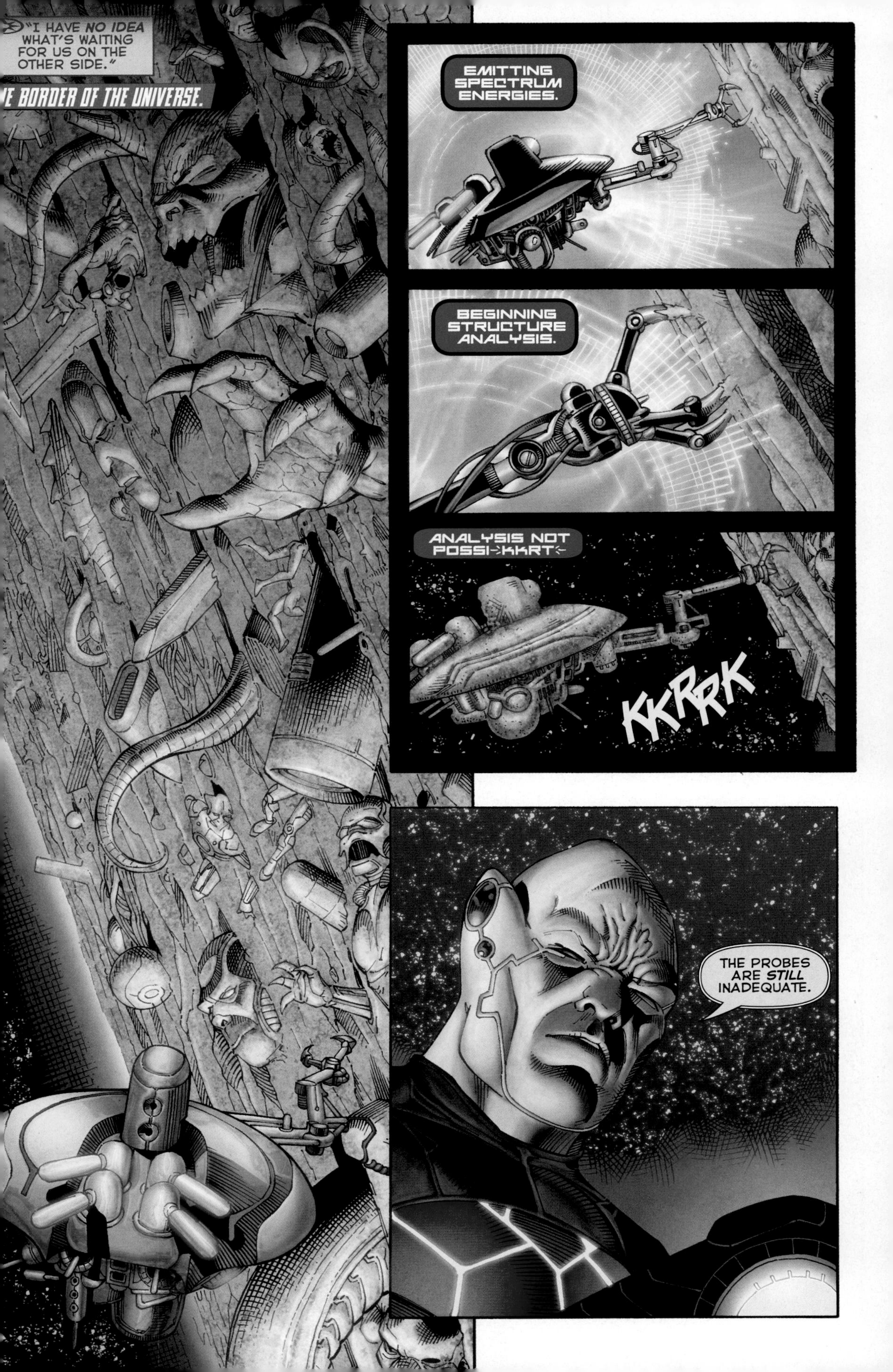
"I HAVE NO IDEA WHAT'S WAITING FOR US ON THE OTHER SIDE."
...E BORDER OF THE UNIVERSE.
EMITTING SPECTRUM ENERGIES.
BEGINNING STRUCTURE ANALYSIS.
ANALYSIS NOT POSSI-KKRT-
KKRRK
THE PROBES ARE STILL INADEQUATE.

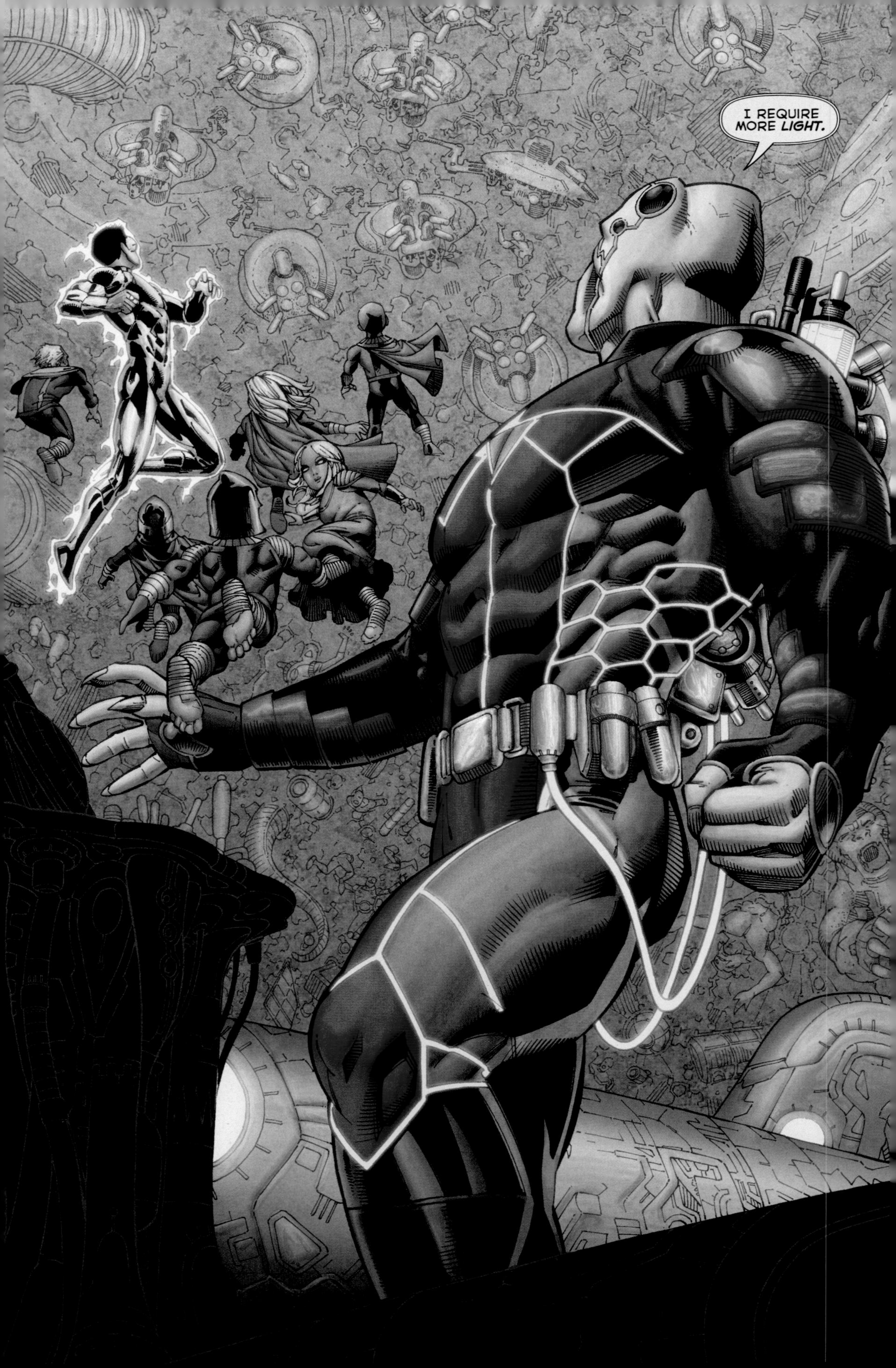
I REQUIRE MORE *LIGHT.*

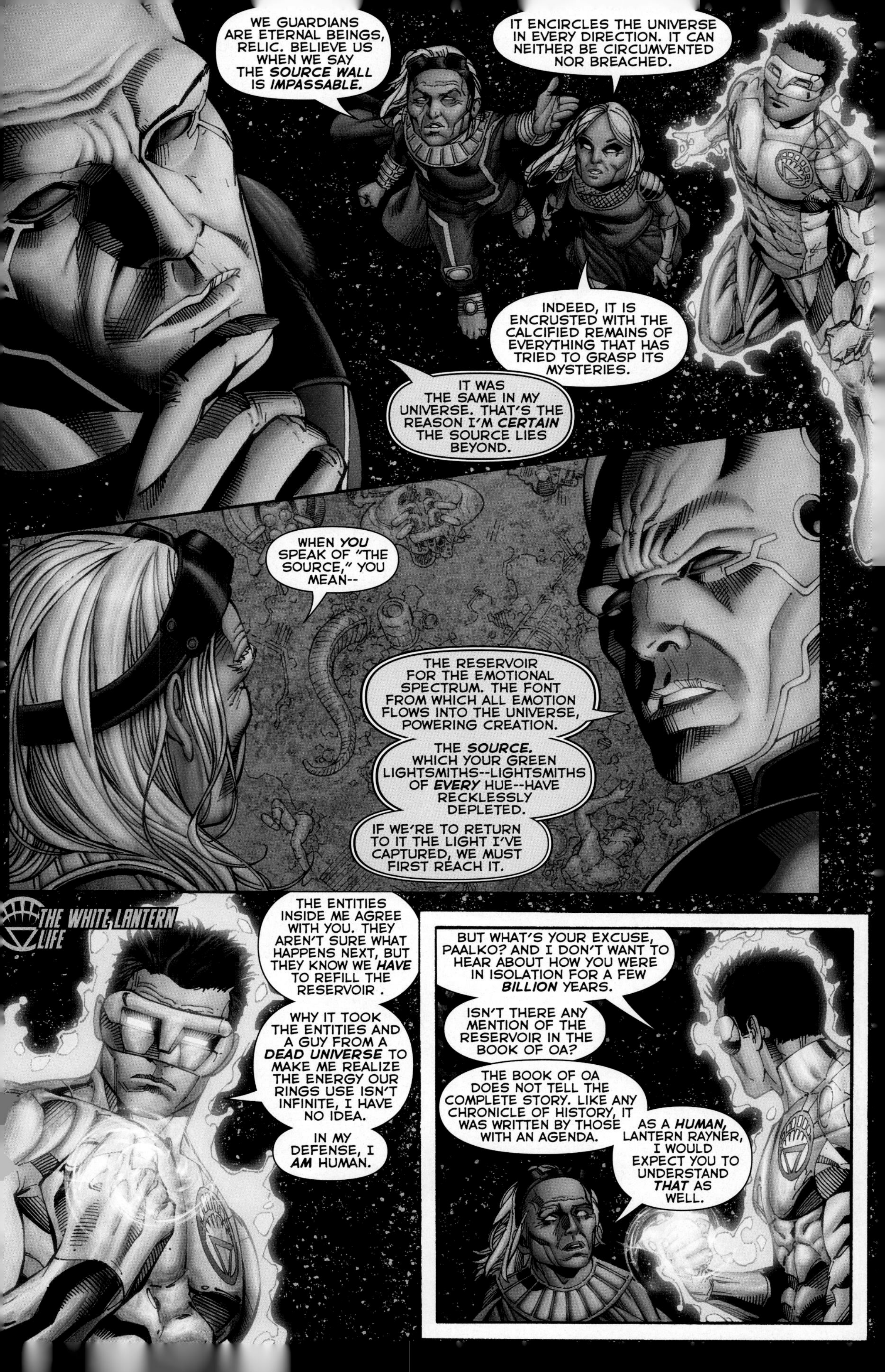

WE GUARDIANS ARE ETERNAL BEINGS, RELIC. BELIEVE US WHEN WE SAY THE SOURCE WALL IS IMPASSABLE.
IT ENCIRCLES THE UNIVERSE IN EVERY DIRECTION. IT CAN NEITHER BE CIRCUMVENTED NOR BREACHED.
INDEED, IT IS ENCRUSTED WITH THE CALCIFIED REMAINS OF EVERYTHING THAT HAS TRIED TO GRASP ITS MYSTERIES.
IT WAS THE SAME IN MY UNIVERSE. THAT'S THE REASON I'M CERTAIN THE SOURCE LIES BEYOND.
WHEN YOU SPEAK OF "THE SOURCE," YOU MEAN--
THE RESERVOIR FOR THE EMOTIONAL SPECTRUM. THE FONT FROM WHICH ALL EMOTION FLOWS INTO THE UNIVERSE, POWERING CREATION.
THE SOURCE. WHICH YOUR GREEN LIGHTSMITHS--LIGHTSMITHS OF EVERY HUE--HAVE RECKLESSLY DEPLETED.
IF WE'RE TO RETURN TO IT THE LIGHT I'VE CAPTURED, WE MUST FIRST REACH IT.
THE WHITE LANTERN LIFE
THE ENTITIES INSIDE ME AGREE WITH YOU. THEY AREN'T SURE WHAT HAPPENS NEXT, BUT THEY KNOW WE HAVE TO REFILL THE RESERVOIR .
WHY IT TOOK THE ENTITIES AND A GUY FROM A DEAD UNIVERSE TO MAKE ME REALIZE THE ENERGY OUR RINGS USE ISN'T INFINITE, I HAVE NO IDEA.
IN MY DEFENSE, I AM HUMAN.
BUT WHAT'S YOUR EXCUSE, PAALKO? AND I DON'T WANT TO HEAR ABOUT HOW YOU WERE IN ISOLATION FOR A FEW BILLION YEARS.
ISN'T THERE ANY MENTION OF THE RESERVOIR IN THE BOOK OF OA?
THE BOOK OF OA DOES NOT TELL THE COMPLETE STORY. LIKE ANY CHRONICLE OF HISTORY, IT WAS WRITTEN BY THOSE WITH AN AGENDA.
AS A HUMAN, LANTERN RAYNER, I WOULD EXPECT YOU TO UNDERSTAND THAT AS WELL.

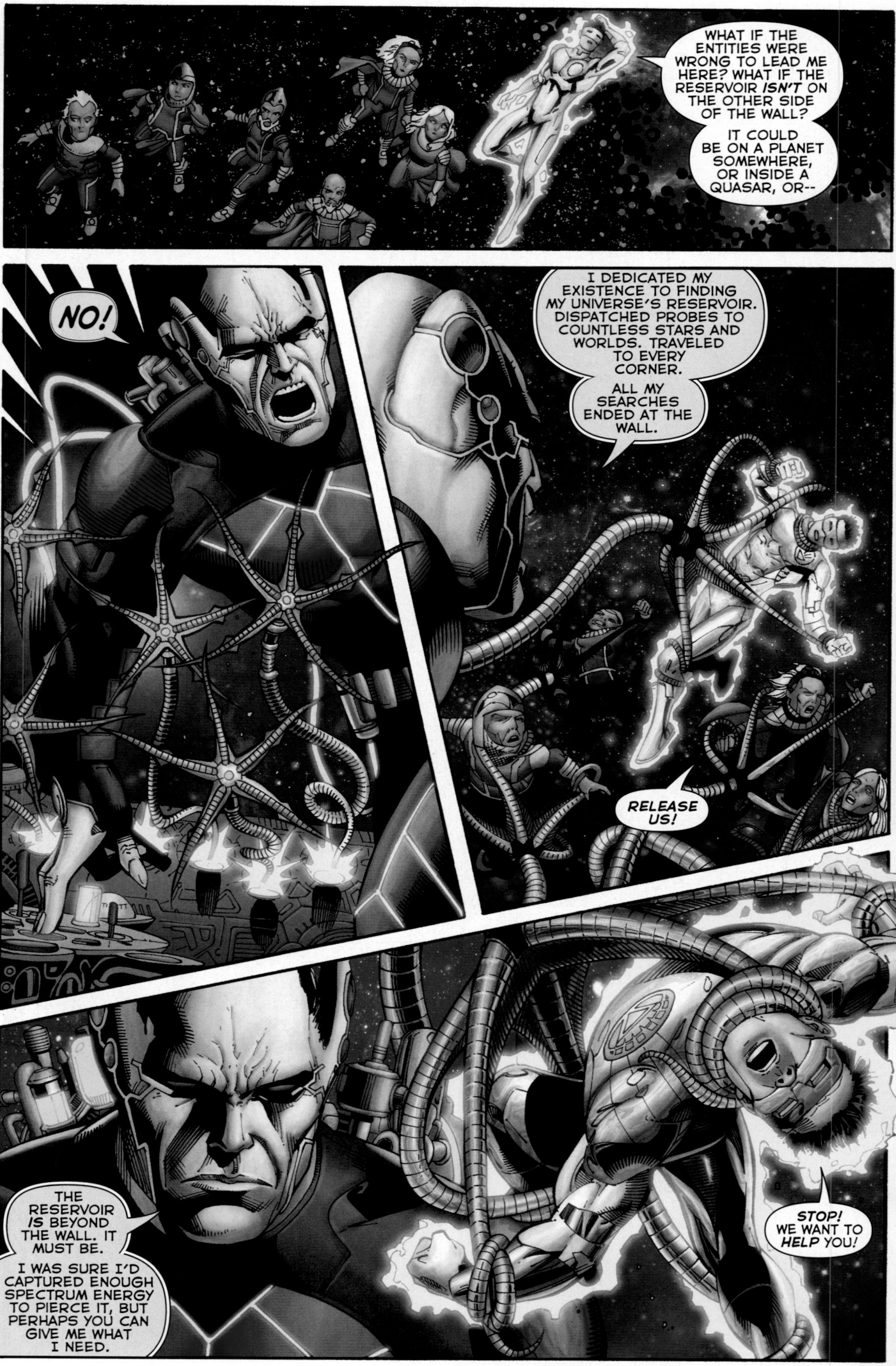

WHAT IF THE ENTITIES WERE WRONG TO LEAD ME HERE? WHAT IF THE RESERVOIR ISN'T ON THE OTHER SIDE OF THE WALL?
IT COULD BE ON A PLANET SOMEWHERE, OR INSIDE A QUASAR, OR--
NO!
I DEDICATED MY EXISTENCE TO FINDING MY UNIVERSE'S RESERVOIR. DISPATCHED PROBES TO COUNTLESS STARS AND WORLDS. TRAVELED TO EVERY CORNER.
ALL MY SEARCHES ENDED AT THE WALL.
RELEASE US!
THE RESERVOIR IS BEYOND THE WALL. IT MUST BE.
I WAS SURE I'D CAPTURED ENOUGH SPECTRUM ENERGY TO PIERCE IT, BUT PERHAPS YOU CAN GIVE ME WHAT I NEED.
STOP! WE WANT TO HELP YOU!

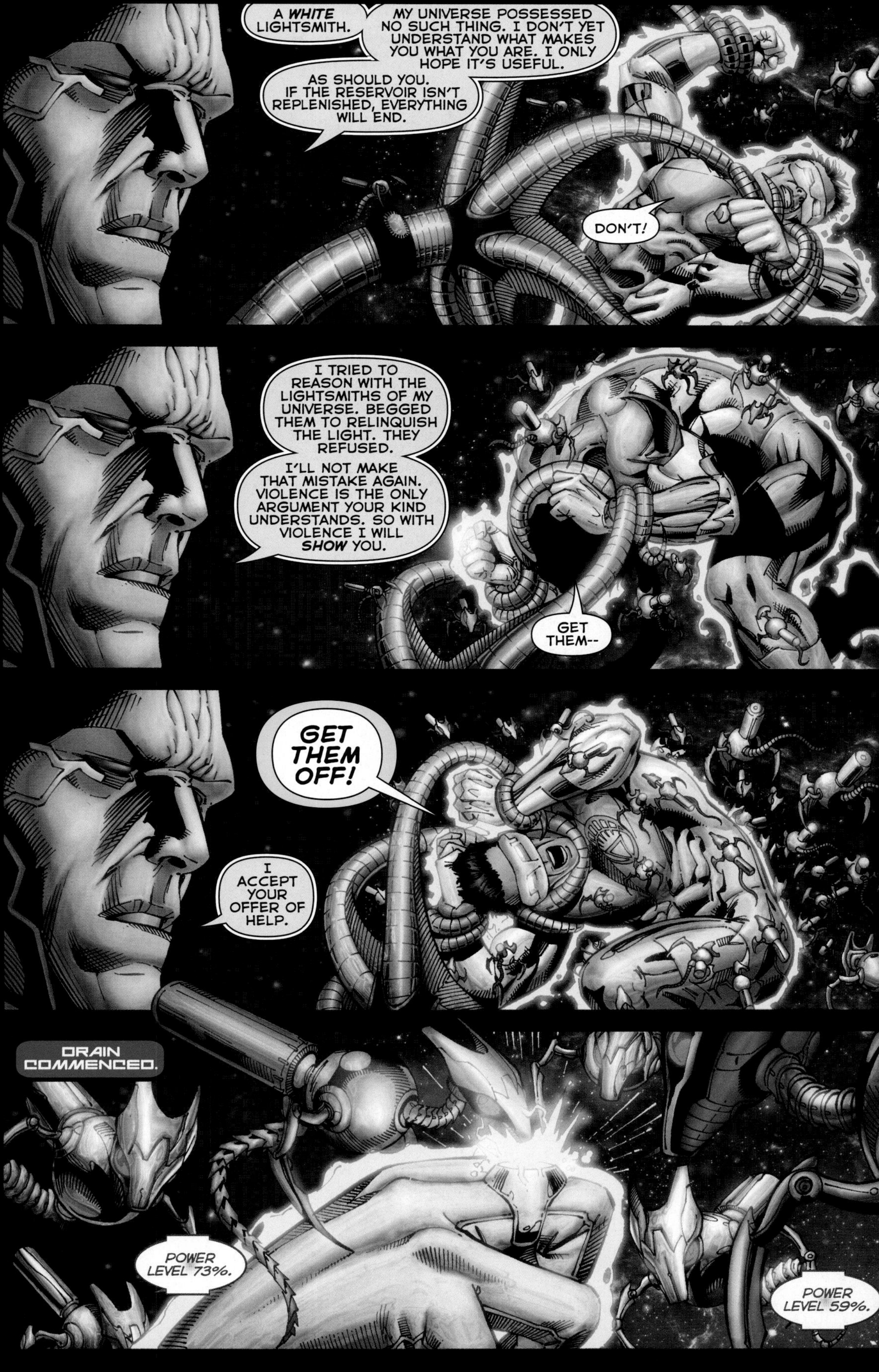
A *WHITE* LIGHTSMITH.
MY UNIVERSE POSSESSED NO SUCH THING. I DON'T YET UNDERSTAND WHAT MAKES YOU WHAT YOU ARE. I ONLY HOPE IT'S USEFUL.
AS SHOULD YOU. IF THE RESERVOIR ISN'T REPLENISHED, EVERYTHING WILL END.
DON'T!
I TRIED TO REASON WITH THE LIGHTSMITHS OF MY UNIVERSE. BEGGED THEM TO RELINQUISH THE LIGHT. THEY REFUSED.
I'LL NOT MAKE THAT MISTAKE AGAIN. VIOLENCE IS THE ONLY ARGUMENT YOUR KIND UNDERSTANDS. SO WITH VIOLENCE I WILL *SHOW* YOU.
GET THEM--
GET THEM OFF!
I ACCEPT YOUR OFFER OF HELP.
DRAIN COMMENCED.
POWER LEVEL 73%.
POWER LEVEL 59%.

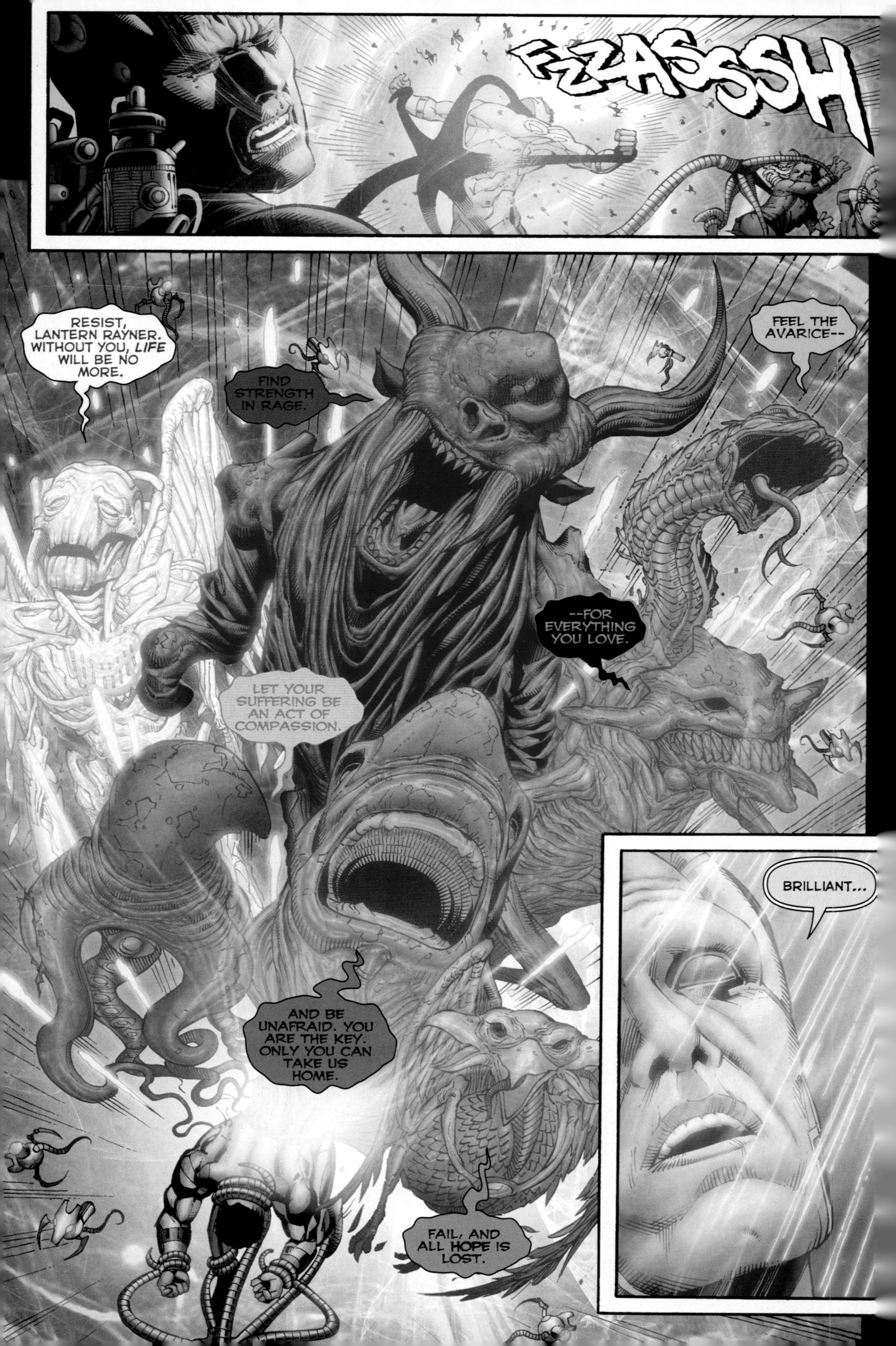
FZZASSSH
RESIST, LANTERN RAYNER. WITHOUT YOU, LIFE WILL BE NO MORE.
FIND STRENGTH IN RAGE.
FEEL THE AVARICE--
--FOR EVERYTHING YOU LOVE.
LET YOUR SUFFERING BE AN ACT OF COMPASSION.
AND BE UNAFRAID. YOU ARE THE KEY. ONLY YOU CAN TAKE US HOME.
FAIL, AND ALL HOPE IS LOST.
BRILLIANT...

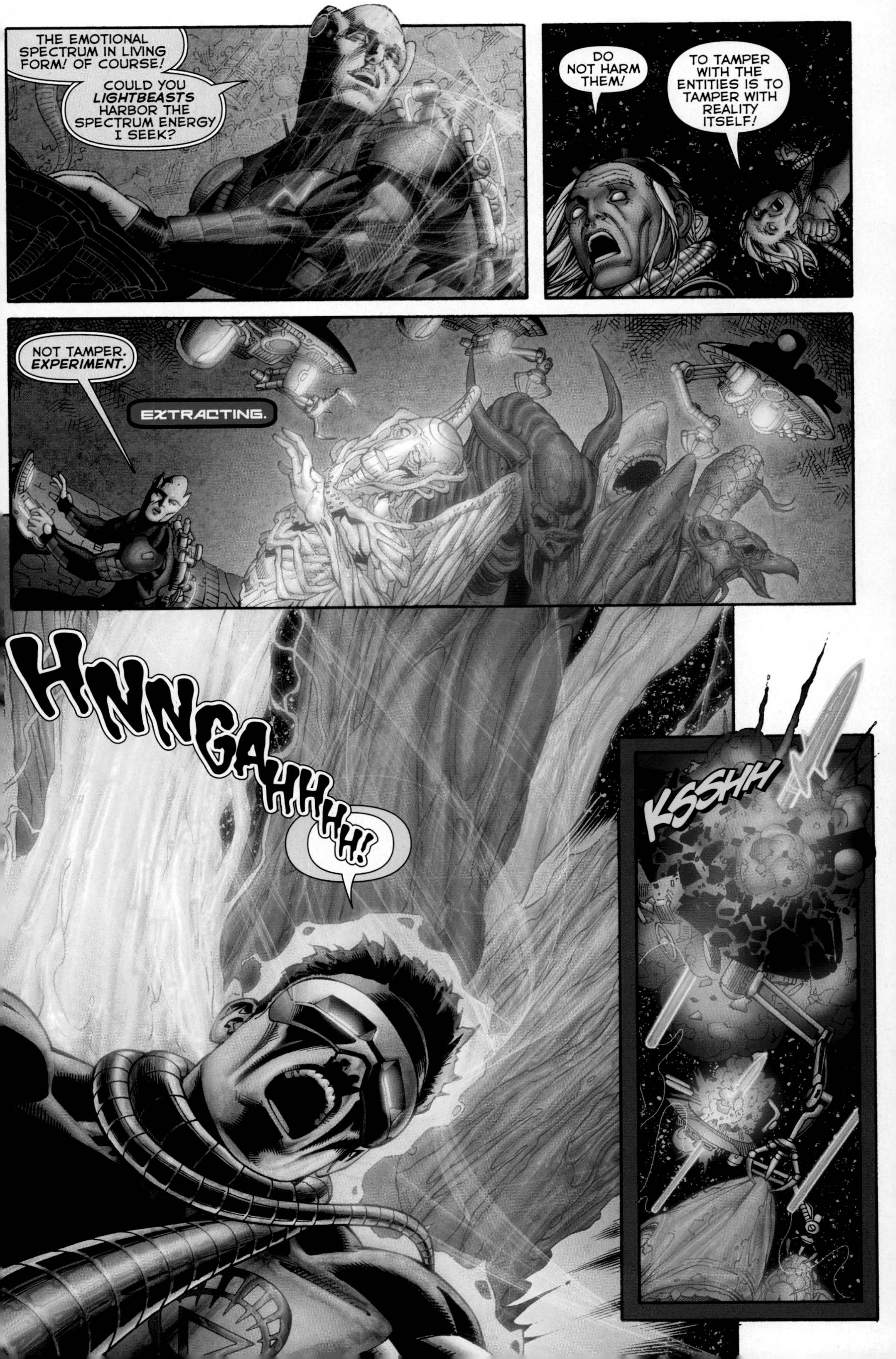
THE EMOTIONAL SPECTRUM IN LIVING FORM! OF COURSE!
COULD YOU LIGHTBEASTS HARBOR THE SPECTRUM ENERGY I SEEK?
DO NOT HARM THEM!
TO TAMPER WITH THE ENTITIES IS TO TAMPER WITH REALITY ITSELF!
NOT TAMPER. EXPERIMENT.
EXTRACTING.
HNNGAHHHHH!
KSSHH

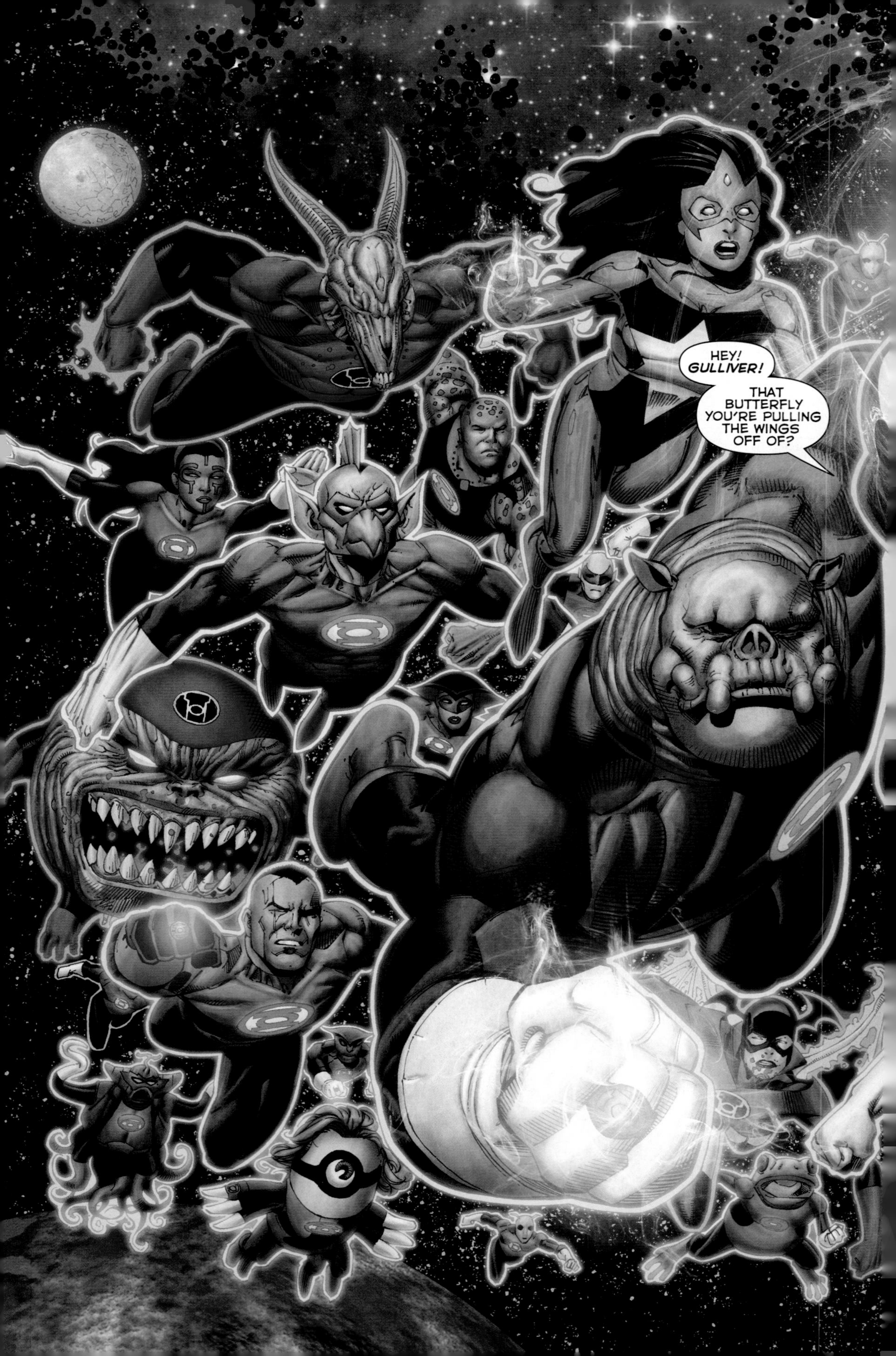
HEY! GULLIVER!
THAT BUTTERFLY YOU'RE PULLING THE WINGS OFF OF?

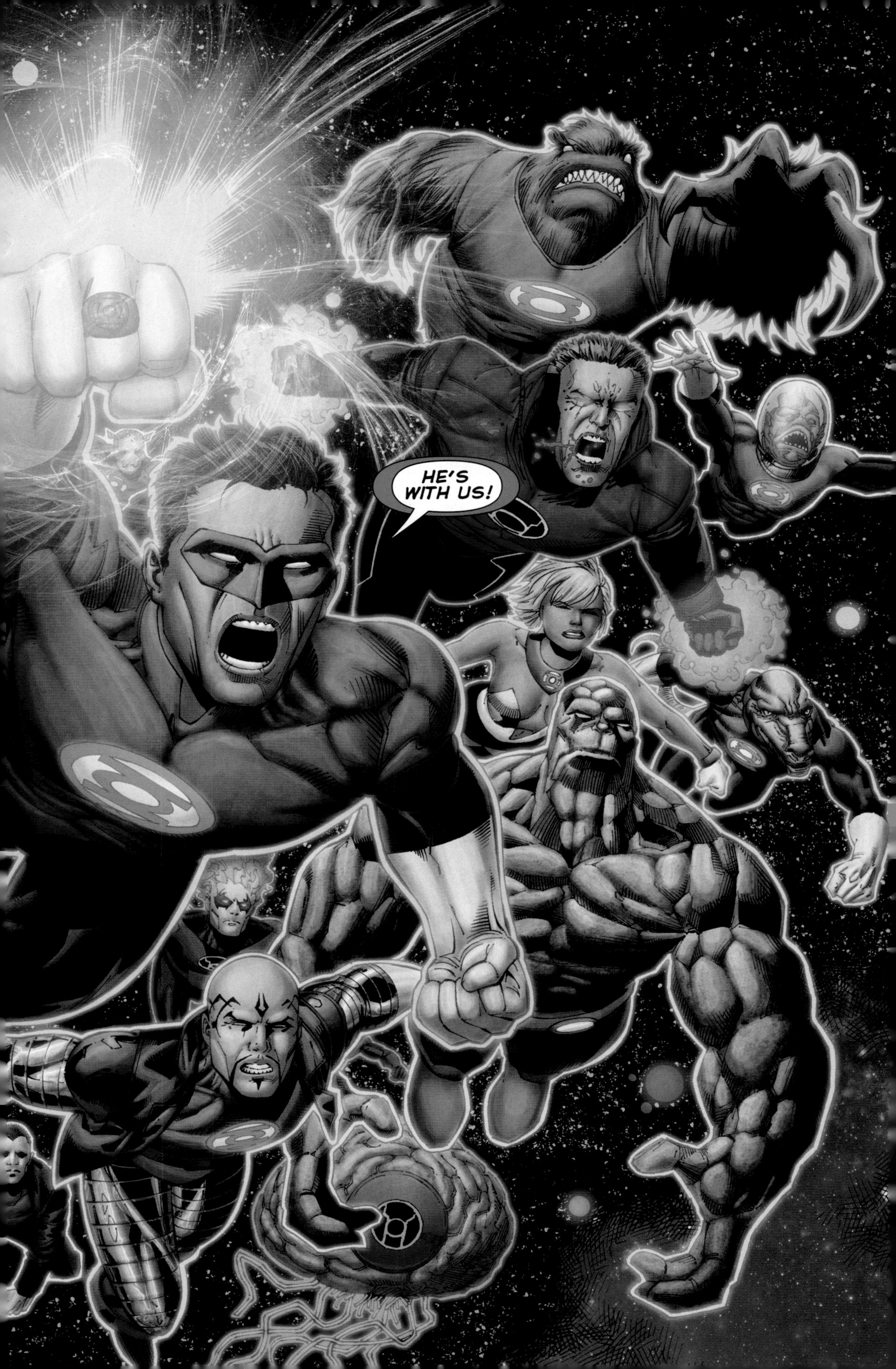
HE'S WITH US!

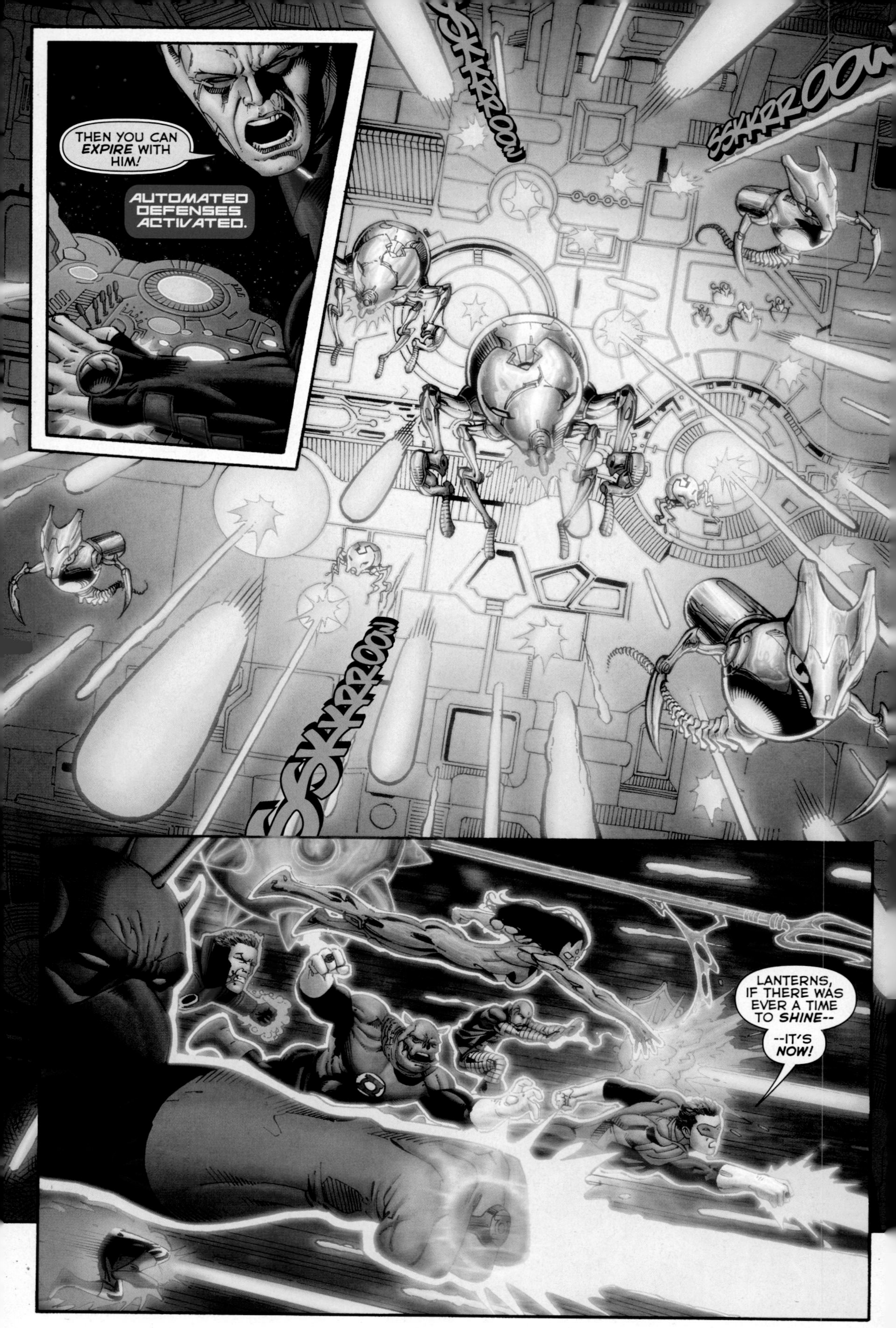

THEN YOU CAN EXPIRE WITH HIM!
AUTOMATED DEFENSES ACTIVATED.
SSKKRROOOW
SSKKRROOW
SSKKRROOW
SSKKRROOW
LANTERNS, IF THERE WAS EVER A TIME TO SHINE--
--IT'S NOW!

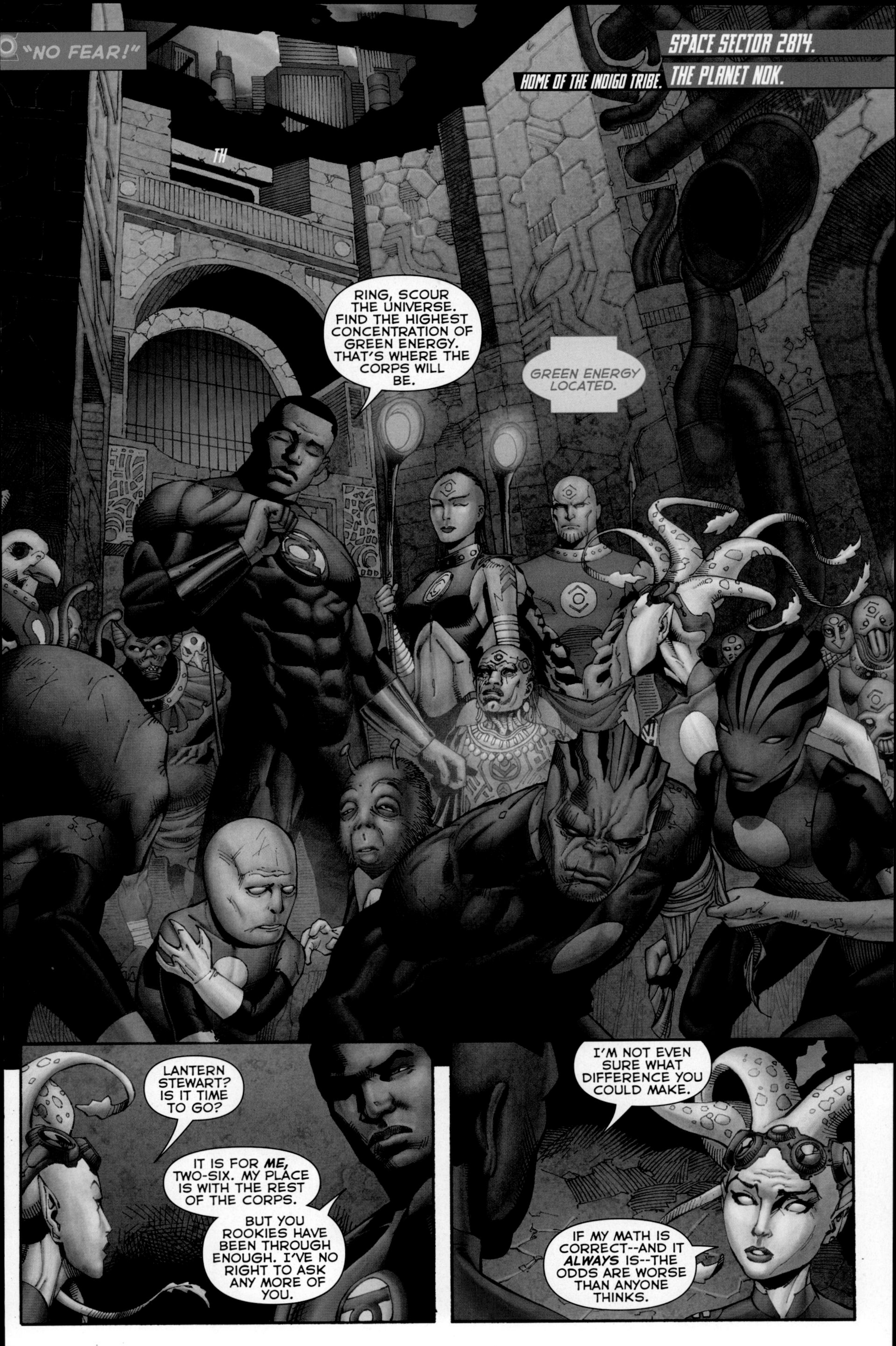
"NO FEAR!"
SPACE SECTOR 2814.
HOME OF THE INDIGO TRIBE. THE PLANET NOK.
TH
RING, SCOUR THE UNIVERSE. FIND THE HIGHEST CONCENTRATION OF GREEN ENERGY. THAT'S WHERE THE CORPS WILL BE.
GREEN ENERGY LOCATED.
LANTERN STEWART? IS IT TIME TO GO?
IT IS FOR ME, TWO-SIX. MY PLACE IS WITH THE REST OF THE CORPS.
BUT YOU ROOKIES HAVE BEEN THROUGH ENOUGH. I'VE NO RIGHT TO ASK ANY MORE OF YOU.
I'M NOT EVEN SURE WHAT DIFFERENCE YOU COULD MAKE.
IF MY MATH IS CORRECT--AND IT ALWAYS IS--THE ODDS ARE WORSE THAN ANYONE THINKS.

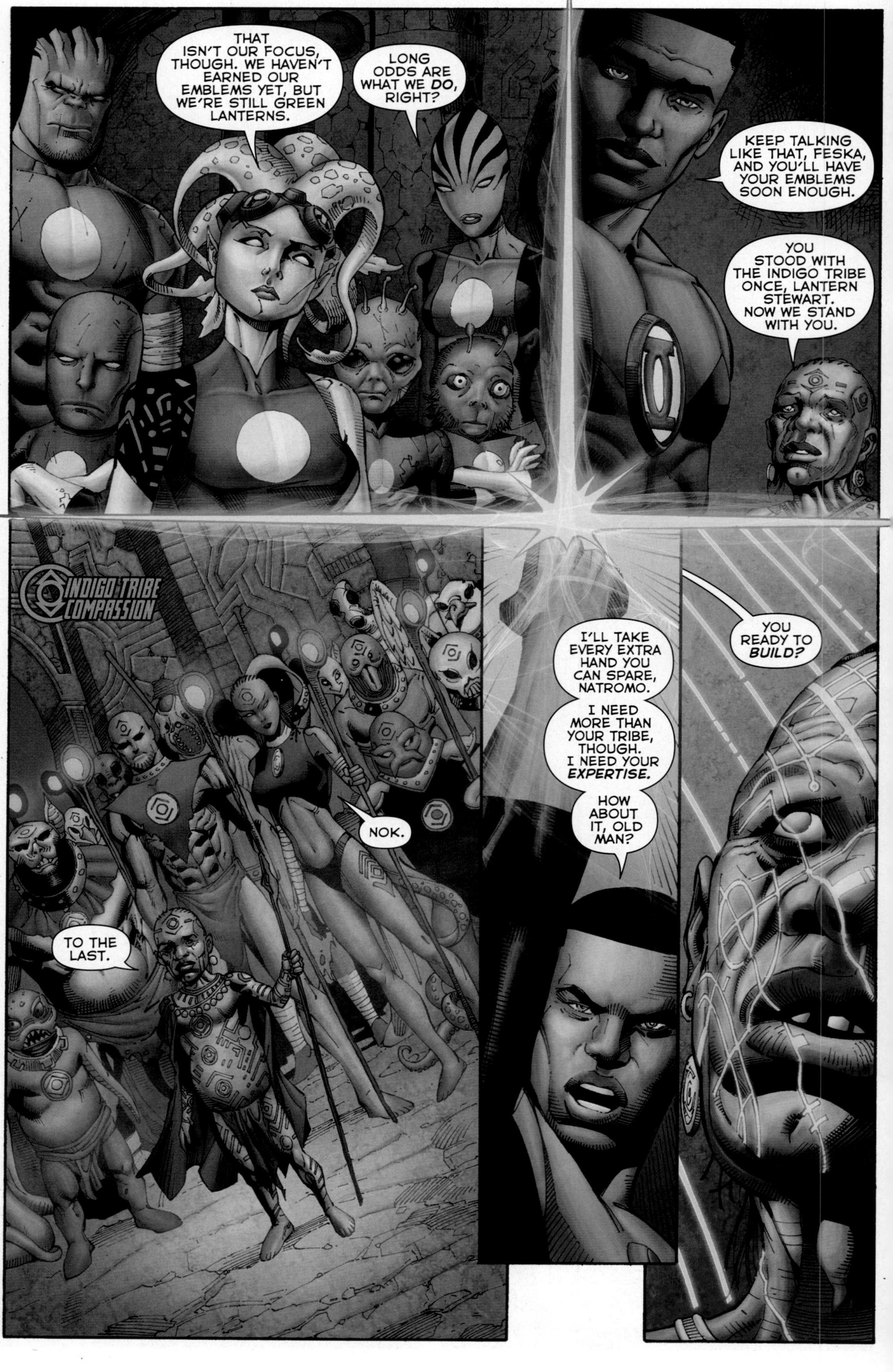
THAT ISN'T OUR FOCUS, THOUGH. WE HAVEN'T EARNED OUR EMBLEMS YET, BUT WE'RE STILL GREEN LANTERNS.
LONG ODDS ARE WHAT WE *DO*, RIGHT?
KEEP TALKING LIKE THAT, FESKA, AND YOU'LL HAVE YOUR EMBLEMS SOON ENOUGH.
YOU STOOD WITH THE INDIGO TRIBE ONCE, LANTERN STEWART. NOW WE STAND WITH YOU.
INDIGO TRIBE COMPASSION
NOK.
TO THE LAST.
I'LL TAKE EVERY EXTRA HAND YOU CAN SPARE, NATROMO.
I NEED MORE THAN YOUR TRIBE, THOUGH. I NEED YOUR ***EXPERTISE.***
HOW ABOUT IT, OLD MAN?
YOU READY TO ***BUILD?***

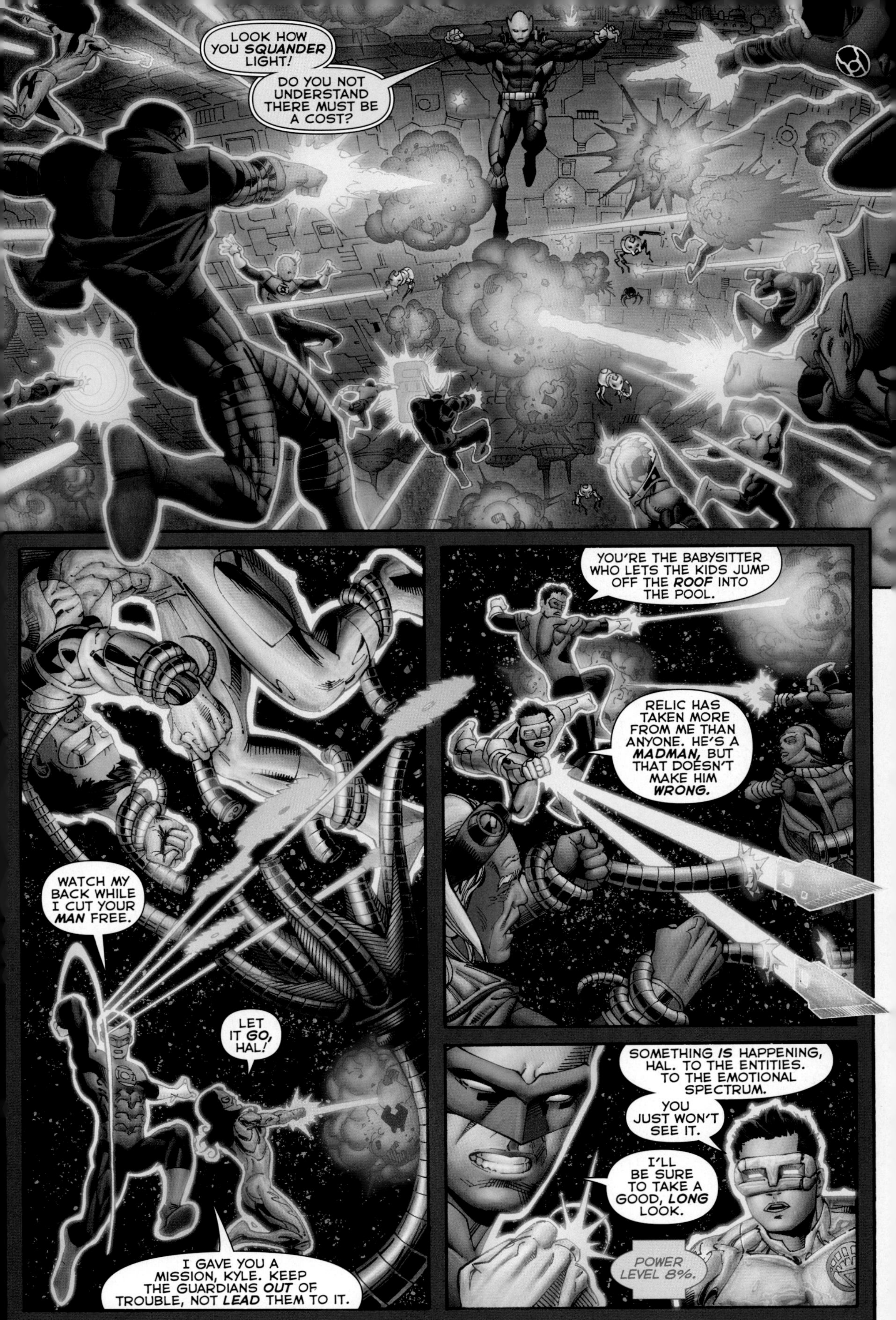

LOOK HOW YOU SQUANDER LIGHT!
DO YOU NOT UNDERSTAND THERE MUST BE A COST?
WATCH MY BACK WHILE I CUT YOUR MAN FREE.
LET IT GO, HAL!
I GAVE YOU A MISSION, KYLE. KEEP THE GUARDIANS OUT OF TROUBLE, NOT LEAD THEM TO IT.
YOU'RE THE BABYSITTER WHO LETS THE KIDS JUMP OFF THE ROOF INTO THE POOL.
RELIC HAS TAKEN MORE FROM ME THAN ANYONE. HE'S A MADMAN, BUT THAT DOESN'T MAKE HIM WRONG.
SOMETHING IS HAPPENING, HAL. TO THE ENTITIES. TO THE EMOTIONAL SPECTRUM.
YOU JUST WON'T SEE IT.
I'LL BE SURE TO TAKE A GOOD, LONG LOOK.
POWER LEVEL 8%.

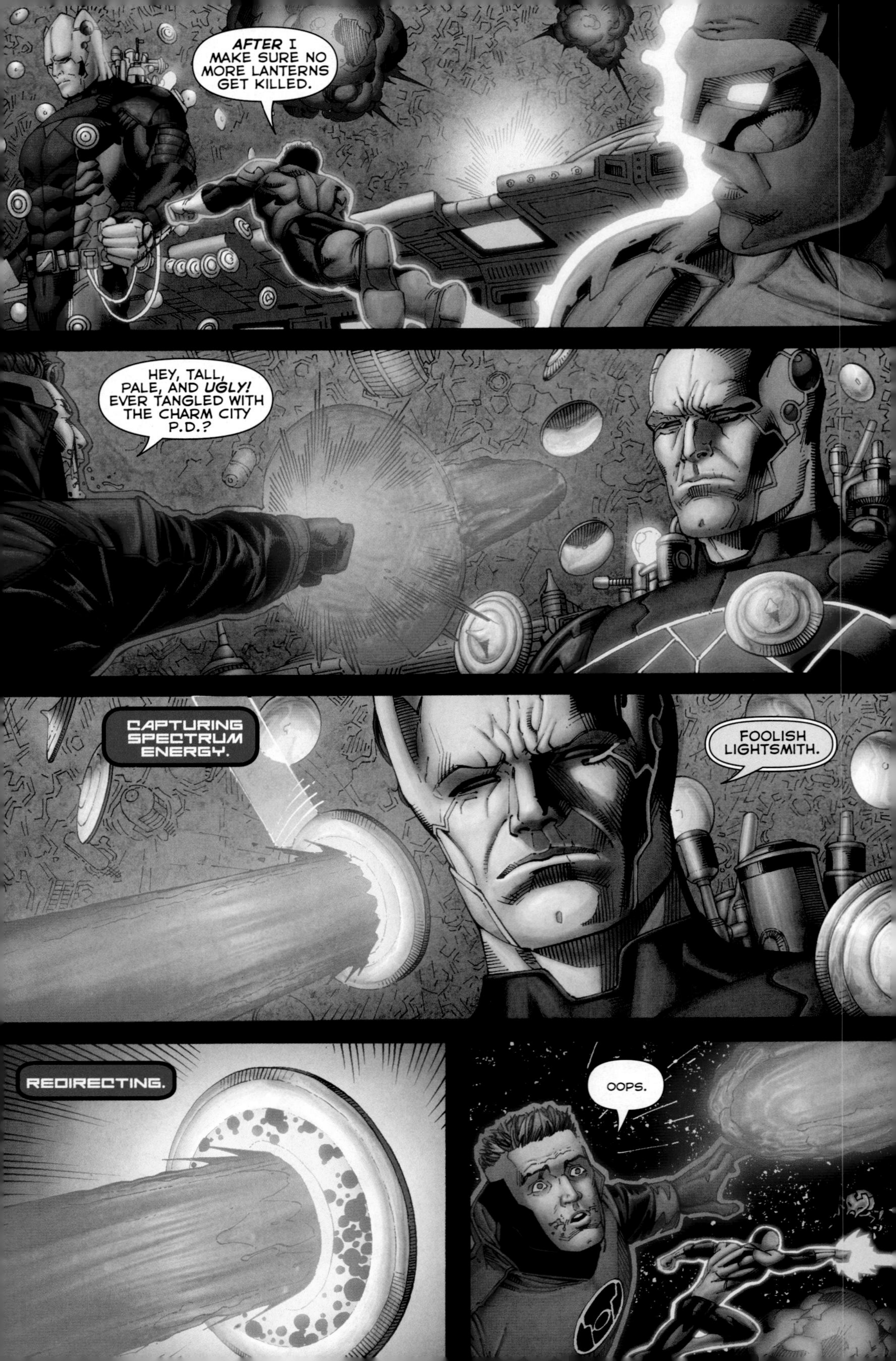
AFTER I MAKE SURE NO MORE LANTERNS GET KILLED.
HEY, TALL, PALE, AND UGLY! EVER TANGLED WITH THE CHARM CITY P.D.?
CAPTURING SPECTRUM ENERGY.
FOOLISH LIGHTSMITH.
REDIRECTING.
OOPS.

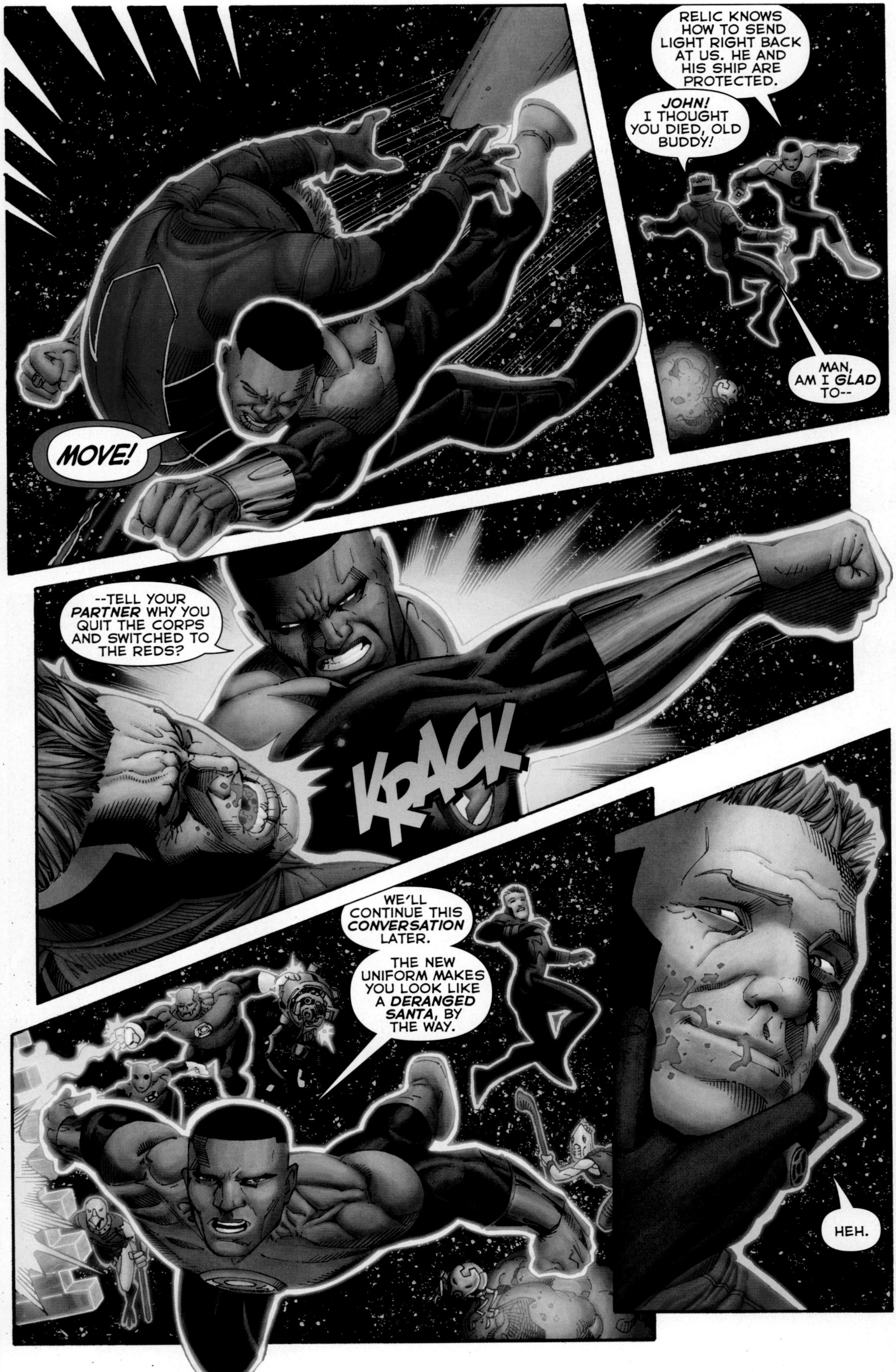
MOVE!
RELIC KNOWS HOW TO SEND LIGHT RIGHT BACK AT US. HE AND HIS SHIP ARE PROTECTED.
JOHN! I THOUGHT YOU DIED, OLD BUDDY!
MAN, AM I GLAD TO--
--TELL YOUR PARTNER WHY YOU QUIT THE CORPS AND SWITCHED TO THE REDS?
KRACK
WE'LL CONTINUE THIS CONVERSATION LATER.
THE NEW UNIFORM MAKES YOU LOOK LIKE A DERANGED SANTA, BY THE WAY.
HEH.

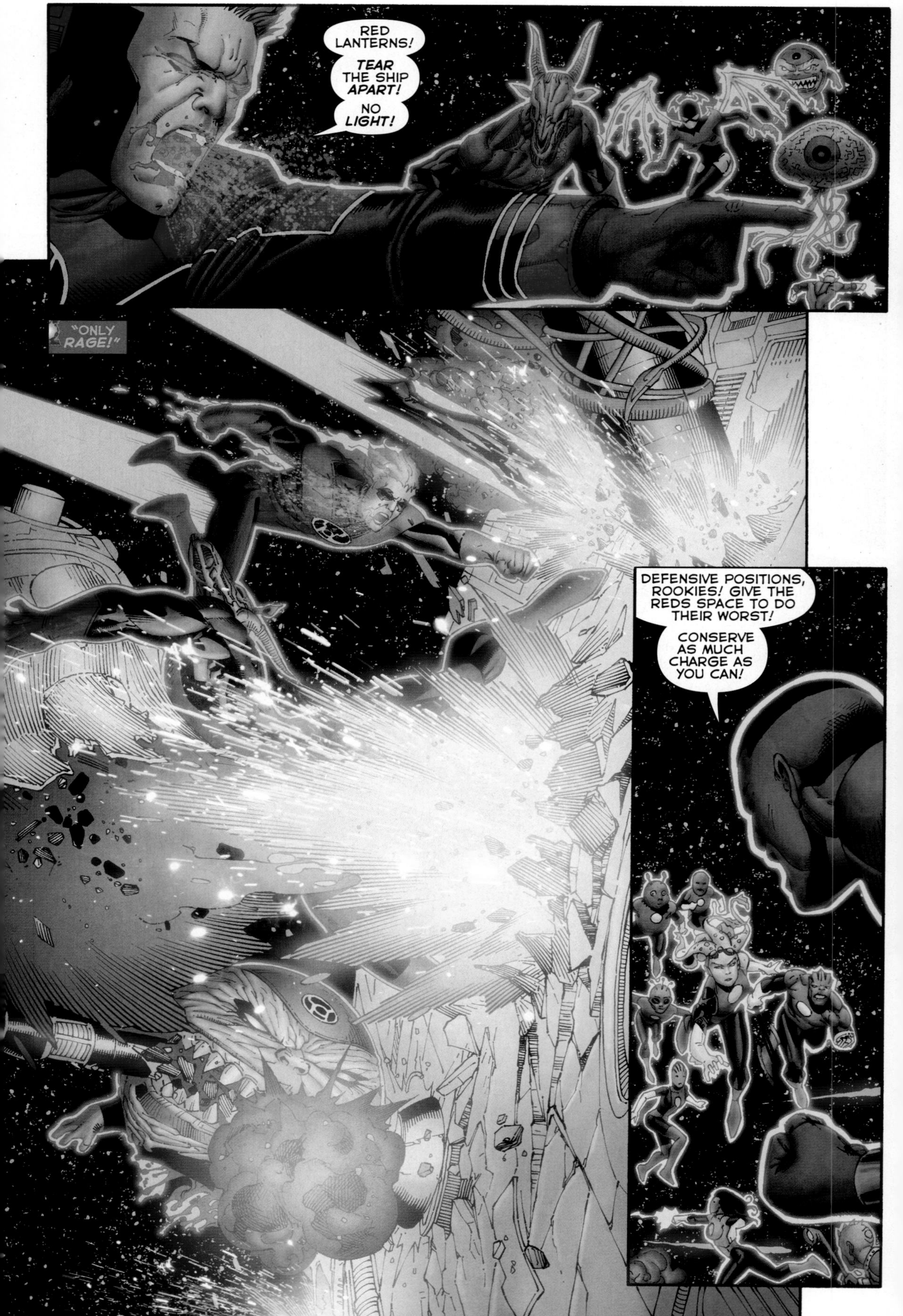
RED LANTERNS! TEAR THE SHIP APART! NO LIGHT!
"ONLY RAGE!"
DEFENSIVE POSITIONS, ROOKIES! GIVE THE REDS SPACE TO DO THEIR WORST!
CONSERVE AS MUCH CHARGE AS YOU CAN!

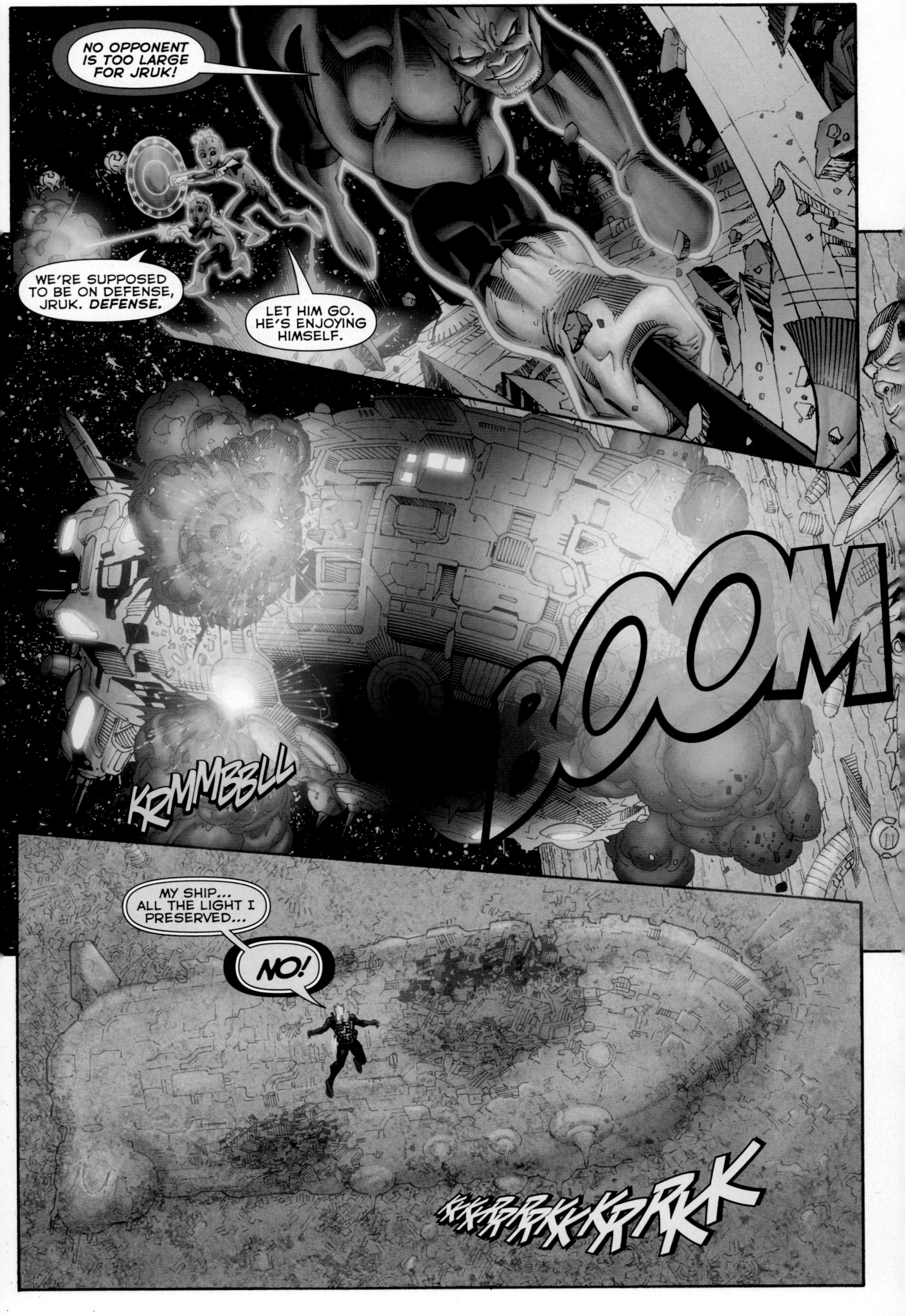
NO OPPONENT IS TOO LARGE FOR JRUK!
WE'RE SUPPOSED TO BE ON DEFENSE, JRUK. *DEFENSE.*
LET HIM GO. HE'S ENJOYING HIMSELF.
BOOM
KRMMBBLL
MY SHIP... ALL THE LIGHT I PRESERVED...
NO!
KKKRPRKKKRRKK

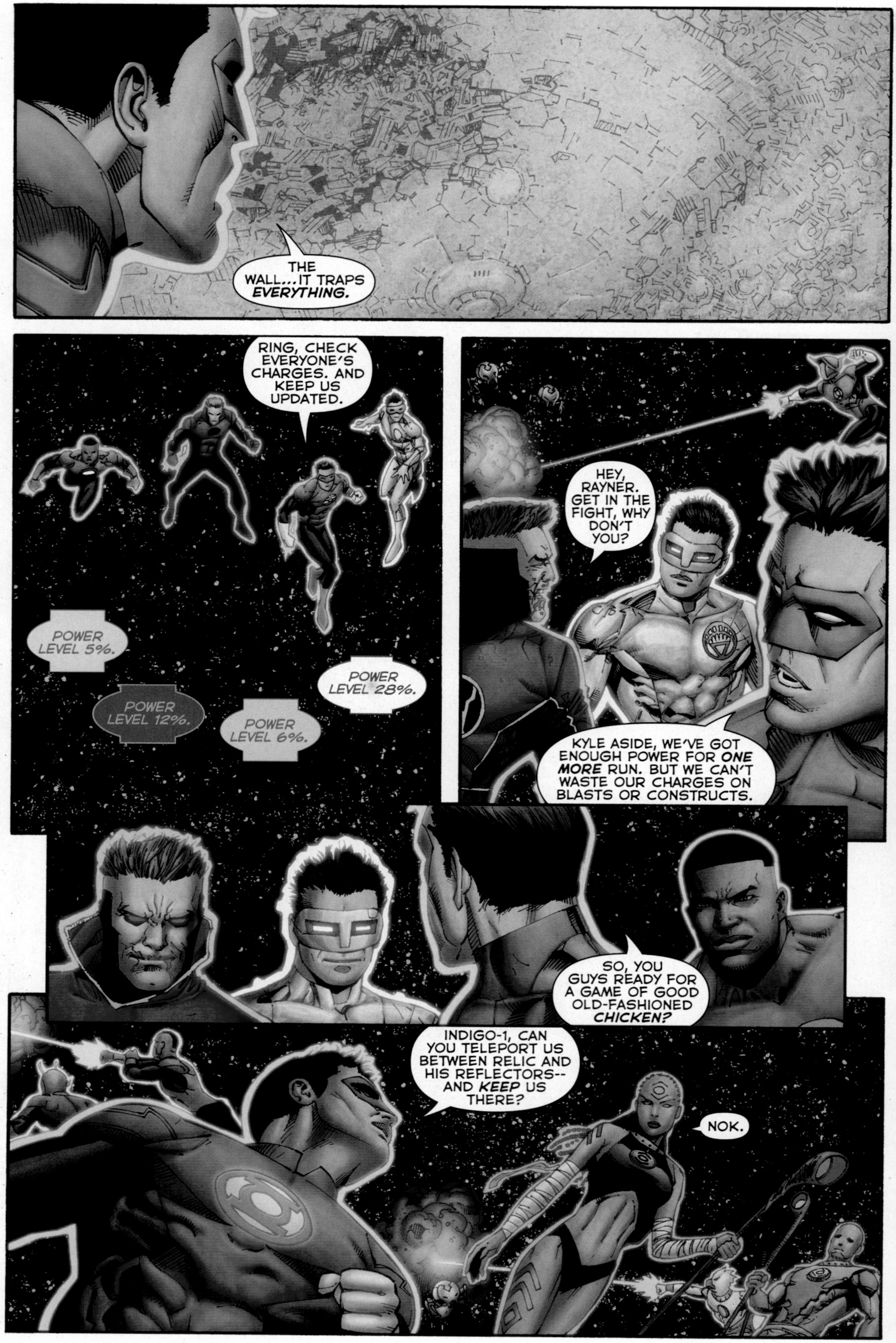
THE WALL...IT TRAPS EVERYTHING.
RING, CHECK EVERYONE'S CHARGES. AND KEEP US UPDATED.
POWER LEVEL 5%.
POWER LEVEL 12%.
POWER LEVEL 6%.
POWER LEVEL 28%.
HEY, RAYNER. GET IN THE FIGHT, WHY DON'T YOU?
KYLE ASIDE, WE'VE GOT ENOUGH POWER FOR ONE MORE RUN. BUT WE CAN'T WASTE OUR CHARGES ON BLASTS OR CONSTRUCTS.
SO, YOU GUYS READY FOR A GAME OF GOOD OLD-FASHIONED CHICKEN?
INDIGO-1, CAN YOU TELEPORT US BETWEEN RELIC AND HIS REFLECTORS-- AND KEEP US THERE?
NOK.

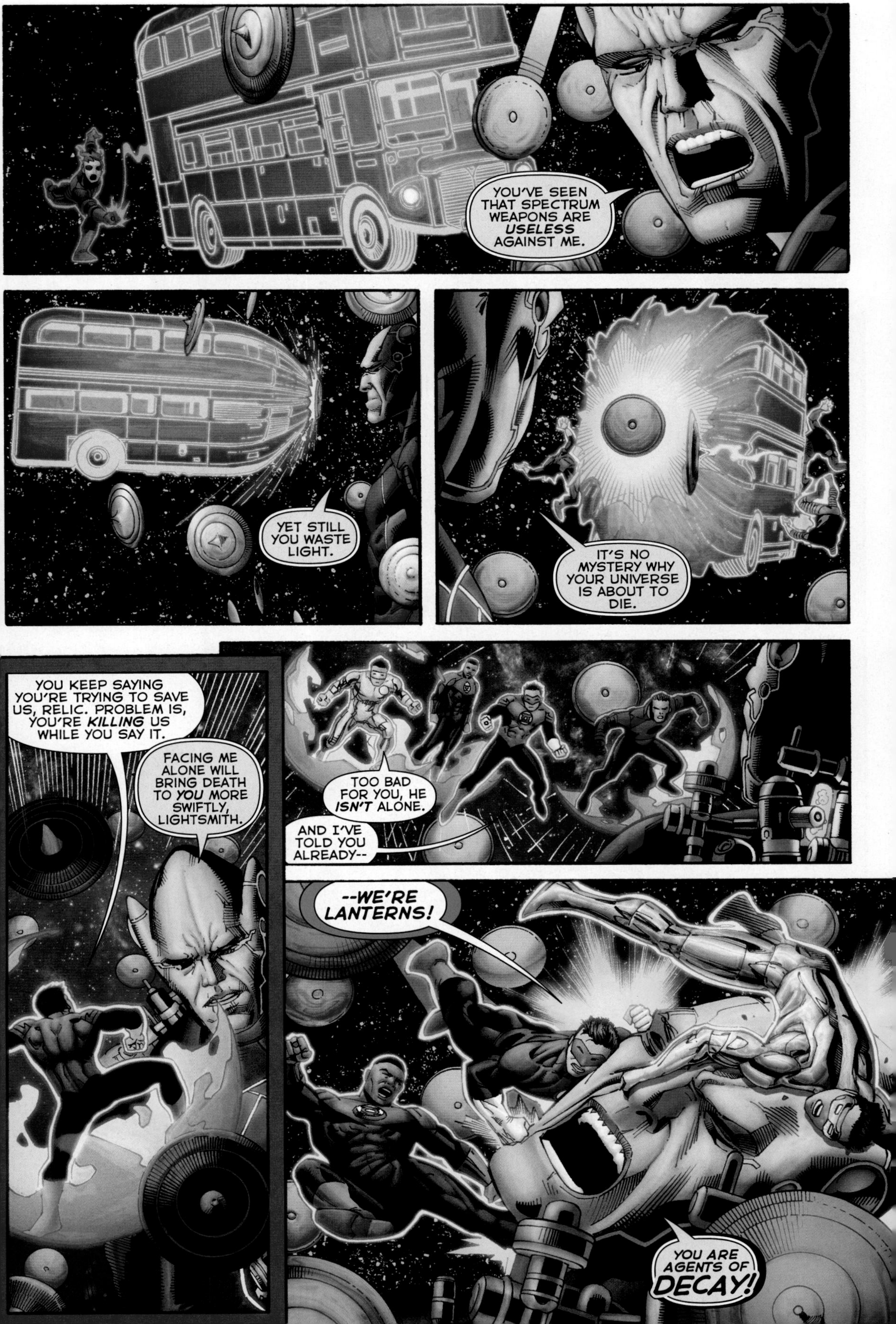
YOU'VE SEEN THAT SPECTRUM WEAPONS ARE USELESS AGAINST ME.
YET STILL YOU WASTE LIGHT.
IT'S NO MYSTERY WHY YOUR UNIVERSE IS ABOUT TO DIE.
YOU KEEP SAYING YOU'RE TRYING TO SAVE US, RELIC. PROBLEM IS, YOU'RE KILLING US WHILE YOU SAY IT.
FACING ME ALONE WILL BRING DEATH TO YOU MORE SWIFTLY, LIGHTSMITH.
TOO BAD FOR YOU, HE ISN'T ALONE.
AND I'VE TOLD YOU ALREADY--
--WE'RE LANTERNS!
YOU ARE AGENTS OF DECAY!

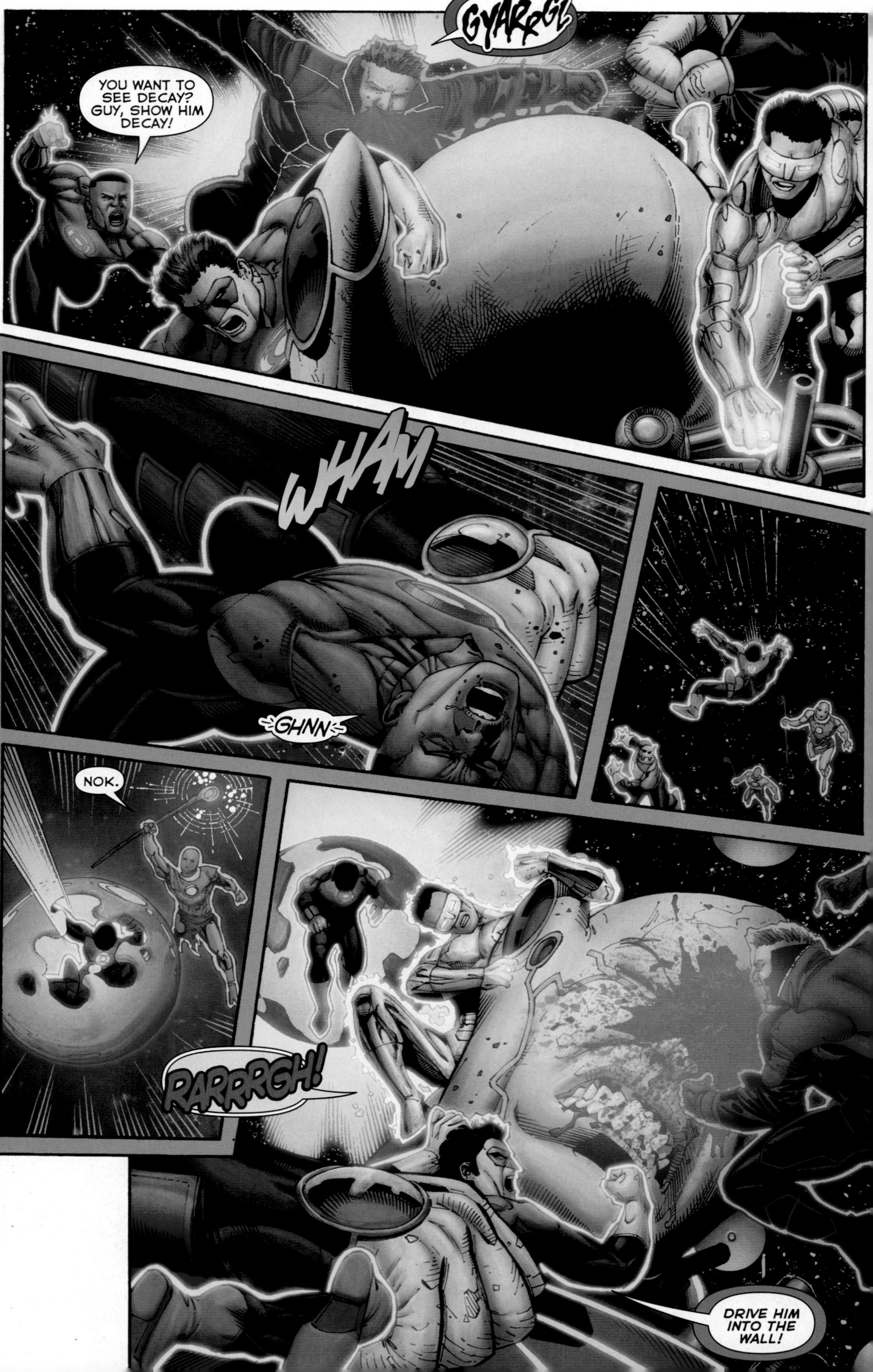
GYARRGL
YOU WANT TO SEE DECAY? GUY, SHOW HIM DECAY!
WHAM
GHNN
NOK.
RARRRGH!
DRIVE HIM INTO THE WALL!

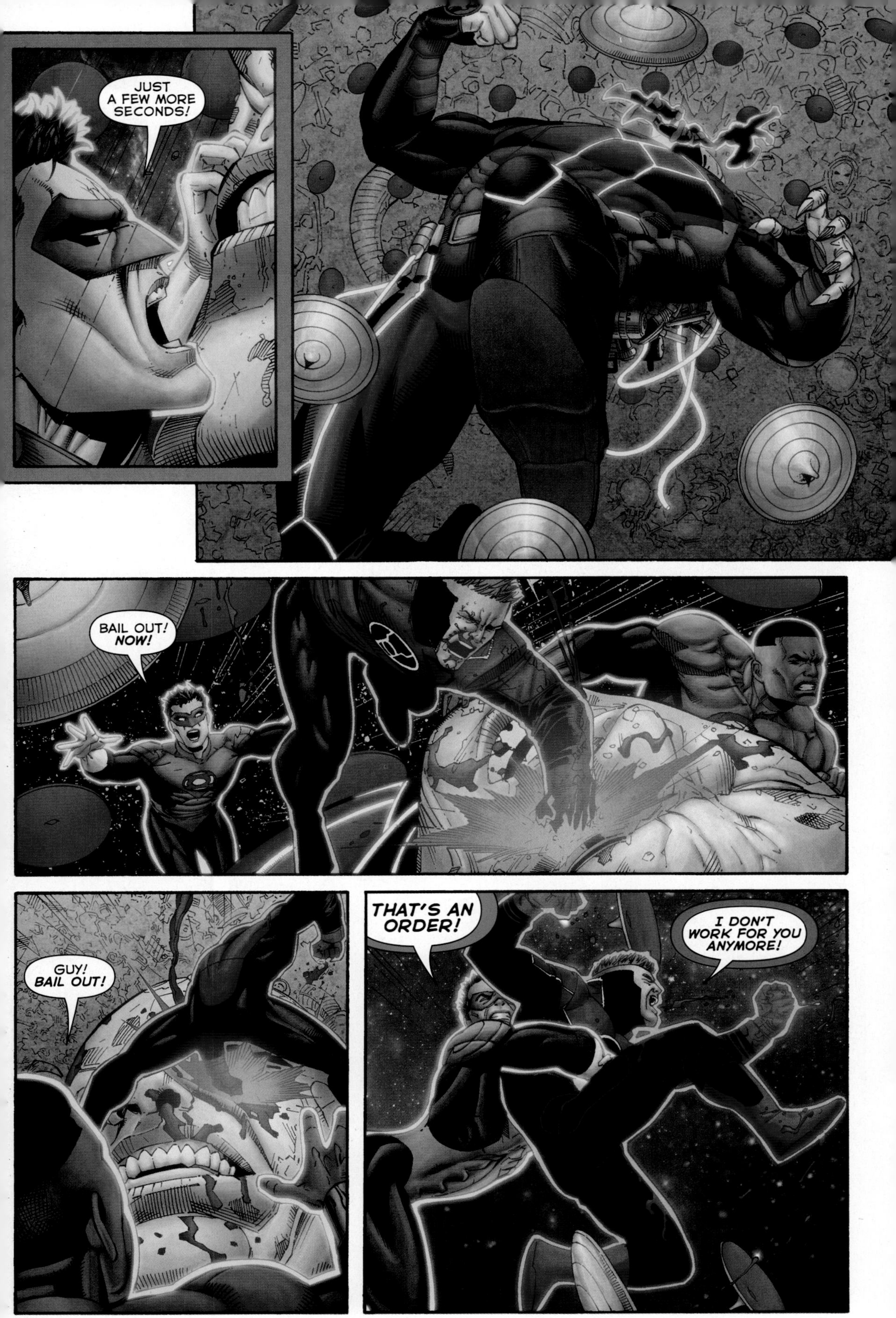
JUST A FEW MORE SECONDS!
BAIL OUT! NOW!
GUY! BAIL OUT!
THAT'S AN ORDER!
I DON'T WORK FOR YOU ANYMORE!

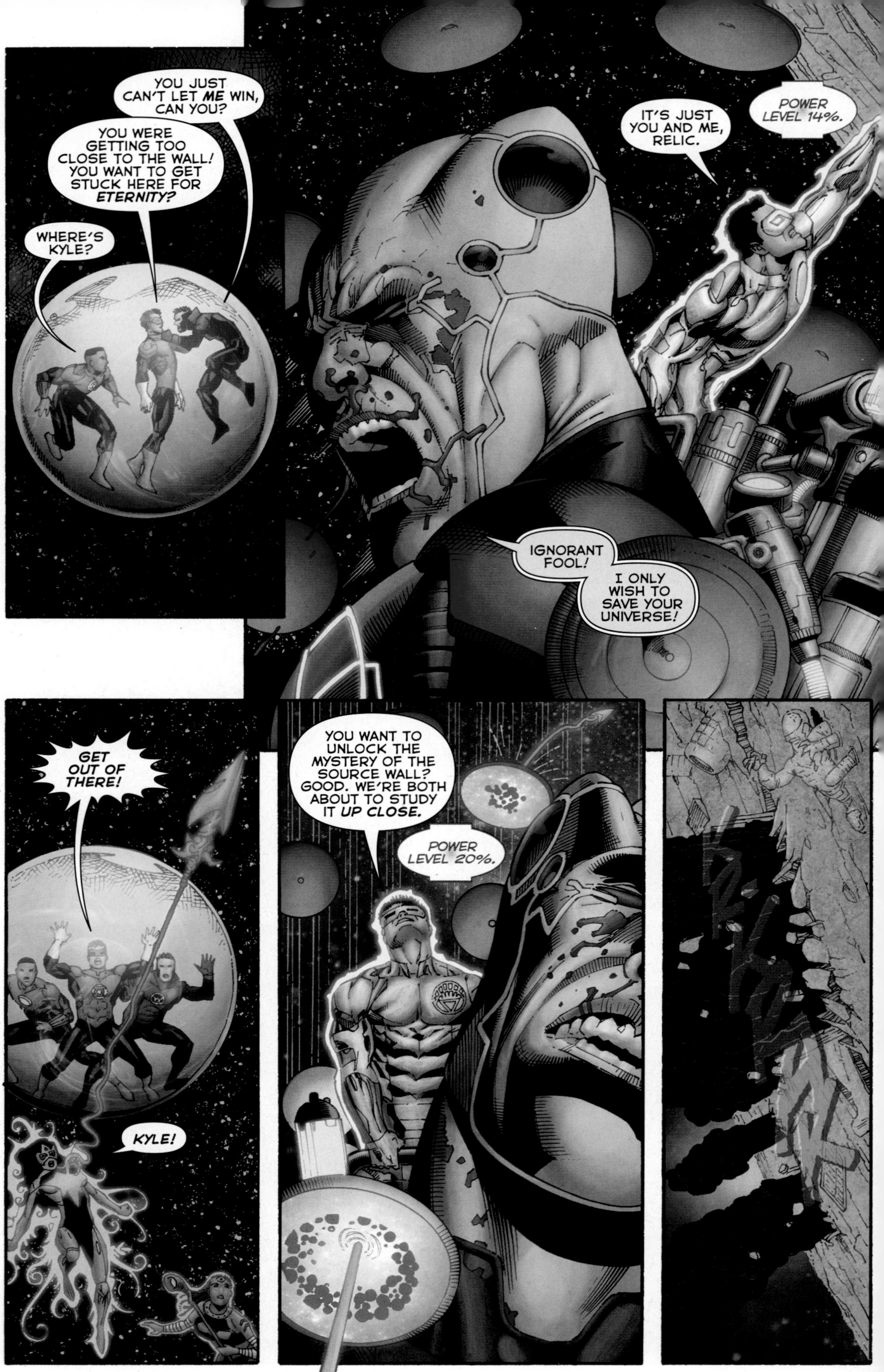

YOU JUST CAN'T LET ME WIN, CAN YOU?
YOU WERE GETTING TOO CLOSE TO THE WALL! YOU WANT TO GET STUCK HERE FOR ETERNITY?
WHERE'S KYLE?
IT'S JUST YOU AND ME, RELIC.
POWER LEVEL 14%.
IGNORANT FOOL!
I ONLY WISH TO SAVE YOUR UNIVERSE!
GET OUT OF THERE!
KYLE!
YOU WANT TO UNLOCK THE MYSTERY OF THE SOURCE WALL? GOOD. WE'RE BOTH ABOUT TO STUDY IT UP CLOSE.
POWER LEVEL 20%.

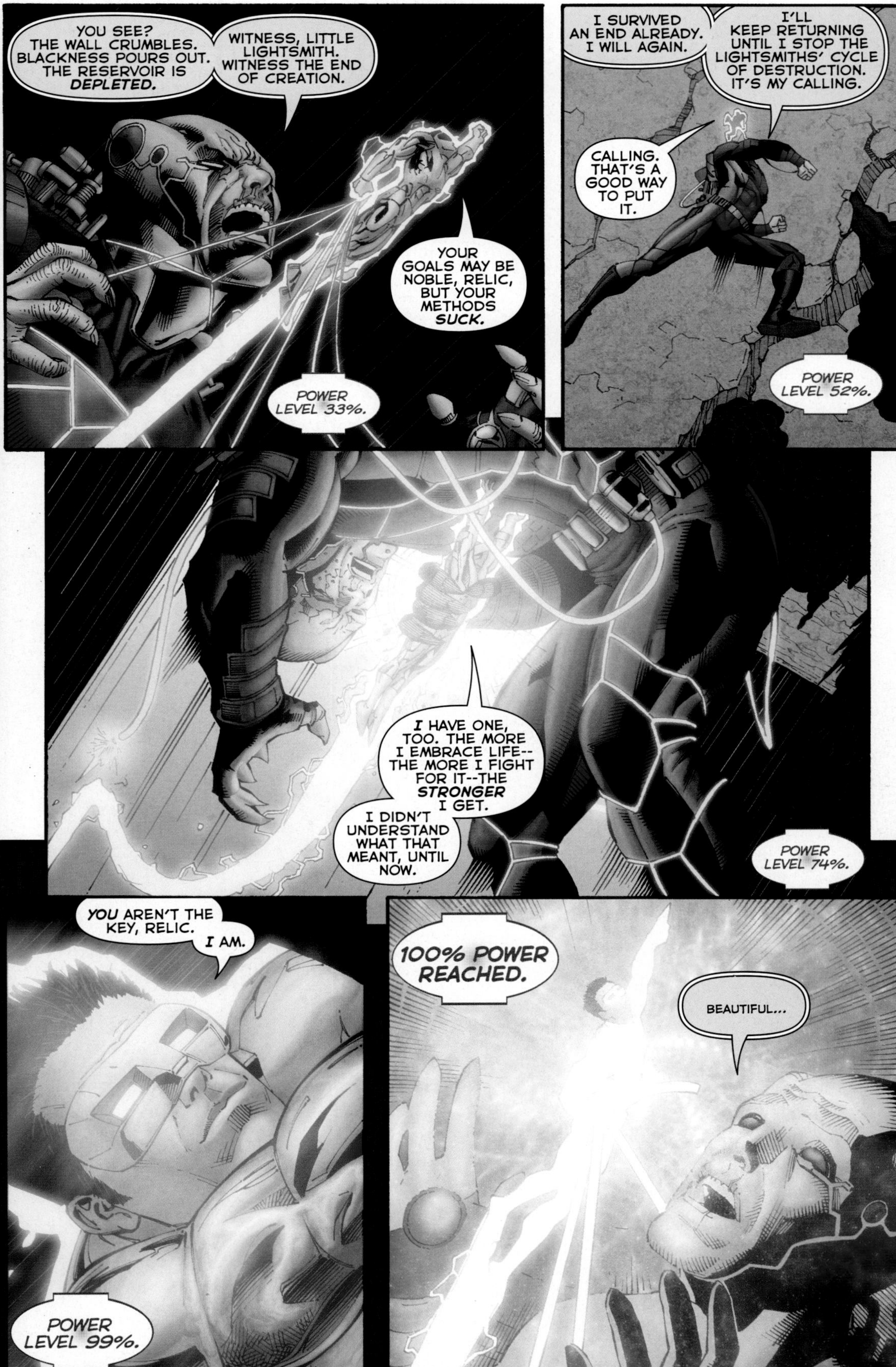
YOU SEE? THE WALL CRUMBLES. BLACKNESS POURS OUT. THE RESERVOIR IS DEPLETED.
WITNESS, LITTLE LIGHTSMITH. WITNESS THE END OF CREATION.
YOUR GOALS MAY BE NOBLE, RELIC, BUT YOUR METHODS SUCK.
POWER LEVEL 33%.
I SURVIVED AN END ALREADY. I WILL AGAIN.
I'LL KEEP RETURNING UNTIL I STOP THE LIGHTSMITHS' CYCLE OF DESTRUCTION. IT'S MY CALLING.
CALLING. THAT'S A GOOD WAY TO PUT IT.
POWER LEVEL 52%.
I HAVE ONE, TOO. THE MORE I EMBRACE LIFE-- THE MORE I FIGHT FOR IT--THE STRONGER I GET.
I DIDN'T UNDERSTAND WHAT THAT MEANT, UNTIL NOW.
POWER LEVEL 74%.
YOU AREN'T THE KEY, RELIC.
I AM.
POWER LEVEL 99%.
100% POWER REACHED.
BEAUTIFUL...

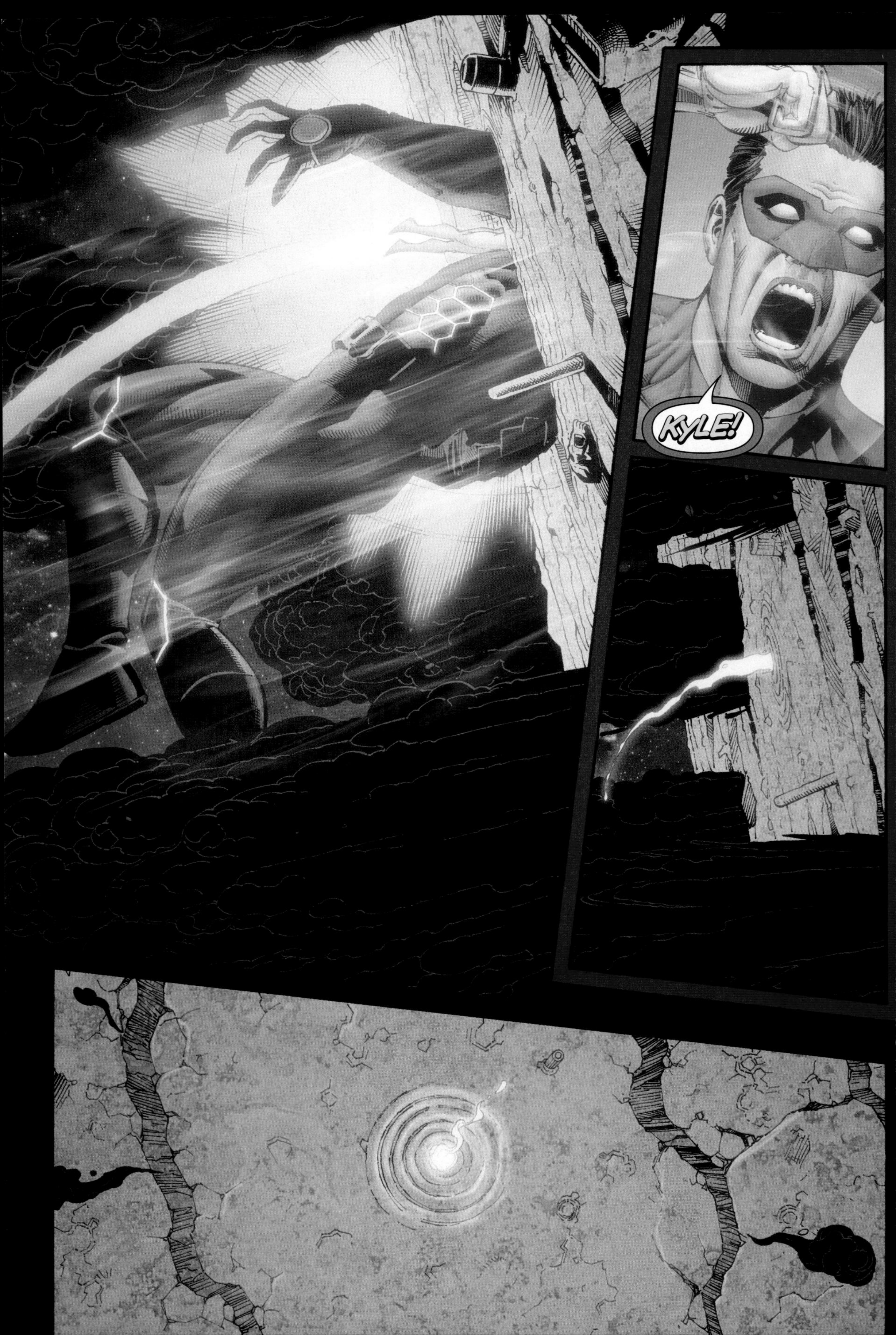
KYLE!

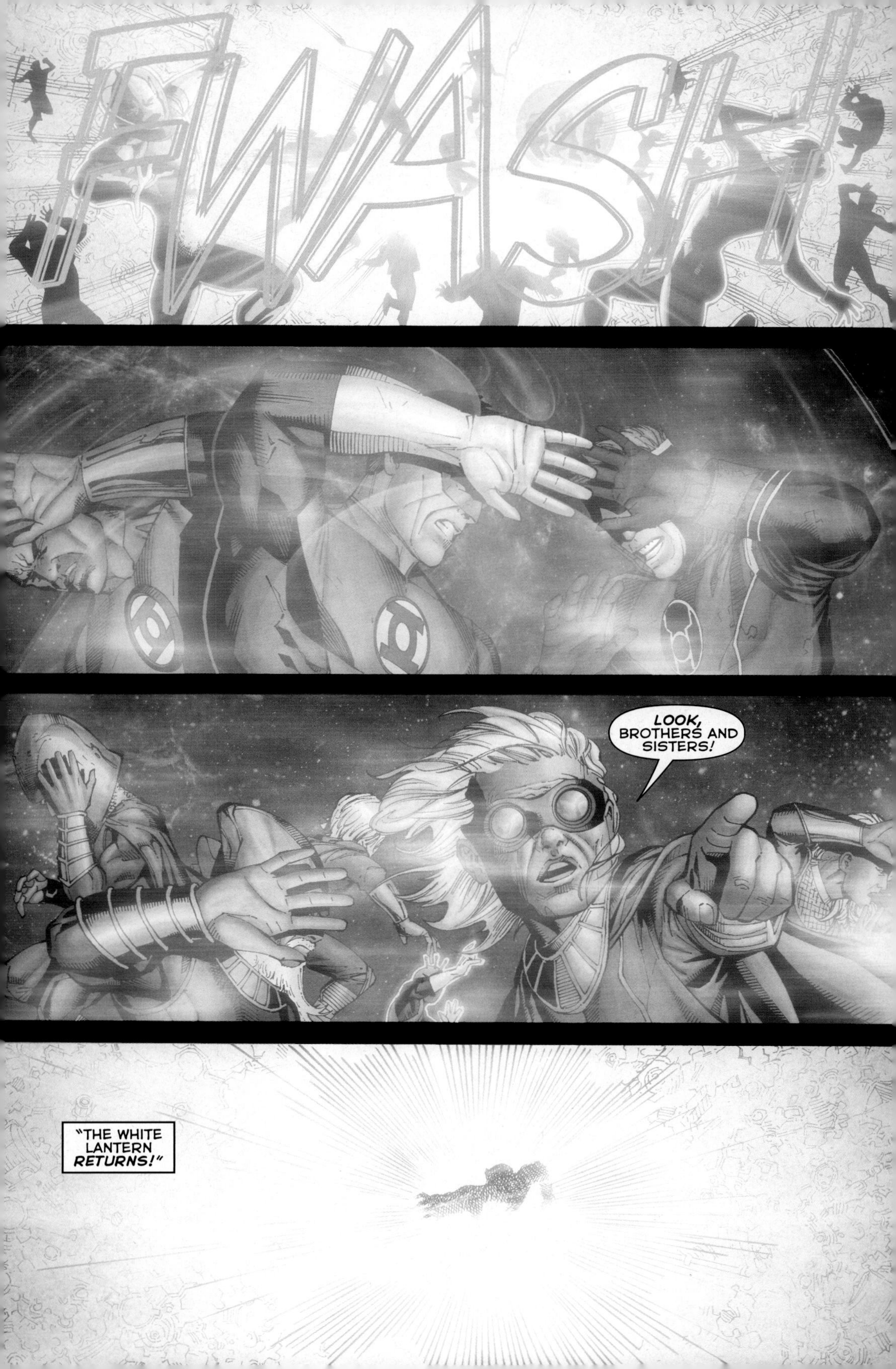
FWASH
LOOK, BROTHERS AND SISTERS!
"THE WHITE LANTERN RETURNS!"

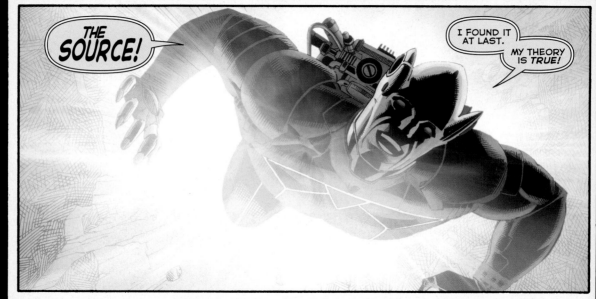

THE SOURCE!

I FOUND IT AT LAST.

MY THEORY IS *TRUE!*

THE RESERVOIR HAS BEEN REPLENISHED.

THE *WHITE LIGHTSMITH* WAS THE SOLUTION!

RESPECT THE OPPORTUNITY YOU'VE BEEN GIVEN.

MY WORK... IS FINISHED.

DMFLLN NNNG

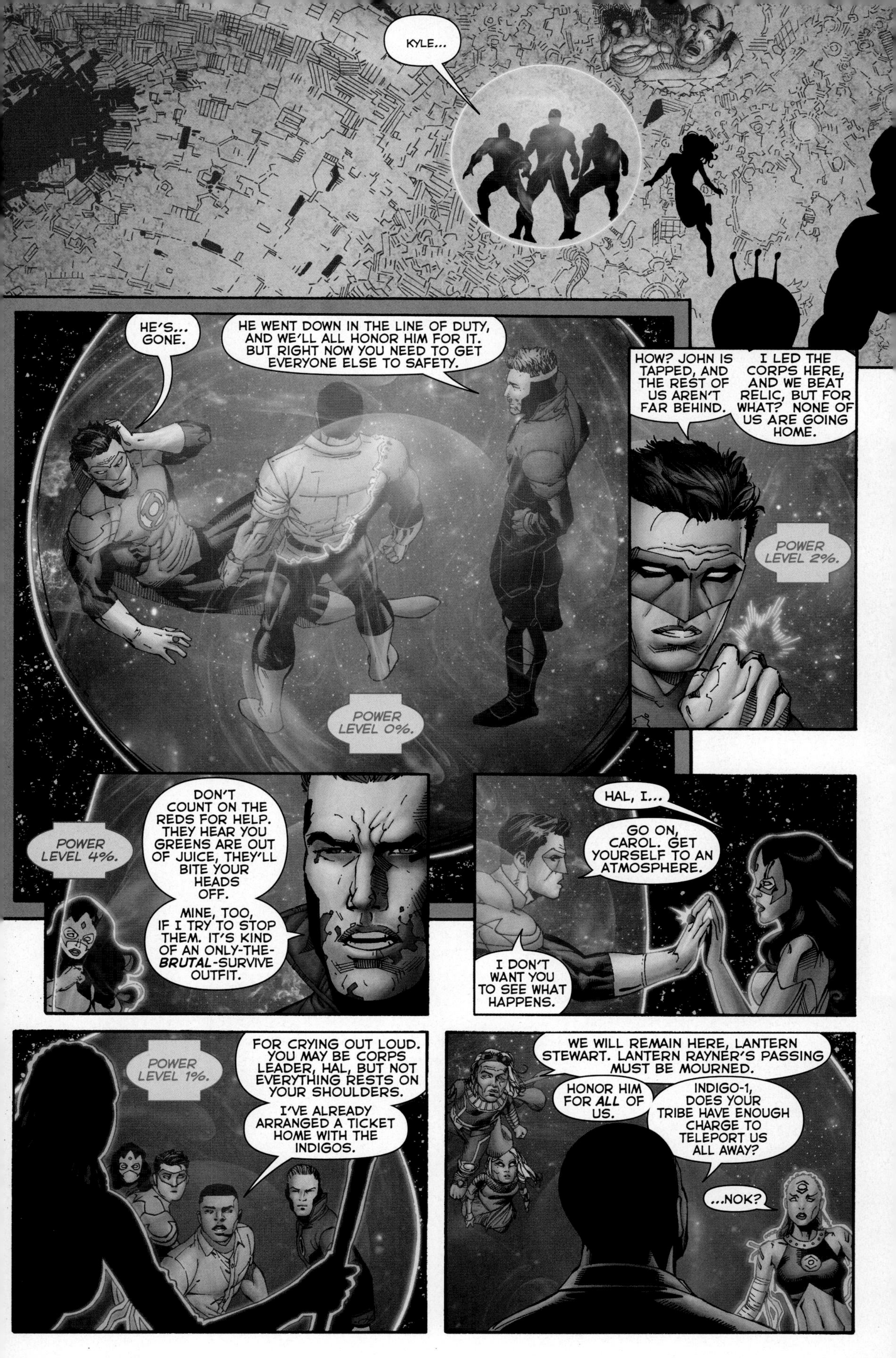
KYLE...
HE'S... GONE.
HE WENT DOWN IN THE LINE OF DUTY, AND WE'LL ALL HONOR HIM FOR IT. BUT RIGHT NOW YOU NEED TO GET EVERYONE ELSE TO SAFETY.
POWER LEVEL 0%.
HOW? JOHN IS TAPPED, AND THE REST OF US AREN'T FAR BEHIND.
I LED THE CORPS HERE, AND WE BEAT RELIC, BUT FOR WHAT? NONE OF US ARE GOING HOME.
POWER LEVEL 2%.
POWER LEVEL 4%.
DON'T COUNT ON THE REDS FOR HELP. THEY HEAR YOU GREENS ARE OUT OF JUICE, THEY'LL BITE YOUR HEADS OFF.
MINE, TOO, IF I TRY TO STOP THEM. IT'S KIND OF AN ONLY-THE-*BRUTAL*-SURVIVE OUTFIT.
HAL, I...
GO ON, CAROL. GET YOURSELF TO AN ATMOSPHERE.
I DON'T WANT YOU TO SEE WHAT HAPPENS.
POWER LEVEL 1%.
FOR CRYING OUT LOUD. YOU MAY BE CORPS LEADER, HAL, BUT NOT EVERYTHING RESTS ON YOUR SHOULDERS.
I'VE ALREADY ARRANGED A TICKET HOME WITH THE INDIGOS.
WE WILL REMAIN HERE, LANTERN STEWART. LANTERN RAYNER'S PASSING MUST BE MOURNED.
HONOR HIM FOR *ALL* OF US.
INDIGO-1, DOES YOUR TRIBE HAVE ENOUGH CHARGE TO TELEPORT US ALL AWAY?
...NOK?

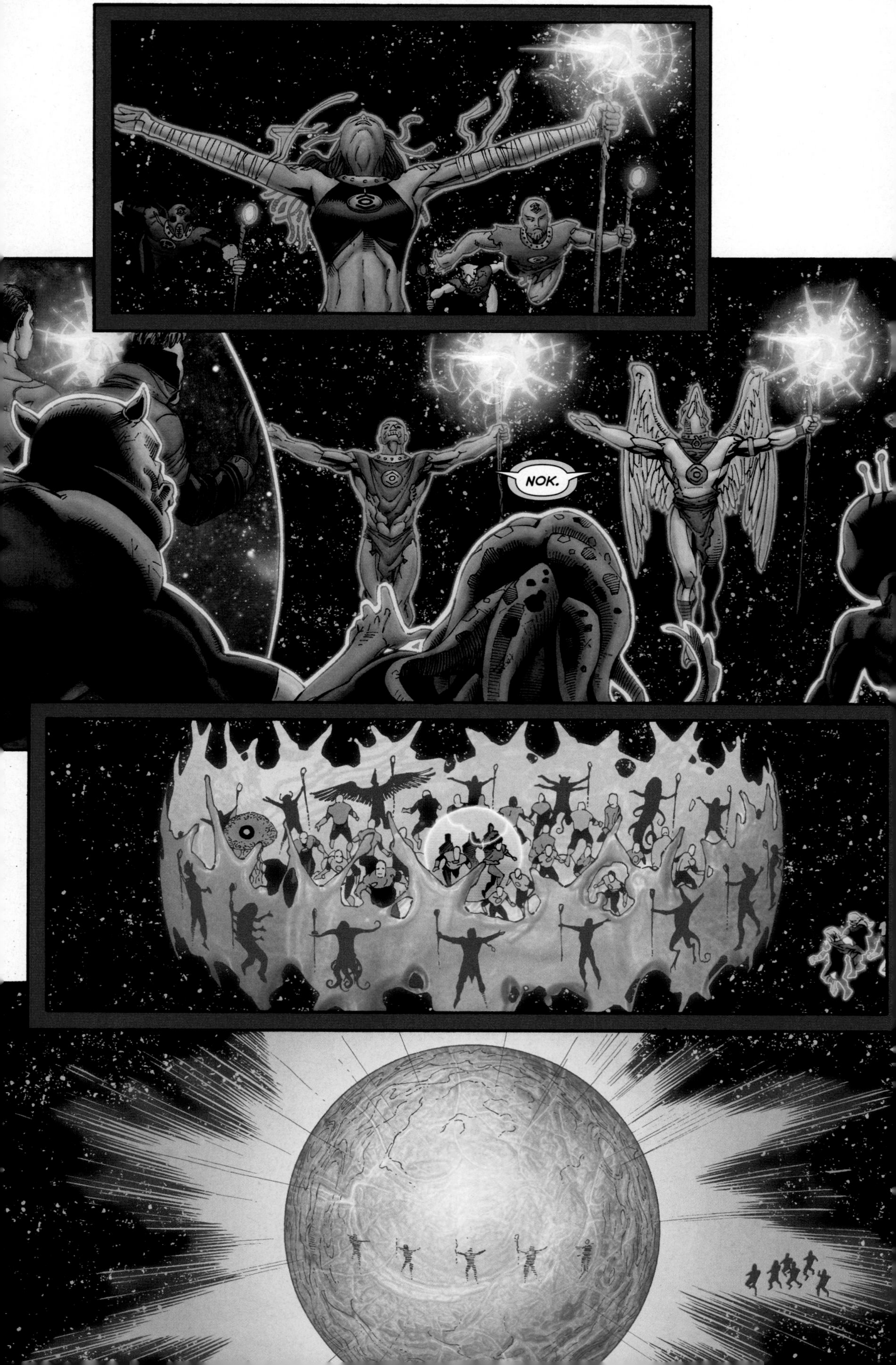
NOK.

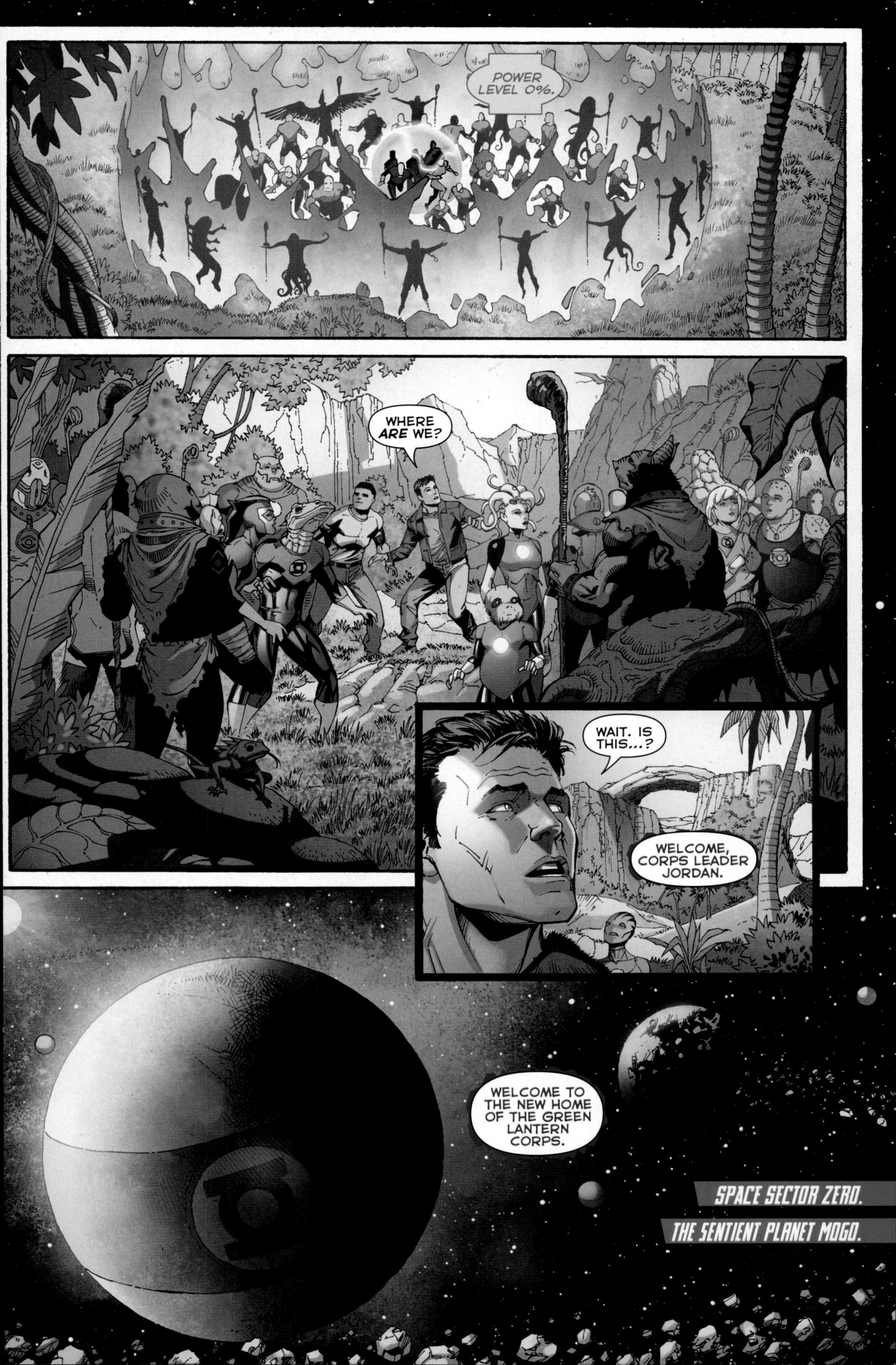
POWER LEVEL 0%.
WHERE ARE WE?
WAIT. IS THIS...?
WELCOME, CORPS LEADER JORDAN.
WELCOME TO THE NEW HOME OF THE GREEN LANTERN CORPS.
SPACE SECTOR ZERO.
THE SENTIENT PLANET MOGO.

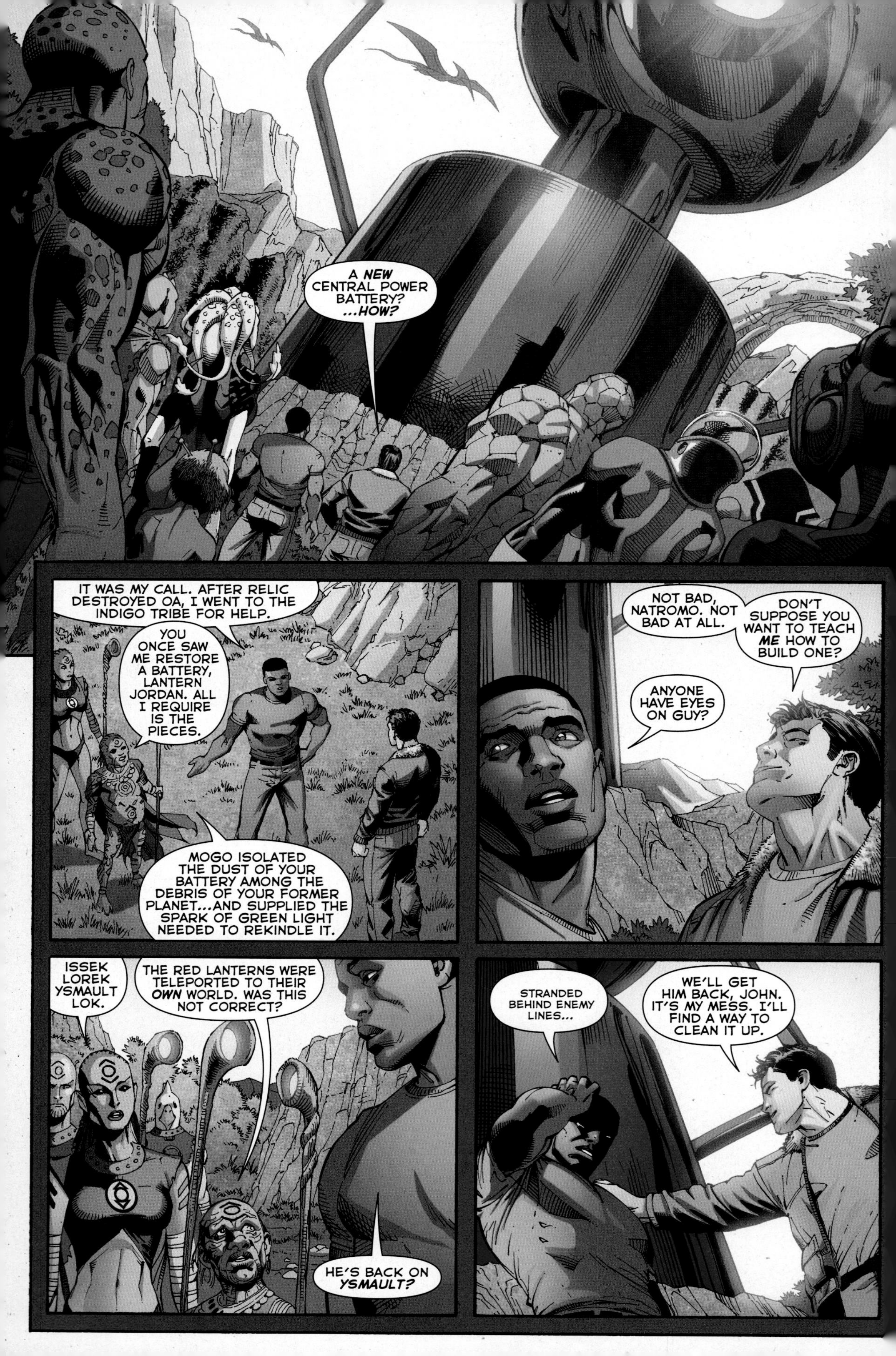
A NEW CENTRAL POWER BATTERY? ...HOW?
IT WAS MY CALL. AFTER RELIC DESTROYED OA, I WENT TO THE INDIGO TRIBE FOR HELP.
YOU ONCE SAW ME RESTORE A BATTERY, LANTERN JORDAN. ALL I REQUIRE IS THE PIECES.
MOGO ISOLATED THE DUST OF YOUR BATTERY AMONG THE DEBRIS OF YOUR FORMER PLANET...AND SUPPLIED THE SPARK OF GREEN LIGHT NEEDED TO REKINDLE IT.
NOT BAD, NATROMO. NOT BAD AT ALL.
DON'T SUPPOSE YOU WANT TO TEACH ME HOW TO BUILD ONE?
ANYONE HAVE EYES ON GUY?
ISSEK LOREK YSMAULT LOK.
THE RED LANTERNS WERE TELEPORTED TO THEIR OWN WORLD. WAS THIS NOT CORRECT?
HE'S BACK ON YSMAULT?
STRANDED BEHIND ENEMY LINES...
WE'LL GET HIM BACK, JOHN. IT'S MY MESS. I'LL FIND A WAY TO CLEAN IT UP.

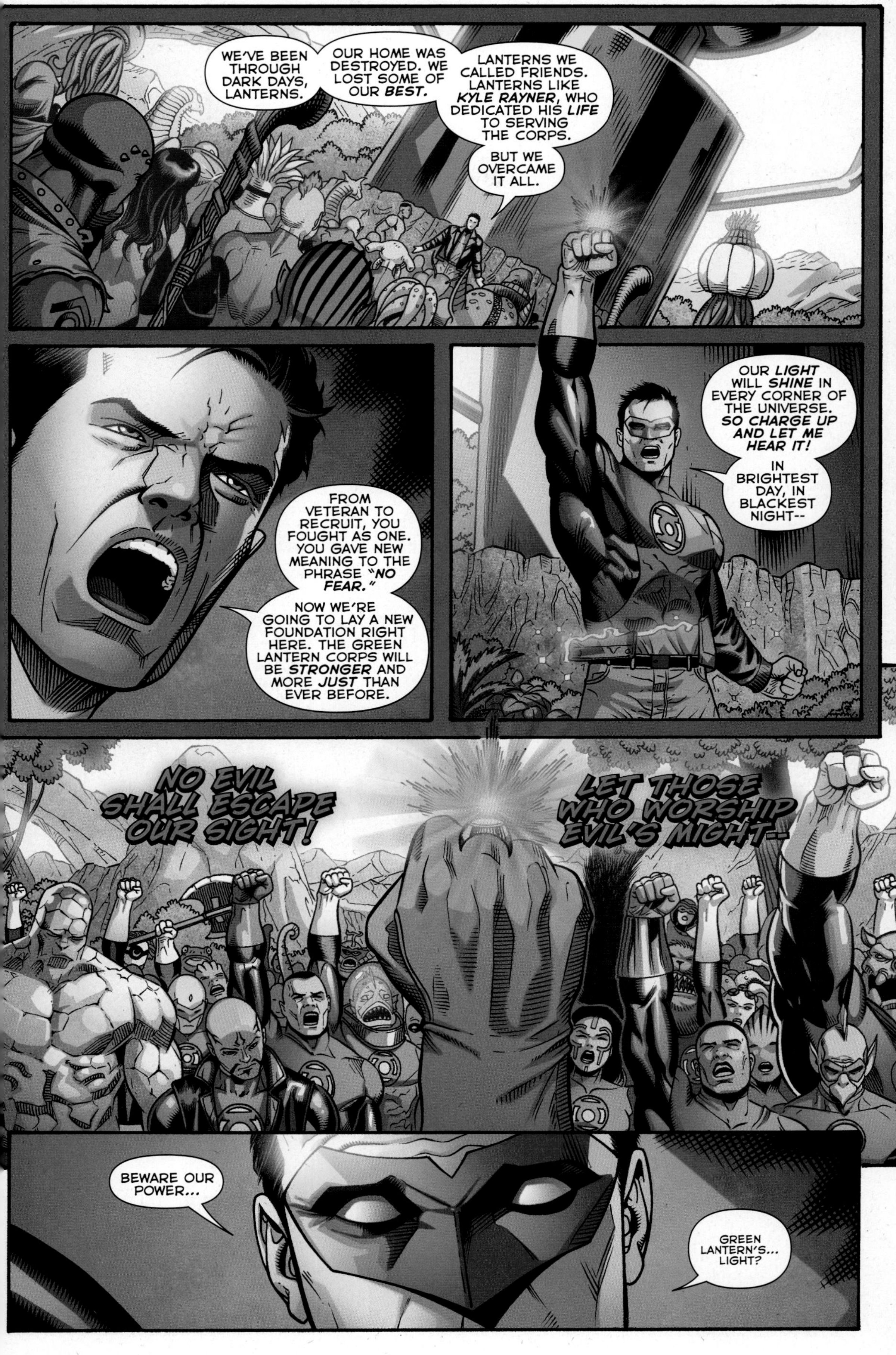
WE'VE BEEN THROUGH DARK DAYS, LANTERNS.
OUR HOME WAS DESTROYED. WE LOST SOME OF OUR *BEST.*
LANTERNS WE CALLED FRIENDS. LANTERNS LIKE *KYLE RAYNER*, WHO DEDICATED HIS *LIFE* TO SERVING THE CORPS.
BUT WE OVERCAME IT ALL.
FROM VETERAN TO RECRUIT, YOU FOUGHT AS ONE. YOU GAVE NEW MEANING TO THE PHRASE *"NO FEAR."*
NOW WE'RE GOING TO LAY A NEW FOUNDATION RIGHT HERE. THE GREEN LANTERN CORPS WILL BE *STRONGER* AND MORE *JUST* THAN EVER BEFORE.
OUR *LIGHT* WILL *SHINE* IN EVERY CORNER OF THE UNIVERSE. *SO CHARGE UP AND LET ME HEAR IT!*
IN BRIGHTEST DAY, IN BLACKEST NIGHT--
NO EVIL SHALL ESCAPE OUR SIGHT!
LET THOSE WHO WORSHIP EVIL'S MIGHT--
BEWARE OUR POWER...
GREEN LANTERN'S... LIGHT?

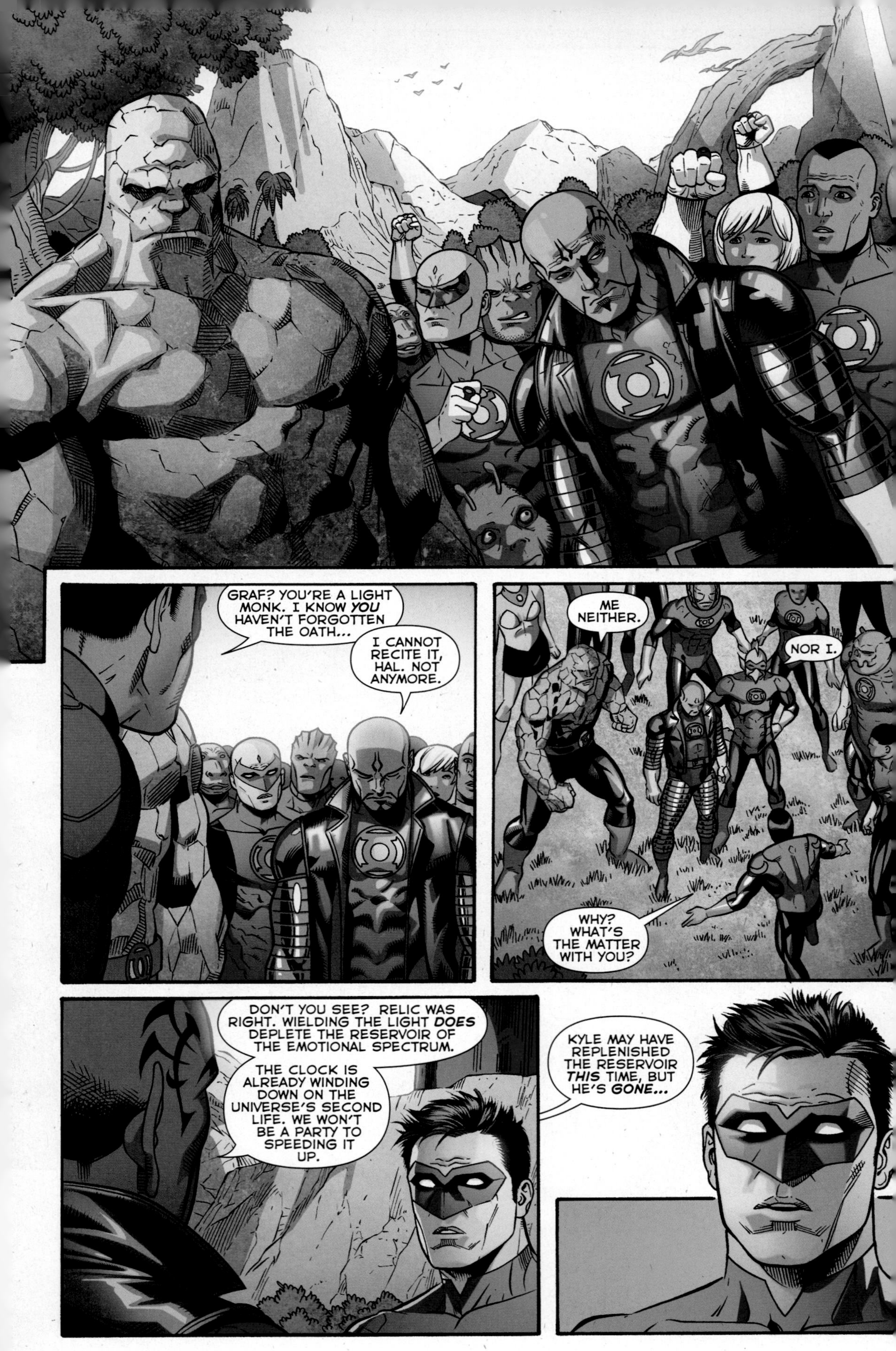
GRAF? YOU'RE A LIGHT MONK. I KNOW YOU HAVEN'T FORGOTTEN THE OATH...
I CANNOT RECITE IT, HAL. NOT ANYMORE.
ME NEITHER.
NOR I.
WHY? WHAT'S THE MATTER WITH YOU?
DON'T YOU SEE? RELIC WAS RIGHT. WIELDING THE LIGHT DOES DEPLETE THE RESERVOIR OF THE EMOTIONAL SPECTRUM.
THE CLOCK IS ALREADY WINDING DOWN ON THE UNIVERSE'S SECOND LIFE. WE WON'T BE A PARTY TO SPEEDING IT UP.
KYLE MAY HAVE REPLENISHED THE RESERVOIR THIS TIME, BUT HE'S GONE...

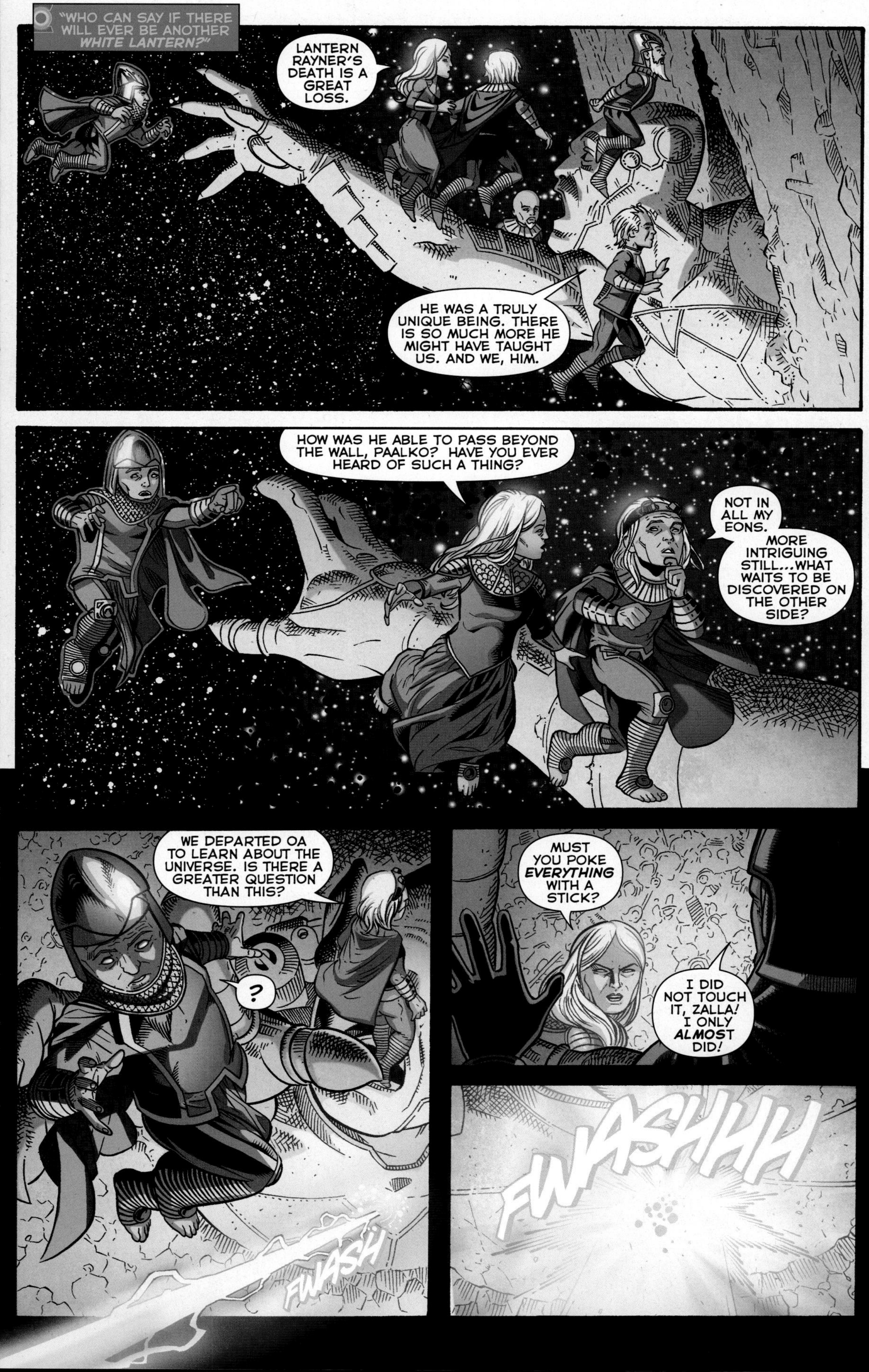
"WHO CAN SAY IF THERE WILL EVER BE ANOTHER *WHITE LANTERN?*"
LANTERN RAYNER'S DEATH IS A GREAT LOSS.
HE WAS A TRULY UNIQUE BEING. THERE IS SO MUCH MORE HE MIGHT HAVE TAUGHT US. AND WE, HIM.
HOW WAS HE ABLE TO PASS BEYOND THE WALL, PAALKO? HAVE YOU EVER HEARD OF SUCH A THING?
NOT IN ALL MY EONS.
MORE INTRIGUING STILL...WHAT WAITS TO BE DISCOVERED ON THE OTHER SIDE?
WE DEPARTED OA TO LEARN ABOUT THE UNIVERSE. IS THERE A GREATER QUESTION THAN THIS?
?
FWASH
MUST YOU POKE **EVERYTHING** WITH A STICK?
I DID NOT TOUCH IT, ZALLA! I ONLY **ALMOST** DID!
FWASHHH

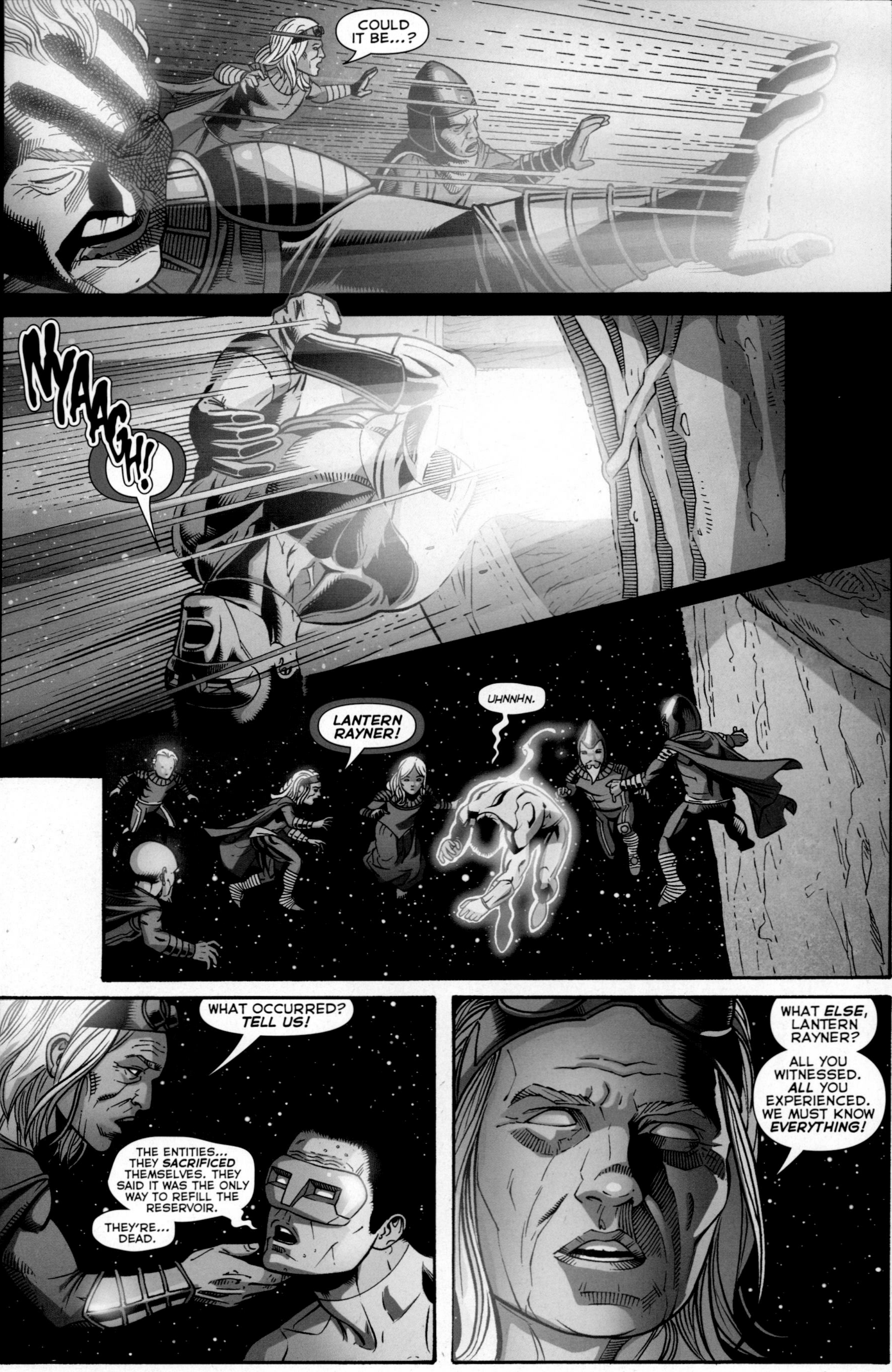
COULD IT BE...?
NYAAAGH!
LANTERN RAYNER!
UHNNHN.
WHAT OCCURRED? TELL US!
THE ENTITIES... THEY SACRIFICED THEMSELVES. THEY SAID IT WAS THE ONLY WAY TO REFILL THE RESERVOIR.
THEY'RE... DEAD.
WHAT ELSE, LANTERN RAYNER?
ALL YOU WITNESSED. ALL YOU EXPERIENCED. WE MUST KNOW EVERYTHING!

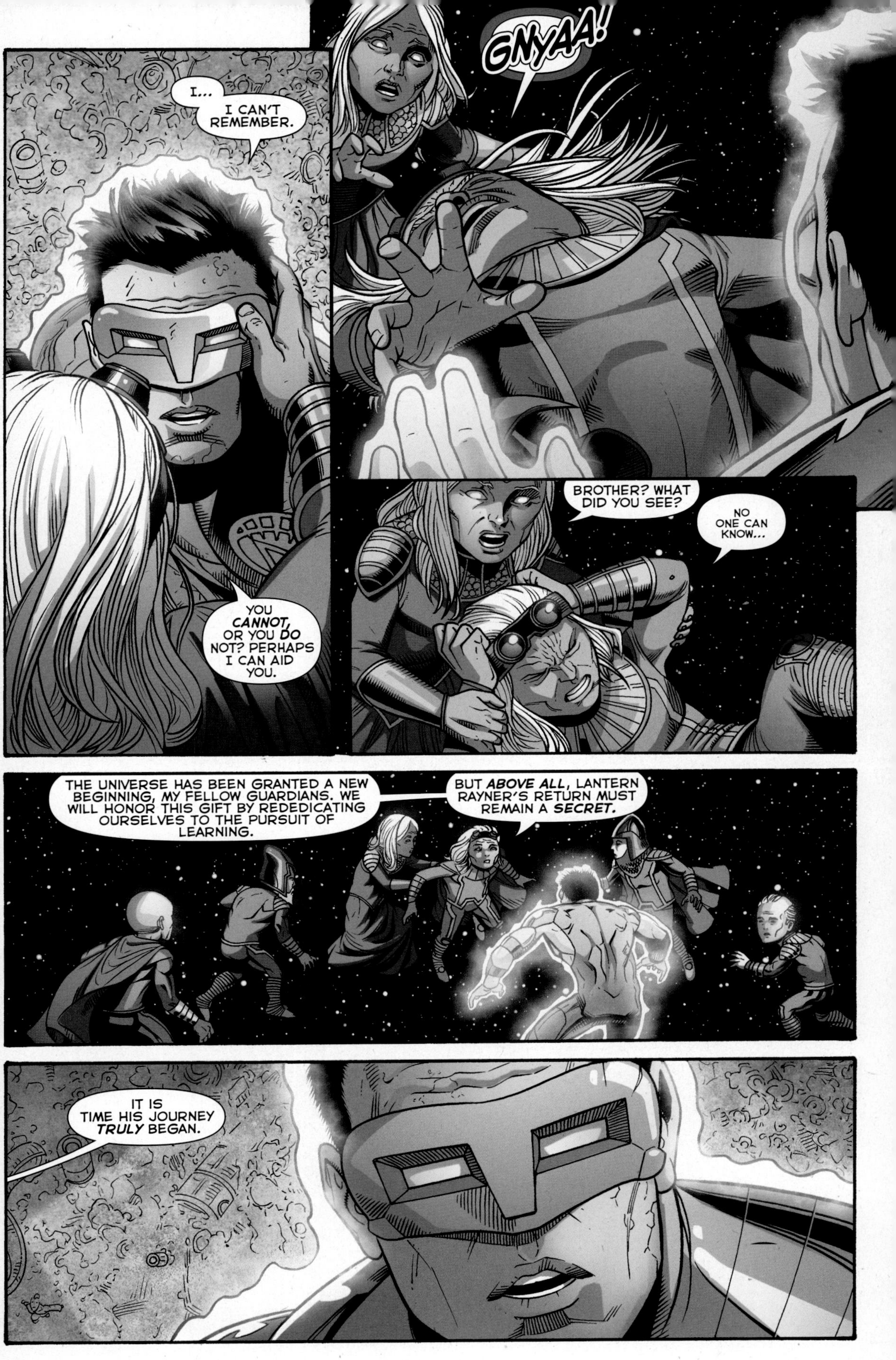
I... I CAN'T REMEMBER.
GNYAA!
YOU CANNOT, OR YOU DO NOT? PERHAPS I CAN AID YOU.
BROTHER? WHAT DID YOU SEE?
NO ONE CAN KNOW...
THE UNIVERSE HAS BEEN GRANTED A NEW BEGINNING, MY FELLOW GUARDIANS. WE WILL HONOR THIS GIFT BY REDEDICATING OURSELVES TO THE PURSUIT OF LEARNING.
BUT ABOVE ALL, LANTERN RAYNER'S RETURN MUST REMAIN A SECRET.
IT IS TIME HIS JOURNEY TRULY BEGAN.

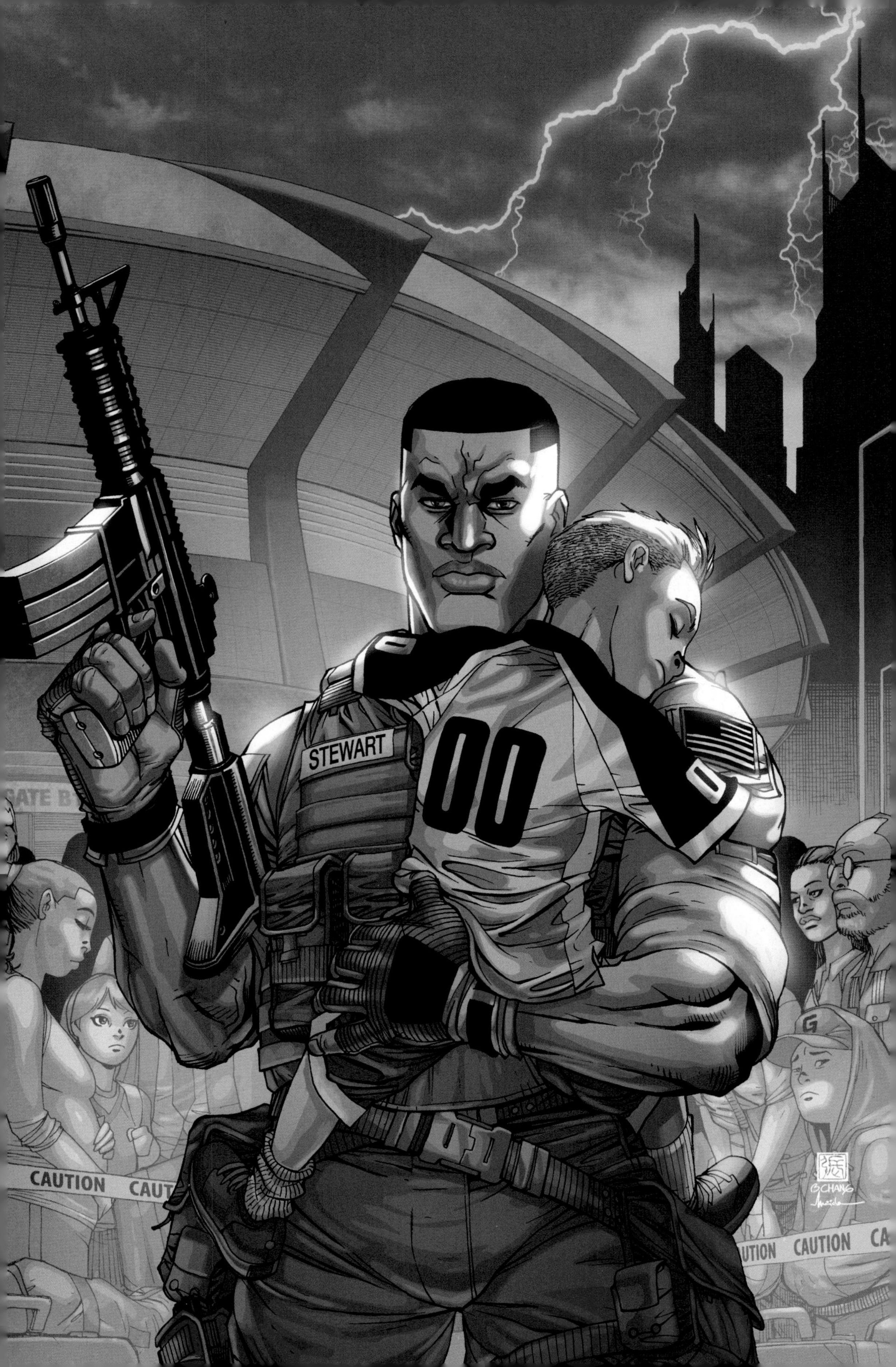
STEWART
00
CAUTION CAUT
UTION CAUTION CA
B CHANG

POWERS THAT BE
VAN JENSEN & ROBERT VENDITTI writers VIC DRUJINIU, IVAN FERNANDEZ & ALLAN JEFFERSON pencillers
JUAN A. CASTRO & ROB LEAN inkers cover art by BERNARD CHANG & MARCELO MAIOLO

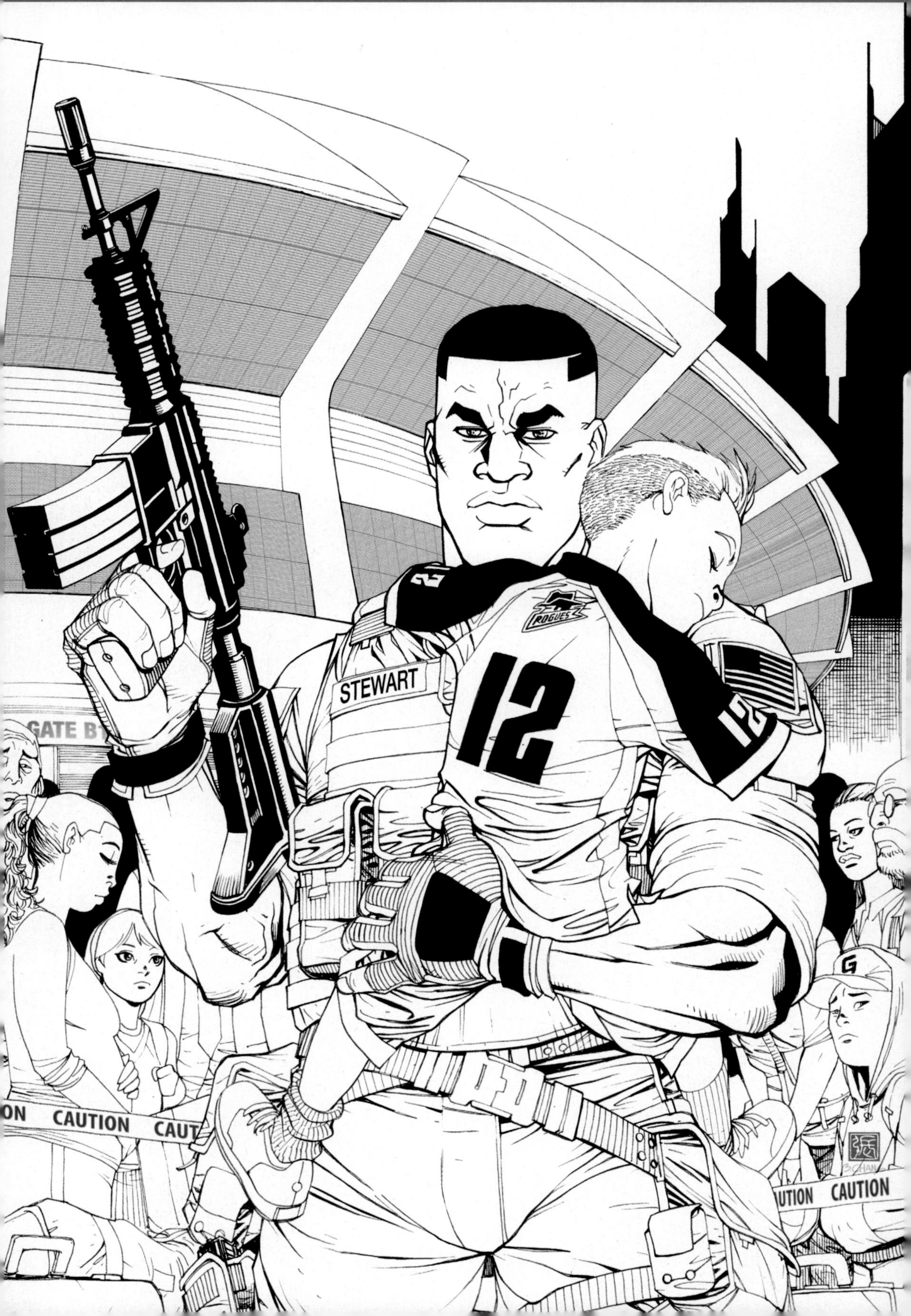

STEWART
12
ROGUES
GATE B
CAUTION
CAUT
ON
CAUTION
UTION

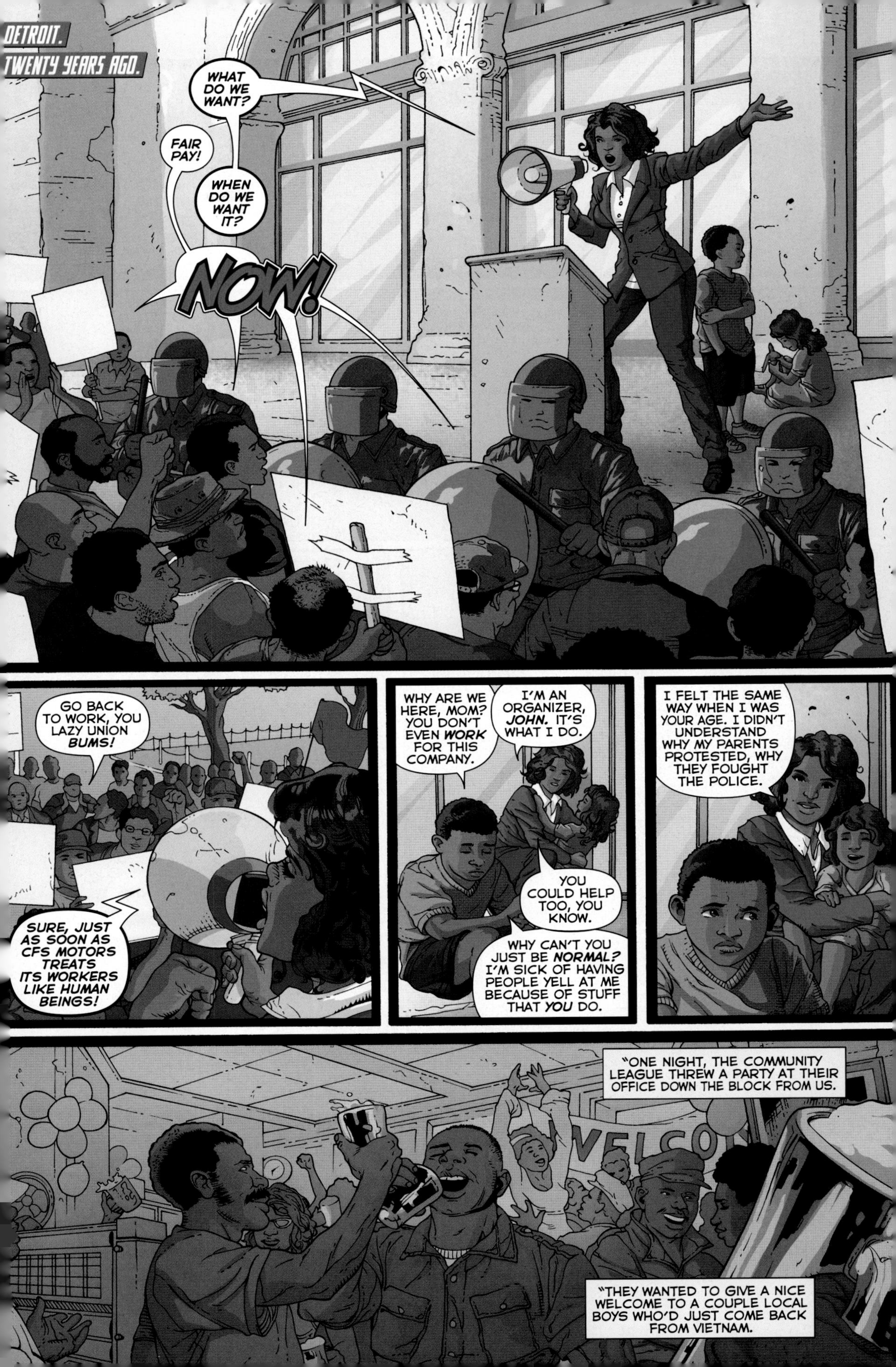
DETROIT.
TWENTY YEARS AGO.
WHAT DO WE WANT?
FAIR PAY!
WHEN DO WE WANT IT?
NOW!
GO BACK TO WORK, YOU LAZY UNION BUMS!
SURE, JUST AS SOON AS CFS MOTORS TREATS ITS WORKERS LIKE HUMAN BEINGS!
WHY ARE WE HERE, MOM? YOU DON'T EVEN WORK FOR THIS COMPANY.
I'M AN ORGANIZER, JOHN. IT'S WHAT I DO.
YOU COULD HELP TOO, YOU KNOW.
WHY CAN'T YOU JUST BE NORMAL? I'M SICK OF HAVING PEOPLE YELL AT ME BECAUSE OF STUFF THAT YOU DO.
I FELT THE SAME WAY WHEN I WAS YOUR AGE. I DIDN'T UNDERSTAND WHY MY PARENTS PROTESTED, WHY THEY FOUGHT THE POLICE.
"ONE NIGHT, THE COMMUNITY LEAGUE THREW A PARTY AT THEIR OFFICE DOWN THE BLOCK FROM US.
"THEY WANTED TO GIVE A NICE WELCOME TO A COUPLE LOCAL BOYS WHO'D JUST COME BACK FROM VIETNAM.

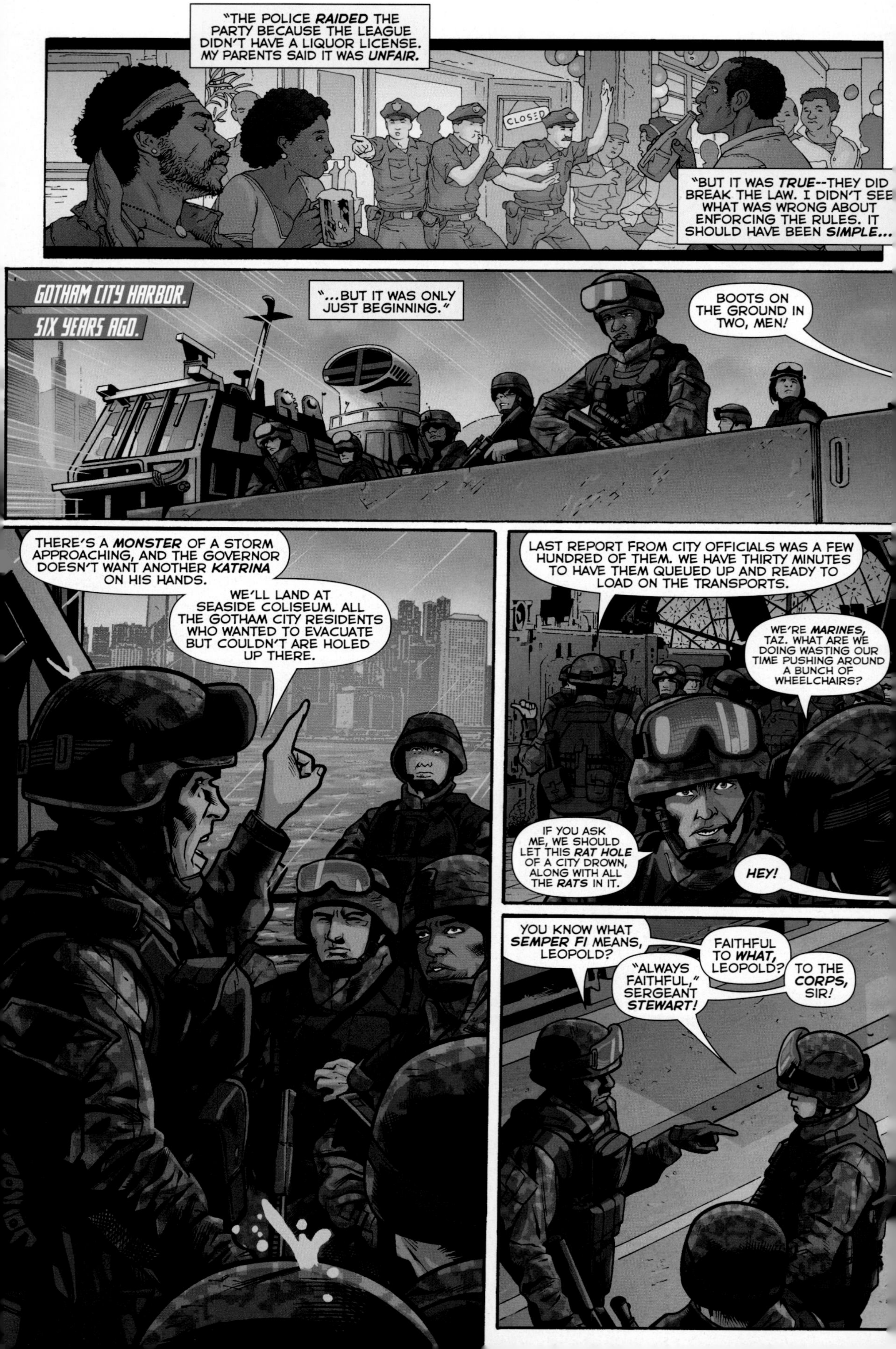
"THE POLICE RAIDED THE PARTY BECAUSE THE LEAGUE DIDN'T HAVE A LIQUOR LICENSE. MY PARENTS SAID IT WAS UNFAIR.
CLOSED
"BUT IT WAS TRUE--THEY DID BREAK THE LAW. I DIDN'T SEE WHAT WAS WRONG ABOUT ENFORCING THE RULES. IT SHOULD HAVE BEEN SIMPLE...
GOTHAM CITY HARBOR.
SIX YEARS AGO.
"...BUT IT WAS ONLY JUST BEGINNING."
BOOTS ON THE GROUND IN TWO, MEN!
THERE'S A MONSTER OF A STORM APPROACHING, AND THE GOVERNOR DOESN'T WANT ANOTHER KATRINA ON HIS HANDS.
WE'LL LAND AT SEASIDE COLISEUM. ALL THE GOTHAM CITY RESIDENTS WHO WANTED TO EVACUATE BUT COULDN'T ARE HOLED UP THERE.
LAST REPORT FROM CITY OFFICIALS WAS A FEW HUNDRED OF THEM. WE HAVE THIRTY MINUTES TO HAVE THEM QUEUED UP AND READY TO LOAD ON THE TRANSPORTS.
WE'RE MARINES, TAZ. WHAT ARE WE DOING WASTING OUR TIME PUSHING AROUND A BUNCH OF WHEELCHAIRS?
IF YOU ASK ME, WE SHOULD LET THIS RAT HOLE OF A CITY DROWN, ALONG WITH ALL THE RATS IN IT.
HEY!
YOU KNOW WHAT SEMPER FI MEANS, LEOPOLD?
"ALWAYS FAITHFUL," SERGEANT STEWART!
FAITHFUL TO WHAT, LEOPOLD?
TO THE CORPS, SIR!

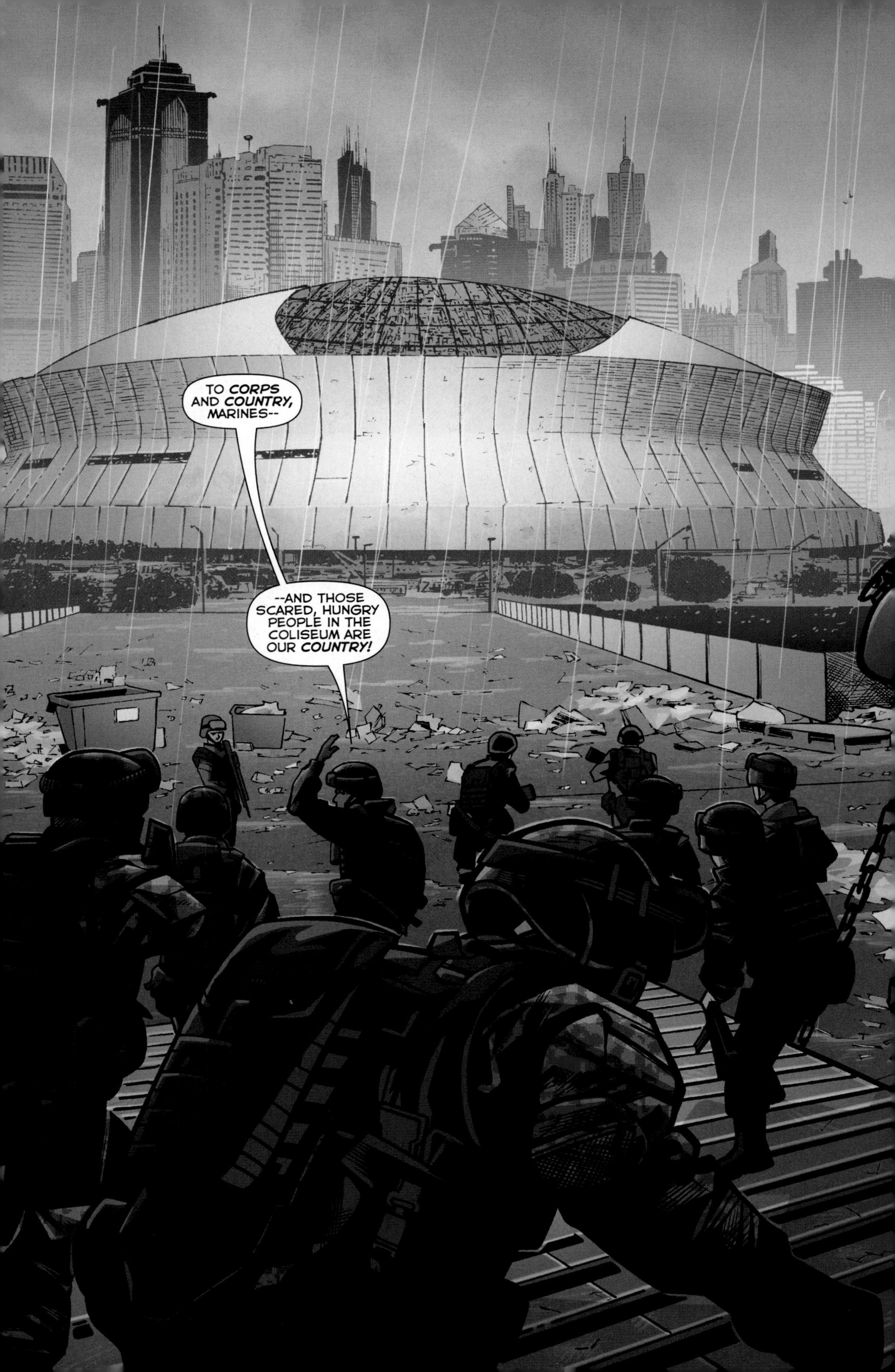
TO CORPS AND COUNTRY, MARINES--
--AND THOSE SCARED, HUNGRY PEOPLE IN THE COLISEUM ARE OUR COUNTRY!

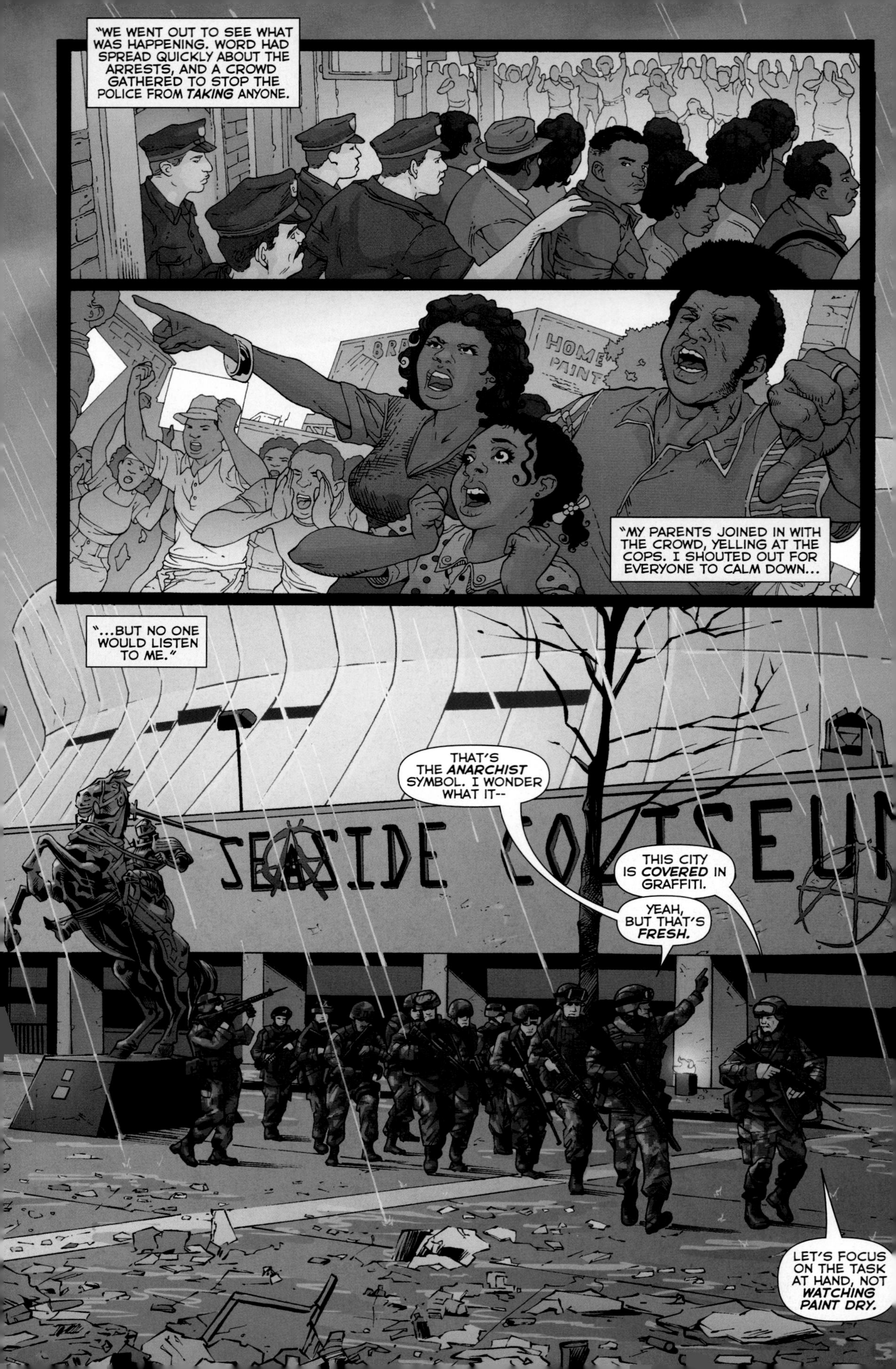

"WE WENT OUT TO SEE WHAT WAS HAPPENING. WORD HAD SPREAD QUICKLY ABOUT THE ARRESTS, AND A CROWD GATHERED TO STOP THE POLICE FROM *TAKING* ANYONE.
HOME PAINT
"MY PARENTS JOINED IN WITH THE CROWD, YELLING AT THE COPS. I SHOUTED OUT FOR EVERYONE TO CALM DOWN...
"...BUT NO ONE WOULD LISTEN TO ME."
THAT'S THE *ANARCHIST* SYMBOL. I WONDER WHAT IT--
SEASIDE COLISEUM
THIS CITY IS *COVERED* IN GRAFFITI.
YEAH, BUT THAT'S *FRESH.*
LET'S FOCUS ON THE TASK AT HAND, NOT *WATCHING PAINT DRY.*

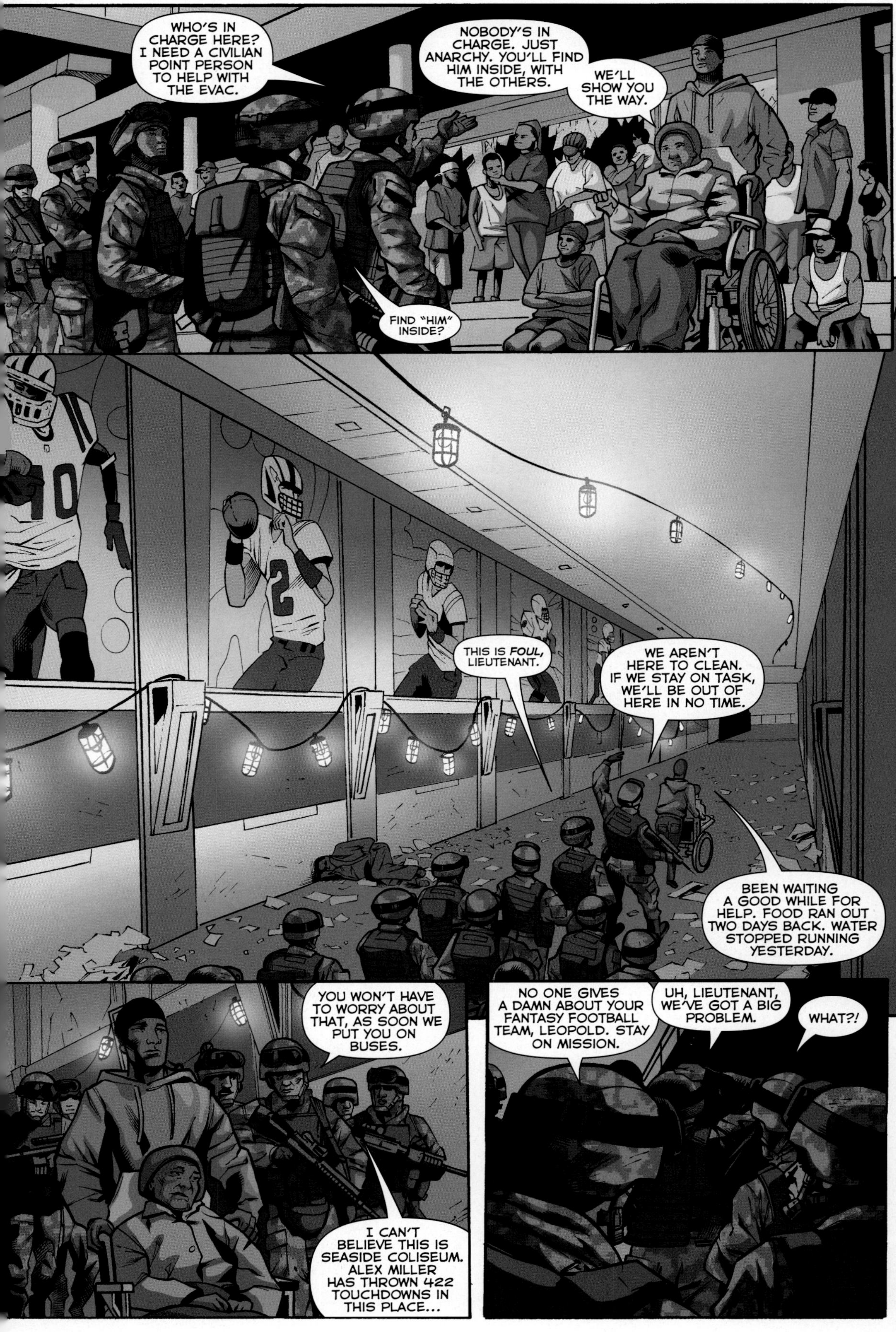
WHO'S IN CHARGE HERE? I NEED A CIVILIAN POINT PERSON TO HELP WITH THE EVAC.
NOBODY'S IN CHARGE. JUST ANARCHY. YOU'LL FIND HIM INSIDE, WITH THE OTHERS.
WE'LL SHOW YOU THE WAY.
FIND "HIM" INSIDE?
THIS IS FOUL, LIEUTENANT.
WE AREN'T HERE TO CLEAN. IF WE STAY ON TASK, WE'LL BE OUT OF HERE IN NO TIME.
BEEN WAITING A GOOD WHILE FOR HELP. FOOD RAN OUT TWO DAYS BACK. WATER STOPPED RUNNING YESTERDAY.
YOU WON'T HAVE TO WORRY ABOUT THAT, AS SOON WE PUT YOU ON BUSES.
I CAN'T BELIEVE THIS IS SEASIDE COLISEUM. ALEX MILLER HAS THROWN 422 TOUCHDOWNS IN THIS PLACE...
NO ONE GIVES A DAMN ABOUT YOUR FANTASY FOOTBALL TEAM, LEOPOLD. STAY ON MISSION.
UH, LIEUTENANT, WE'VE GOT A BIG PROBLEM.
WHAT?!

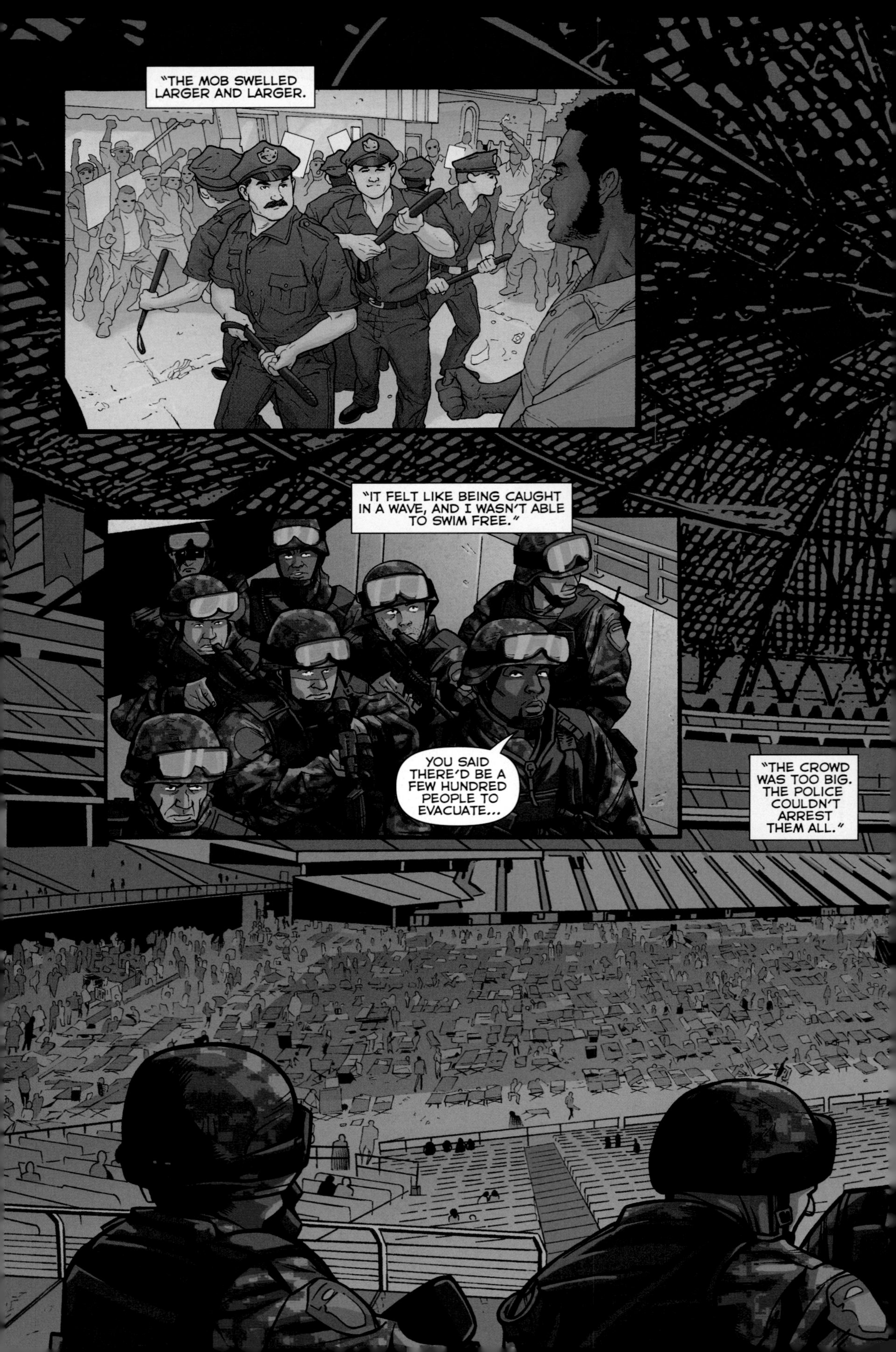
"THE MOB SWELLED LARGER AND LARGER.
"IT FELT LIKE BEING CAUGHT IN A WAVE, AND I WASN'T ABLE TO SWIM FREE."
YOU SAID THERE'D BE A FEW HUNDRED PEOPLE TO EVACUATE...
"THE CROWD WAS TOO BIG. THE POLICE COULDN'T ARREST THEM ALL."

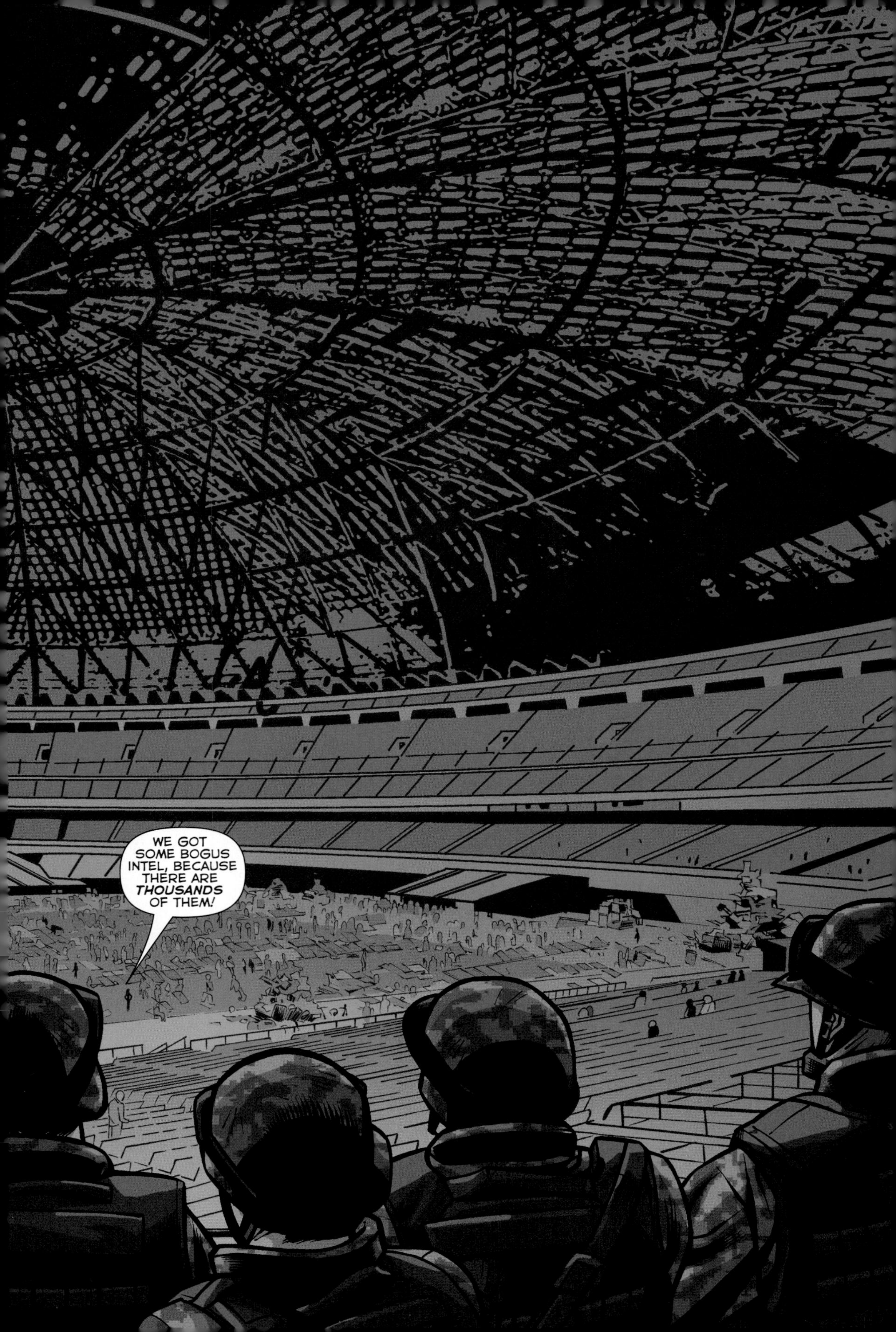
WE GOT SOME BOGUS INTEL, BECAUSE THERE ARE *THOUSANDS* OF THEM!

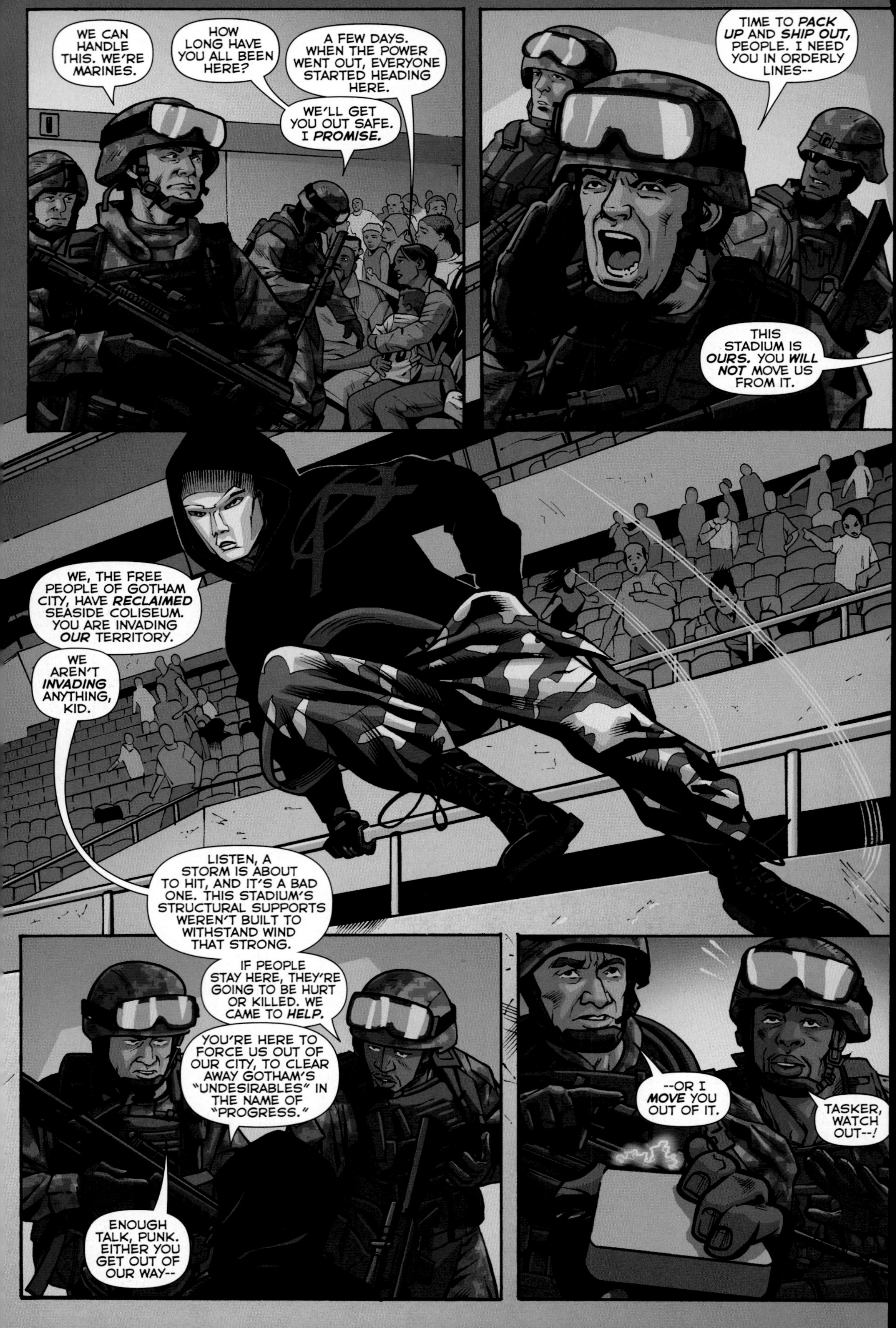
WE CAN HANDLE THIS. WE'RE MARINES.
HOW LONG HAVE YOU ALL BEEN HERE?
A FEW DAYS. WHEN THE POWER WENT OUT, EVERYONE STARTED HEADING HERE.
WE'LL GET YOU OUT SAFE. I PROMISE.
TIME TO PACK UP AND SHIP OUT, PEOPLE. I NEED YOU IN ORDERLY LINES--
THIS STADIUM IS OURS. YOU WILL NOT MOVE US FROM IT.
WE, THE FREE PEOPLE OF GOTHAM CITY, HAVE RECLAIMED SEASIDE COLISEUM. YOU ARE INVADING OUR TERRITORY.
WE AREN'T INVADING ANYTHING, KID.
LISTEN, A STORM IS ABOUT TO HIT, AND IT'S A BAD ONE. THIS STADIUM'S STRUCTURAL SUPPORTS WEREN'T BUILT TO WITHSTAND WIND THAT STRONG.
IF PEOPLE STAY HERE, THEY'RE GOING TO BE HURT OR KILLED. WE CAME TO HELP.
YOU'RE HERE TO FORCE US OUT OF OUR CITY, TO CLEAR AWAY GOTHAM'S "UNDESIRABLES" IN THE NAME OF "PROGRESS."
ENOUGH TALK, PUNK. EITHER YOU GET OUT OF OUR WAY--
--OR I MOVE YOU OUT OF IT.
TASKER, WATCH OUT--!

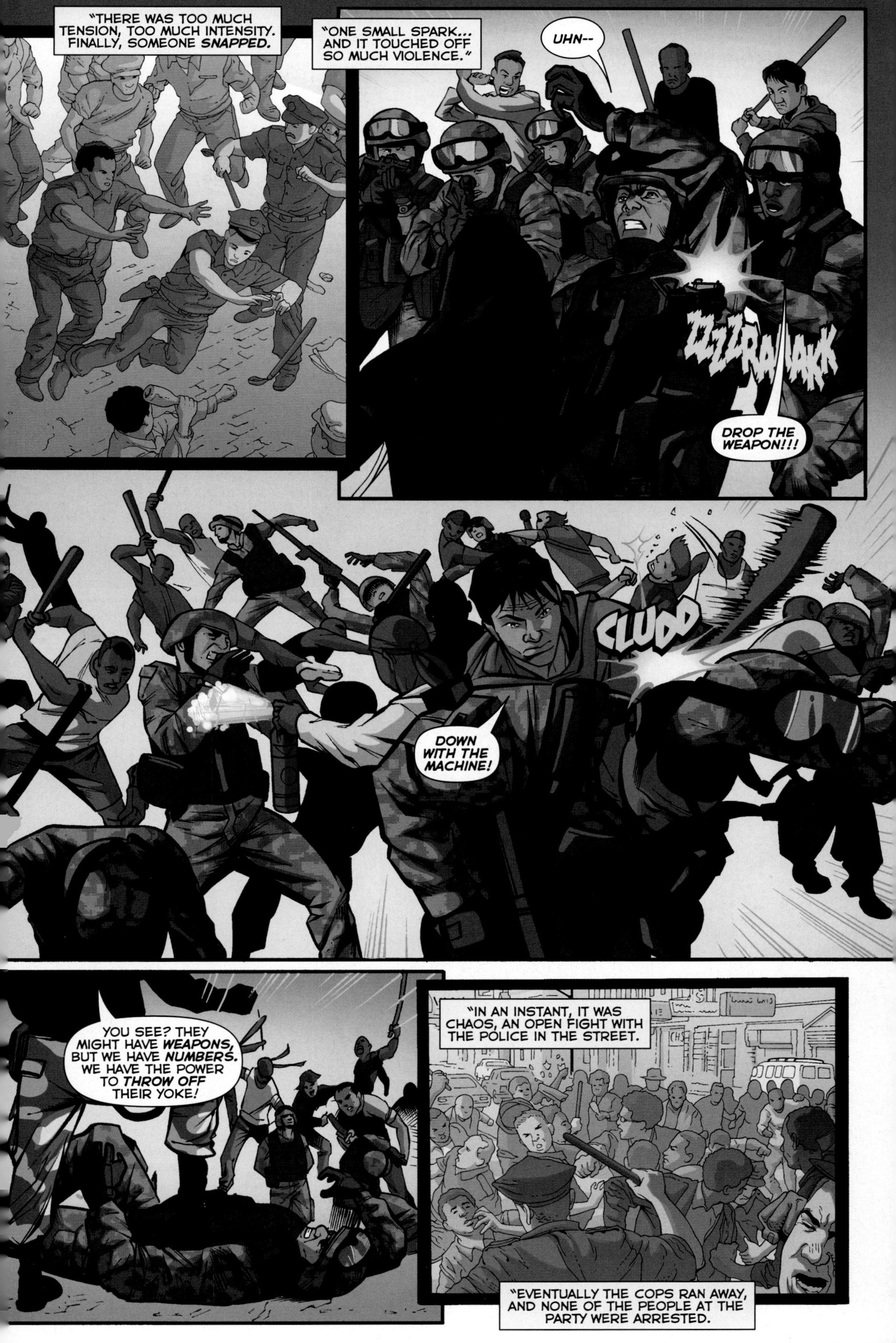
"THERE WAS TOO MUCH TENSION, TOO MUCH INTENSITY. FINALLY, SOMEONE *SNAPPED.*
"ONE SMALL SPARK... AND IT TOUCHED OFF SO MUCH VIOLENCE."
UHN--
ZZZZRAKKK
DROP THE WEAPON!!!
CLUDD
DOWN WITH THE MACHINE!
YOU SEE? THEY MIGHT HAVE *WEAPONS,* BUT WE HAVE *NUMBERS.* WE HAVE THE POWER TO *THROW OFF* THEIR YOKE!
"IN AN INSTANT, IT WAS CHAOS, AN OPEN FIGHT WITH THE POLICE IN THE STREET.
"EVENTUALLY THE COPS RAN AWAY, AND NONE OF THE PEOPLE AT THE PARTY WERE ARRESTED.

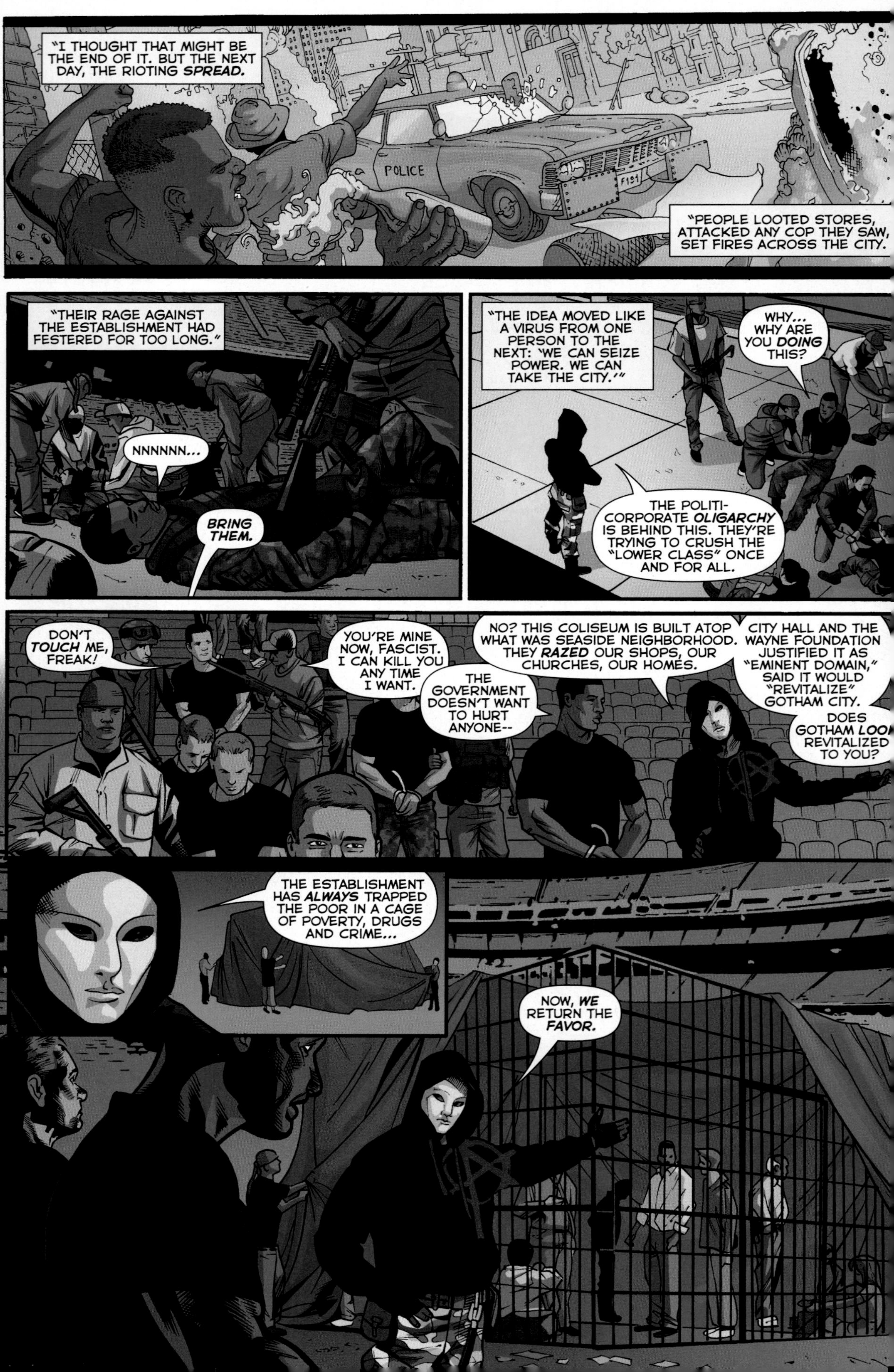
"I THOUGHT THAT MIGHT BE THE END OF IT. BUT THE NEXT DAY, THE RIOTING SPREAD.
POLICE
"PEOPLE LOOTED STORES, ATTACKED ANY COP THEY SAW, SET FIRES ACROSS THE CITY.
"THEIR RAGE AGAINST THE ESTABLISHMENT HAD FESTERED FOR TOO LONG."
NNNNNN...
BRING THEM.
"THE IDEA MOVED LIKE A VIRUS FROM ONE PERSON TO THE NEXT: 'WE CAN SEIZE POWER. WE CAN TAKE THE CITY.'"
WHY... WHY ARE YOU DOING THIS?
THE POLITI-CORPORATE OLIGARCHY IS BEHIND THIS. THEY'RE TRYING TO CRUSH THE "LOWER CLASS" ONCE AND FOR ALL.
DON'T TOUCH ME, FREAK!
YOU'RE MINE NOW, FASCIST. I CAN KILL YOU ANY TIME I WANT.
THE GOVERNMENT DOESN'T WANT TO HURT ANYONE--
NO? THIS COLISEUM IS BUILT ATOP WHAT WAS SEASIDE NEIGHBORHOOD. THEY RAZED OUR SHOPS, OUR CHURCHES, OUR HOMES.
CITY HALL AND THE WAYNE FOUNDATION JUSTIFIED IT AS "EMINENT DOMAIN," SAID IT WOULD "REVITALIZE" GOTHAM CITY.
DOES GOTHAM LOOK REVITALIZED TO YOU?
THE ESTABLISHMENT HAS ALWAYS TRAPPED THE POOR IN A CAGE OF POVERTY, DRUGS AND CRIME...
NOW, WE RETURN THE FAVOR.

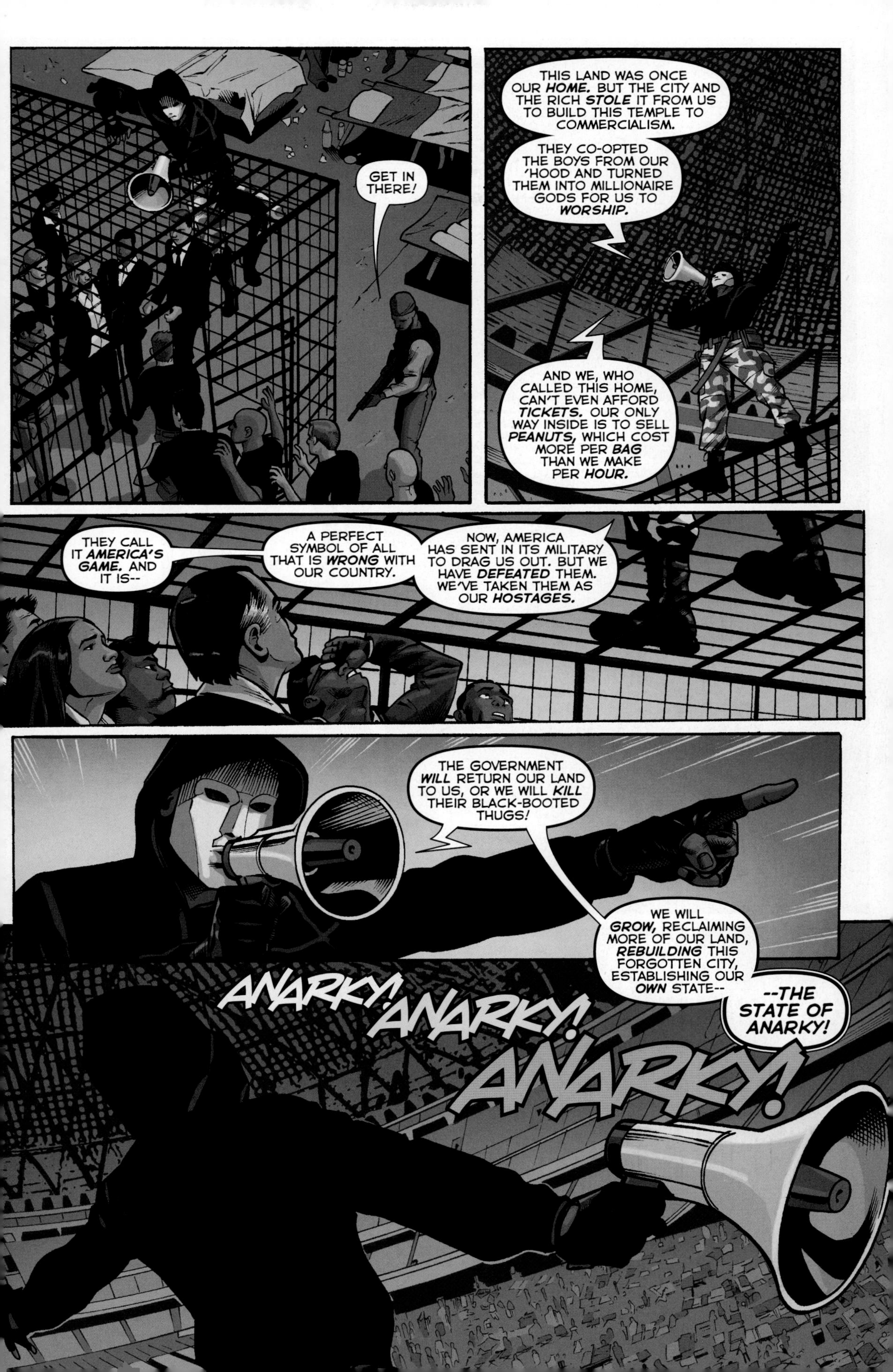
GET IN THERE!
THIS LAND WAS ONCE OUR HOME. BUT THE CITY AND THE RICH STOLE IT FROM US TO BUILD THIS TEMPLE TO COMMERCIALISM.
THEY CO-OPTED THE BOYS FROM OUR 'HOOD AND TURNED THEM INTO MILLIONAIRE GODS FOR US TO WORSHIP.
AND WE, WHO CALLED THIS HOME, CAN'T EVEN AFFORD TICKETS. OUR ONLY WAY INSIDE IS TO SELL PEANUTS, WHICH COST MORE PER BAG THAN WE MAKE PER HOUR.
THEY CALL IT AMERICA'S GAME. AND IT IS--
A PERFECT SYMBOL OF ALL THAT IS WRONG WITH OUR COUNTRY.
NOW, AMERICA HAS SENT IN ITS MILITARY TO DRAG US OUT. BUT WE HAVE DEFEATED THEM. WE'VE TAKEN THEM AS OUR HOSTAGES.
THE GOVERNMENT WILL RETURN OUR LAND TO US, OR WE WILL KILL THEIR BLACK-BOOTED THUGS!
WE WILL GROW, RECLAIMING MORE OF OUR LAND, REBUILDING THIS FORGOTTEN CITY, ESTABLISHING OUR OWN STATE--
--THE STATE OF ANARKY!
ANARKY! ANARKY! ANARKY!

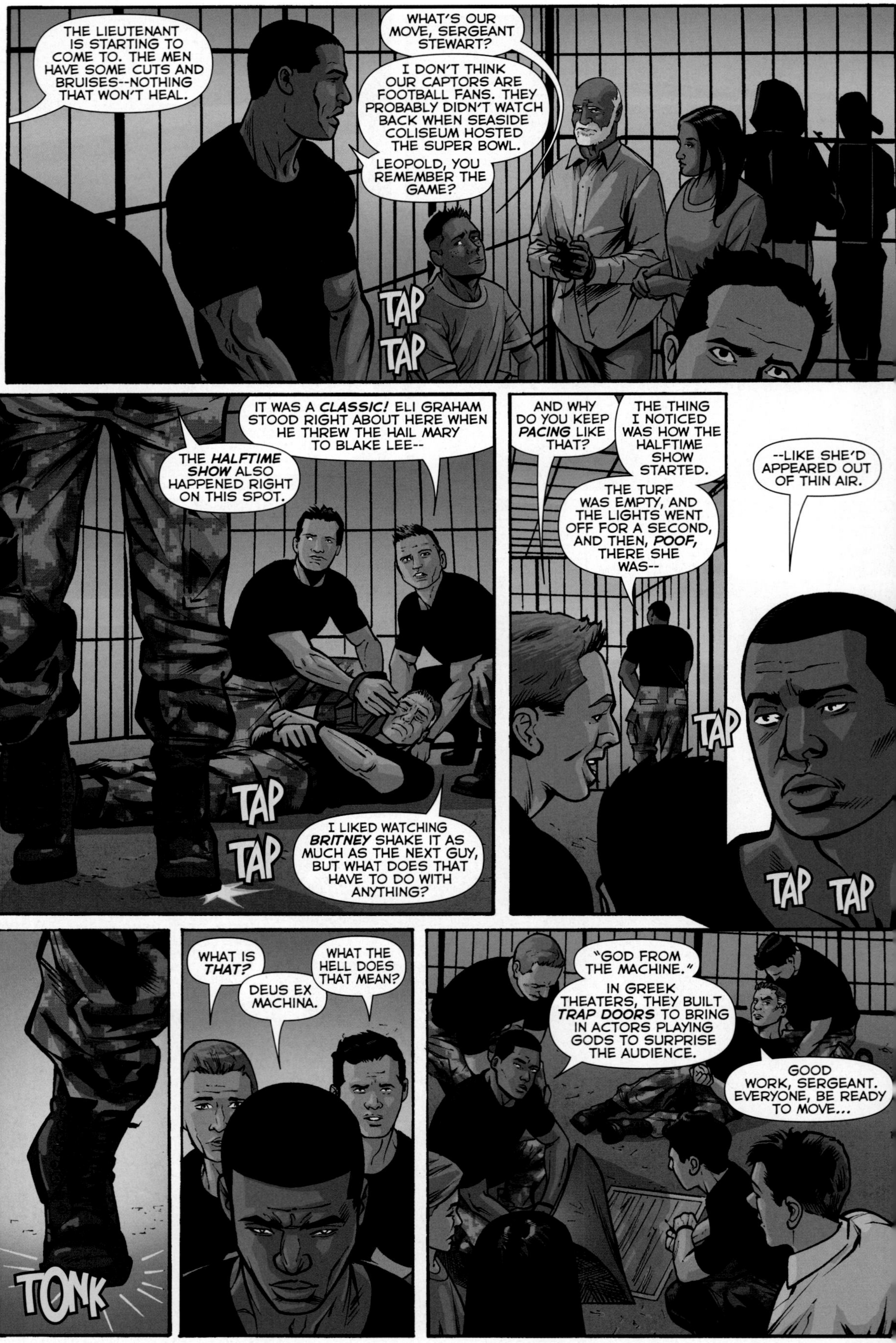
THE LIEUTENANT IS STARTING TO COME TO. THE MEN HAVE SOME CUTS AND BRUISES--NOTHING THAT WON'T HEAL.
WHAT'S OUR MOVE, SERGEANT STEWART?
I DON'T THINK OUR CAPTORS ARE FOOTBALL FANS. THEY PROBABLY DIDN'T WATCH BACK WHEN SEASIDE COLISEUM HOSTED THE SUPER BOWL.
LEOPOLD, YOU REMEMBER THE GAME?
TAP
TAP
IT WAS A *CLASSIC!* ELI GRAHAM STOOD RIGHT ABOUT HERE WHEN HE THREW THE HAIL MARY TO BLAKE LEE--
THE *HALFTIME SHOW* ALSO HAPPENED RIGHT ON THIS SPOT.
TAP
TAP
I LIKED WATCHING *BRITNEY* SHAKE IT AS MUCH AS THE NEXT GUY, BUT WHAT DOES THAT HAVE TO DO WITH ANYTHING?
AND WHY DO YOU KEEP *PACING* LIKE THAT?
THE THING I NOTICED WAS HOW THE HALFTIME SHOW STARTED.
THE TURF WAS EMPTY, AND THE LIGHTS WENT OFF FOR A SECOND, AND THEN, *POOF,* THERE SHE WAS--
TAP
--LIKE SHE'D APPEARED OUT OF THIN AIR.
TAP TAP
TONK
WHAT IS *THAT?*
DEUS EX MACHINA.
WHAT THE HELL DOES THAT MEAN?
"GOD FROM THE MACHINE."
IN GREEK THEATERS, THEY BUILT *TRAP DOORS* TO BRING IN ACTORS PLAYING GODS TO SURPRISE THE AUDIENCE.
GOOD WORK, SERGEANT. EVERYONE, BE READY TO MOVE...

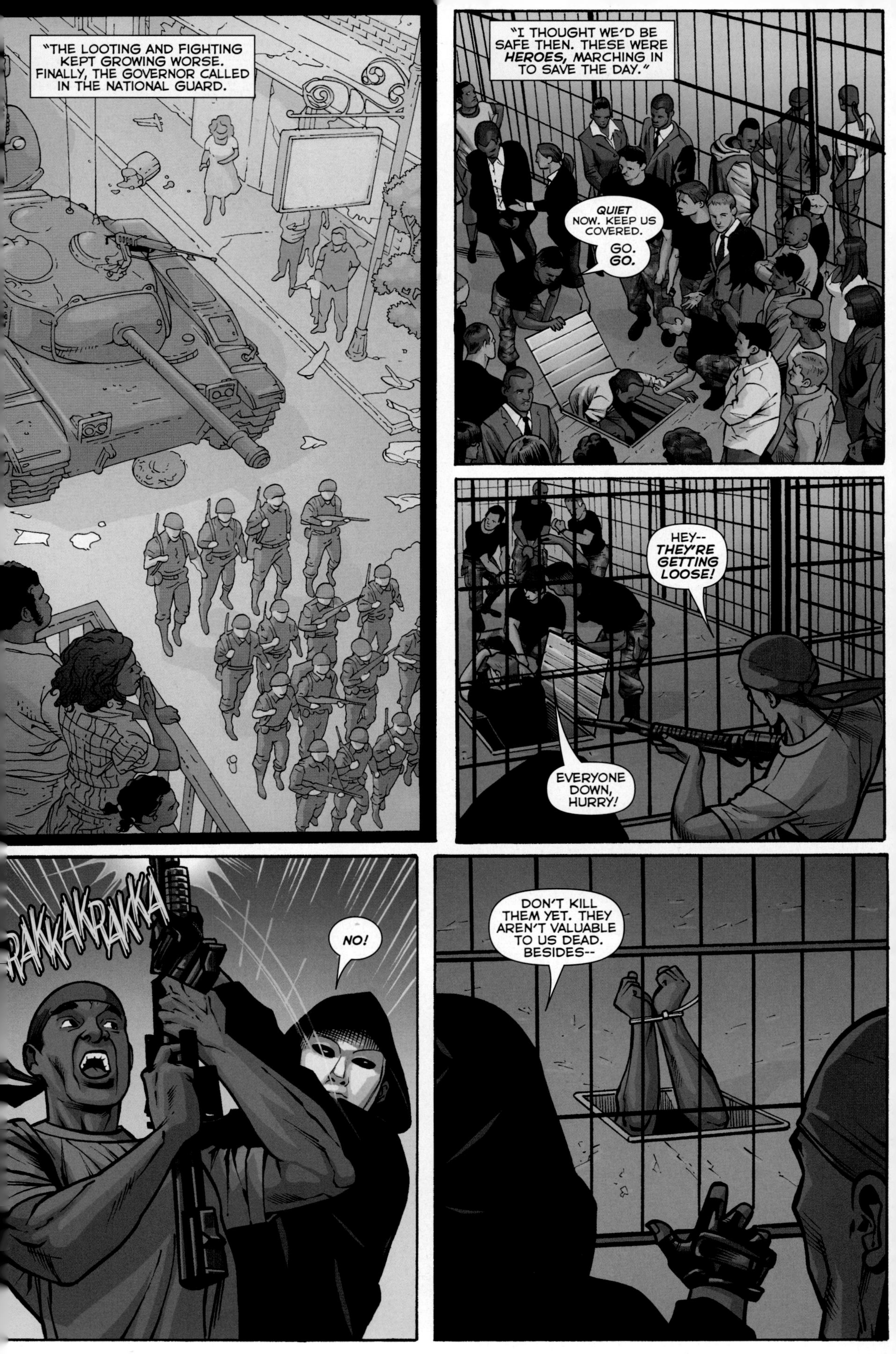

"THE LOOTING AND FIGHTING KEPT GROWING WORSE. FINALLY, THE GOVERNOR CALLED IN THE NATIONAL GUARD.
"I THOUGHT WE'D BE SAFE THEN. THESE WERE *HEROES,* MARCHING IN TO SAVE THE DAY."
QUIET NOW. KEEP US COVERED.
GO. *GO.*
HEY-- *THEY'RE GETTING LOOSE!*
EVERYONE DOWN, HURRY!
RAKKAKRAKKA
NO!
DON'T KILL THEM YET. THEY AREN'T VALUABLE TO US DEAD. BESIDES--

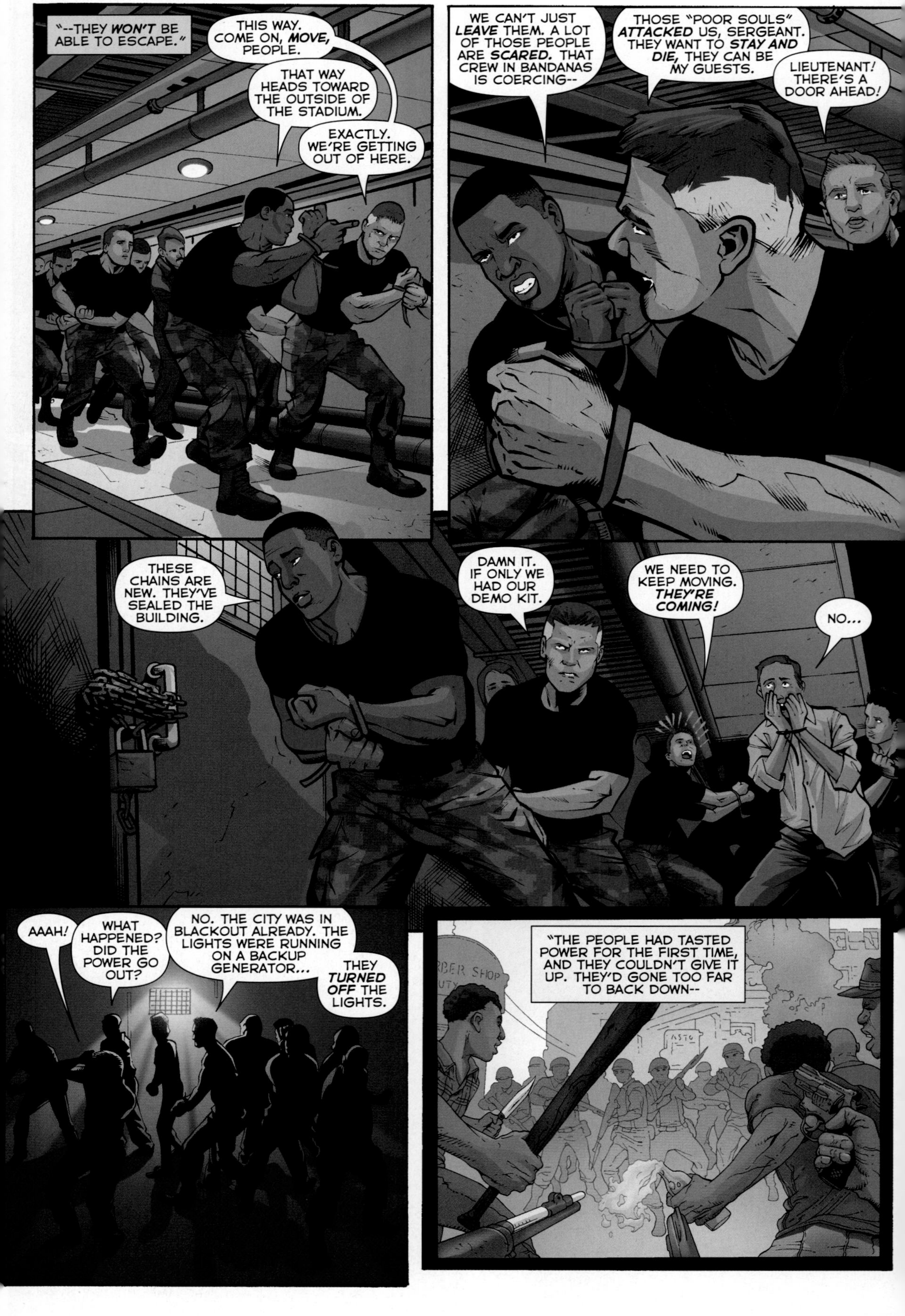
"--THEY WON'T BE ABLE TO ESCAPE."
THIS WAY. COME ON, MOVE, PEOPLE.
THAT WAY HEADS TOWARD THE OUTSIDE OF THE STADIUM.
EXACTLY. WE'RE GETTING OUT OF HERE.
WE CAN'T JUST LEAVE THEM. A LOT OF THOSE PEOPLE ARE SCARED. THAT CREW IN BANDANAS IS COERCING--
THOSE "POOR SOULS" ATTACKED US, SERGEANT. THEY WANT TO STAY AND DIE, THEY CAN BE MY GUESTS.
LIEUTENANT! THERE'S A DOOR AHEAD!
THESE CHAINS ARE NEW. THEY'VE SEALED THE BUILDING.
DAMN IT. IF ONLY WE HAD OUR DEMO KIT.
WE NEED TO KEEP MOVING. THEY'RE COMING!
NO...
AAAH!
WHAT HAPPENED? DID THE POWER GO OUT?
NO. THE CITY WAS IN BLACKOUT ALREADY. THE LIGHTS WERE RUNNING ON A BACKUP GENERATOR...
THEY TURNED OFF THE LIGHTS.
"THE PEOPLE HAD TASTED POWER FOR THE FIRST TIME, AND THEY COULDN'T GIVE IT UP. THEY'D GONE TOO FAR TO BACK DOWN--

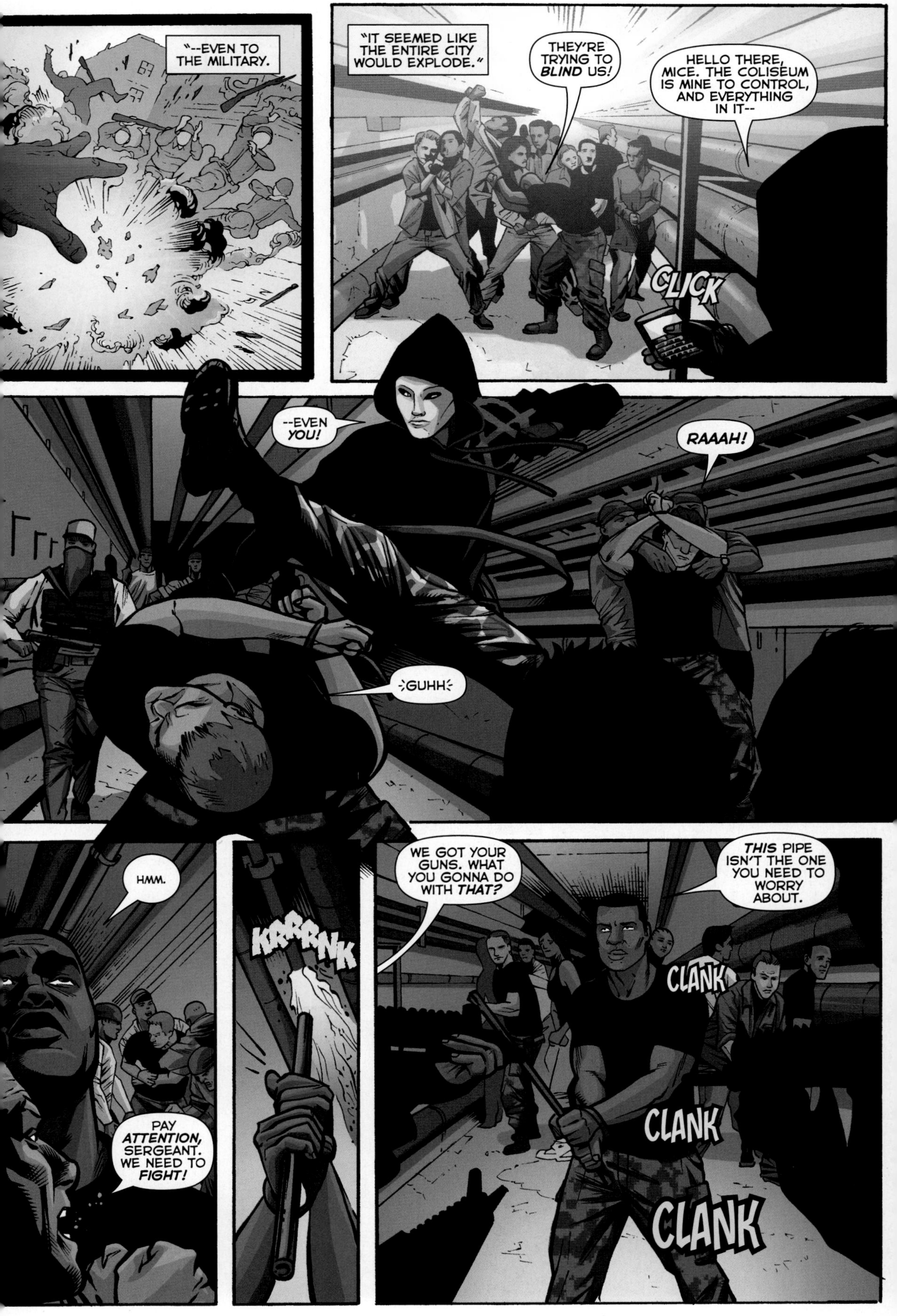
"--EVEN TO THE MILITARY.
"IT SEEMED LIKE THE ENTIRE CITY WOULD EXPLODE."
THEY'RE TRYING TO *BLIND* US!
HELLO THERE, MICE. THE COLISEUM IS MINE TO CONTROL, AND EVERYTHING IN IT--
CLICK
--EVEN *YOU!*
RAAAH!
GUHH
HMM.
PAY *ATTENTION,* SERGEANT. WE NEED TO *FIGHT!*
KRRRNK
WE GOT YOUR GUNS. WHAT YOU GONNA DO WITH *THAT?*
THIS PIPE ISN'T THE ONE YOU NEED TO WORRY ABOUT.
CLANK
CLANK
CLANK

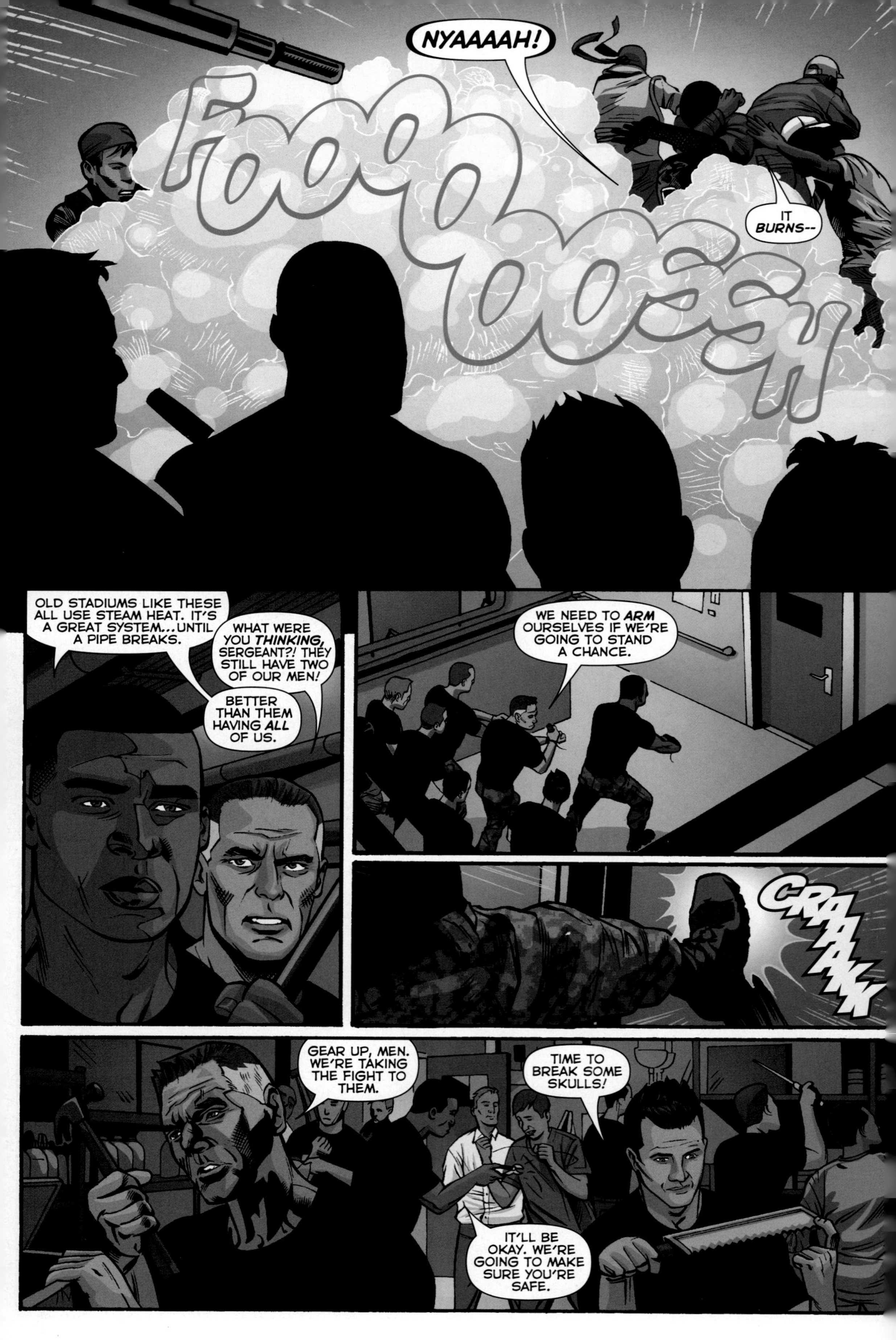
NYAAAAH!
FOOOOOOSSH
IT BURNS--
OLD STADIUMS LIKE THESE ALL USE STEAM HEAT. IT'S A GREAT SYSTEM...UNTIL A PIPE BREAKS.
WHAT WERE YOU THINKING, SERGEANT?! THEY STILL HAVE TWO OF OUR MEN!
BETTER THAN THEM HAVING ALL OF US.
WE NEED TO ARM OURSELVES IF WE'RE GOING TO STAND A CHANCE.
CRAAAKK
GEAR UP, MEN. WE'RE TAKING THE FIGHT TO THEM.
TIME TO BREAK SOME SKULLS!
IT'LL BE OKAY. WE'RE GOING TO MAKE SURE YOU'RE SAFE.

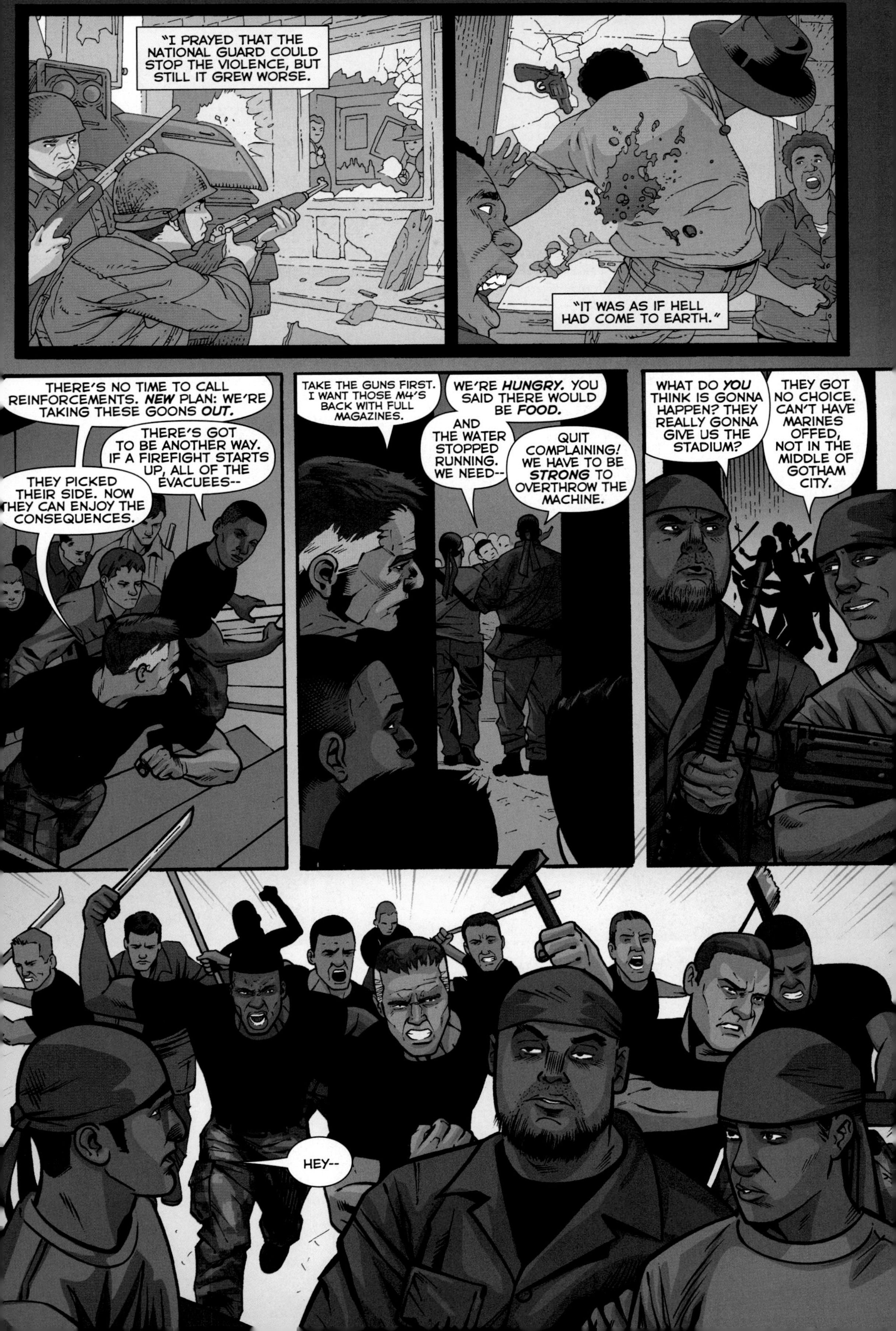
"I PRAYED THAT THE NATIONAL GUARD COULD STOP THE VIOLENCE, BUT STILL IT GREW WORSE.
"IT WAS AS IF HELL HAD COME TO EARTH."
THERE'S NO TIME TO CALL REINFORCEMENTS. NEW PLAN: WE'RE TAKING THESE GOONS OUT.
THERE'S GOT TO BE ANOTHER WAY. IF A FIREFIGHT STARTS UP, ALL OF THE EVACUEES--
THEY PICKED THEIR SIDE. NOW THEY CAN ENJOY THE CONSEQUENCES.
TAKE THE GUNS FIRST. I WANT THOSE M4'S BACK WITH FULL MAGAZINES.
WE'RE HUNGRY. YOU SAID THERE WOULD BE FOOD.
AND THE WATER STOPPED RUNNING. WE NEED--
QUIT COMPLAINING! WE HAVE TO BE STRONG TO OVERTHROW THE MACHINE.
WHAT DO YOU THINK IS GONNA HAPPEN? THEY REALLY GONNA GIVE US THE STADIUM?
THEY GOT NO CHOICE. CAN'T HAVE MARINES OFFED, NOT IN THE MIDDLE OF GOTHAM CITY.
HEY--

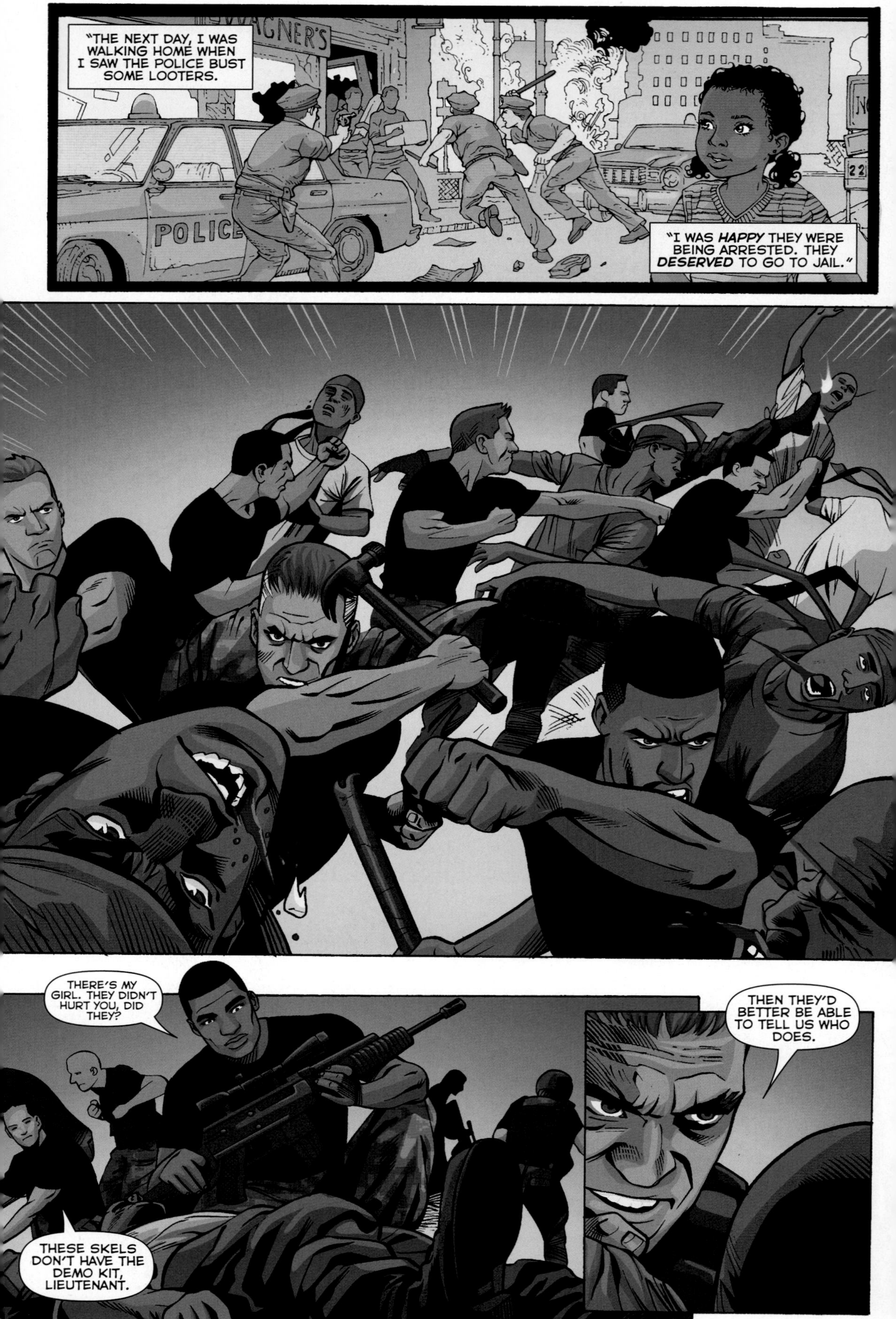
"THE NEXT DAY, I WAS WALKING HOME WHEN I SAW THE POLICE BUST SOME LOOTERS.
WAGNER'S
POLICE
"I WAS *HAPPY* THEY WERE BEING ARRESTED. THEY *DESERVED* TO GO TO JAIL."
THERE'S MY GIRL. THEY DIDN'T HURT YOU, DID THEY?
THESE SKELS DON'T HAVE THE DEMO KIT, LIEUTENANT.
THEN THEY'D BETTER BE ABLE TO TELL US WHO DOES.

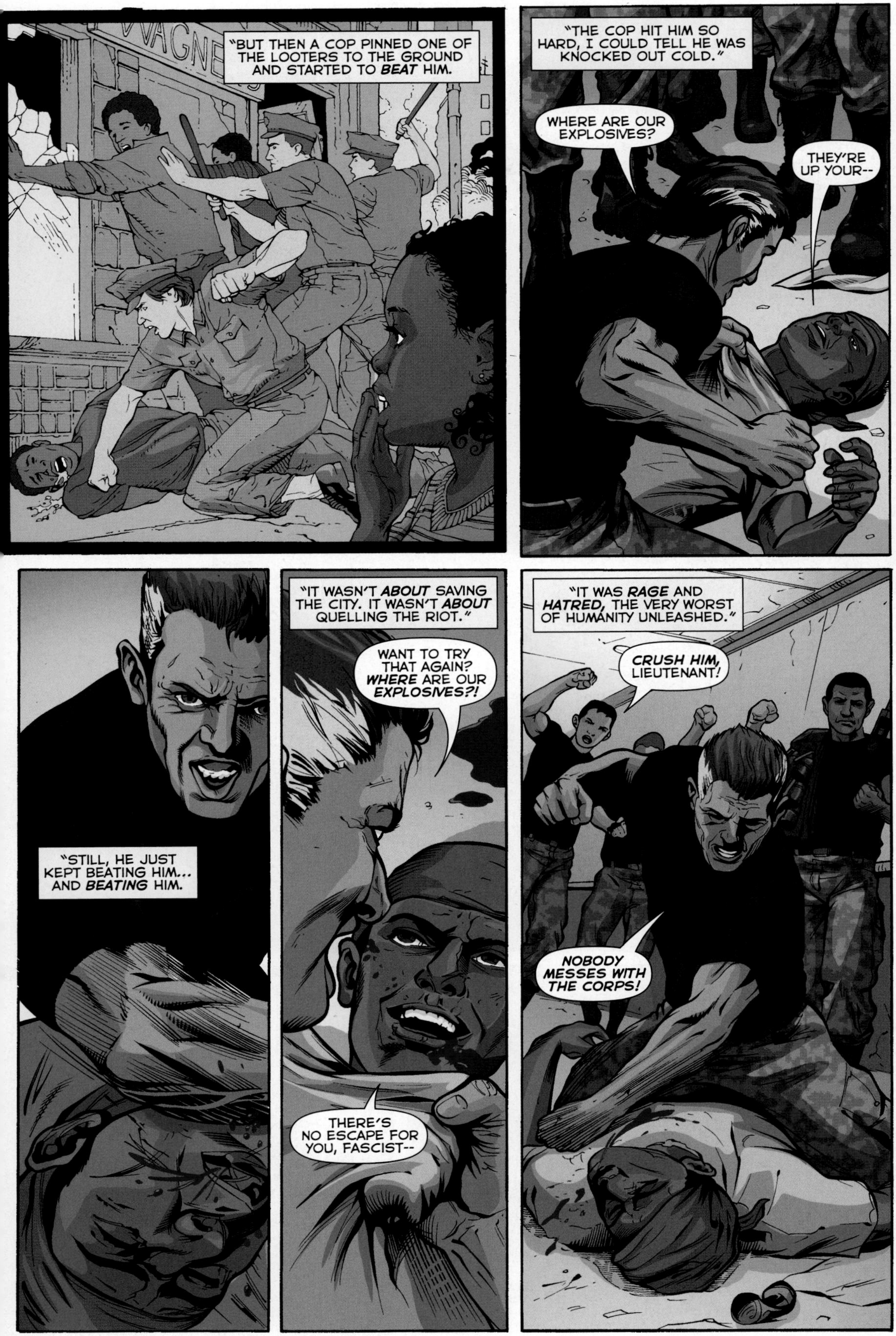
"BUT THEN A COP PINNED ONE OF THE LOOTERS TO THE GROUND AND STARTED TO *BEAT* HIM.
"THE COP HIT HIM SO HARD, I COULD TELL HE WAS KNOCKED OUT COLD."
WHERE ARE OUR EXPLOSIVES?
THEY'RE UP YOUR--
"STILL, HE JUST KEPT BEATING HIM... AND *BEATING* HIM.
"IT WASN'T *ABOUT* SAVING THE CITY. IT WASN'T *ABOUT* QUELLING THE RIOT."
WANT TO TRY THAT AGAIN? *WHERE* ARE OUR *EXPLOSIVES?!*
THERE'S NO ESCAPE FOR YOU, FASCIST--
"IT WAS *RAGE* AND *HATRED,* THE VERY WORST OF HUMANITY UNLEASHED."
CRUSH HIM, LIEUTENANT!
NOBODY MESSES WITH THE CORPS!

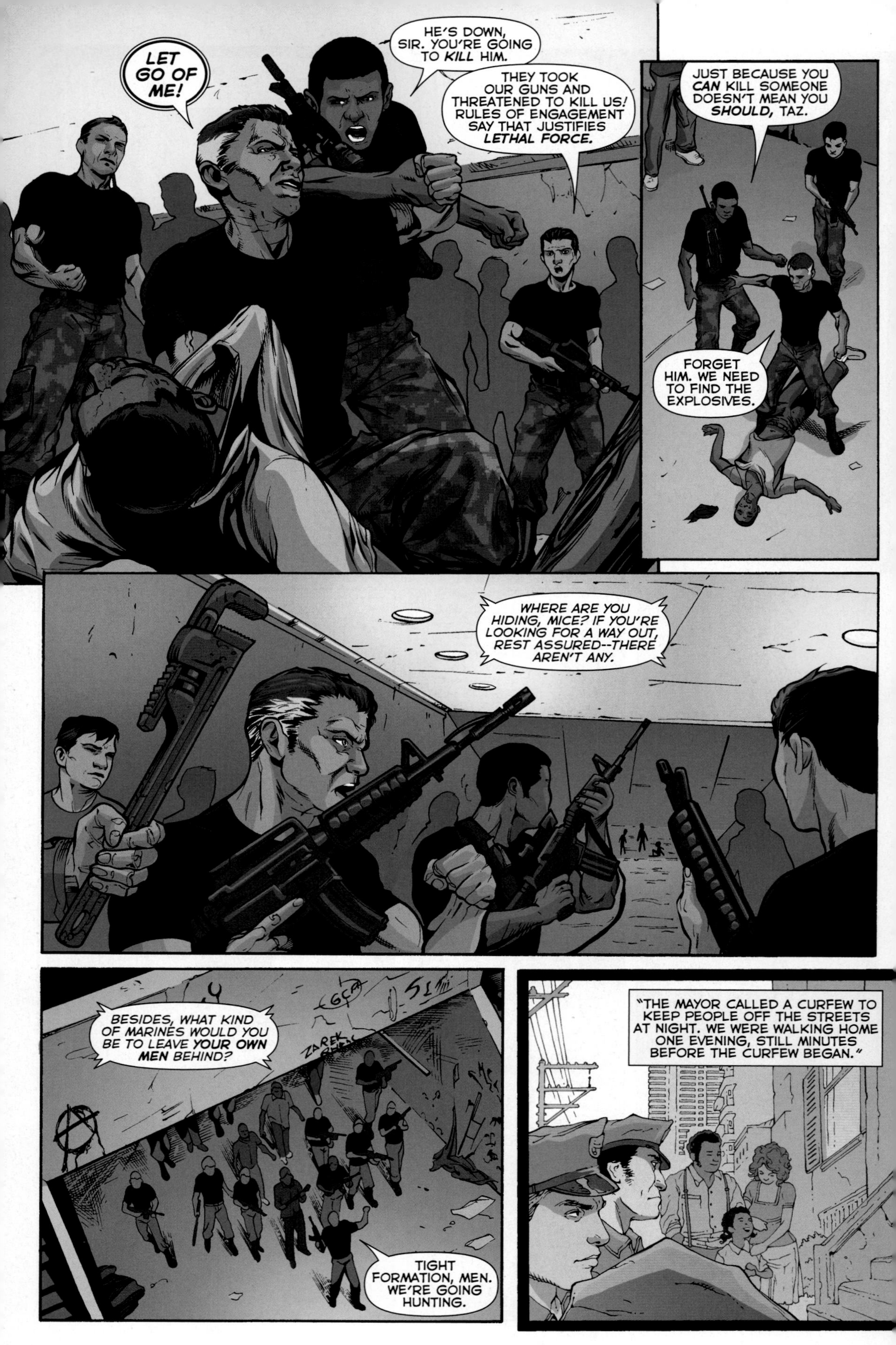
LET GO OF ME!
HE'S DOWN, SIR. YOU'RE GOING TO KILL HIM.
THEY TOOK OUR GUNS AND THREATENED TO KILL US! RULES OF ENGAGEMENT SAY THAT JUSTIFIES LETHAL FORCE.
JUST BECAUSE YOU CAN KILL SOMEONE DOESN'T MEAN YOU SHOULD, TAZ.
FORGET HIM. WE NEED TO FIND THE EXPLOSIVES.
WHERE ARE YOU HIDING, MICE? IF YOU'RE LOOKING FOR A WAY OUT, REST ASSURED--THERE AREN'T ANY.
BESIDES, WHAT KIND OF MARINES WOULD YOU BE TO LEAVE YOUR OWN MEN BEHIND?
TIGHT FORMATION, MEN. WE'RE GOING HUNTING.
"THE MAYOR CALLED A CURFEW TO KEEP PEOPLE OFF THE STREETS AT NIGHT. WE WERE WALKING HOME ONE EVENING, STILL MINUTES BEFORE THE CURFEW BEGAN."

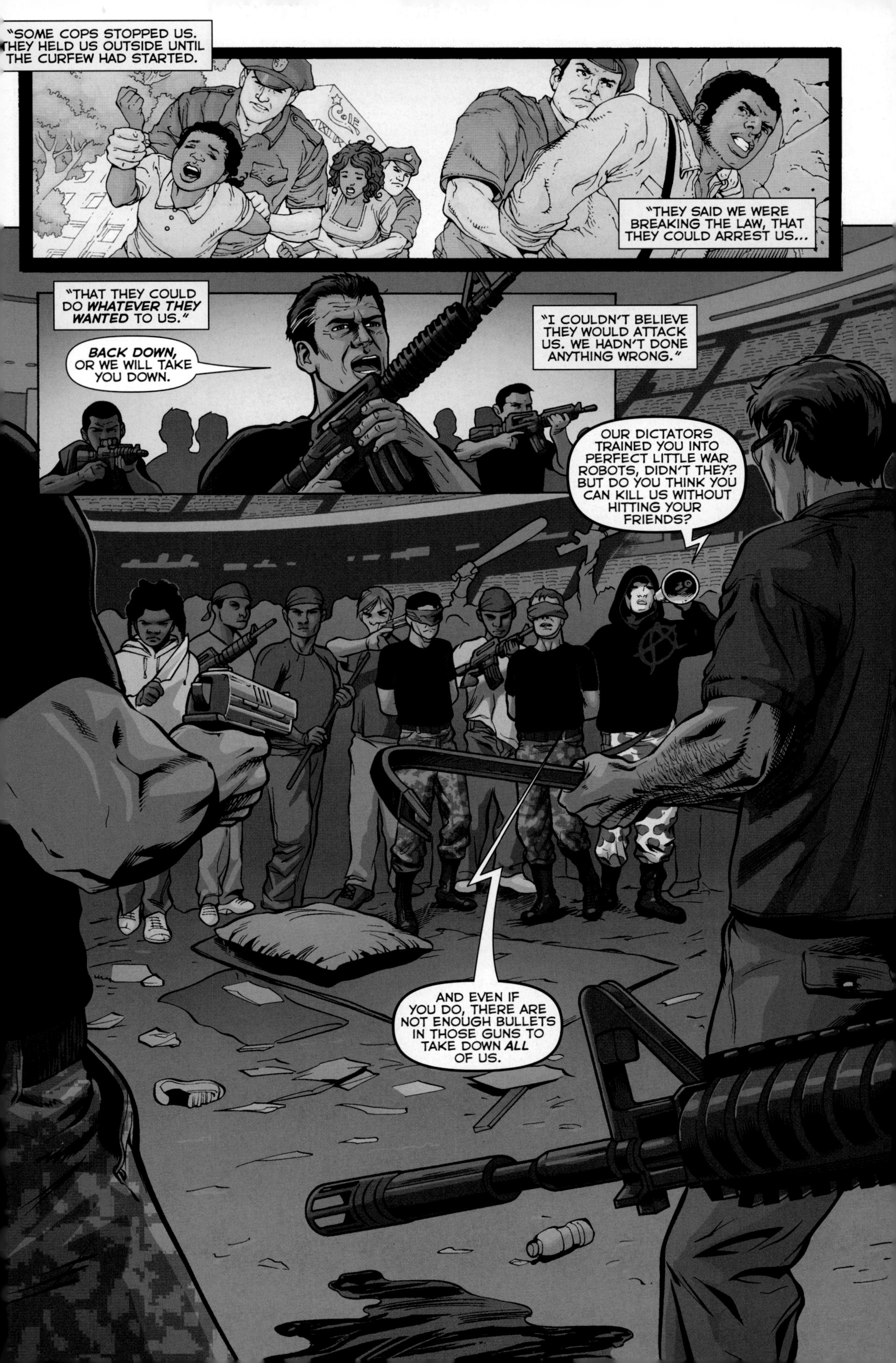
"SOME COPS STOPPED US. THEY HELD US OUTSIDE UNTIL THE CURFEW HAD STARTED.
"THEY SAID WE WERE BREAKING THE LAW, THAT THEY COULD ARREST US...
"THAT THEY COULD DO *WHATEVER THEY WANTED* TO US."
BACK DOWN, OR WE WILL TAKE YOU DOWN.
"I COULDN'T BELIEVE THEY WOULD ATTACK US. WE HADN'T DONE ANYTHING WRONG."
OUR DICTATORS TRAINED YOU INTO PERFECT LITTLE WAR ROBOTS, DIDN'T THEY? BUT DO YOU THINK YOU CAN KILL US WITHOUT HITTING YOUR FRIENDS?
AND EVEN IF YOU DO, THERE ARE NOT ENOUGH BULLETS IN THOSE GUNS TO TAKE DOWN *ALL* OF US.

"THERE COULD BE NO JUSTICE, NO FAIRNESS, NO *HOPE*."

BE READY TO *FIRE*, MEN!

THEY'RE BEING MANIPULATED. WE NEED TO TAKE OUT THE *LEADER*, NOT THE *FOLLOWERS*--

SHUT YOUR MOUTH AND *POINT YOUR RIFLE*, SERGEANT!

AIM FOR *CENTER MASS!*

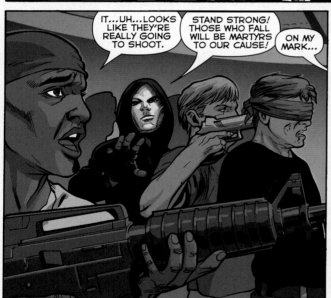

IT...UH...LOOKS LIKE THEY'RE REALLY GOING TO SHOOT.

STAND STRONG! THOSE WHO FALL WILL BE MARTYRS TO OUR CAUSE!

ON MY MARK...

READY...

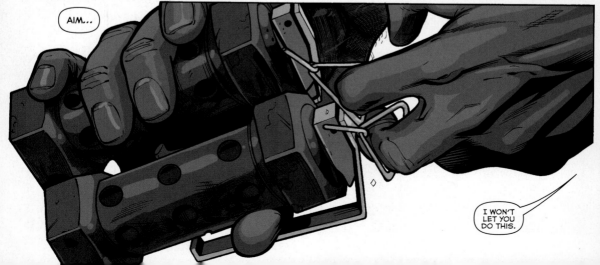

AIM...

I WON'T LET YOU DO THIS.

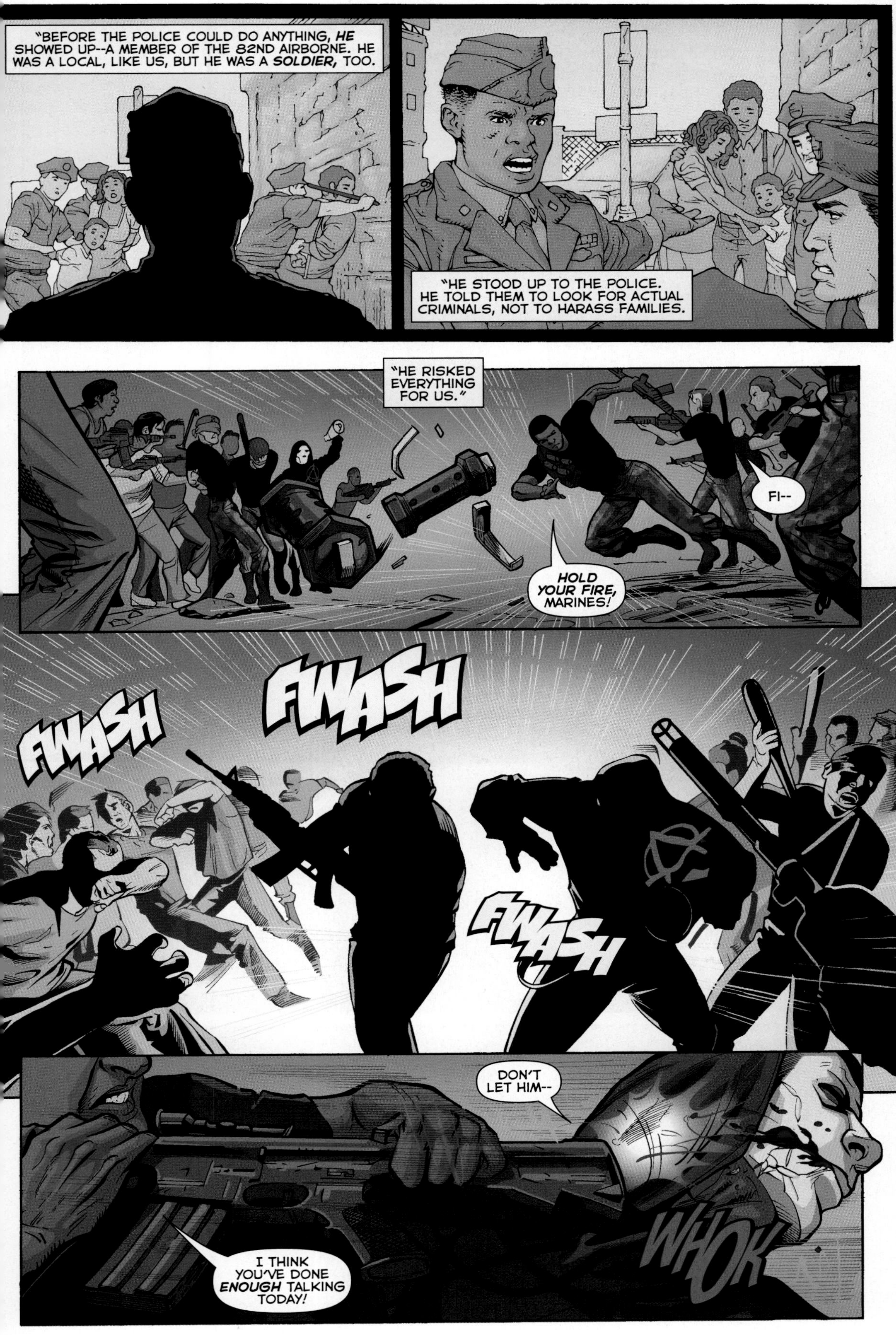

"BEFORE THE POLICE COULD DO ANYTHING, *HE* SHOWED UP--A MEMBER OF THE 82ND AIRBORNE. HE WAS A LOCAL, LIKE US, BUT HE WAS A *SOLDIER,* TOO.
"HE STOOD UP TO THE POLICE. HE TOLD THEM TO LOOK FOR ACTUAL CRIMINALS, NOT TO HARASS FAMILIES.
"HE RISKED EVERYTHING FOR US."
FI--
HOLD YOUR FIRE, MARINES!
FWASH
FWASH
FWASH
DON'T LET HIM--
I THINK YOU'VE DONE *ENOUGH* TALKING TODAY!
WHOK

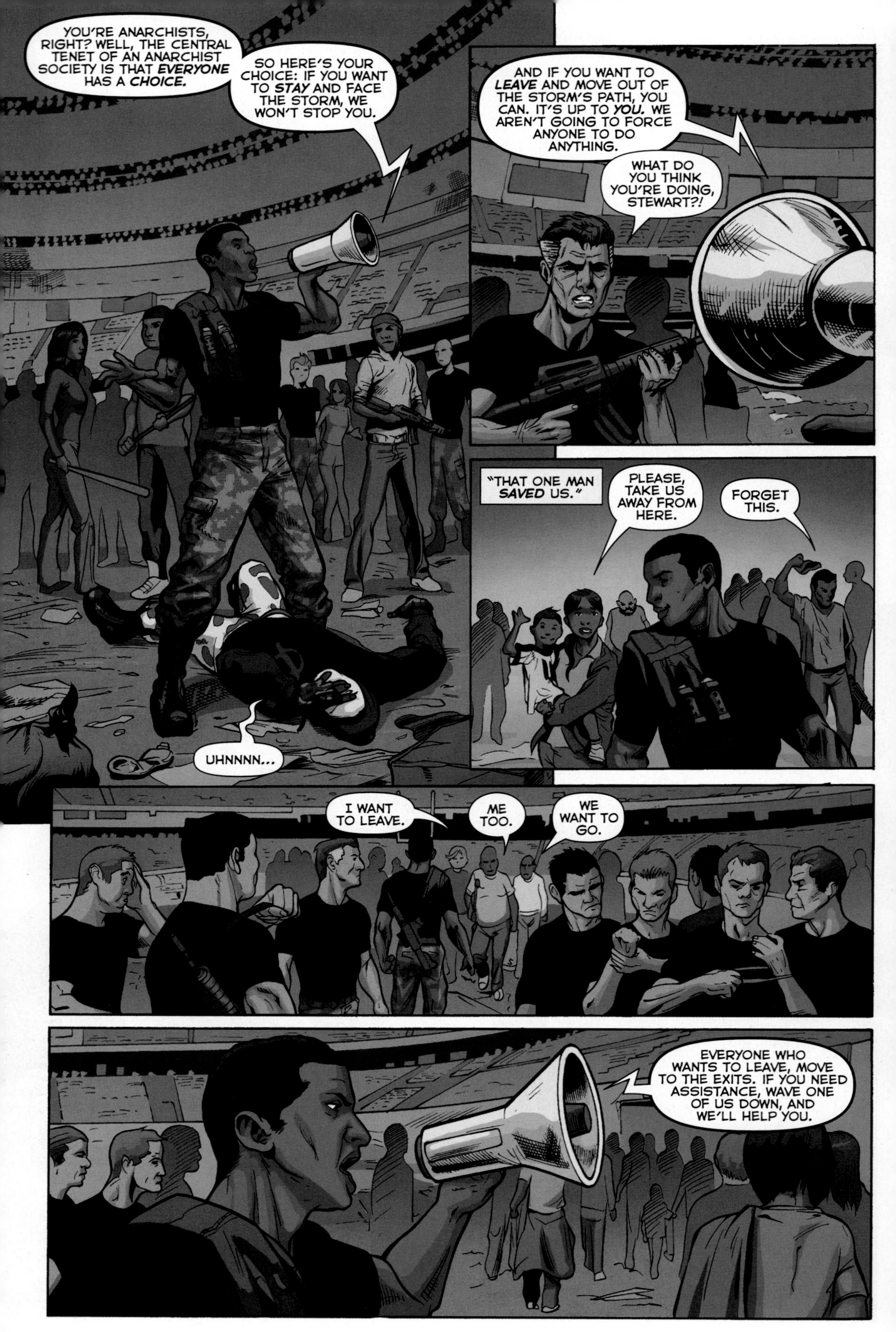
YOU'RE ANARCHISTS, RIGHT? WELL, THE CENTRAL TENET OF AN ANARCHIST SOCIETY IS THAT EVERYONE HAS A CHOICE.
SO HERE'S YOUR CHOICE: IF YOU WANT TO STAY AND FACE THE STORM, WE WON'T STOP YOU.
UHNNNN...
AND IF YOU WANT TO LEAVE AND MOVE OUT OF THE STORM'S PATH, YOU CAN. IT'S UP TO YOU. WE AREN'T GOING TO FORCE ANYONE TO DO ANYTHING.
WHAT DO YOU THINK YOU'RE DOING, STEWART?!
"THAT ONE MAN SAVED US."
PLEASE, TAKE US AWAY FROM HERE.
FORGET THIS.
I WANT TO LEAVE.
ME TOO.
WE WANT TO GO.
EVERYONE WHO WANTS TO LEAVE, MOVE TO THE EXITS. IF YOU NEED ASSISTANCE, WAVE ONE OF US DOWN, AND WE'LL HELP YOU.

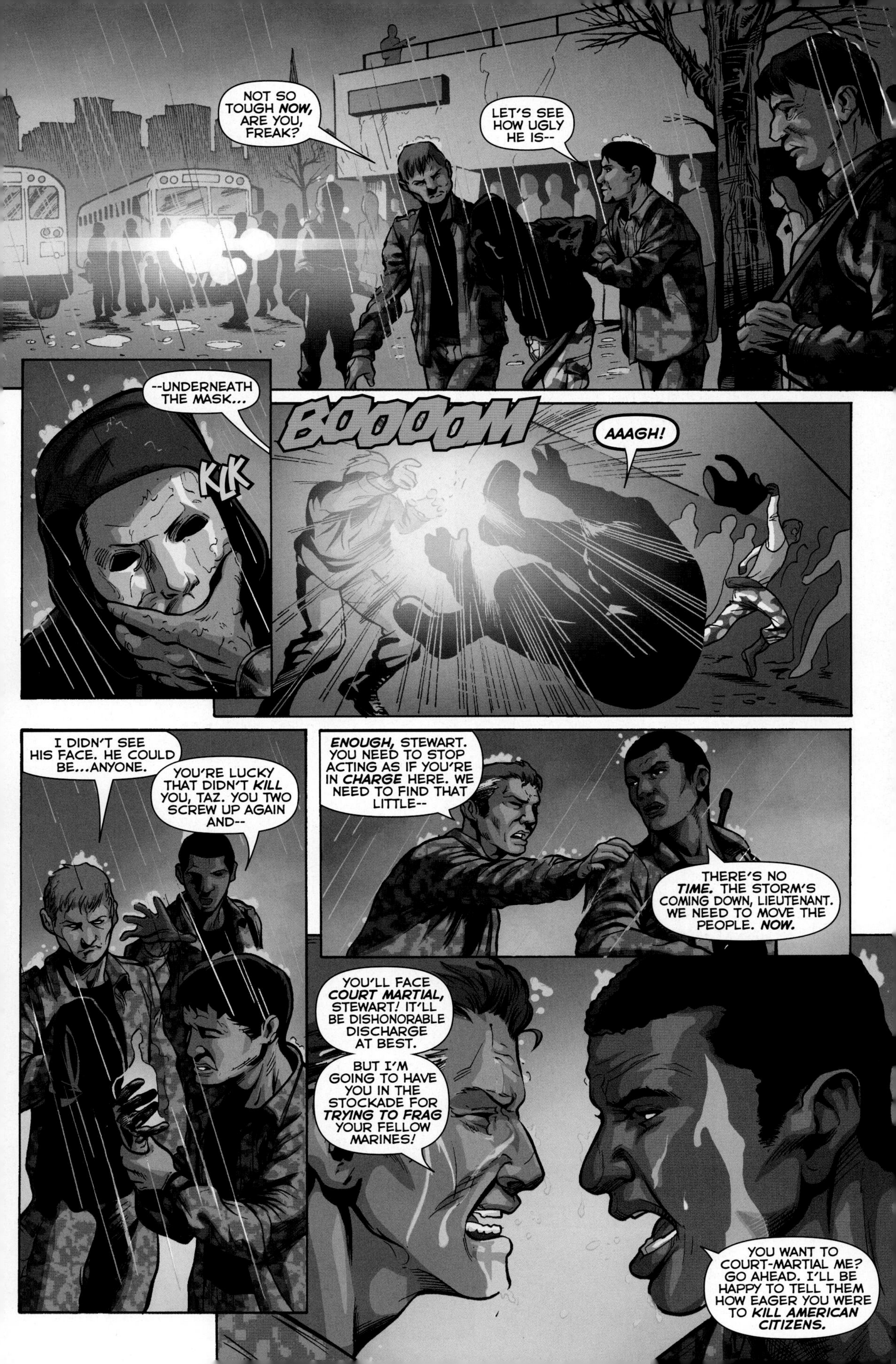
NOT SO TOUGH NOW, ARE YOU, FREAK?
LET'S SEE HOW UGLY HE IS--
--UNDERNEATH THE MASK...
KLK
BOOOOM
AAAGH!
I DIDN'T SEE HIS FACE. HE COULD BE...ANYONE.
YOU'RE LUCKY THAT DIDN'T KILL YOU, TAZ. YOU TWO SCREW UP AGAIN AND--
ENOUGH, STEWART. YOU NEED TO STOP ACTING AS IF YOU'RE IN CHARGE HERE. WE NEED TO FIND THAT LITTLE--
THERE'S NO TIME. THE STORM'S COMING DOWN, LIEUTENANT. WE NEED TO MOVE THE PEOPLE. NOW.
YOU'LL FACE COURT MARTIAL, STEWART! IT'LL BE DISHONORABLE DISCHARGE AT BEST.
BUT I'M GOING TO HAVE YOU IN THE STOCKADE FOR TRYING TO FRAG YOUR FELLOW MARINES!
YOU WANT TO COURT-MARTIAL ME? GO AHEAD. I'LL BE HAPPY TO TELL THEM HOW EAGER YOU WERE TO KILL AMERICAN CITIZENS.

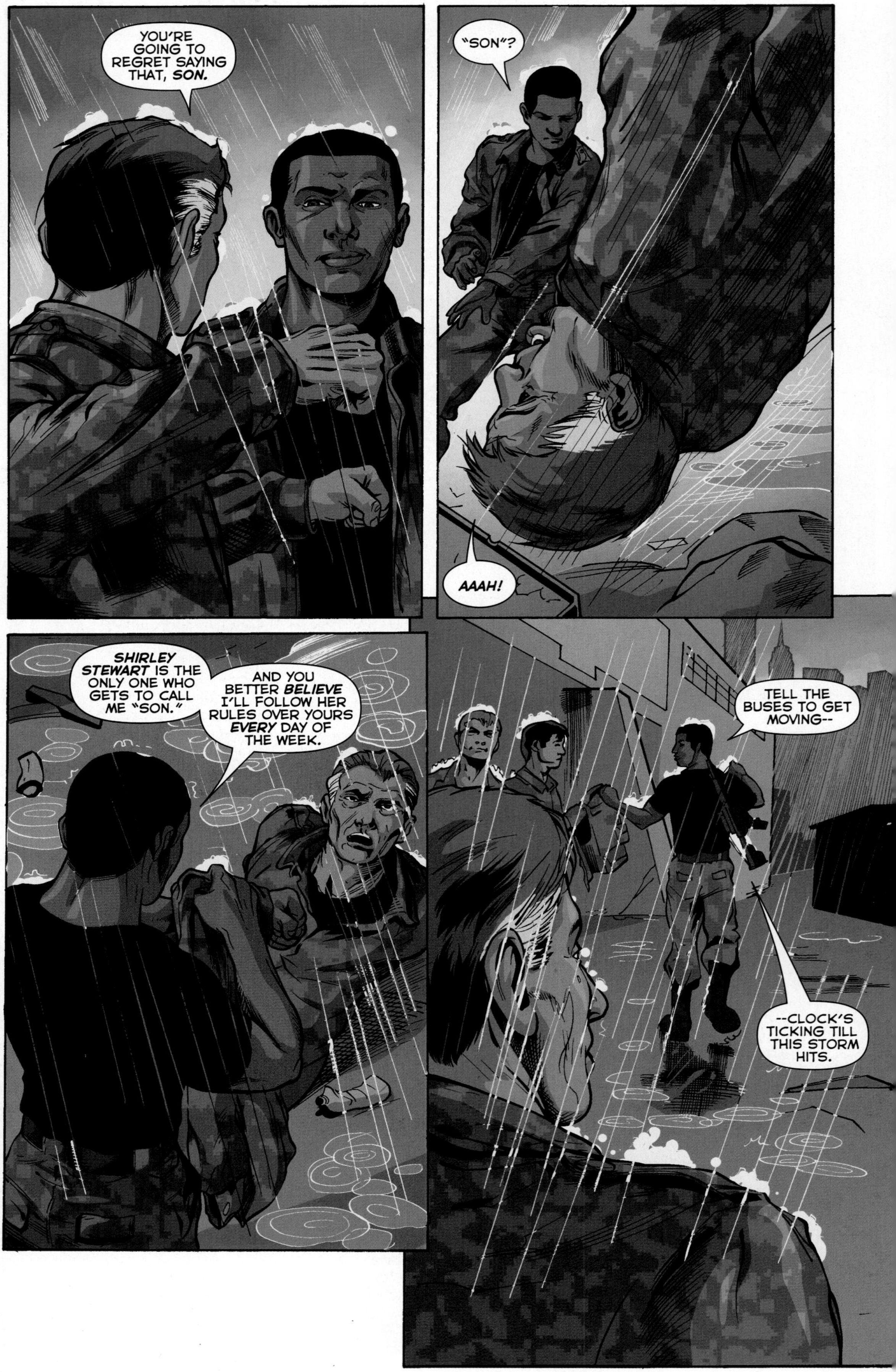
YOU'RE GOING TO REGRET SAYING THAT, SON.
"SON"?
AAAH!
SHIRLEY STEWART IS THE ONLY ONE WHO GETS TO CALL ME "SON."
AND YOU BETTER BELIEVE I'LL FOLLOW HER RULES OVER YOURS EVERY DAY OF THE WEEK.
TELL THE BUSES TO GET MOVING--
--CLOCK'S TICKING TILL THIS STORM HITS.

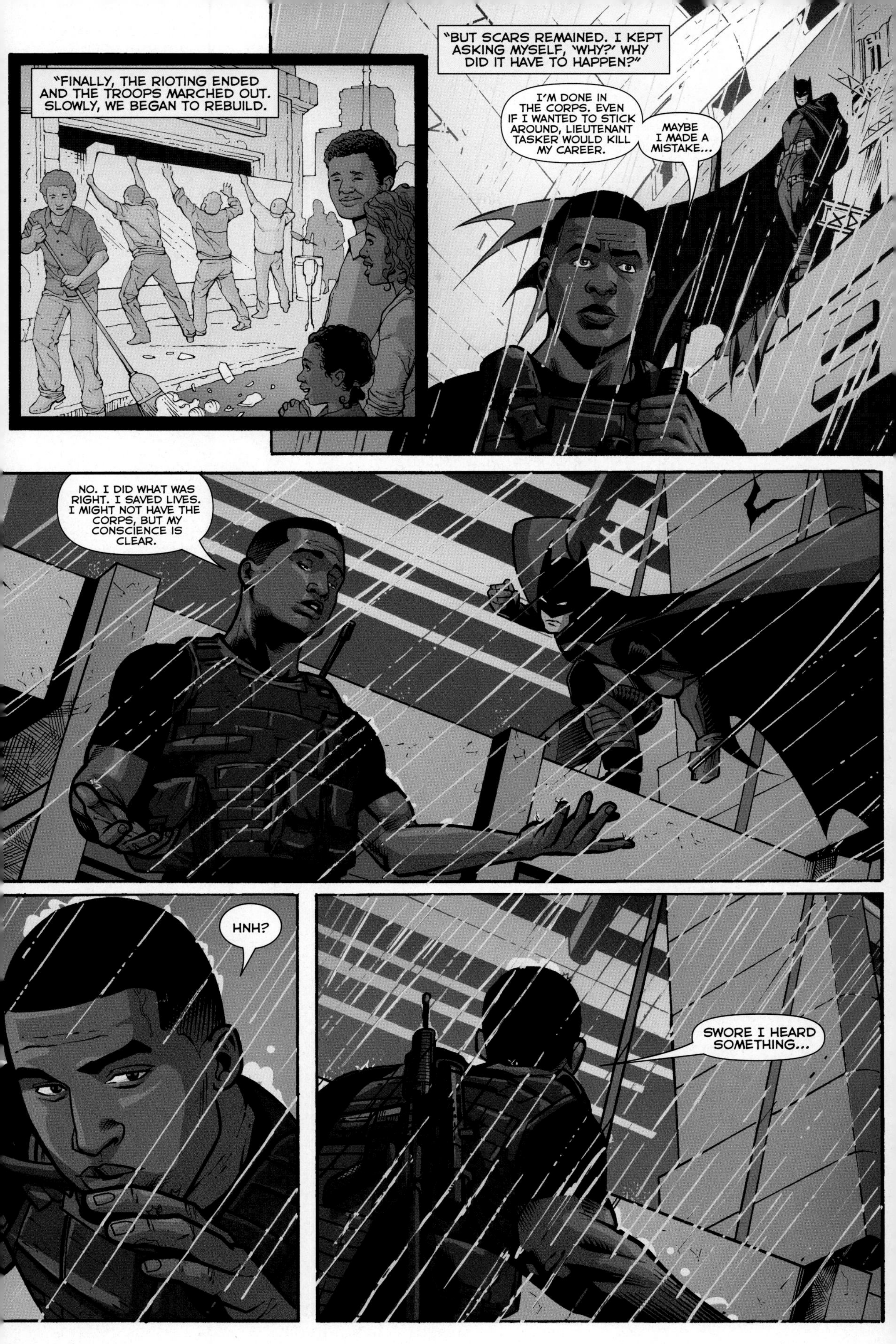
"FINALLY, THE RIOTING ENDED AND THE TROOPS MARCHED OUT. SLOWLY, WE BEGAN TO REBUILD.
"BUT SCARS REMAINED. I KEPT ASKING MYSELF, 'WHY?' WHY DID IT HAVE TO HAPPEN?"
I'M DONE IN THE CORPS. EVEN IF I WANTED TO STICK AROUND, LIEUTENANT TASKER WOULD KILL MY CAREER.
MAYBE I MADE A MISTAKE...
NO. I DID WHAT WAS RIGHT. I SAVED LIVES. I MIGHT NOT HAVE THE CORPS, BUT MY CONSCIENCE IS CLEAR.
HNH?
SWORE I HEARD SOMETHING...

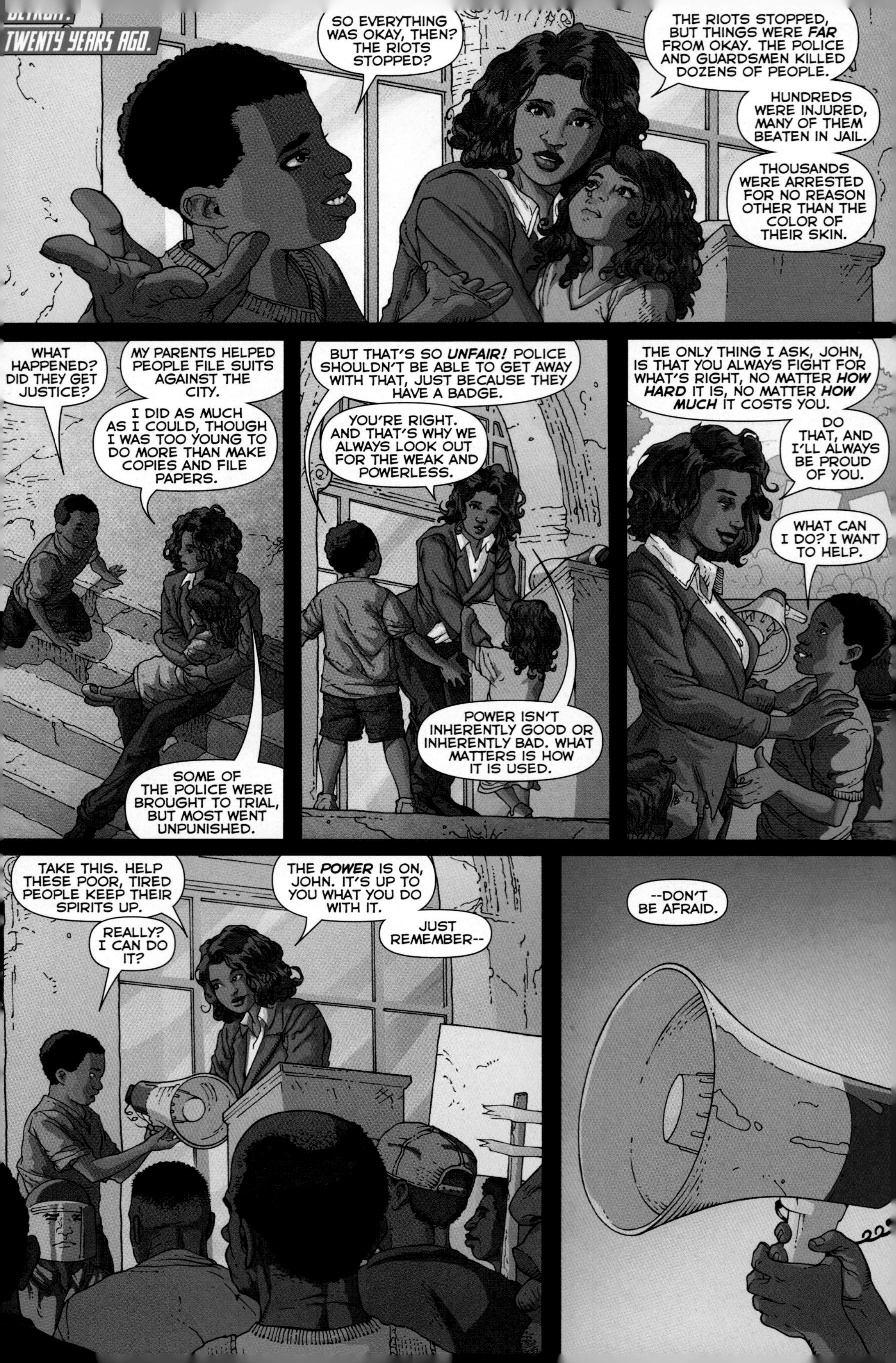
TWENTY YEARS AGO.
SO EVERYTHING WAS OKAY, THEN? THE RIOTS STOPPED?
THE RIOTS STOPPED, BUT THINGS WERE FAR FROM OKAY. THE POLICE AND GUARDSMEN KILLED DOZENS OF PEOPLE.
HUNDREDS WERE INJURED, MANY OF THEM BEATEN IN JAIL.
THOUSANDS WERE ARRESTED FOR NO REASON OTHER THAN THE COLOR OF THEIR SKIN.
WHAT HAPPENED? DID THEY GET JUSTICE?
MY PARENTS HELPED PEOPLE FILE SUITS AGAINST THE CITY.
I DID AS MUCH AS I COULD, THOUGH I WAS TOO YOUNG TO DO MORE THAN MAKE COPIES AND FILE PAPERS.
SOME OF THE POLICE WERE BROUGHT TO TRIAL, BUT MOST WENT UNPUNISHED.
BUT THAT'S SO UNFAIR! POLICE SHOULDN'T BE ABLE TO GET AWAY WITH THAT, JUST BECAUSE THEY HAVE A BADGE.
YOU'RE RIGHT. AND THAT'S WHY WE ALWAYS LOOK OUT FOR THE WEAK AND POWERLESS.
POWER ISN'T INHERENTLY GOOD OR INHERENTLY BAD. WHAT MATTERS IS HOW IT IS USED.
THE ONLY THING I ASK, JOHN, IS THAT YOU ALWAYS FIGHT FOR WHAT'S RIGHT, NO MATTER HOW HARD IT IS, NO MATTER HOW MUCH IT COSTS YOU.
DO THAT, AND I'LL ALWAYS BE PROUD OF YOU.
WHAT CAN I DO? I WANT TO HELP.
TAKE THIS. HELP THESE POOR, TIRED PEOPLE KEEP THEIR SPIRITS UP.
REALLY? I CAN DO IT?
THE POWER IS ON, JOHN. IT'S UP TO YOU WHAT YOU DO WITH IT.
JUST REMEMBER--
--DON'T BE AFRAID.

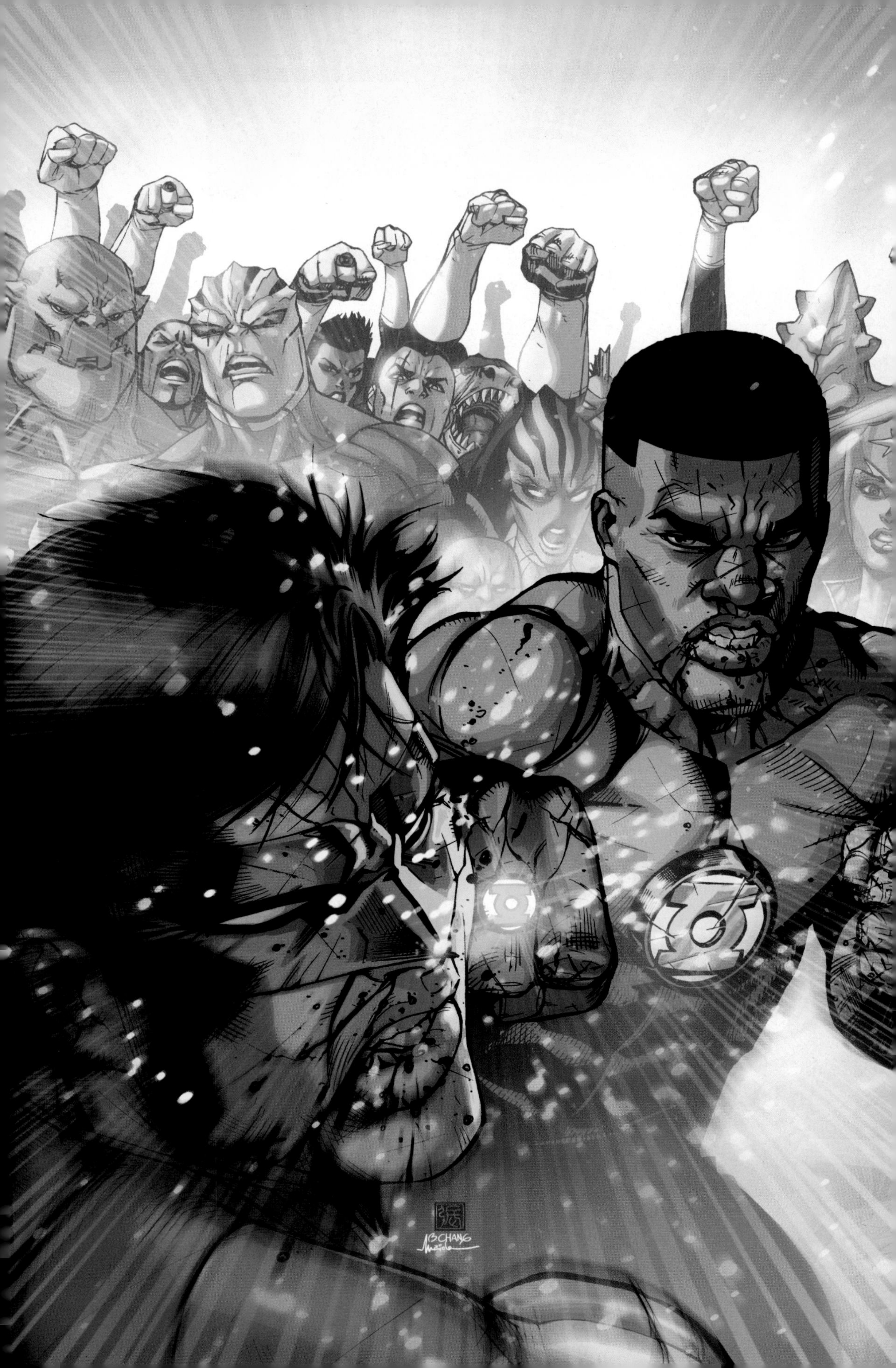

HOMECOMING

VAN JENSEN & ROBERT VENDITTI writers BERNARD CHANG artist cover art by BERNARD CHANG & MARCELO MAIOLO

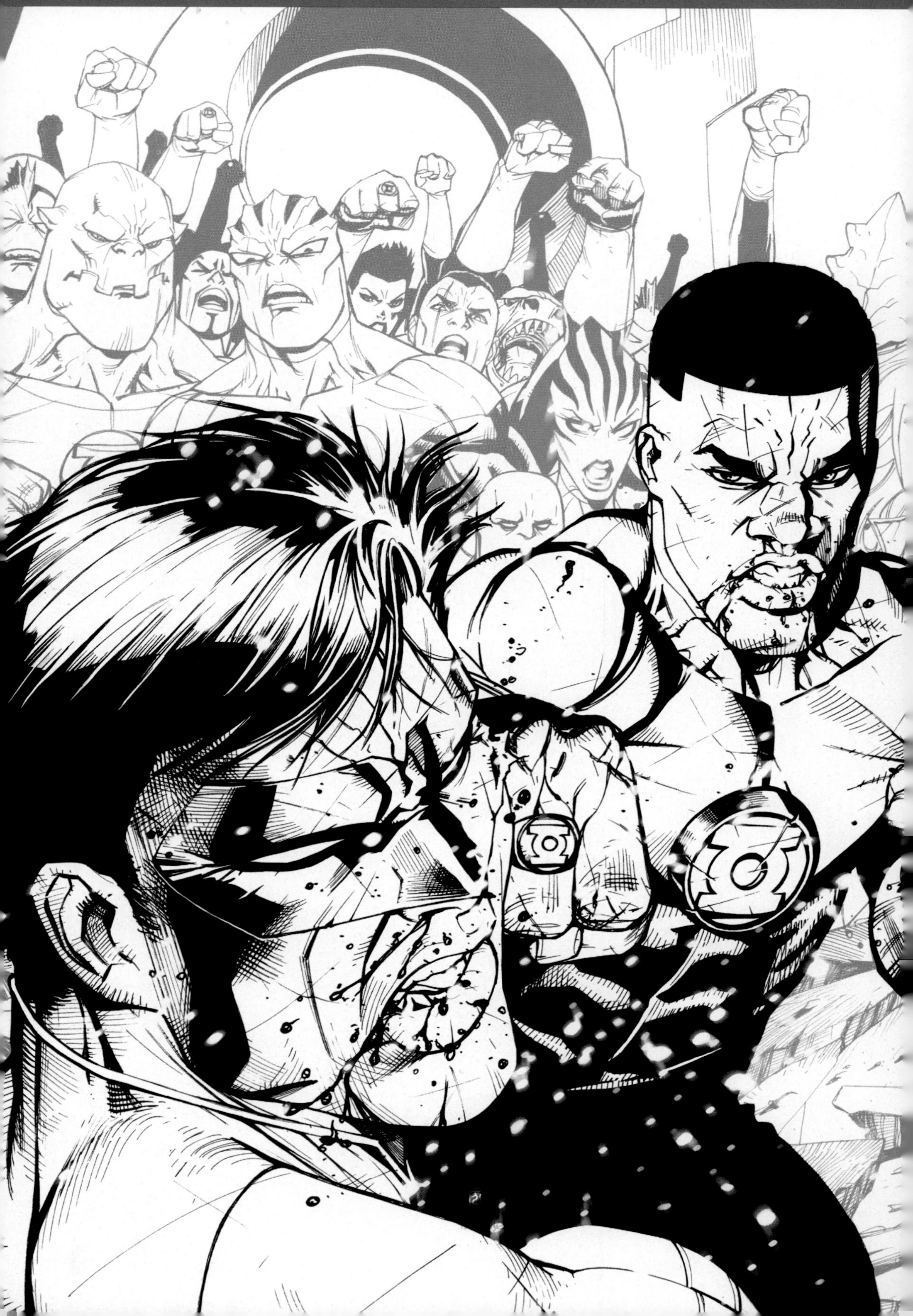

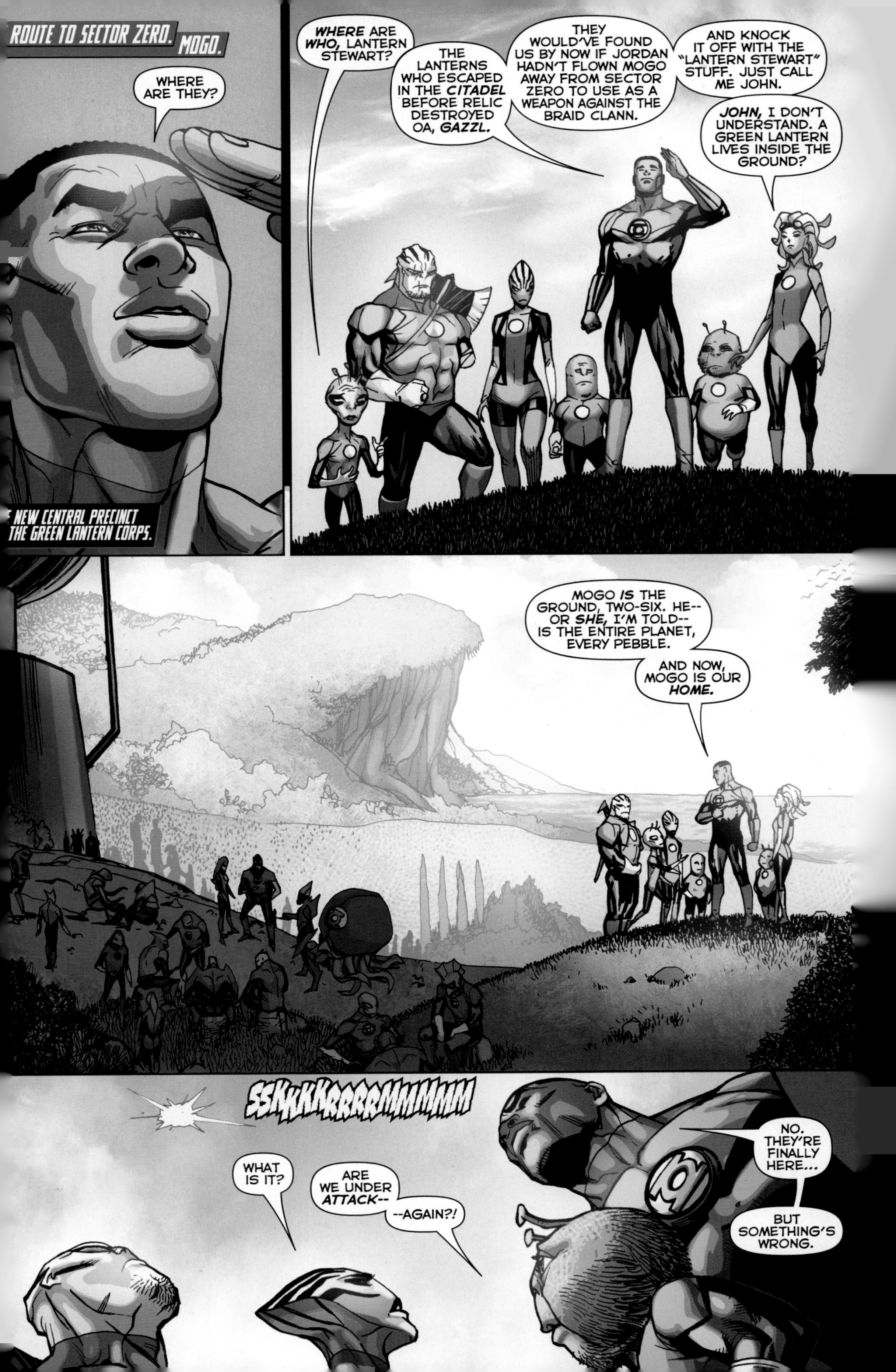
ROUTE TO SECTOR ZERO.
MOGO.
WHERE ARE THEY?
NEW CENTRAL PRECINCT
THE GREEN LANTERN CORPS.
WHERE ARE WHO, LANTERN STEWART?
THE LANTERNS WHO ESCAPED IN THE CITADEL BEFORE RELIC DESTROYED OA, GAZZL.
THEY WOULD'VE FOUND US BY NOW IF JORDAN HADN'T FLOWN MOGO AWAY FROM SECTOR ZERO TO USE AS A WEAPON AGAINST THE BRAID CLANN.
AND KNOCK IT OFF WITH THE "LANTERN STEWART" STUFF. JUST CALL ME JOHN.
JOHN, I DON'T UNDERSTAND. A GREEN LANTERN LIVES INSIDE THE GROUND?
MOGO IS THE GROUND, TWO-SIX. HE-- OR SHE, I'M TOLD-- IS THE ENTIRE PLANET, EVERY PEBBLE.
AND NOW, MOGO IS OUR HOME.
SSKKKKRRRRMMMMM
WHAT IS IT?
ARE WE UNDER ATTACK--
--AGAIN?!
NO. THEY'RE FINALLY HERE...
BUT SOMETHING'S WRONG.

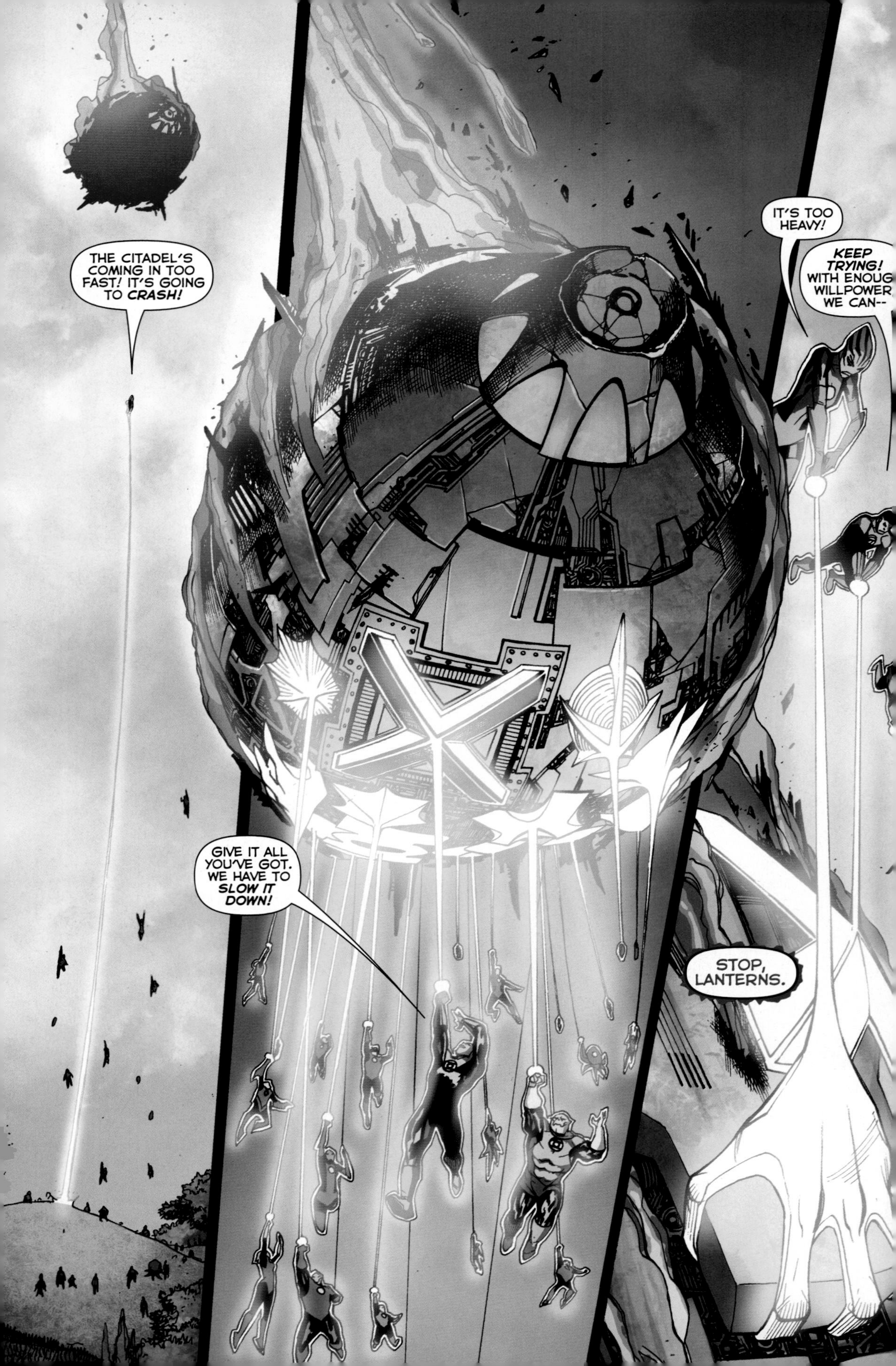
THE CITADEL'S COMING IN TOO FAST! IT'S GOING TO CRASH!
IT'S TOO HEAVY!
KEEP TRYING! WITH ENOUG WILLPOWER WE CAN--
GIVE IT ALL YOU'VE GOT. WE HAVE TO SLOW IT DOWN!
STOP, LANTERNS.

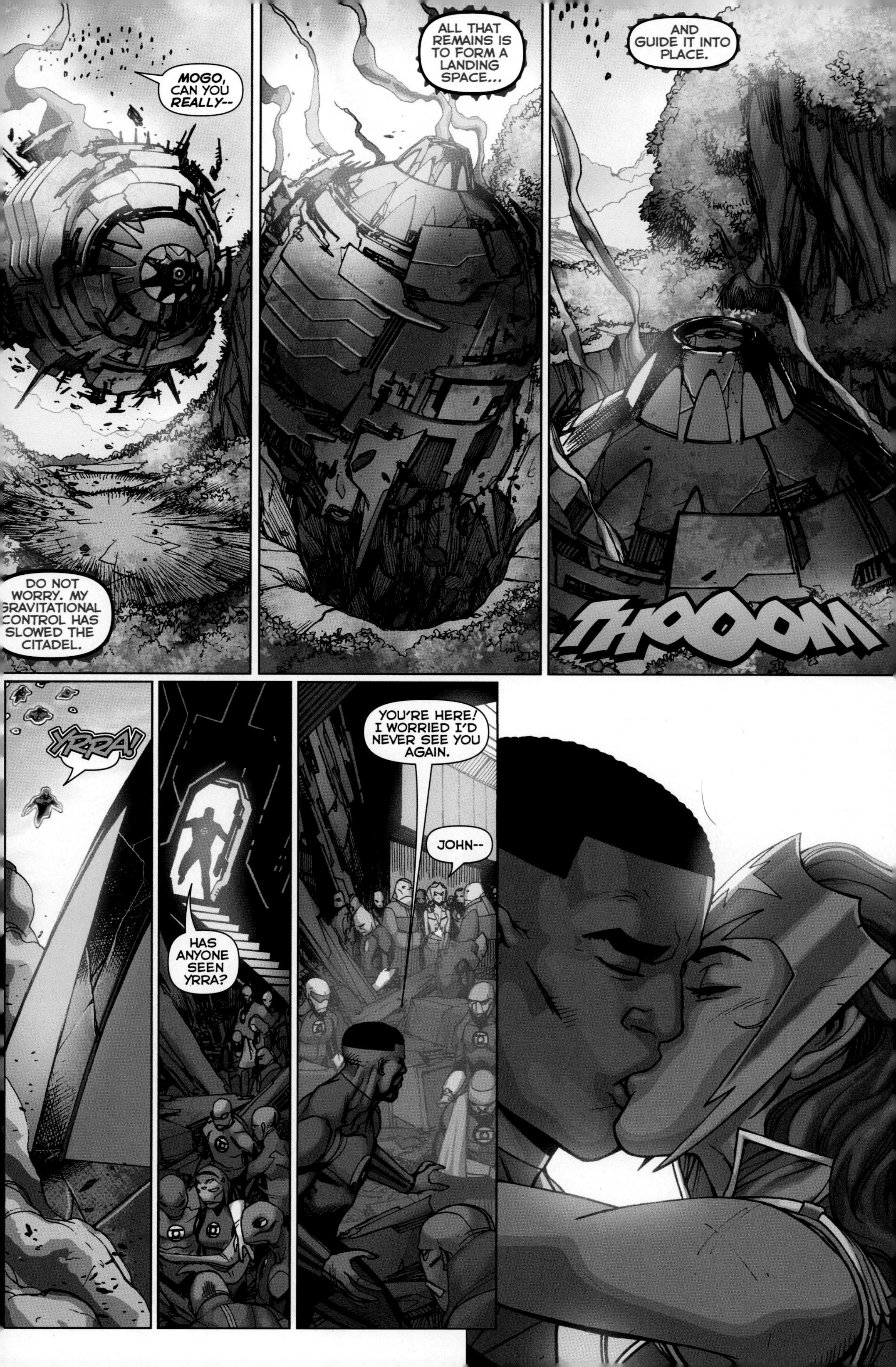
MOGO, CAN YOU REALLY--
DO NOT WORRY. MY GRAVITATIONAL CONTROL HAS SLOWED THE CITADEL.
ALL THAT REMAINS IS TO FORM A LANDING SPACE...
AND GUIDE IT INTO PLACE.
THOOOM
YRRA!
HAS ANYONE SEEN YRRA?
YOU'RE HERE! I WORRIED I'D NEVER SEE YOU AGAIN.
JOHN--

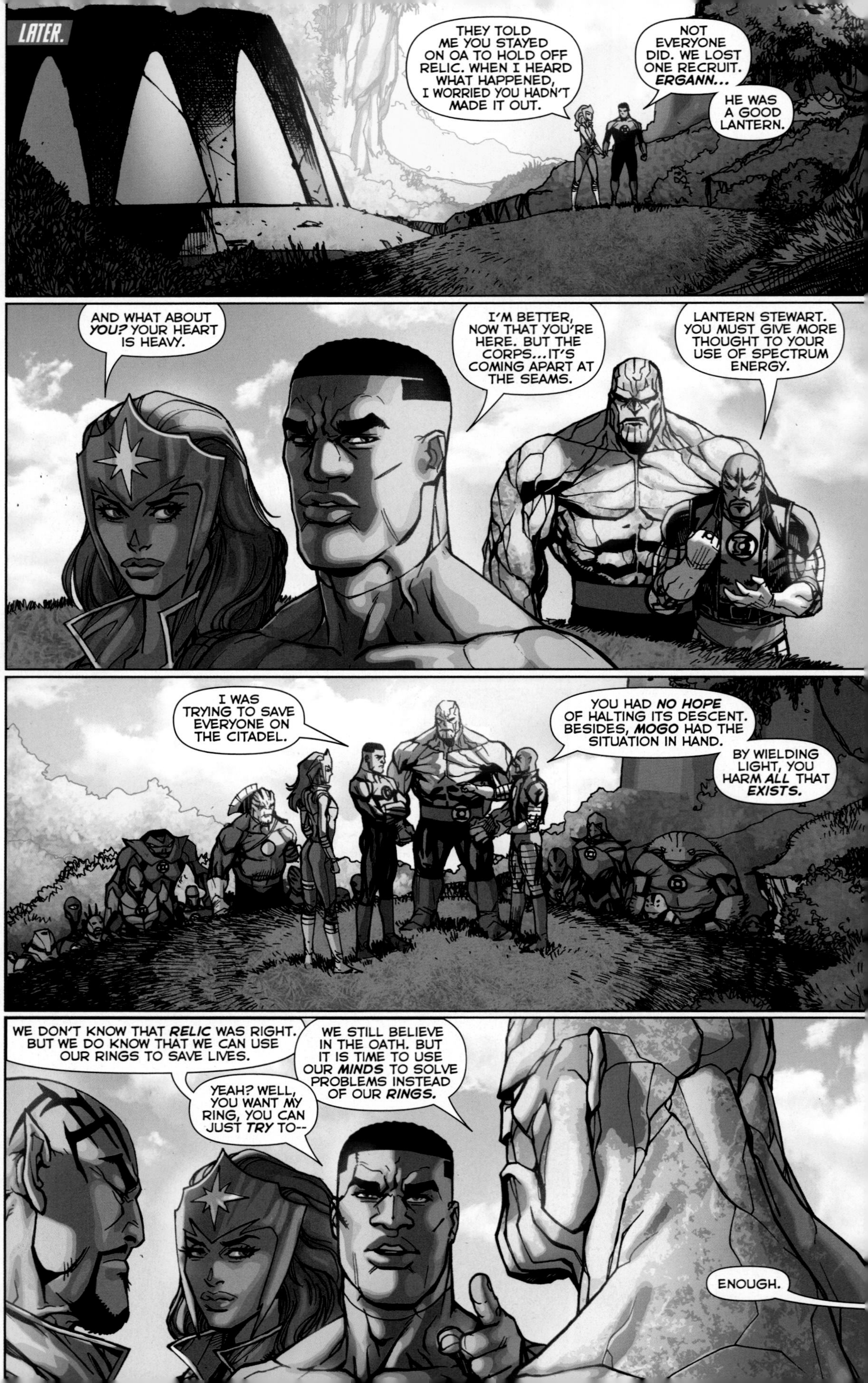
LATER.
THEY TOLD ME YOU STAYED ON OA TO HOLD OFF RELIC. WHEN I HEARD WHAT HAPPENED, I WORRIED YOU HADN'T MADE IT OUT.
NOT EVERYONE DID. WE LOST ONE RECRUIT. ERGANN...
HE WAS A GOOD LANTERN.
AND WHAT ABOUT YOU? YOUR HEART IS HEAVY.
I'M BETTER, NOW THAT YOU'RE HERE. BUT THE CORPS...IT'S COMING APART AT THE SEAMS.
LANTERN STEWART. YOU MUST GIVE MORE THOUGHT TO YOUR USE OF SPECTRUM ENERGY.
I WAS TRYING TO SAVE EVERYONE ON THE CITADEL.
YOU HAD NO HOPE OF HALTING ITS DESCENT. BESIDES, MOGO HAD THE SITUATION IN HAND.
BY WIELDING LIGHT, YOU HARM ALL THAT EXISTS.
WE DON'T KNOW THAT RELIC WAS RIGHT. BUT WE DO KNOW THAT WE CAN USE OUR RINGS TO SAVE LIVES.
WE STILL BELIEVE IN THE OATH. BUT IT IS TIME TO USE OUR MINDS TO SOLVE PROBLEMS INSTEAD OF OUR RINGS.
YEAH? WELL, YOU WANT MY RING, YOU CAN JUST TRY TO--
ENOUGH.

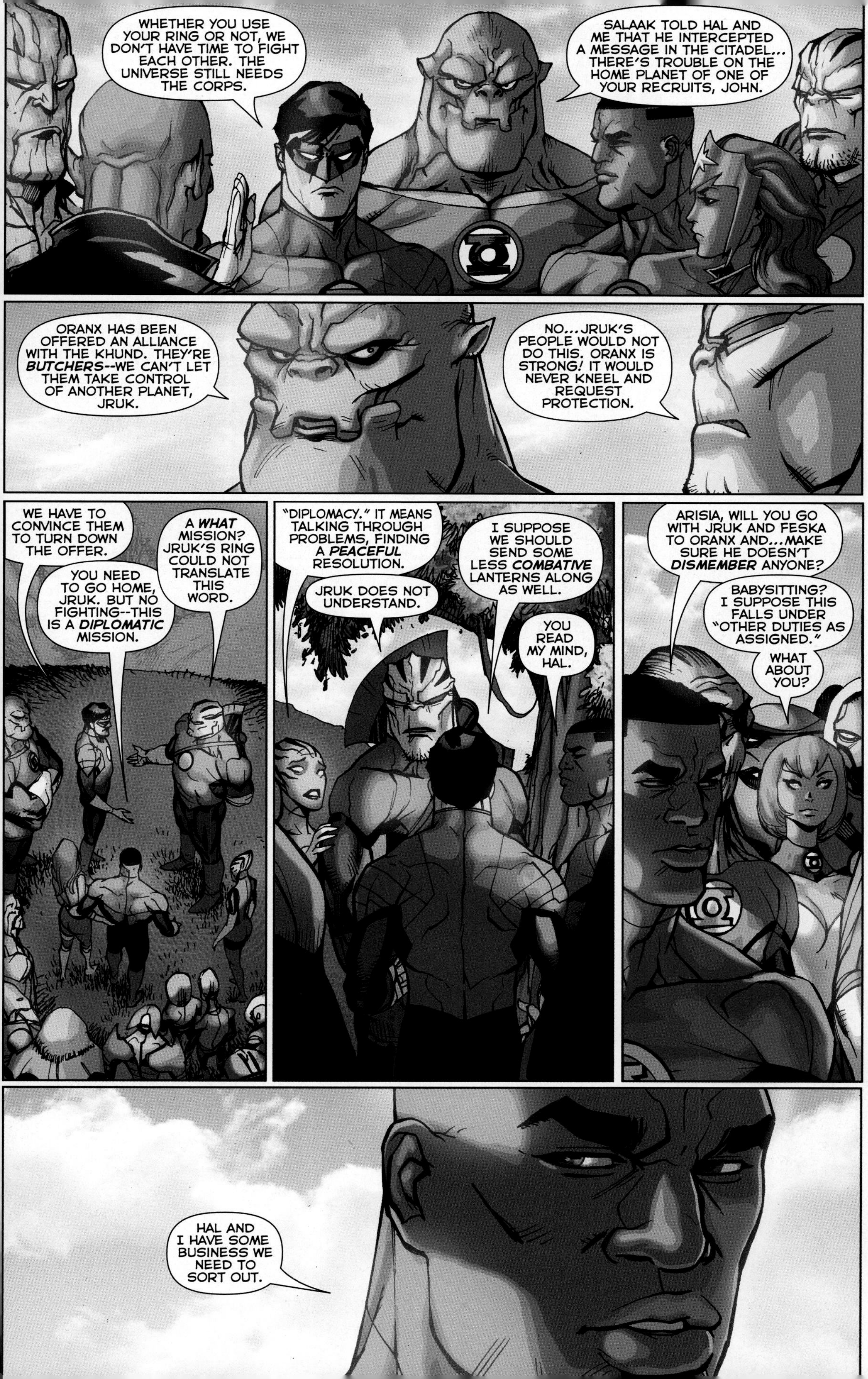
WHETHER YOU USE YOUR RING OR NOT, WE DON'T HAVE TIME TO FIGHT EACH OTHER. THE UNIVERSE STILL NEEDS THE CORPS.
SALAAK TOLD HAL AND ME THAT HE INTERCEPTED A MESSAGE IN THE CITADEL... THERE'S TROUBLE ON THE HOME PLANET OF ONE OF YOUR RECRUITS, JOHN.
ORANX HAS BEEN OFFERED AN ALLIANCE WITH THE KHUND. THEY'RE BUTCHERS--WE CAN'T LET THEM TAKE CONTROL OF ANOTHER PLANET, JRUK.
NO... JRUK'S PEOPLE WOULD NOT DO THIS. ORANX IS STRONG! IT WOULD NEVER KNEEL AND REQUEST PROTECTION.
WE HAVE TO CONVINCE THEM TO TURN DOWN THE OFFER.
YOU NEED TO GO HOME, JRUK. BUT NO FIGHTING--THIS IS A DIPLOMATIC MISSION.
A WHAT MISSION? JRUK'S RING COULD NOT TRANSLATE THIS WORD.
"DIPLOMACY." IT MEANS TALKING THROUGH PROBLEMS, FINDING A PEACEFUL RESOLUTION.
JRUK DOES NOT UNDERSTAND.
I SUPPOSE WE SHOULD SEND SOME LESS COMBATIVE LANTERNS ALONG AS WELL.
YOU READ MY MIND, HAL.
ARISIA, WILL YOU GO WITH JRUK AND FESKA TO ORANX AND... MAKE SURE HE DOESN'T DISMEMBER ANYONE?
BABYSITTING? I SUPPOSE THIS FALLS UNDER "OTHER DUTIES AS ASSIGNED."
WHAT ABOUT YOU?
HAL AND I HAVE SOME BUSINESS WE NEED TO SORT OUT.

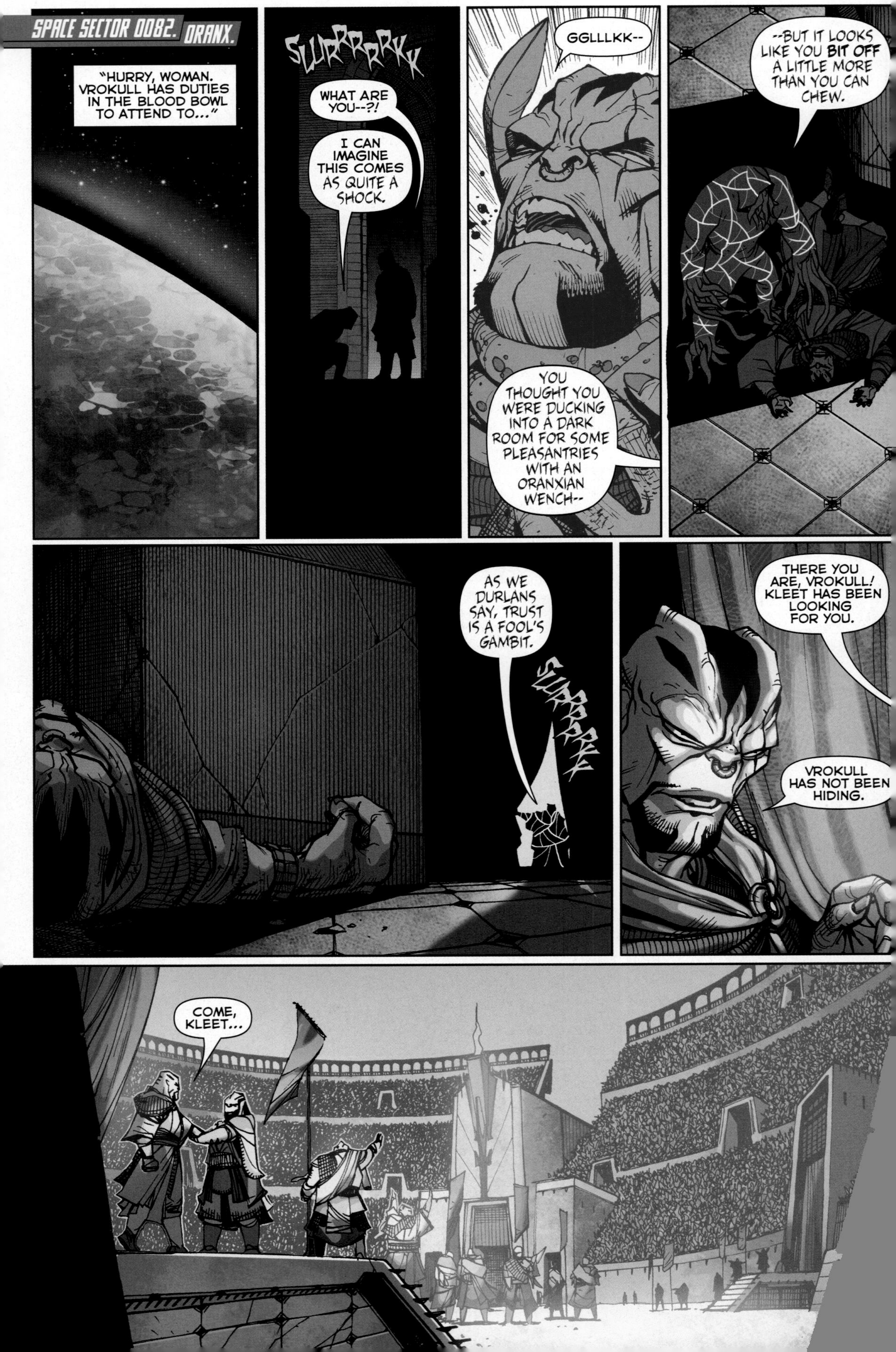
SPACE SECTOR 0082. ORANX.
"HURRY, WOMAN. VROKULL HAS DUTIES IN THE BLOOD BOWL TO ATTEND TO..."
SURRRRRKK
WHAT ARE YOU--?!
I CAN IMAGINE THIS COMES AS QUITE A SHOCK.
GGLLLKK--
YOU THOUGHT YOU WERE DUCKING INTO A DARK ROOM FOR SOME PLEASANTRIES WITH AN ORANXIAN WENCH--
--BUT IT LOOKS LIKE YOU BIT OFF A LITTLE MORE THAN YOU CAN CHEW.
AS WE DURLANS SAY, TRUST IS A FOOL'S GAMBIT.
SURRRRKK
THERE YOU ARE, VROKULL! KLEET HAS BEEN LOOKING FOR YOU.
VROKULL HAS NOT BEEN HIDING.
COME, KLEET...

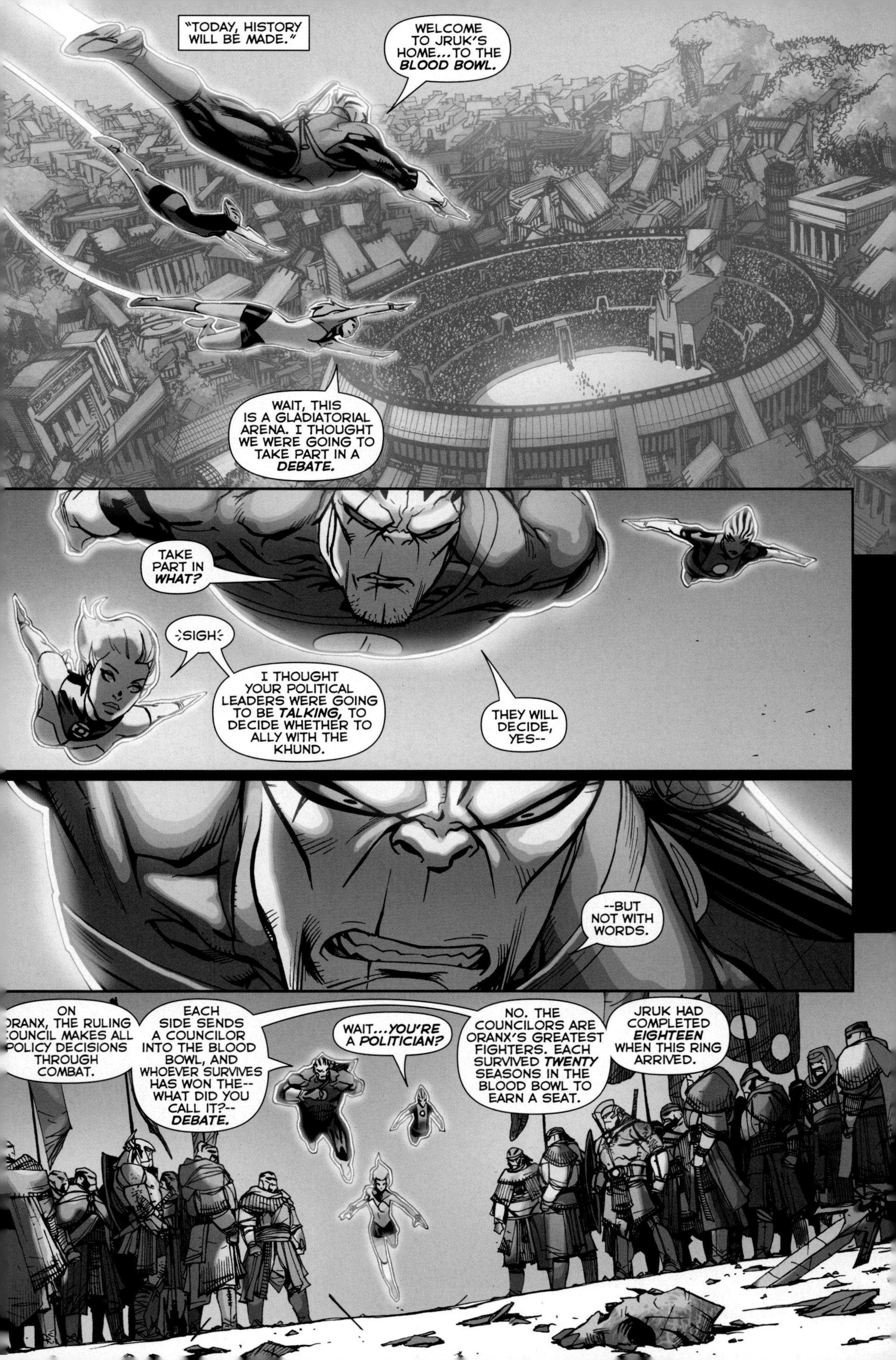

"TODAY, HISTORY WILL BE MADE."
WELCOME TO JRUK'S HOME... TO THE BLOOD BOWL.
WAIT, THIS IS A GLADIATORIAL ARENA. I THOUGHT WE WERE GOING TO TAKE PART IN A DEBATE.
TAKE PART IN WHAT?
SIGH
I THOUGHT YOUR POLITICAL LEADERS WERE GOING TO BE TALKING, TO DECIDE WHETHER TO ALLY WITH THE KHUND.
THEY WILL DECIDE, YES--
--BUT NOT WITH WORDS.
ON ORANX, THE RULING COUNCIL MAKES ALL POLICY DECISIONS THROUGH COMBAT.
EACH SIDE SENDS A COUNCILOR INTO THE BLOOD BOWL, AND WHOEVER SURVIVES HAS WON THE-- WHAT DID YOU CALL IT?-- DEBATE.
WAIT... YOU'RE A POLITICIAN?
NO. THE COUNCILORS ARE ORANX'S GREATEST FIGHTERS. EACH SURVIVED TWENTY SEASONS IN THE BLOOD BOWL TO EARN A SEAT.
JRUK HAD COMPLETED EIGHTEEN WHEN THIS RING ARRIVED.

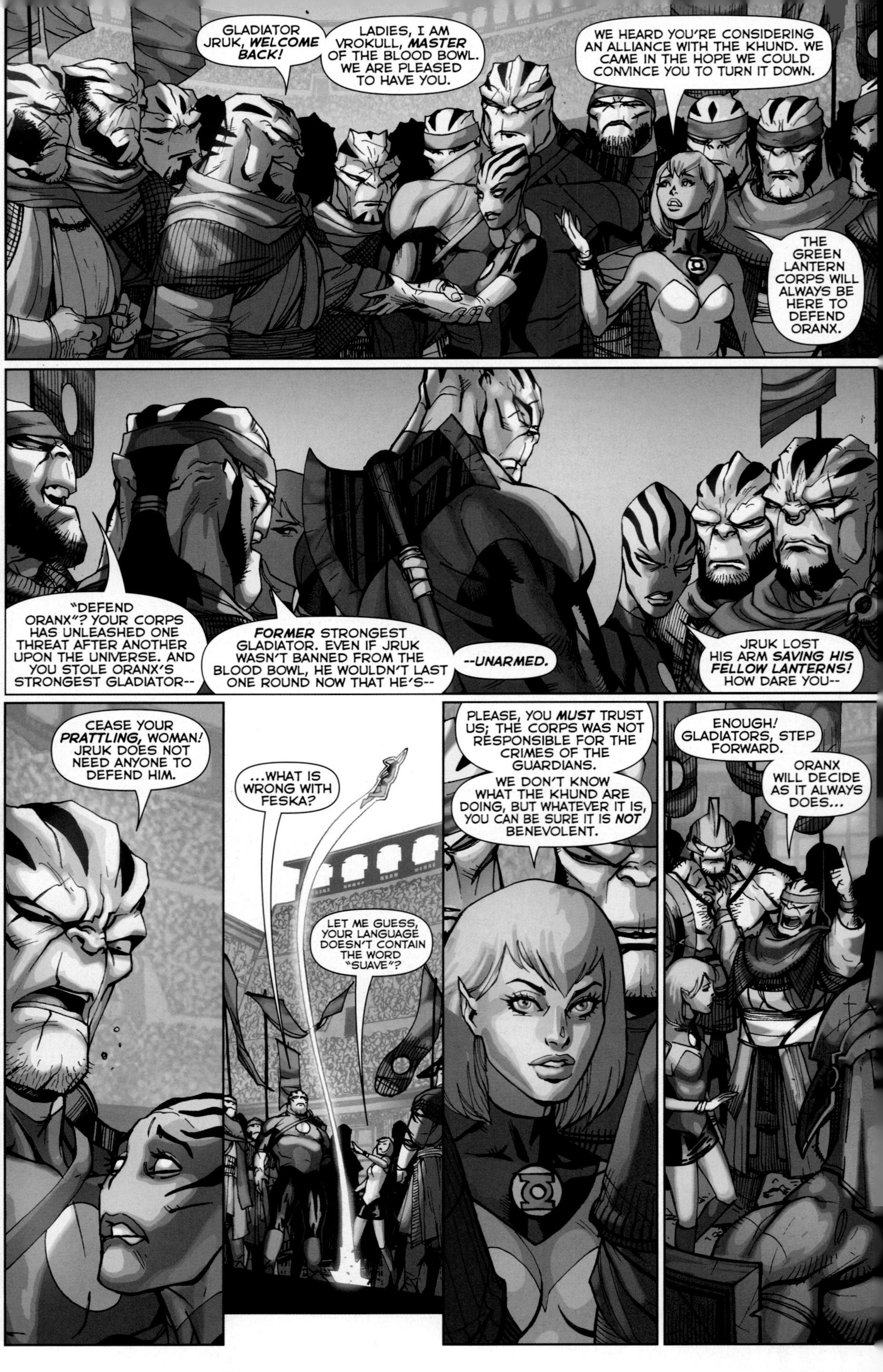
GLADIATOR JRUK, WELCOME BACK!
LADIES, I AM VROKULL, MASTER OF THE BLOOD BOWL. WE ARE PLEASED TO HAVE YOU.
WE HEARD YOU'RE CONSIDERING AN ALLIANCE WITH THE KHUND. WE CAME IN THE HOPE WE COULD CONVINCE YOU TO TURN IT DOWN.
THE GREEN LANTERN CORPS WILL ALWAYS BE HERE TO DEFEND ORANX.
"DEFEND ORANX"? YOUR CORPS HAS UNLEASHED ONE THREAT AFTER ANOTHER UPON THE UNIVERSE. AND YOU STOLE ORANX'S STRONGEST GLADIATOR--
FORMER STRONGEST GLADIATOR. EVEN IF JRUK WASN'T BANNED FROM THE BLOOD BOWL, HE WOULDN'T LAST ONE ROUND NOW THAT HE'S--
--UNARMED.
JRUK LOST HIS ARM SAVING HIS FELLOW LANTERNS! HOW DARE YOU--
CEASE YOUR PRATTLING, WOMAN! JRUK DOES NOT NEED ANYONE TO DEFEND HIM.
...WHAT IS WRONG WITH FESKA?
LET ME GUESS, YOUR LANGUAGE DOESN'T CONTAIN THE WORD "SUAVE"?
PLEASE, YOU MUST TRUST US; THE CORPS WAS NOT RESPONSIBLE FOR THE CRIMES OF THE GUARDIANS.
WE DON'T KNOW WHAT THE KHUND ARE DOING, BUT WHATEVER IT IS, YOU CAN BE SURE IT IS NOT BENEVOLENT.
ENOUGH! GLADIATORS, STEP FORWARD.
ORANX WILL DECIDE AS IT ALWAYS DOES...

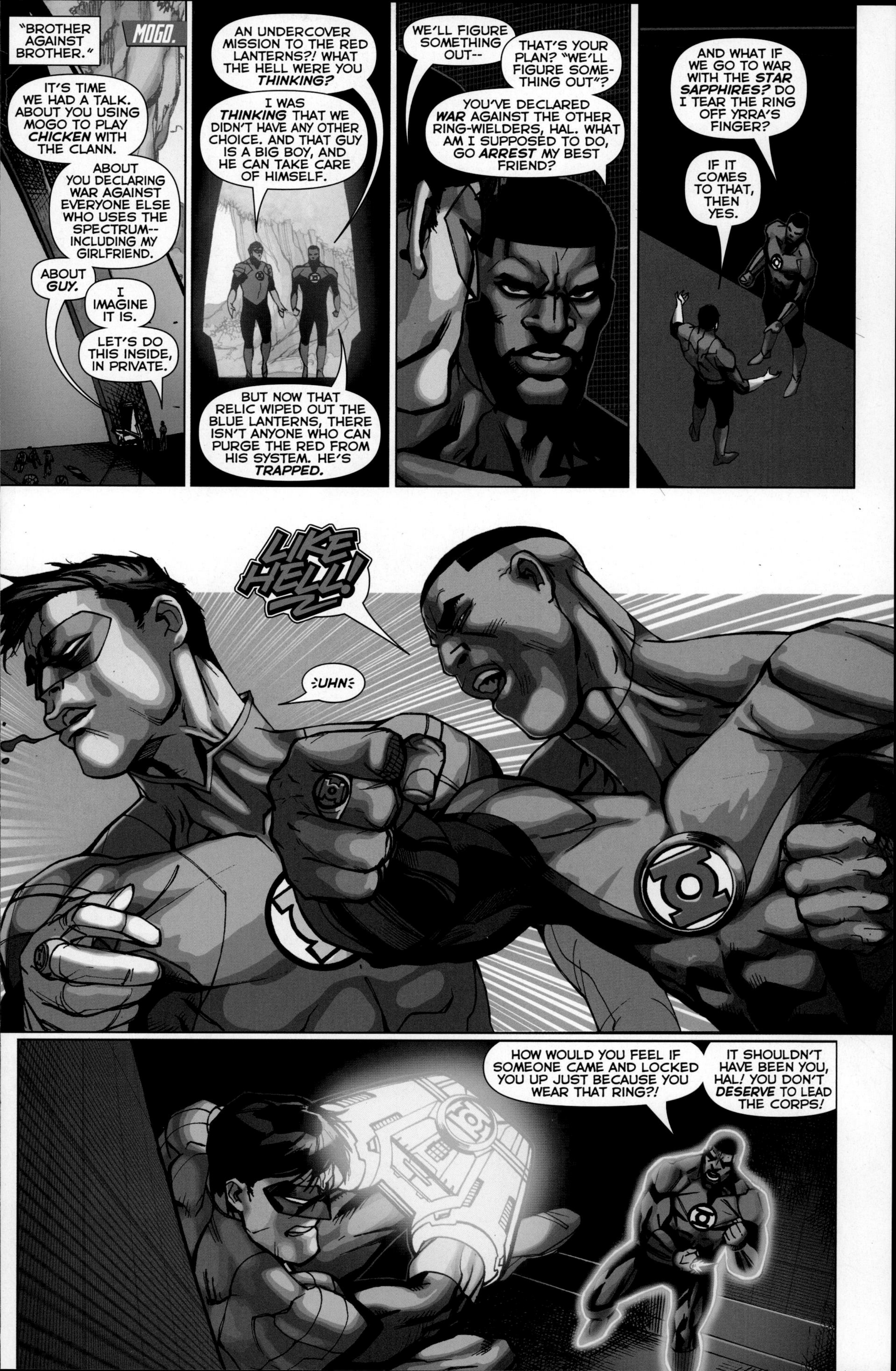
"BROTHER AGAINST BROTHER."
MOGO.
IT'S TIME WE HAD A TALK. ABOUT YOU USING MOGO TO PLAY CHICKEN WITH THE CLANN.
ABOUT YOU DECLARING WAR AGAINST EVERYONE ELSE WHO USES THE SPECTRUM-- INCLUDING MY GIRLFRIEND.
ABOUT GUY.
I IMAGINE IT IS.
LET'S DO THIS INSIDE, IN PRIVATE.
AN UNDERCOVER MISSION TO THE RED LANTERNS?! WHAT THE HELL WERE YOU THINKING?
I WAS THINKING THAT WE DIDN'T HAVE ANY OTHER CHOICE. AND THAT GUY IS A BIG BOY, AND HE CAN TAKE CARE OF HIMSELF.
BUT NOW THAT RELIC WIPED OUT THE BLUE LANTERNS, THERE ISN'T ANYONE WHO CAN PURGE THE RED FROM HIS SYSTEM. HE'S TRAPPED.
WE'LL FIGURE SOMETHING OUT--
THAT'S YOUR PLAN? "WE'LL FIGURE SOMETHING OUT"?
YOU'VE DECLARED WAR AGAINST THE OTHER RING-WIELDERS, HAL. WHAT AM I SUPPOSED TO DO, GO ARREST MY BEST FRIEND?
AND WHAT IF WE GO TO WAR WITH THE STAR SAPPHIRES? DO I TEAR THE RING OFF YRRA'S FINGER?
IF IT COMES TO THAT, THEN YES.
LIKE HELL!
UHN
HOW WOULD YOU FEEL IF SOMEONE CAME AND LOCKED YOU UP JUST BECAUSE YOU WEAR THAT RING?!
IT SHOULDN'T HAVE BEEN YOU, HAL! YOU DON'T DESERVE TO LEAD THE CORPS!

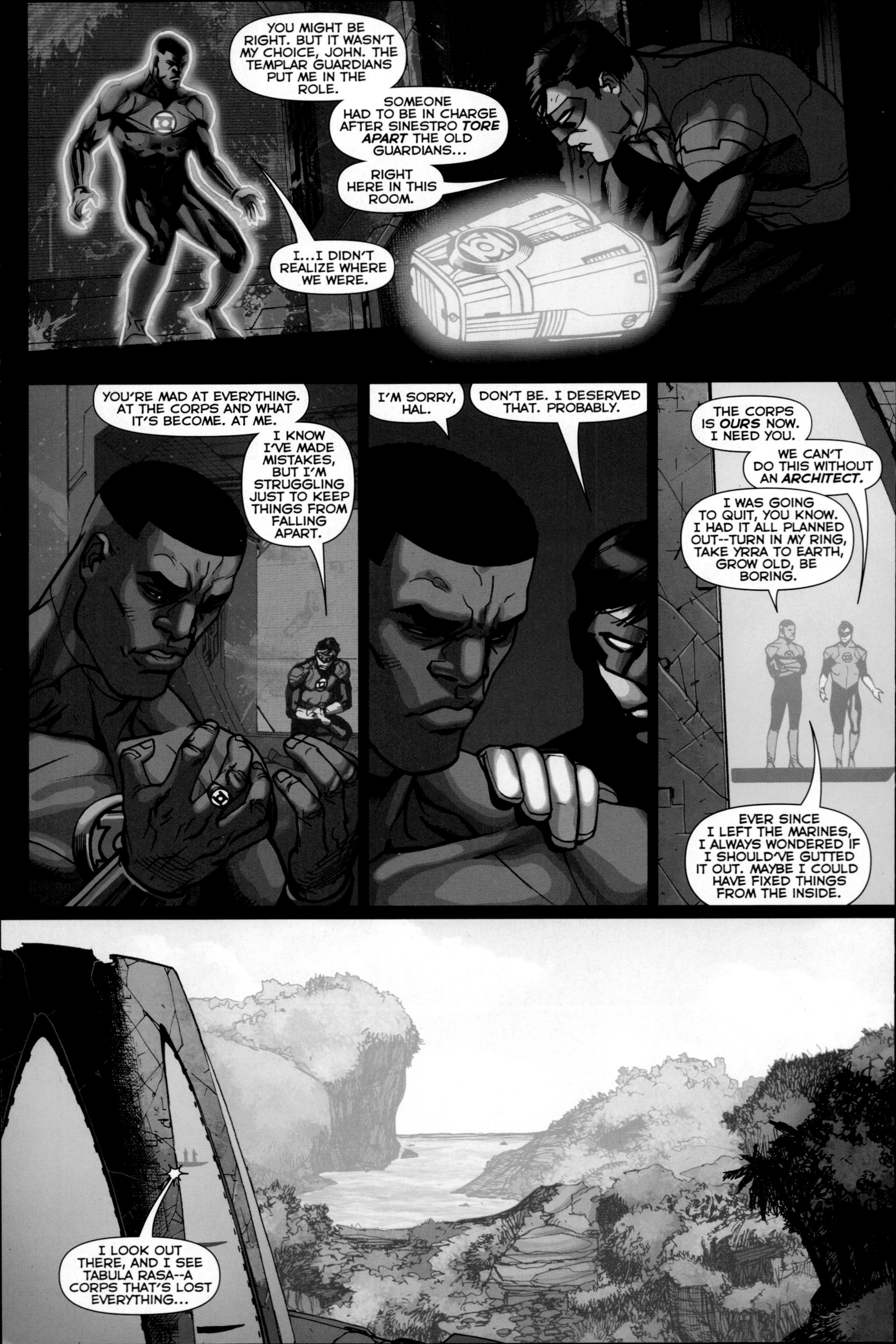

YOU MIGHT BE RIGHT. BUT IT WASN'T MY CHOICE, JOHN. THE TEMPLAR GUARDIANS PUT ME IN THE ROLE.
SOMEONE HAD TO BE IN CHARGE AFTER SINESTRO *TORE APART* THE OLD GUARDIANS...
RIGHT HERE IN THIS ROOM.
I...I DIDN'T REALIZE WHERE WE WERE.
YOU'RE MAD AT EVERYTHING. AT THE CORPS AND WHAT IT'S BECOME. AT ME.
I KNOW I'VE MADE MISTAKES, BUT I'M STRUGGLING JUST TO KEEP THINGS FROM FALLING APART.
I'M SORRY, HAL.
DON'T BE. I DESERVED THAT. PROBABLY.
THE CORPS IS *OURS* NOW. I NEED YOU.
WE CAN'T DO THIS WITHOUT AN *ARCHITECT.*
I WAS GOING TO QUIT, YOU KNOW. I HAD IT ALL PLANNED OUT--TURN IN MY RING, TAKE YRRA TO EARTH, GROW OLD, BE BORING.
EVER SINCE I LEFT THE MARINES, I ALWAYS WONDERED IF I SHOULD'VE GUTTED IT OUT. MAYBE I COULD HAVE FIXED THINGS FROM THE INSIDE.
I LOOK OUT THERE, AND I SEE TABULA RASA--A CORPS THAT'S LOST EVERYTHING...

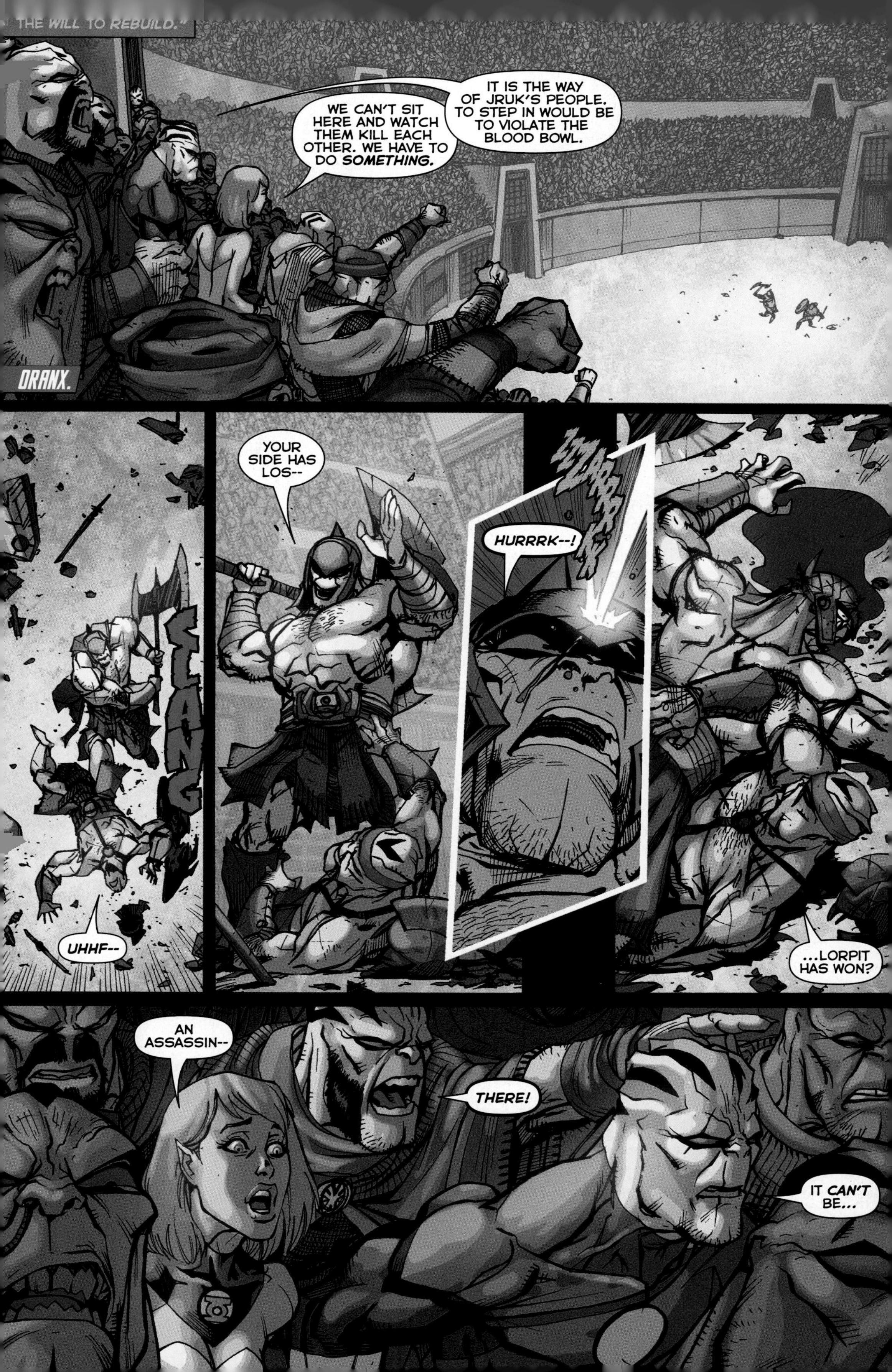
"THE WILL TO REBUILD."
ORANX.
WE CAN'T SIT HERE AND WATCH THEM KILL EACH OTHER. WE HAVE TO DO SOMETHING.
IT IS THE WAY OF JRUK'S PEOPLE. TO STEP IN WOULD BE TO VIOLATE THE BLOOD BOWL.
CLANG
UHHF--
YOUR SIDE HAS LOS--
HURRRK--!
...LORPIT HAS WON?
AN ASSASSIN--
THERE!
IT CAN'T BE...

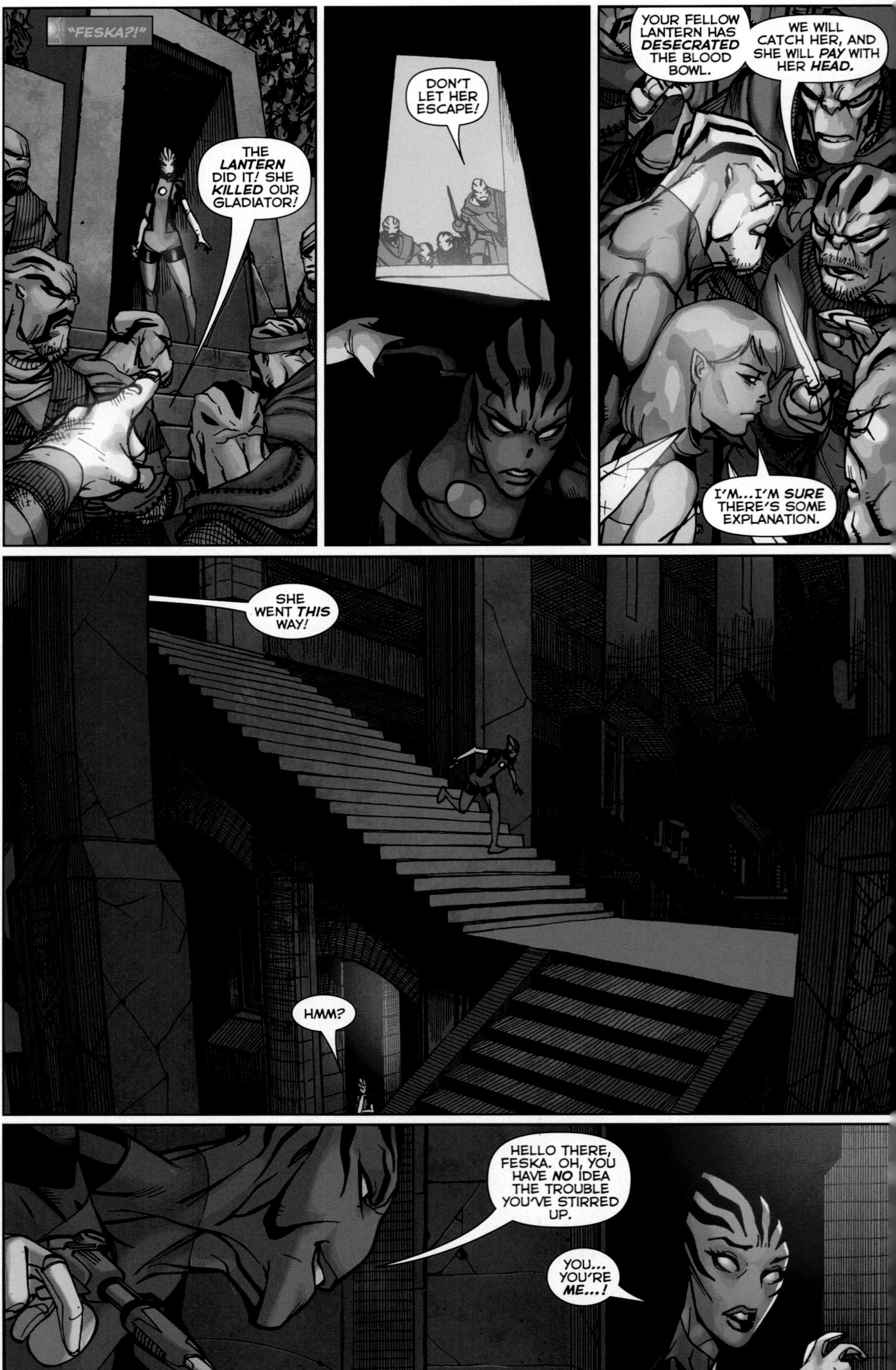
"FESKA?!"
THE LANTERN DID IT! SHE KILLED OUR GLADIATOR!
DON'T LET HER ESCAPE!
YOUR FELLOW LANTERN HAS DESECRATED THE BLOOD BOWL.
WE WILL CATCH HER, AND SHE WILL PAY WITH HER HEAD.
I'M...I'M SURE THERE'S SOME EXPLANATION.
SHE WENT THIS WAY!
HMM?
HELLO THERE, FESKA. OH, YOU HAVE NO IDEA THE TROUBLE YOU'VE STIRRED UP.
YOU... YOU'RE ME...!

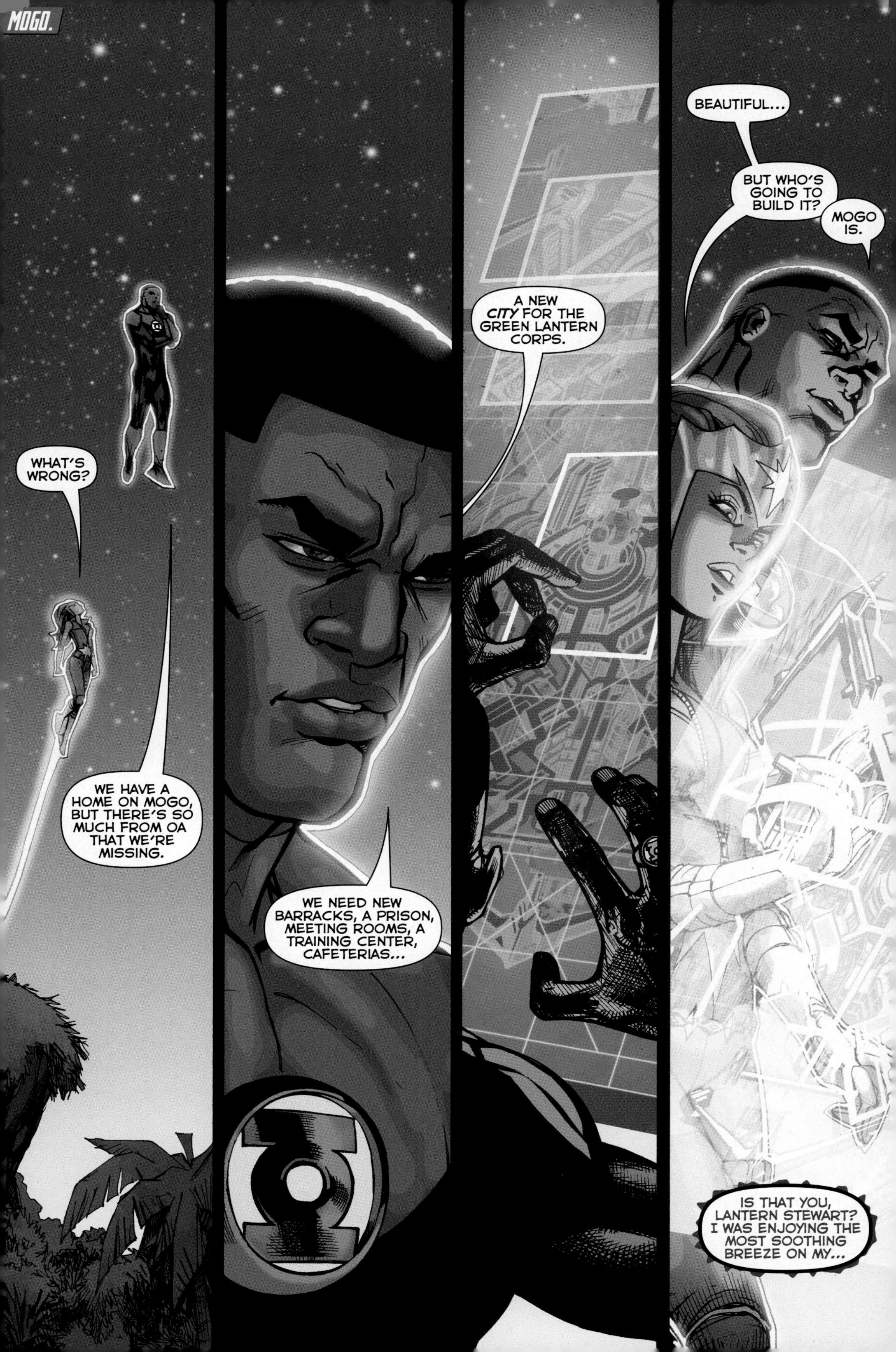
MOGO.
WHAT'S WRONG?
WE HAVE A HOME ON MOGO, BUT THERE'S SO MUCH FROM OA THAT WE'RE MISSING.
WE NEED NEW BARRACKS, A PRISON, MEETING ROOMS, A TRAINING CENTER, CAFETERIAS...
A NEW CITY FOR THE GREEN LANTERN CORPS.
BEAUTIFUL...
BUT WHO'S GOING TO BUILD IT?
MOGO IS.
IS THAT YOU, LANTERN STEWART? I WAS ENJOYING THE MOST SOOTHING BREEZE ON MY...

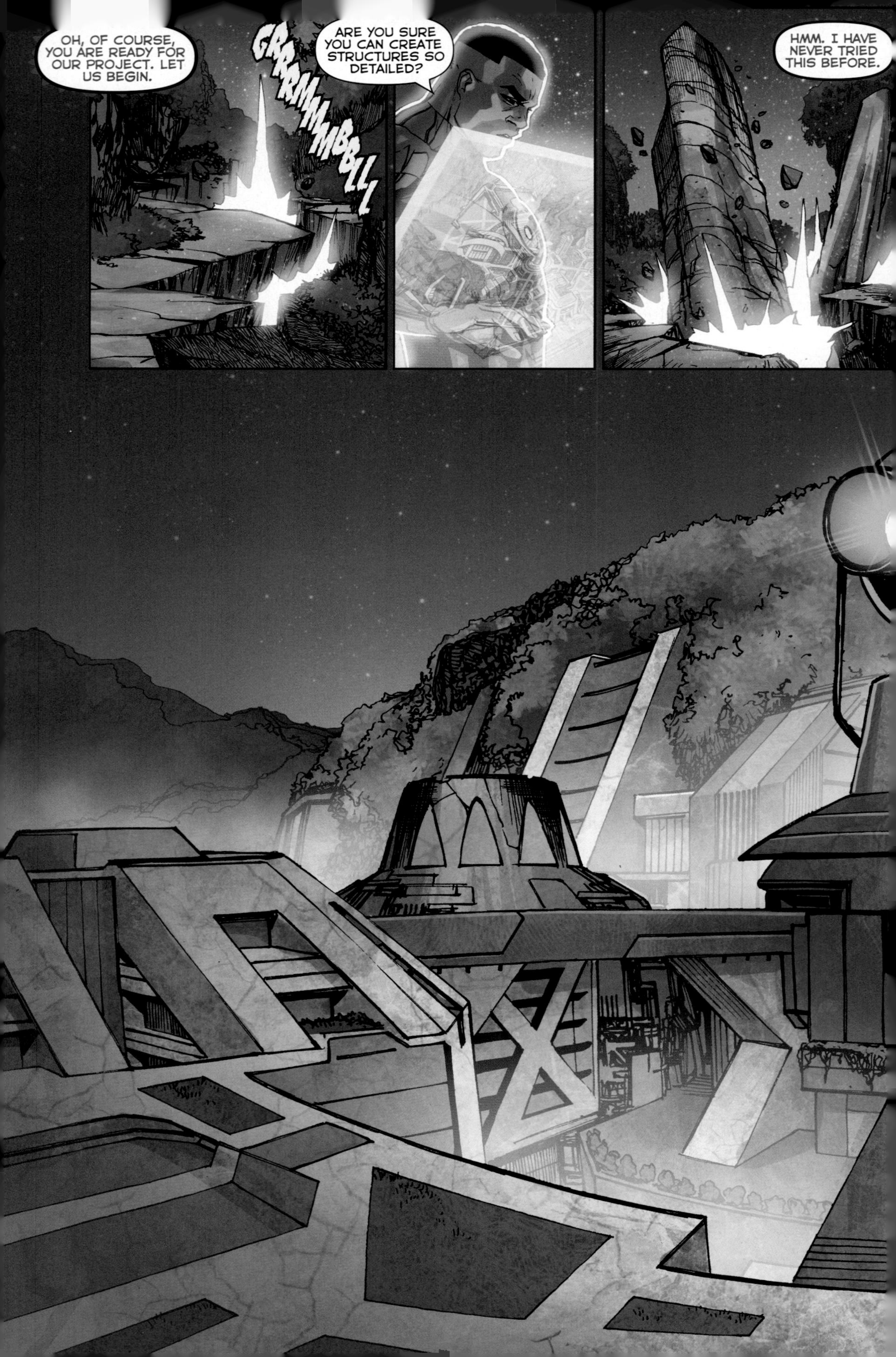
OH, OF COURSE, YOU ARE READY FOR OUR PROJECT. LET US BEGIN.
GRRRMMMBBLLL
ARE YOU SURE YOU CAN CREATE STRUCTURES SO DETAILED?
HMM. I HAVE NEVER TRIED THIS BEFORE.

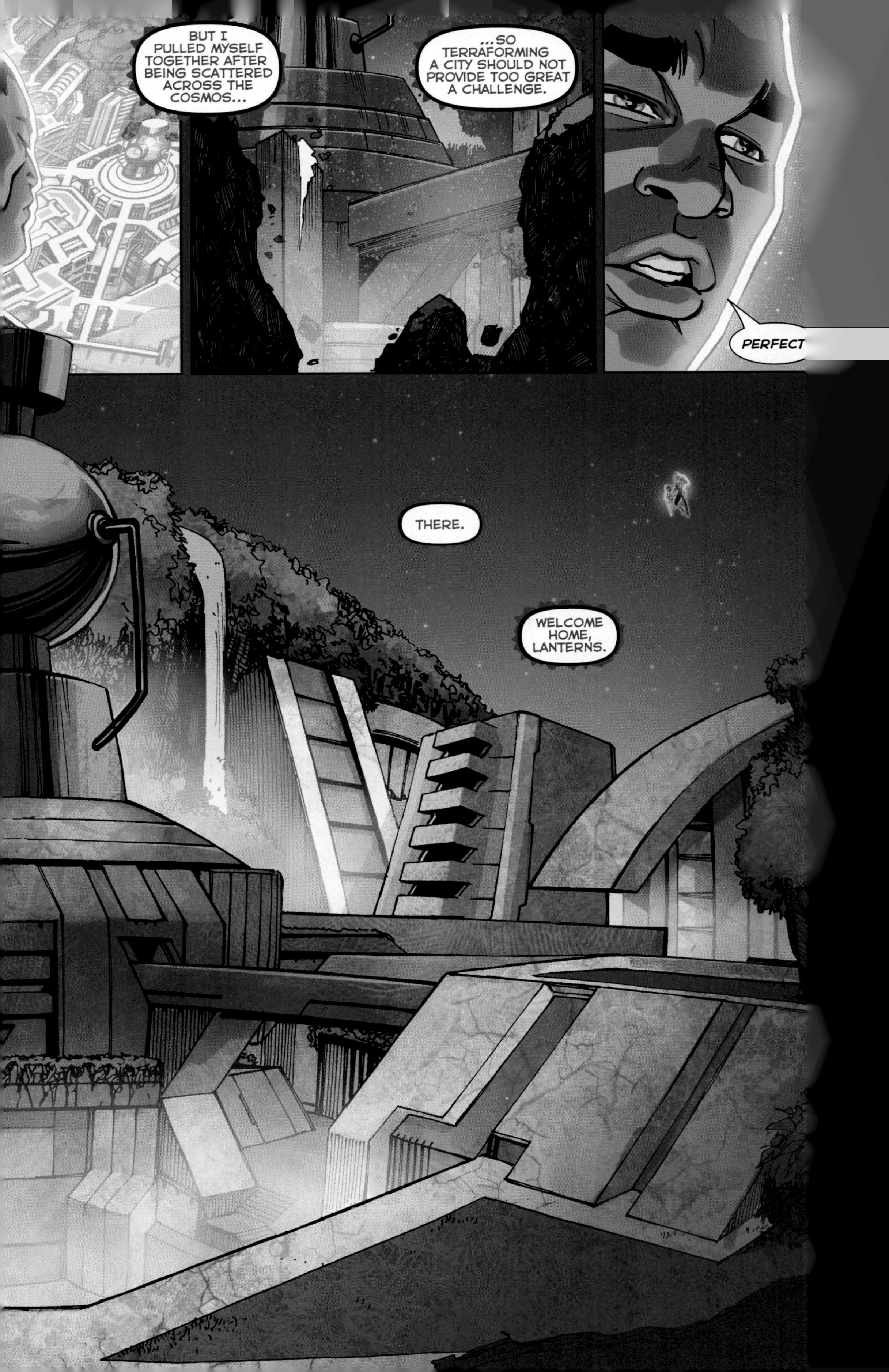
BUT I PULLED MYSELF TOGETHER AFTER BEING SCATTERED ACROSS THE COSMOS...
...SO TERRAFORMING A CITY SHOULD NOT PROVIDE TOO GREAT A CHALLENGE.
PERFECT
THERE.
WELCOME HOME, LANTERNS.

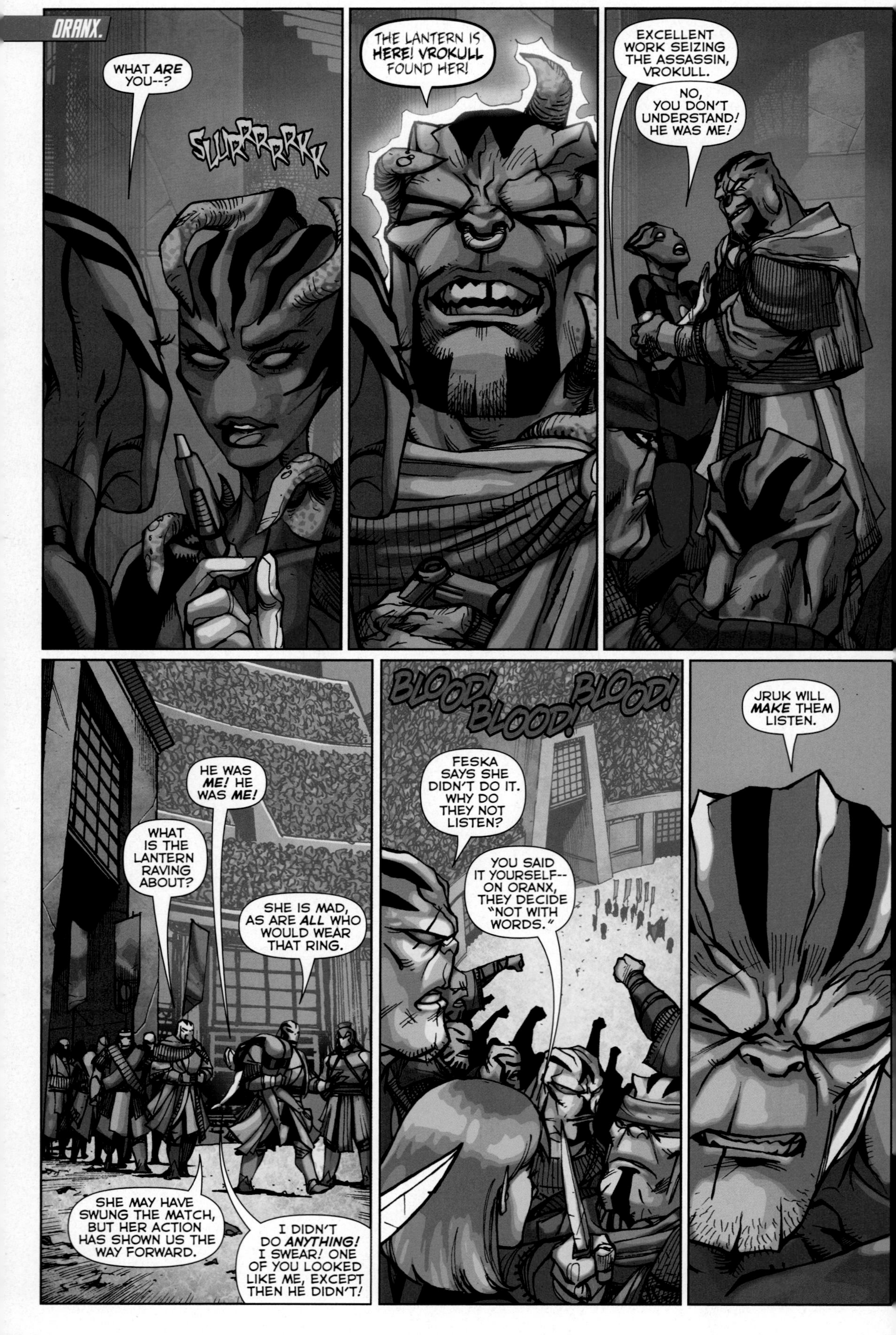
ORANX.
WHAT ARE YOU--?
SLURRRRRKK
THE LANTERN IS HERE! VROKULL FOUND HER!
EXCELLENT WORK SEIZING THE ASSASSIN, VROKULL.
NO, YOU DON'T UNDERSTAND! HE WAS ME!
HE WAS ME! HE WAS ME!
WHAT IS THE LANTERN RAVING ABOUT?
SHE IS MAD, AS ARE ALL WHO WOULD WEAR THAT RING.
SHE MAY HAVE SWUNG THE MATCH, BUT HER ACTION HAS SHOWN US THE WAY FORWARD.
I DIDN'T DO ANYTHING! I SWEAR! ONE OF YOU LOOKED LIKE ME, EXCEPT THEN HE DIDN'T!
BLOOD! BLOOD! BLOOD!
FESKA SAYS SHE DIDN'T DO IT. WHY DO THEY NOT LISTEN?
YOU SAID IT YOURSELF-- ON ORANX, THEY DECIDE "NOT WITH WORDS."
JRUK WILL MAKE THEM LISTEN.

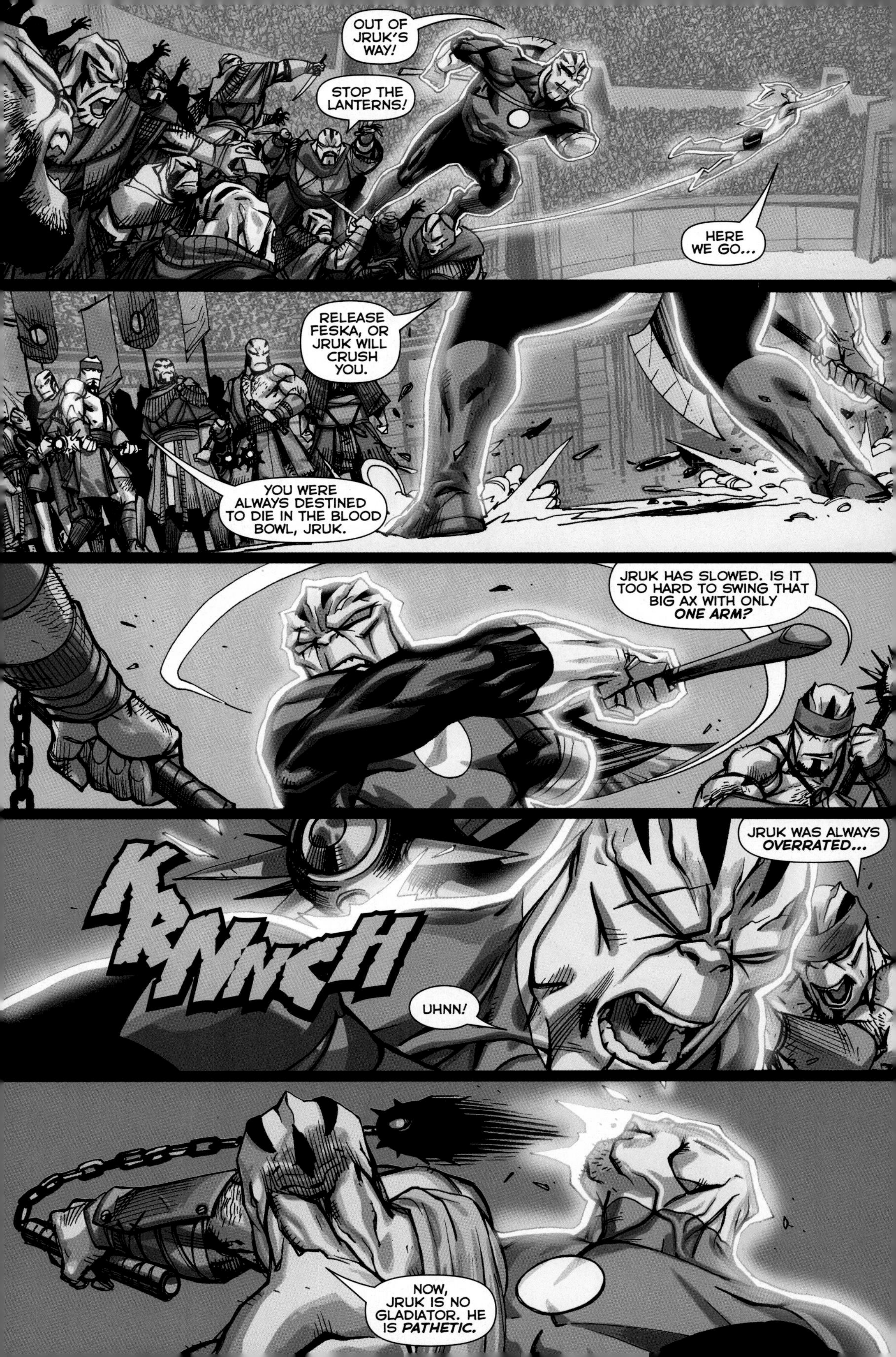
OUT OF JRUK'S WAY!
STOP THE LANTERNS!
HERE WE GO...
RELEASE FESKA, OR JRUK WILL CRUSH YOU.
YOU WERE ALWAYS DESTINED TO DIE IN THE BLOOD BOWL, JRUK.
JRUK HAS SLOWED. IS IT TOO HARD TO SWING THAT BIG AX WITH ONLY *ONE ARM?*
KRNNCH
JRUK WAS ALWAYS *OVERRATED...*
UHNN!
NOW, JRUK IS NO GLADIATOR. HE IS *PATHETIC.*

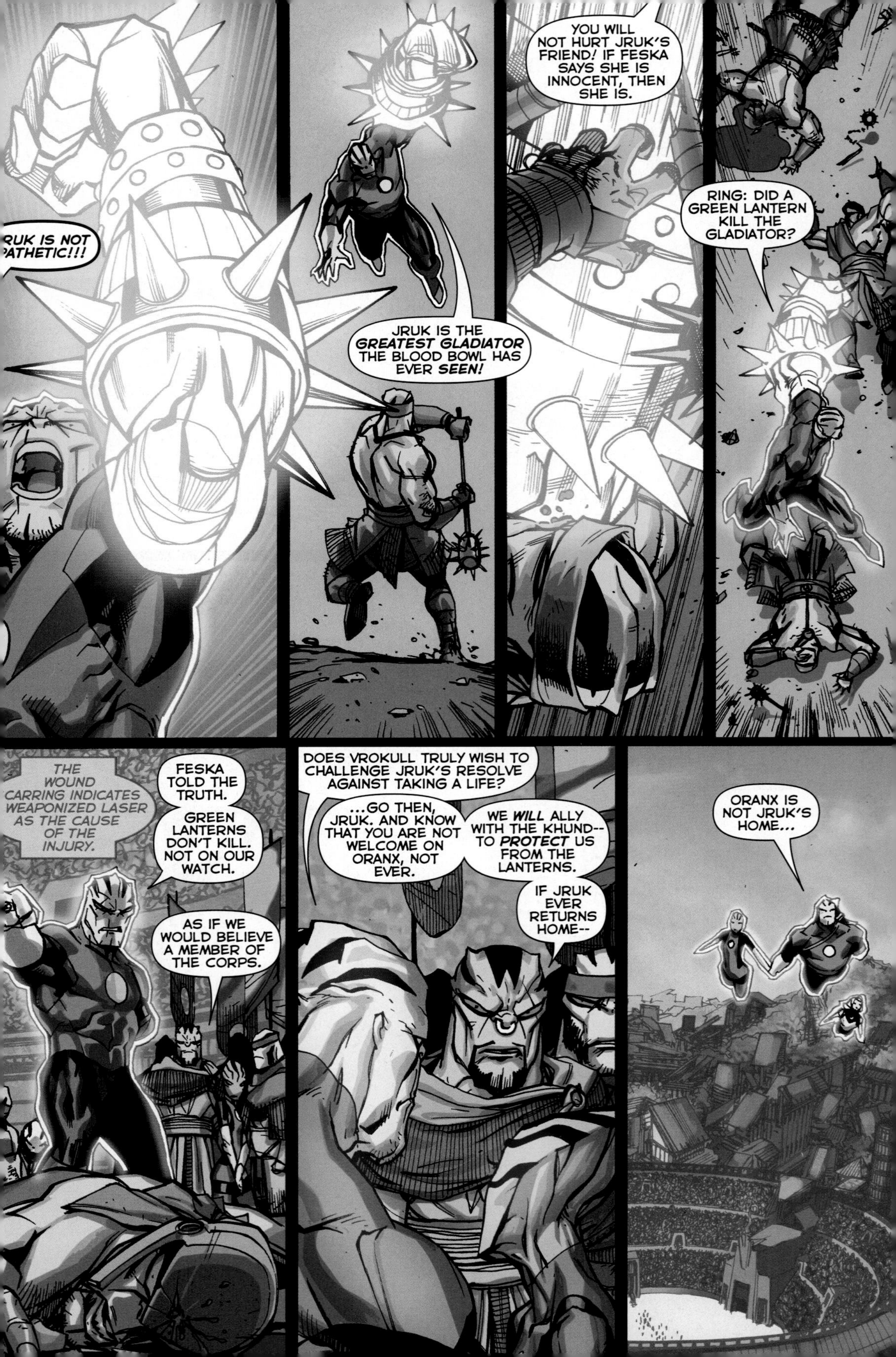

JRUK IS NOT PATHETIC!!!
JRUK IS THE GREATEST GLADIATOR THE BLOOD BOWL HAS EVER SEEN!
YOU WILL NOT HURT JRUK'S FRIEND! IF FESKA SAYS SHE IS INNOCENT, THEN SHE IS.
RING: DID A GREEN LANTERN KILL THE GLADIATOR?
THE WOUND CARRING INDICATES WEAPONIZED LASER AS THE CAUSE OF THE INJURY.
FESKA TOLD THE TRUTH.
GREEN LANTERNS DON'T KILL. NOT ON OUR WATCH.
AS IF WE WOULD BELIEVE A MEMBER OF THE CORPS.
DOES VROKULL TRULY WISH TO CHALLENGE JRUK'S RESOLVE AGAINST TAKING A LIFE?
...GO THEN, JRUK. AND KNOW THAT YOU ARE NOT WELCOME ON ORANX, NOT EVER.
WE WILL ALLY WITH THE KHUND-- TO PROTECT US FROM THE LANTERNS.
IF JRUK EVER RETURNS HOME--
ORANX IS NOT JRUK'S HOME...

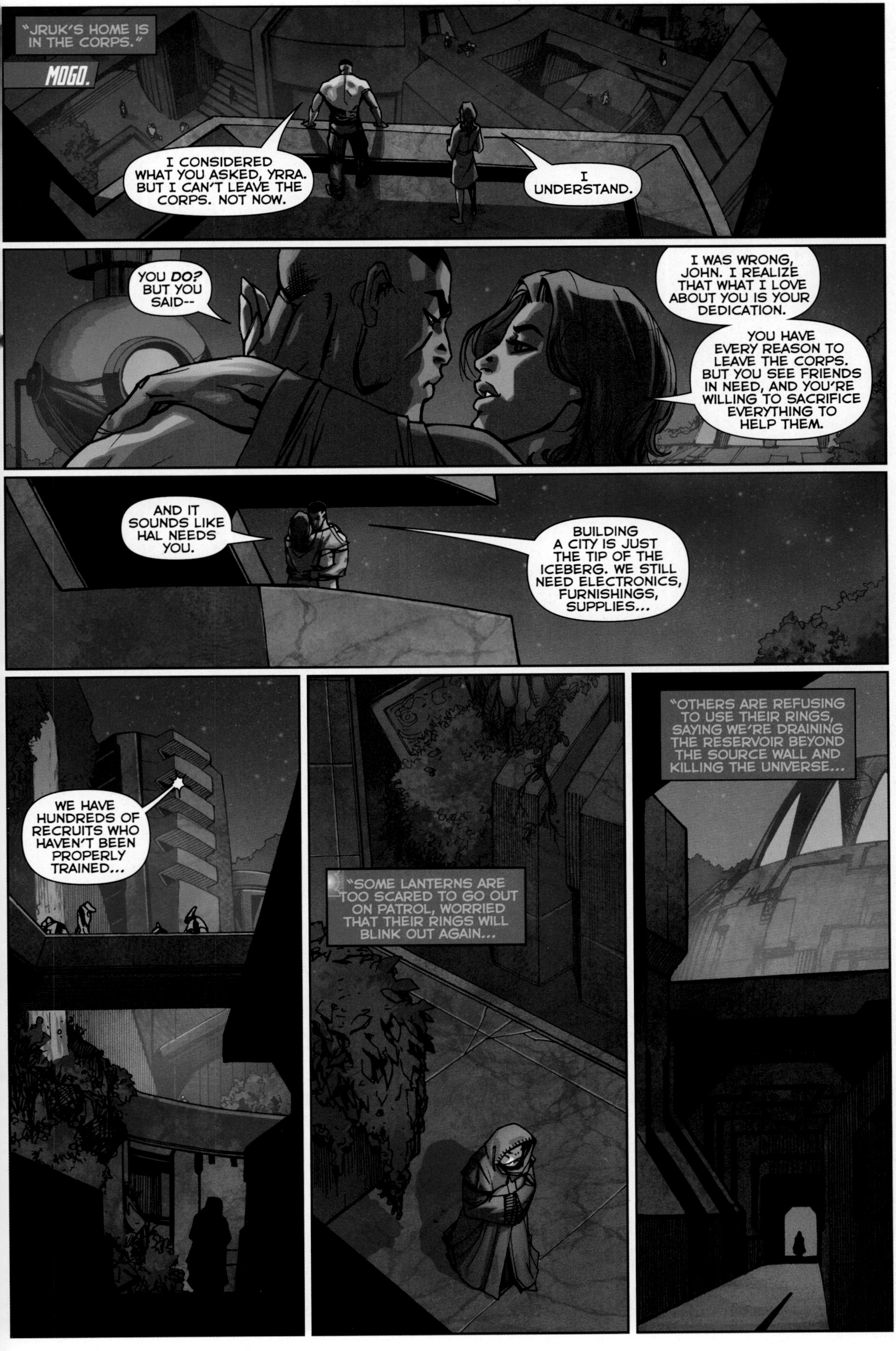
"JRUK'S HOME IS IN THE CORPS."
MOGO.
I CONSIDERED WHAT YOU ASKED, YRRA. BUT I CAN'T LEAVE THE CORPS. NOT NOW.
I UNDERSTAND.
YOU DO? BUT YOU SAID--
I WAS WRONG, JOHN. I REALIZE THAT WHAT I LOVE ABOUT YOU IS YOUR DEDICATION.
YOU HAVE EVERY REASON TO LEAVE THE CORPS. BUT YOU SEE FRIENDS IN NEED, AND YOU'RE WILLING TO SACRIFICE EVERYTHING TO HELP THEM.
AND IT SOUNDS LIKE HAL NEEDS YOU.
BUILDING A CITY IS JUST THE TIP OF THE ICEBERG. WE STILL NEED ELECTRONICS, FURNISHINGS, SUPPLIES...
WE HAVE HUNDREDS OF RECRUITS WHO HAVEN'T BEEN PROPERLY TRAINED...
"SOME LANTERNS ARE TOO SCARED TO GO OUT ON PATROL, WORRIED THAT THEIR RINGS WILL BLINK OUT AGAIN...
"OTHERS ARE REFUSING TO USE THEIR RINGS, SAYING WE'RE DRAINING THE RESERVOIR BEYOND THE SOURCE WALL AND KILLING THE UNIVERSE...

"ONE OF MY FRIENDS, THE ONLY PERSON WHO CAN REFILL THE RESERVOIR, IS DEAD..."

"AND MY CLOSEST FRIEND IS STUCK AS A RED LANTERN, WITH NO HOPE OF ESCAPING..."

"THE WHOLE UNIVERSE TREATS US LIKE WE'RE VILLAINS, NOT HEROES..."

"AND THE SHAPE-SHIFTERS THAT ATTACKED YOU ARE STILL ON THE LOOSE, *SOMEWHERE* OUT THERE."

SLUURRRRK

WE HAVE REJOINED THE CORPS ON MOGO. THEY ARE REBUILDING.

SEVERAL OF THE ROBOTS CONTROLLED BY RELIC WERE DISABLED IN THE CITADEL. WE'VE GATHERED THEM HERE.

GOOD. CONTACT YOUR **SIBLING.** THE DEVICES MUST BE DELIVERED TO OUR PARTNERS.

RELIC MIGHT HAVE FAILED IN HIS QUEST TO DESTROY THE CORPS--

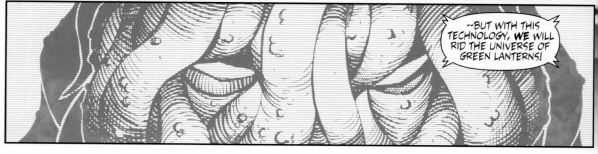

--BUT WITH THIS TECHNOLOGY, **WE** WILL RID THE UNIVERSE OF GREEN LANTERNS!

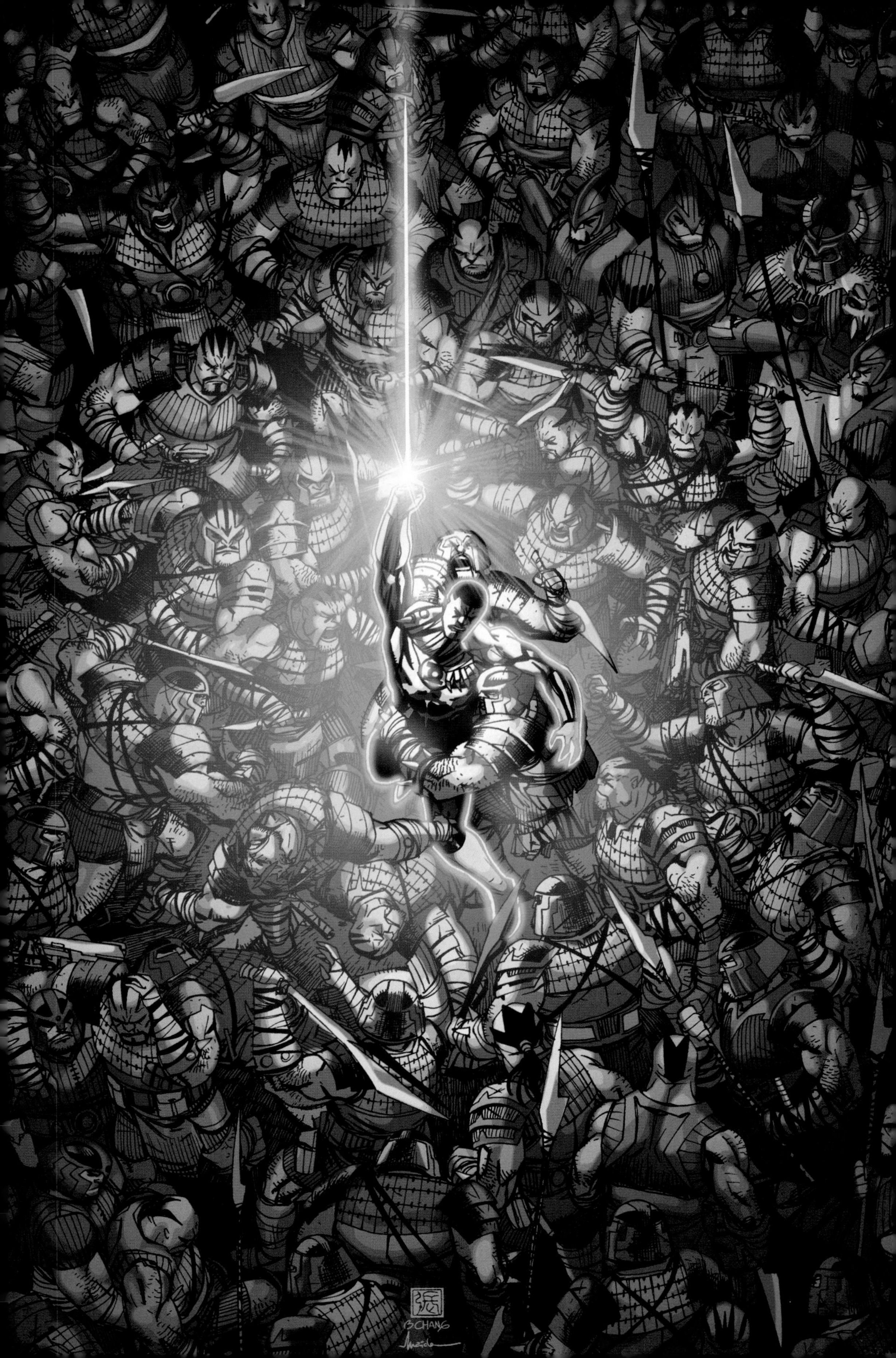
B CHANG

FORENSICS

VAN JENSEN & ROBERT VENDITTI writers BERNARD CHANG & SEAN CHEN pencillers BERNARD CHANG & WALDEN WONG inkers
cover art by BERNARD CHANG & MARCELO MAIOLO

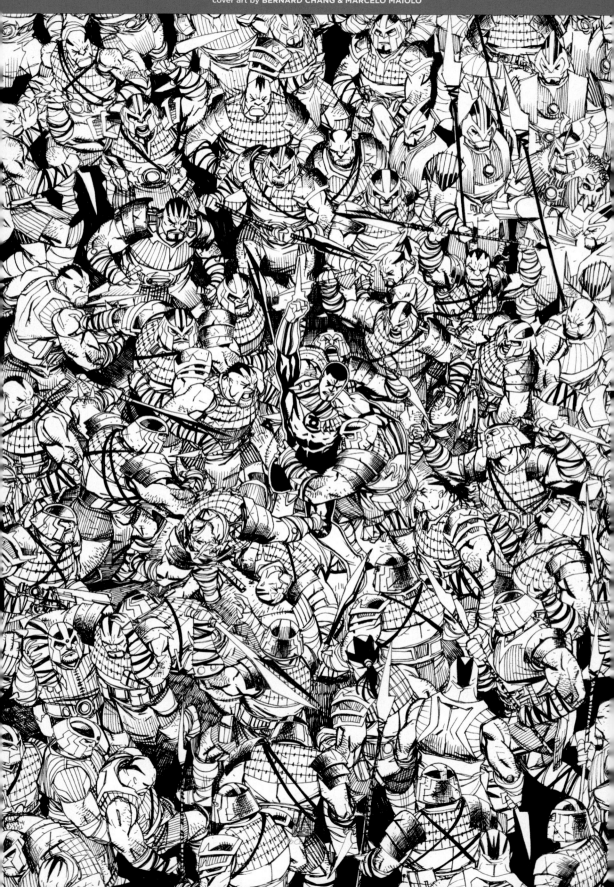

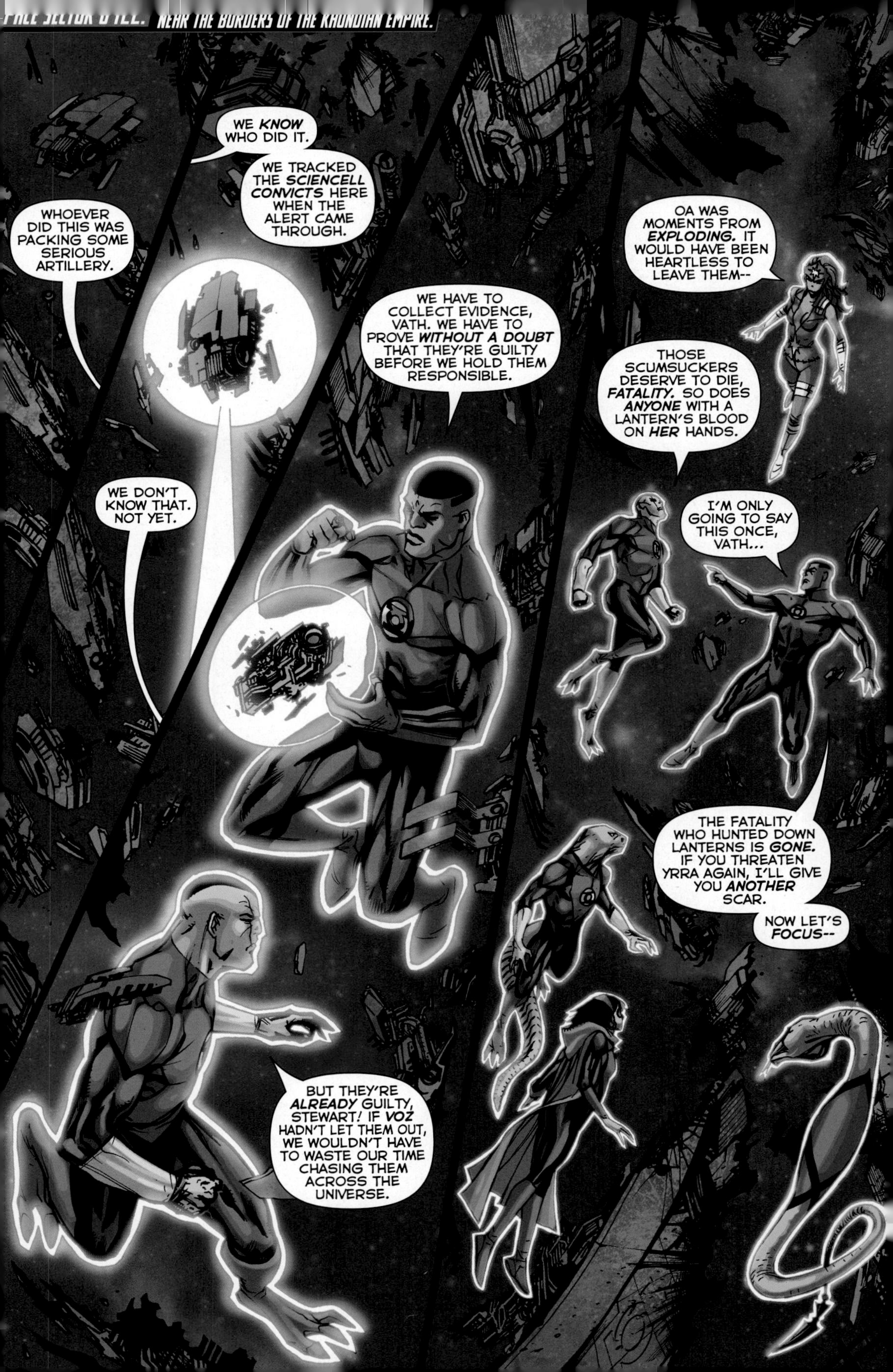
NEAR THE BORDERS OF THE KHUNDIAN EMPIRE.
WHOEVER DID THIS WAS PACKING SOME SERIOUS ARTILLERY.
WE KNOW WHO DID IT.
WE TRACKED THE SCIENCELL CONVICTS HERE WHEN THE ALERT CAME THROUGH.
WE DON'T KNOW THAT. NOT YET.
WE HAVE TO COLLECT EVIDENCE, VATH. WE HAVE TO PROVE WITHOUT A DOUBT THAT THEY'RE GUILTY BEFORE WE HOLD THEM RESPONSIBLE.
BUT THEY'RE ALREADY GUILTY, STEWART! IF VOZ HADN'T LET THEM OUT, WE WOULDN'T HAVE TO WASTE OUR TIME CHASING THEM ACROSS THE UNIVERSE.
OA WAS MOMENTS FROM EXPLODING. IT WOULD HAVE BEEN HEARTLESS TO LEAVE THEM--
THOSE SCUMSUCKERS DESERVE TO DIE, FATALITY. SO DOES ANYONE WITH A LANTERN'S BLOOD ON HER HANDS.
I'M ONLY GOING TO SAY THIS ONCE, VATH...
THE FATALITY WHO HUNTED DOWN LANTERNS IS GONE. IF YOU THREATEN YRRA AGAIN, I'LL GIVE YOU ANOTHER SCAR.
NOW LET'S FOCUS--

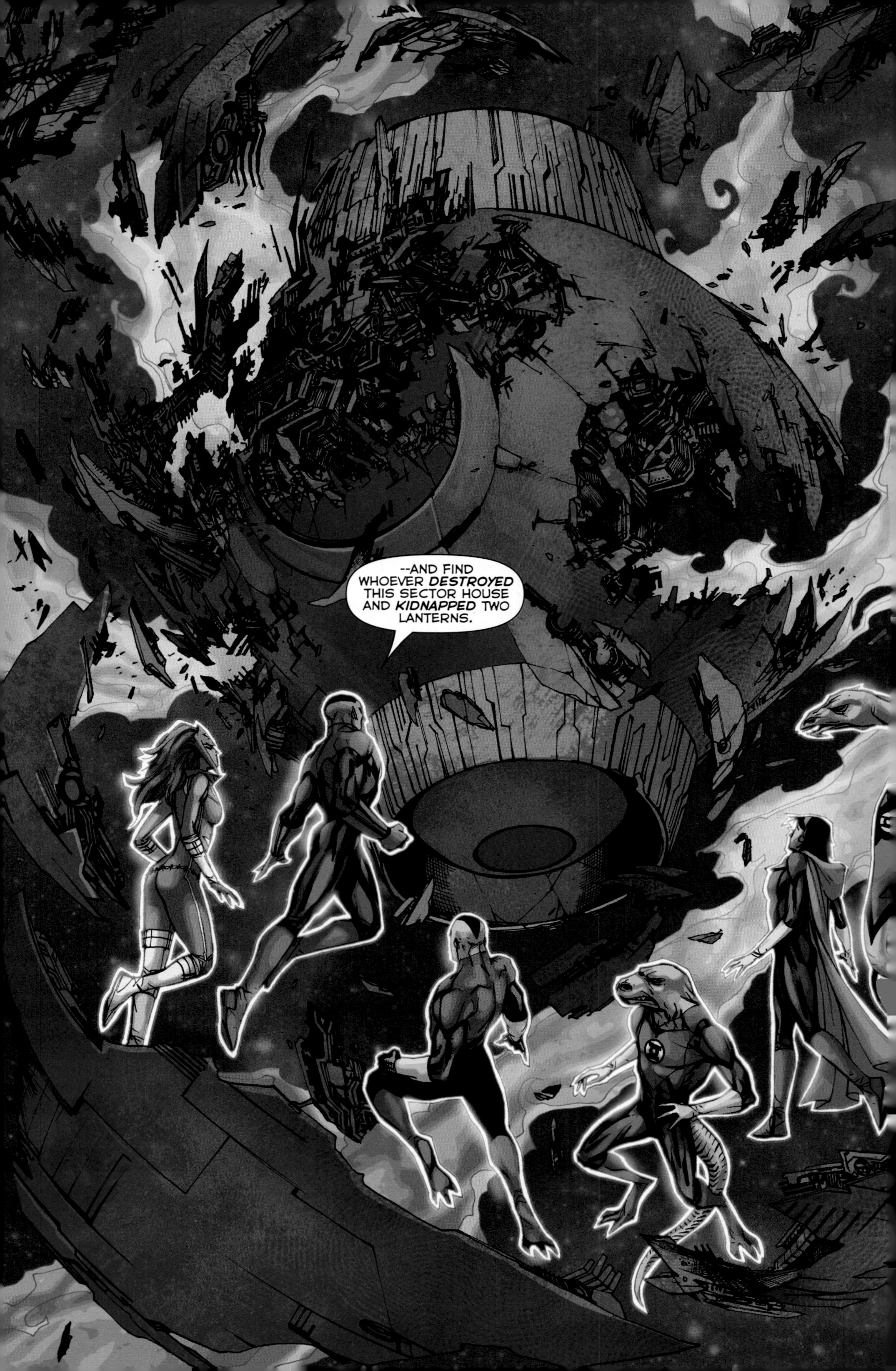
--AND FIND WHOEVER DESTROYED THIS SECTOR HOUSE AND KIDNAPPED TWO LANTERNS.

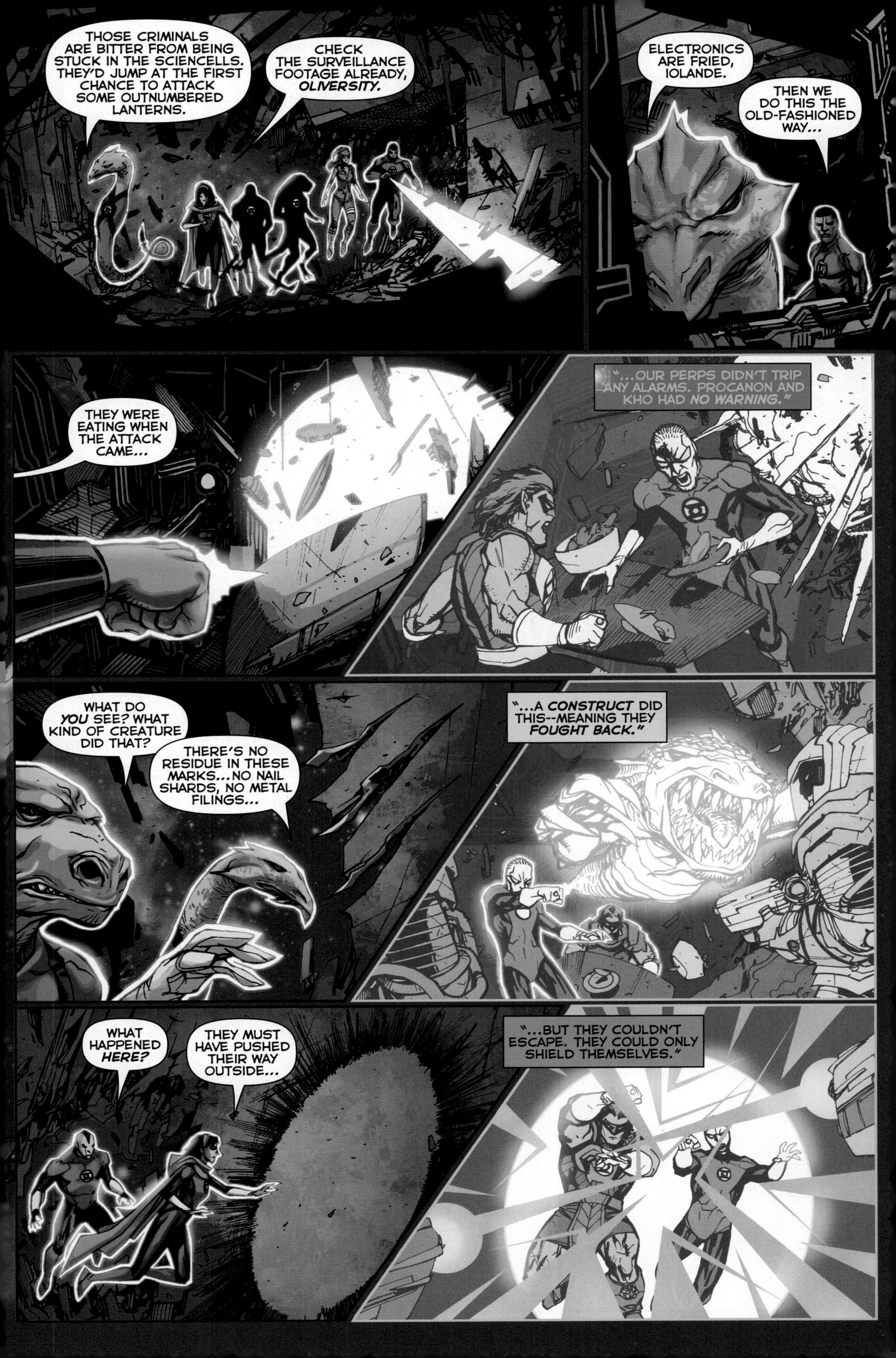
THOSE CRIMINALS ARE BITTER FROM BEING STUCK IN THE SCIENCELLS. THEY'D JUMP AT THE FIRST CHANCE TO ATTACK SOME OUTNUMBERED LANTERNS.
CHECK THE SURVEILLANCE FOOTAGE ALREADY, OLIVERSITY.
ELECTRONICS ARE FRIED, IOLANDE.
THEN WE DO THIS THE OLD-FASHIONED WAY...
THEY WERE EATING WHEN THE ATTACK CAME...
"...OUR PERPS DIDN'T TRIP ANY ALARMS. PROCANON AND KHO HAD NO WARNING."
WHAT DO YOU SEE? WHAT KIND OF CREATURE DID THAT?
THERE'S NO RESIDUE IN THESE MARKS...NO NAIL SHARDS, NO METAL FILINGS...
"...A CONSTRUCT DID THIS--MEANING THEY FOUGHT BACK."
WHAT HAPPENED HERE?
THEY MUST HAVE PUSHED THEIR WAY OUTSIDE...
"...BUT THEY COULDN'T ESCAPE. THEY COULD ONLY SHIELD THEMSELVES."

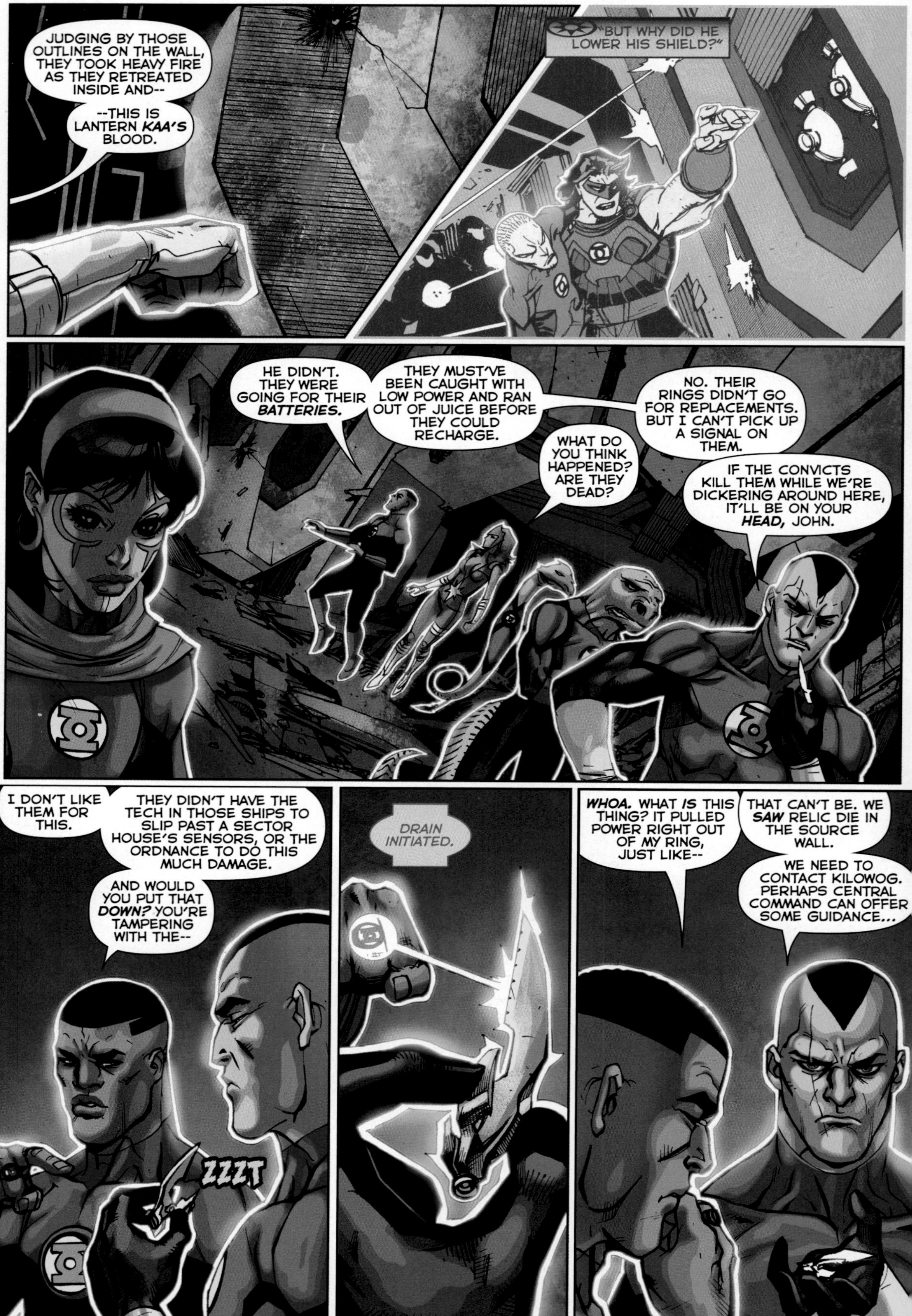
JUDGING BY THOSE OUTLINES ON THE WALL, THEY TOOK HEAVY FIRE AS THEY RETREATED INSIDE AND--
--THIS IS LANTERN KAA'S BLOOD.
"BUT WHY DID HE LOWER HIS SHIELD?"
HE DIDN'T. THEY WERE GOING FOR THEIR BATTERIES.
THEY MUST'VE BEEN CAUGHT WITH LOW POWER AND RAN OUT OF JUICE BEFORE THEY COULD RECHARGE.
NO. THEIR RINGS DIDN'T GO FOR REPLACEMENTS. BUT I CAN'T PICK UP A SIGNAL ON THEM.
WHAT DO YOU THINK HAPPENED? ARE THEY DEAD?
IF THE CONVICTS KILL THEM WHILE WE'RE DICKERING AROUND HERE, IT'LL BE ON YOUR HEAD, JOHN.
I DON'T LIKE THEM FOR THIS.
THEY DIDN'T HAVE THE TECH IN THOSE SHIPS TO SLIP PAST A SECTOR HOUSE'S SENSORS, OR THE ORDNANCE TO DO THIS MUCH DAMAGE.
AND WOULD YOU PUT THAT DOWN? YOU'RE TAMPERING WITH THE--
ZZZT
DRAIN INITIATED.
WHOA. WHAT IS THIS THING? IT PULLED POWER RIGHT OUT OF MY RING, JUST LIKE--
THAT CAN'T BE. WE SAW RELIC DIE IN THE SOURCE WALL.
WE NEED TO CONTACT KILOWOG. PERHAPS CENTRAL COMMAND CAN OFFER SOME GUIDANCE...

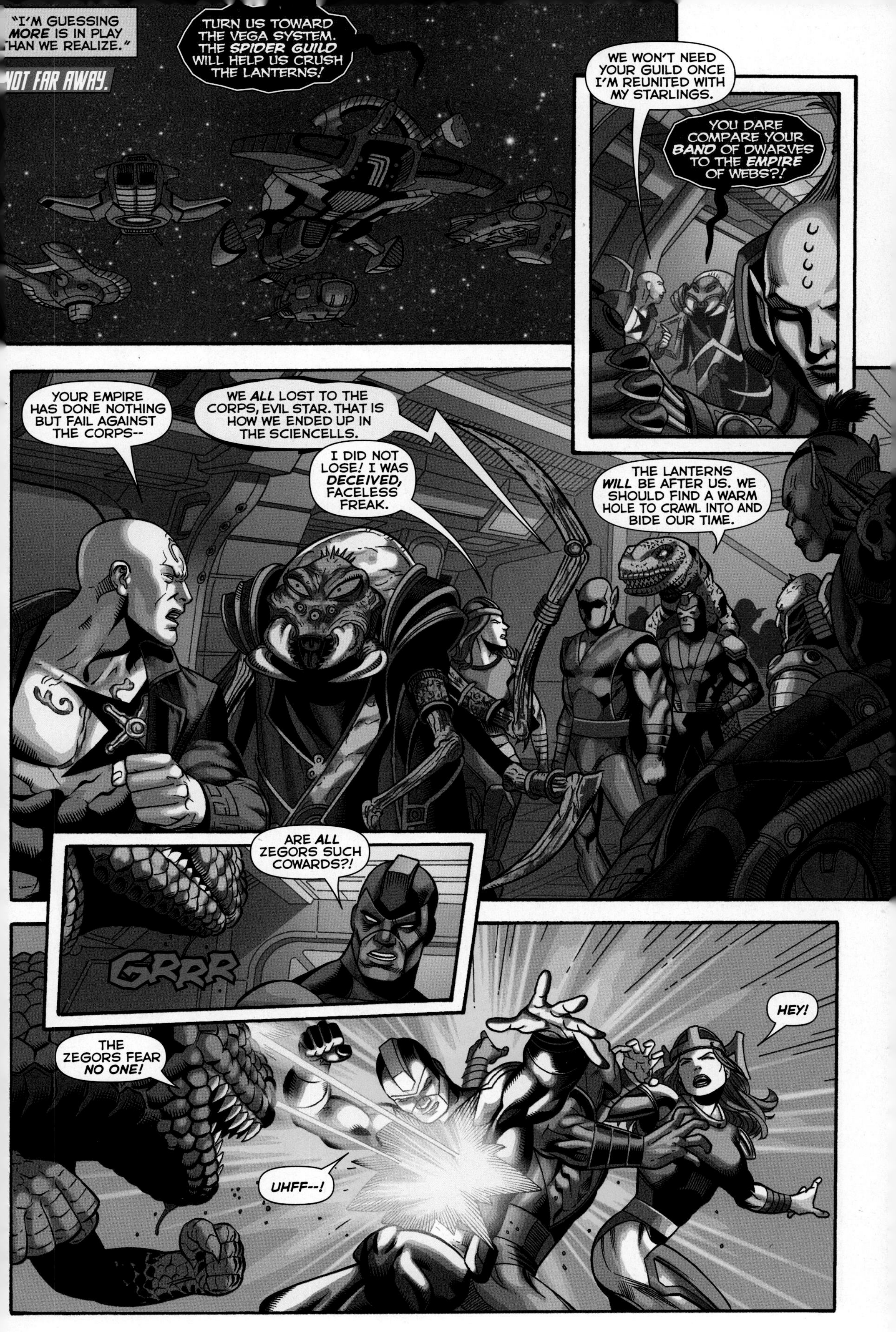

"I'M GUESSING MORE IS IN PLAY THAN WE REALIZE."
NOT FAR AWAY.
TURN US TOWARD THE VEGA SYSTEM. THE SPIDER GUILD WILL HELP US CRUSH THE LANTERNS!
WE WON'T NEED YOUR GUILD ONCE I'M REUNITED WITH MY STARLINGS.
YOU DARE COMPARE YOUR BAND OF DWARVES TO THE EMPIRE OF WEBS?!
YOUR EMPIRE HAS DONE NOTHING BUT FAIL AGAINST THE CORPS--
WE ALL LOST TO THE CORPS, EVIL STAR. THAT IS HOW WE ENDED UP IN THE SCIENCELLS.
I DID NOT LOSE! I WAS DECEIVED, FACELESS FREAK.
THE LANTERNS WILL BE AFTER US. WE SHOULD FIND A WARM HOLE TO CRAWL INTO AND BIDE OUR TIME.
ARE ALL ZEGORS SUCH COWARDS?!
GRRR
THE ZEGORS FEAR NO ONE!
HEY!
UHFF--!

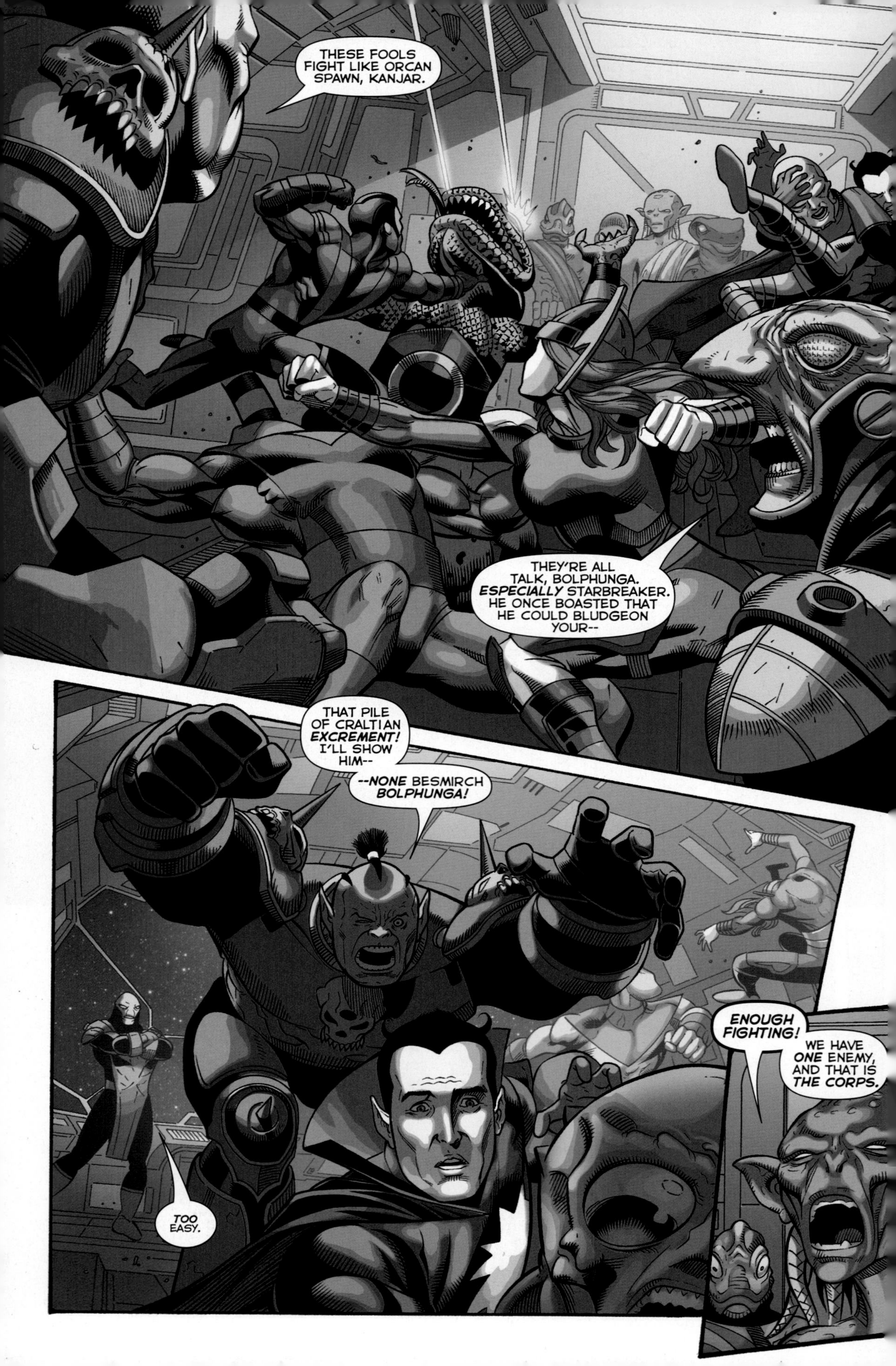

THESE FOOLS FIGHT LIKE ORCAN SPAWN, KANJAR.
THEY'RE ALL TALK, BOLPHUNGA. *ESPECIALLY* STARBREAKER. HE ONCE BOASTED THAT HE COULD BLUDGEON YOUR--
THAT PILE OF CRALTIAN *EXCREMENT!* I'LL SHOW HIM--
--*NONE* BESMIRCH *BOLPHUNGA!*
TOO EASY.
ENOUGH FIGHTING!
WE HAVE *ONE* ENEMY, AND THAT IS *THE CORPS.*

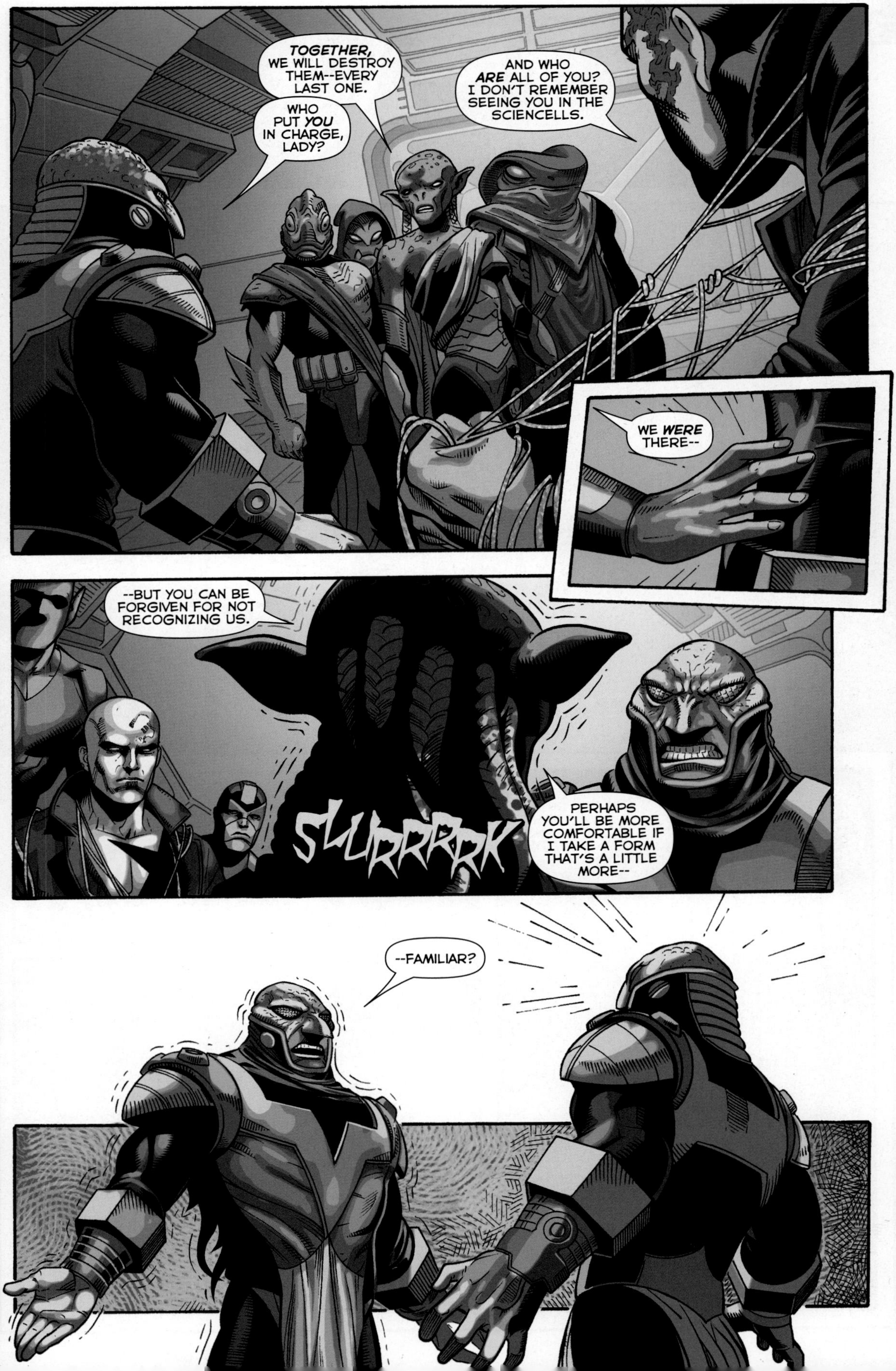
TOGETHER, WE WILL DESTROY THEM--EVERY LAST ONE.
WHO PUT YOU IN CHARGE, LADY?
AND WHO ARE ALL OF YOU? I DON'T REMEMBER SEEING YOU IN THE SCIENCELLS.
WE WERE THERE--
--BUT YOU CAN BE FORGIVEN FOR NOT RECOGNIZING US.
SLURRRRK
PERHAPS YOU'LL BE MORE COMFORTABLE IF I TAKE A FORM THAT'S A LITTLE MORE--
--FAMILIAR?

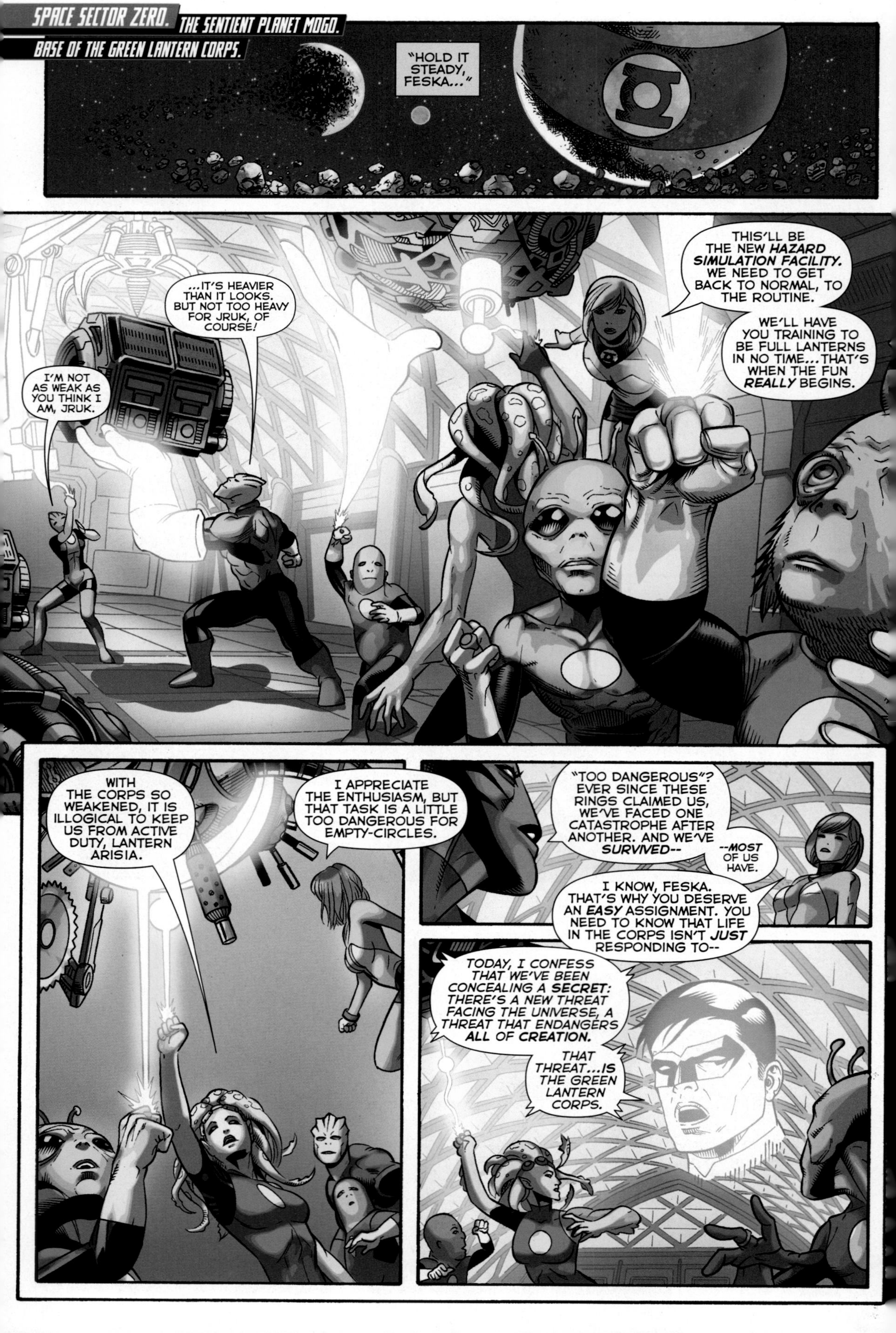

SPACE SECTOR ZERO.
THE SENTIENT PLANET MOGO.
BASE OF THE GREEN LANTERN CORPS.
"HOLD IT STEADY, FESKA..."
I'M NOT AS WEAK AS YOU THINK I AM, JRUK.
...IT'S HEAVIER THAN IT LOOKS. BUT NOT TOO HEAVY FOR JRUK, OF COURSE!
THIS'LL BE THE NEW HAZARD SIMULATION FACILITY. WE NEED TO GET BACK TO NORMAL, TO THE ROUTINE.
WE'LL HAVE YOU TRAINING TO BE FULL LANTERNS IN NO TIME...THAT'S WHEN THE FUN REALLY BEGINS.
WITH THE CORPS SO WEAKENED, IT IS ILLOGICAL TO KEEP US FROM ACTIVE DUTY, LANTERN ARISIA.
I APPRECIATE THE ENTHUSIASM, BUT THAT TASK IS A LITTLE TOO DANGEROUS FOR EMPTY-CIRCLES.
"TOO DANGEROUS"? EVER SINCE THESE RINGS CLAIMED US, WE'VE FACED ONE CATASTROPHE AFTER ANOTHER. AND WE'VE SURVIVED--
--MOST OF US HAVE.
I KNOW, FESKA. THAT'S WHY YOU DESERVE AN EASY ASSIGNMENT. YOU NEED TO KNOW THAT LIFE IN THE CORPS ISN'T JUST RESPONDING TO--
TODAY, I CONFESS THAT WE'VE BEEN CONCEALING A SECRET: THERE'S A NEW THREAT FACING THE UNIVERSE, A THREAT THAT ENDANGERS ALL OF CREATION.
THAT THREAT...IS THE GREEN LANTERN CORPS.

IT WAS RECENTLY PROVEN THAT THE EMOTIONAL SPECTRUM CHANNELED THROUGH OUR RINGS ORIGINATES FROM A *RESERVOIR.*

THIS RESERVOIR CONTAINS A FINITE AMOUNT OF ENERGY. WHEN THAT ENERGY IS EXHAUSTED, THE UNIVERSE ENDS.

WHAT IS HAL *DOING?!* RING: WHERE IS THIS TRANSMISSION BEING BROADCAST?

LANTERN JORDAN OPENED HE TRANSMISSION TO ALL SECTORS.

WAIT...

"MY *FAMILY'S* HEARING THIS?"

SPACE SECTOR 2525. THE SLUMS OF ZAROX.

IF YOU THINK THAT MEANS THE GREEN LANTERN CORPS WILL CEASE USING THE MOST POWERFUL WEAPONS IN THE UNIVERSE--

--YOU'RE WRONG.

GRANDMA, DOES THIS MEAN MOM IS...BAD?

SPACE SECTOR 0082. HE BLOOD BOWL OF ORANX.

SEE? WE CHOSE WISELY IN ALLYING WITH THE KHUND AGAINST THE LANTERNS!

WE'VE DEEMED THE DRAINING OF THE EMOTIONAL SPECTRUM TO BE A *NECESSARY* COST, WHETHER IT HARMS ALL OF YOU OR NOT.

WE WILL, HOWEVER, LESSEN THE COST BY TAKING DOWN *ANYONE* WHO WIELDS A RING AND ISN'T AN OFFICER OF THE CORPS.

SPACE SECTOR 1632. THE ORATORIUM OF RHOON.

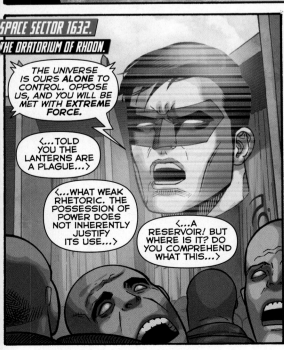

THE UNIVERSE IS OURS ALONE TO CONTROL. OPPOSE US, AND YOU WILL BE MET WITH *EXTREME* FORCE.

‹...TOLD YOU THE LANTERNS ARE A PLAGUE...›

‹...WHAT WEAK RHETORIC. THE POSSESSION OF POWER DOES NOT INHERENTLY JUSTIFY ITS USE...›

‹...A RESERVOIR! BUT WHERE IS IT? DO YOU COMPREHEND WHAT THIS...›

SPACE SECTOR 0422.

THE *NEW* ERA OF THE CORPS STARTS NOW. YOU HAVE BEEN WARNED.

HAS HE LOST HIS *MIND?!* EVERY CIVILIZATION IN THE UNIVERSE WILL *DESPISE* US.

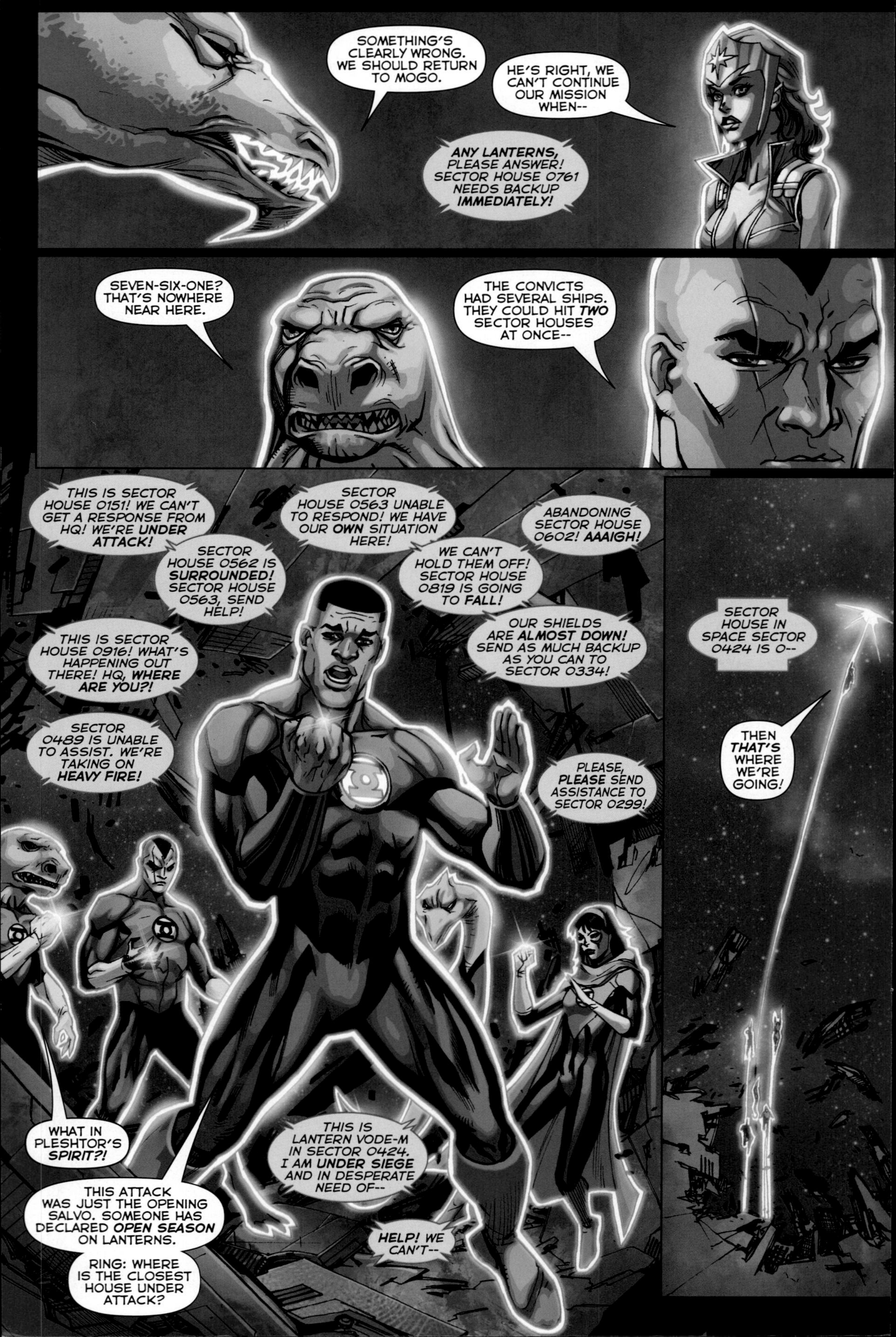
SOMETHING'S CLEARLY WRONG. WE SHOULD RETURN TO MOGO.
HE'S RIGHT, WE CAN'T CONTINUE OUR MISSION WHEN--
ANY LANTERNS, PLEASE ANSWER! SECTOR HOUSE 0761 NEEDS BACKUP IMMEDIATELY!
SEVEN-SIX-ONE? THAT'S NOWHERE NEAR HERE.
THE CONVICTS HAD SEVERAL SHIPS. THEY COULD HIT TWO SECTOR HOUSES AT ONCE--
THIS IS SECTOR HOUSE 0151! WE CAN'T GET A RESPONSE FROM HQ! WE'RE UNDER ATTACK!
SECTOR HOUSE 0563 UNABLE TO RESPOND! WE HAVE OUR OWN SITUATION HERE!
ABANDONING SECTOR HOUSE 0602! AAAIGH!
SECTOR HOUSE 0562 IS SURROUNDED! SECTOR HOUSE 0563, SEND HELP!
WE CAN'T HOLD THEM OFF! SECTOR HOUSE 0819 IS GOING TO FALL!
THIS IS SECTOR HOUSE 0916! WHAT'S HAPPENING OUT THERE! HQ, WHERE ARE YOU?!
OUR SHIELDS ARE ALMOST DOWN! SEND AS MUCH BACKUP AS YOU CAN TO SECTOR 0334!
SECTOR 0489 IS UNABLE TO ASSIST. WE'RE TAKING ON HEAVY FIRE!
PLEASE, PLEASE SEND ASSISTANCE TO SECTOR 0299!
WHAT IN PLESHTOR'S SPIRIT?!
THIS IS LANTERN VODE-M IN SECTOR 0424. I AM UNDER SIEGE AND IN DESPERATE NEED OF--
THIS ATTACK WAS JUST THE OPENING SALVO. SOMEONE HAS DECLARED OPEN SEASON ON LANTERNS.
RING: WHERE IS THE CLOSEST HOUSE UNDER ATTACK?
HELP! WE CAN'T--
SECTOR HOUSE IN SPACE SECTOR 0424 IS O--
THEN THAT'S WHERE WE'RE GOING!

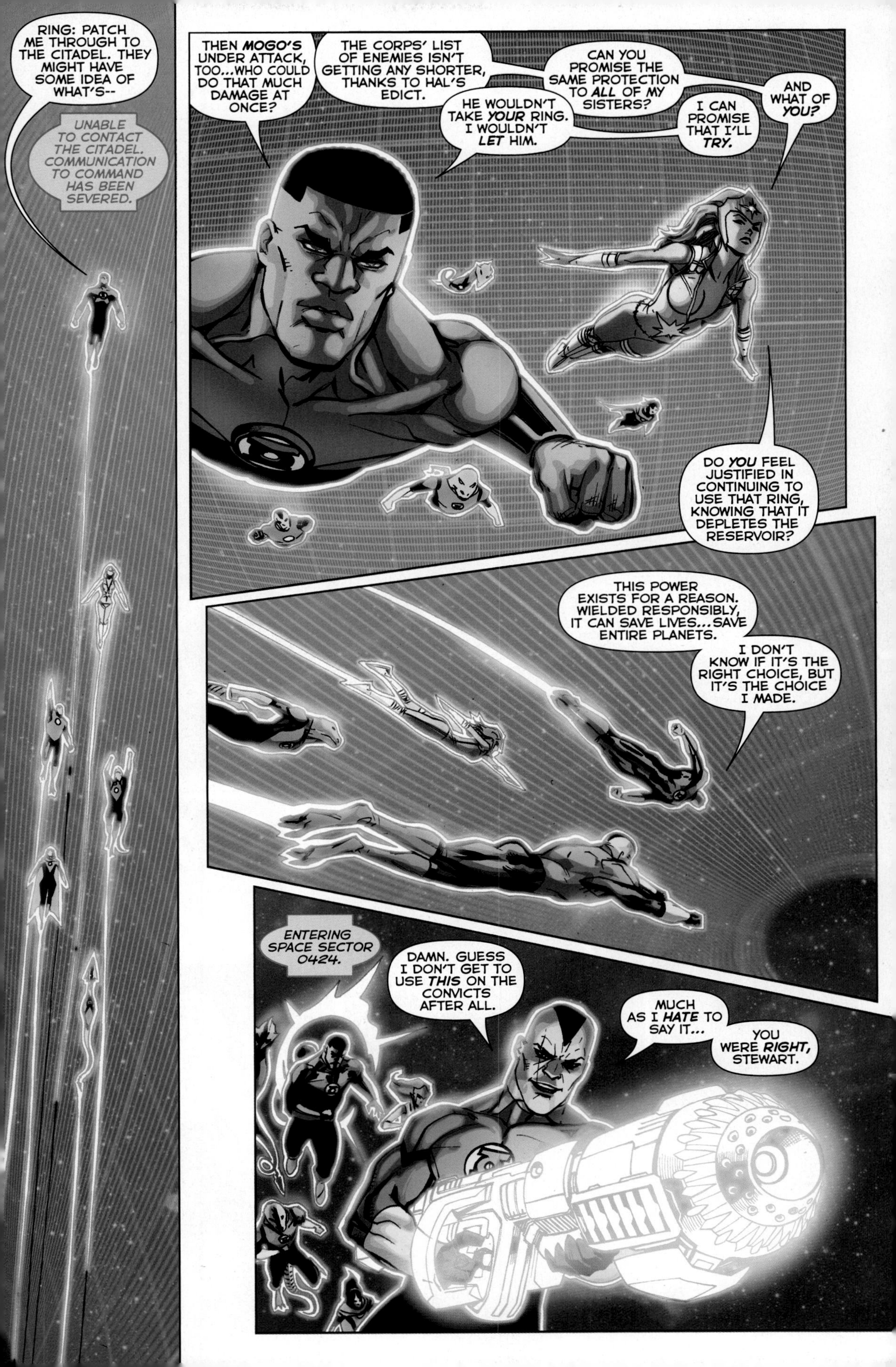
RING: PATCH ME THROUGH TO THE CITADEL. THEY MIGHT HAVE SOME IDEA OF WHAT'S--
UNABLE TO CONTACT THE CITADEL. COMMUNICATION TO COMMAND HAS BEEN SEVERED.
THEN MOGO'S UNDER ATTACK, TOO...WHO COULD DO THAT MUCH DAMAGE AT ONCE?
THE CORPS' LIST OF ENEMIES ISN'T GETTING ANY SHORTER, THANKS TO HAL'S EDICT.
CAN YOU PROMISE THE SAME PROTECTION TO ALL OF MY SISTERS?
HE WOULDN'T TAKE YOUR RING. I WOULDN'T LET HIM.
I CAN PROMISE THAT I'LL TRY.
AND WHAT OF YOU?
DO YOU FEEL JUSTIFIED IN CONTINUING TO USE THAT RING, KNOWING THAT IT DEPLETES THE RESERVOIR?
THIS POWER EXISTS FOR A REASON. WIELDED RESPONSIBLY, IT CAN SAVE LIVES...SAVE ENTIRE PLANETS.
I DON'T KNOW IF IT'S THE RIGHT CHOICE, BUT IT'S THE CHOICE I MADE.
ENTERING SPACE SECTOR 0424.
DAMN. GUESS I DON'T GET TO USE THIS ON THE CONVICTS AFTER ALL.
MUCH AS I HATE TO SAY IT...
YOU WERE RIGHT, STEWART.

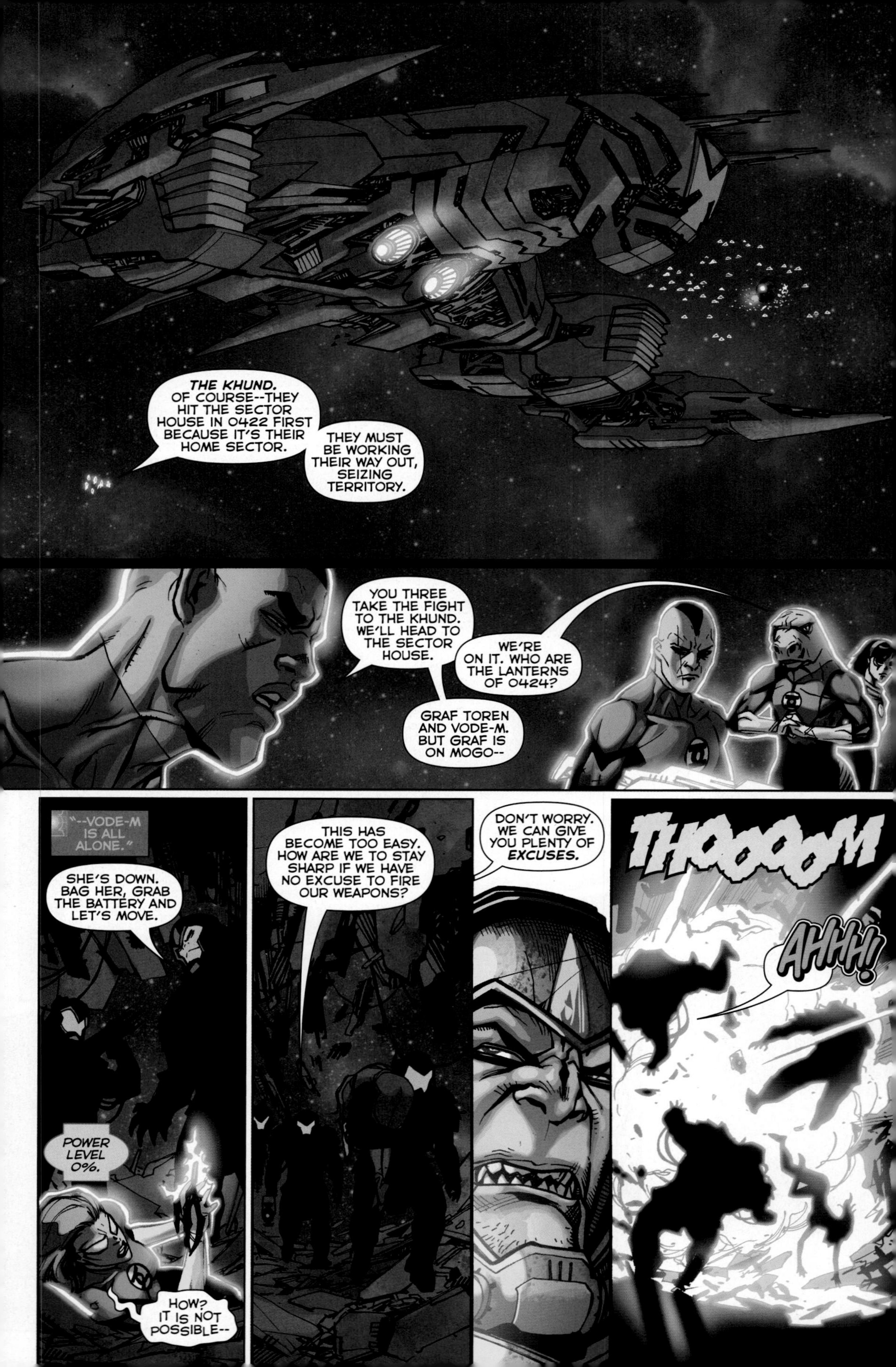

THE KHUND. OF COURSE--THEY HIT THE SECTOR HOUSE IN 0422 FIRST BECAUSE IT'S THEIR HOME SECTOR.
THEY MUST BE WORKING THEIR WAY OUT, SEIZING TERRITORY.
YOU THREE TAKE THE FIGHT TO THE KHUND. WE'LL HEAD TO THE SECTOR HOUSE.
WE'RE ON IT. WHO ARE THE LANTERNS OF 0424?
GRAF TOREN AND VODE-M. BUT GRAF IS ON MOGO--
"--VODE-M IS ALL ALONE."
SHE'S DOWN. BAG HER, GRAB THE BATTERY AND LET'S MOVE.
POWER LEVEL 0%.
HOW? IT IS NOT POSSIBLE--
THIS HAS BECOME TOO EASY. HOW ARE WE TO STAY SHARP IF WE HAVE NO EXCUSE TO FIRE OUR WEAPONS?
DON'T WORRY. WE CAN GIVE YOU PLENTY OF EXCUSES.
THOOOOM
AHHH!

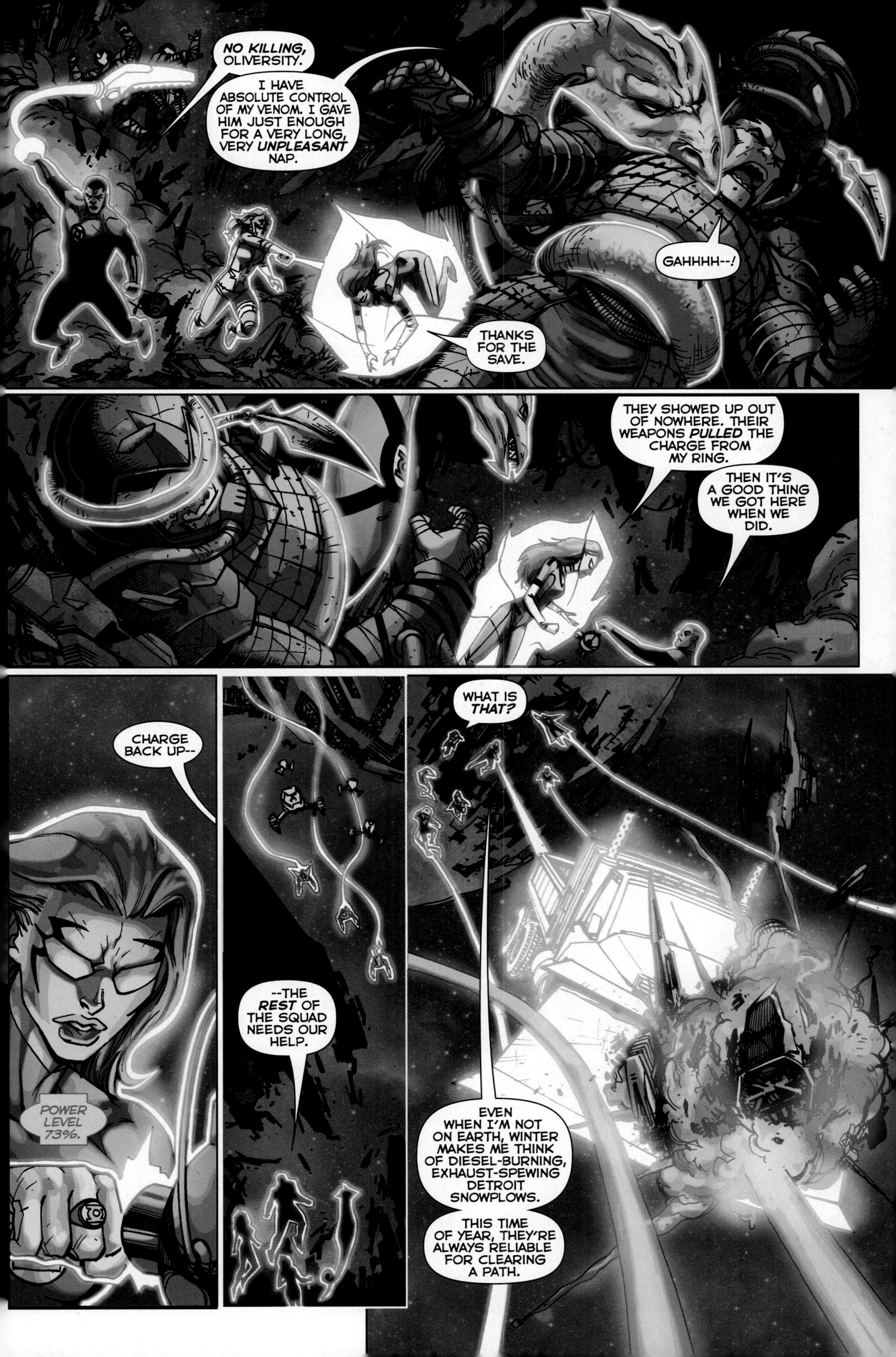
NO KILLING, OLIVERSITY.
I HAVE ABSOLUTE CONTROL OF MY VENOM. I GAVE HIM JUST ENOUGH FOR A VERY LONG, VERY UNPLEASANT NAP.
GAHHHH--!
THANKS FOR THE SAVE.
THEY SHOWED UP OUT OF NOWHERE. THEIR WEAPONS PULLED THE CHARGE FROM MY RING.
THEN IT'S A GOOD THING WE GOT HERE WHEN WE DID.
CHARGE BACK UP--
POWER LEVEL 73%.
--THE REST OF THE SQUAD NEEDS OUR HELP.
WHAT IS THAT?
EVEN WHEN I'M NOT ON EARTH, WINTER MAKES ME THINK OF DIESEL-BURNING, EXHAUST-SPEWING DETROIT SNOWPLOWS.
THIS TIME OF YEAR, THEY'RE ALWAYS RELIABLE FOR CLEARING A PATH.

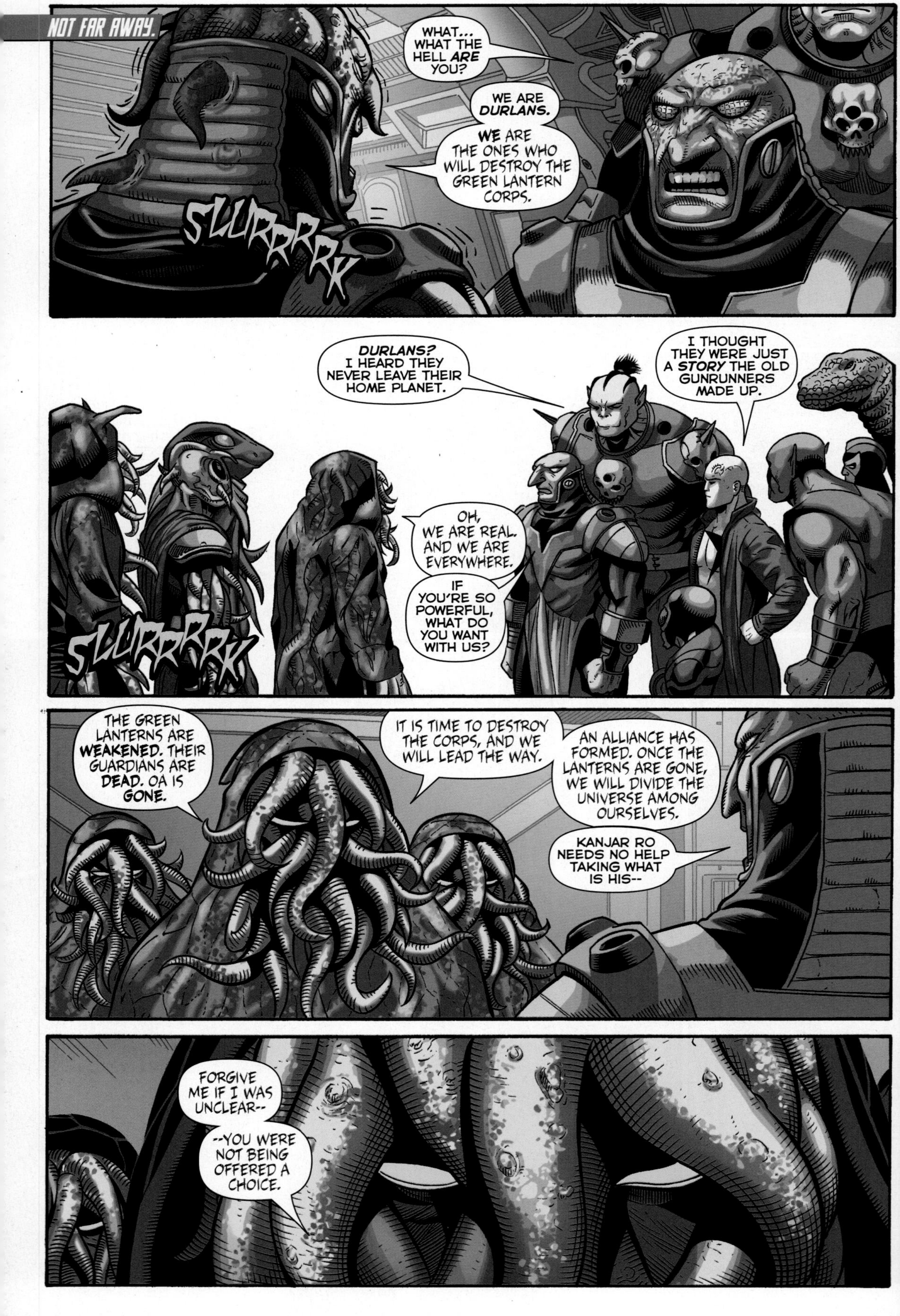
NOT FAR AWAY.
WHAT... WHAT THE HELL ARE YOU?
WE ARE DURLANS.
WE ARE THE ONES WHO WILL DESTROY THE GREEN LANTERN CORPS.
SLURRRRK
DURLANS? I HEARD THEY NEVER LEAVE THEIR HOME PLANET.
I THOUGHT THEY WERE JUST A STORY THE OLD GUNRUNNERS MADE UP.
OH, WE ARE REAL. AND WE ARE EVERYWHERE.
IF YOU'RE SO POWERFUL, WHAT DO YOU WANT WITH US?
SLURRRRK
THE GREEN LANTERNS ARE WEAKENED. THEIR GUARDIANS ARE DEAD. OA IS GONE.
IT IS TIME TO DESTROY THE CORPS, AND WE WILL LEAD THE WAY.
AN ALLIANCE HAS FORMED. ONCE THE LANTERNS ARE GONE, WE WILL DIVIDE THE UNIVERSE AMONG OURSELVES.
KANJAR RO NEEDS NO HELP TAKING WHAT IS HIS--
FORGIVE ME IF I WAS UNCLEAR--
--YOU WERE NOT BEING OFFERED A CHOICE.

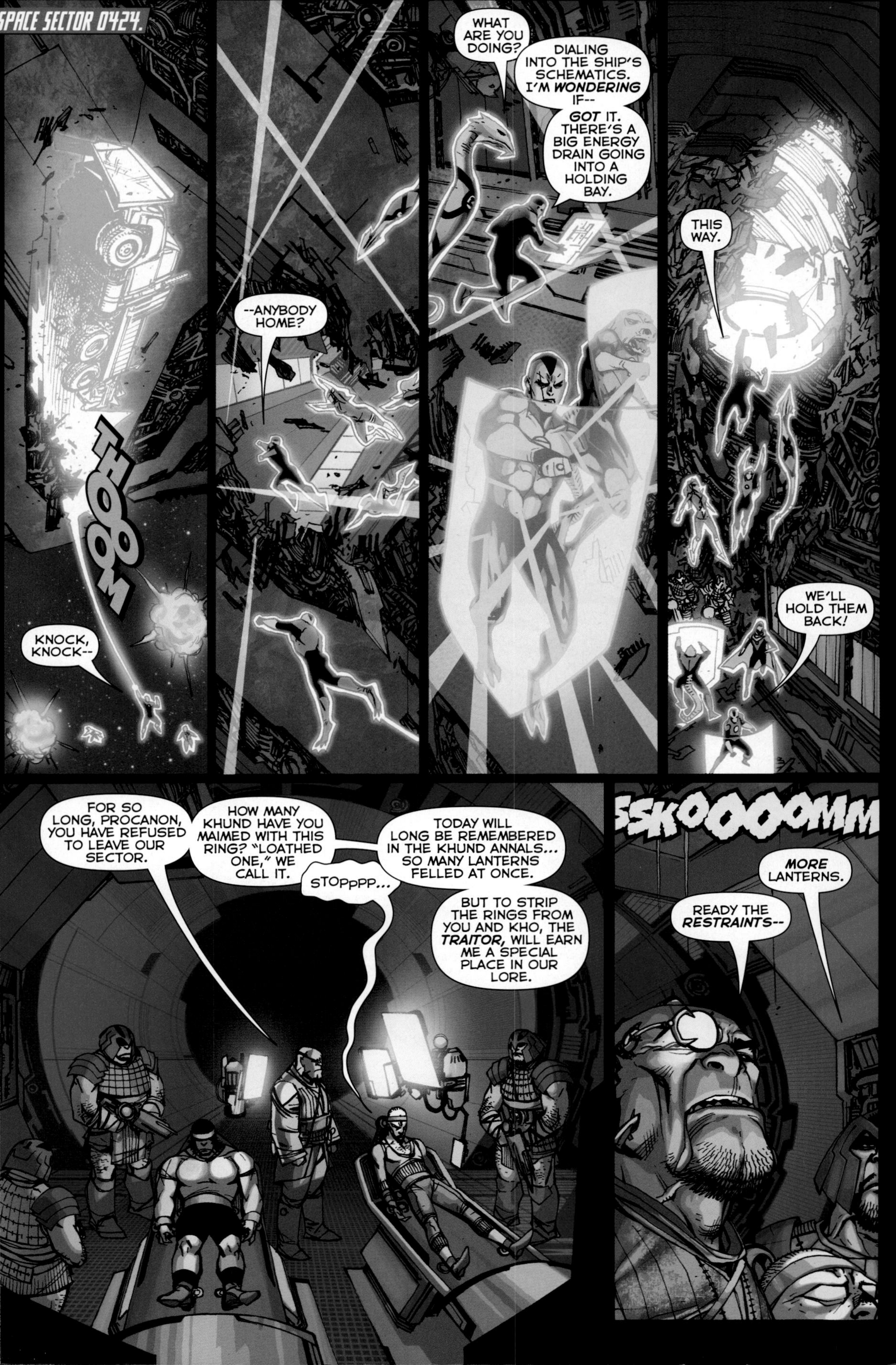
SPACE SECTOR 0424.
THOOOOM
KNOCK, KNOCK--
--ANYBODY HOME?
WHAT ARE YOU DOING?
DIALING INTO THE SHIP'S SCHEMATICS. I'M WONDERING IF--
GOT IT. THERE'S A BIG ENERGY DRAIN GOING INTO A HOLDING BAY.
THIS WAY.
WE'LL HOLD THEM BACK!
FOR SO LONG, PROCANON, YOU HAVE REFUSED TO LEAVE OUR SECTOR.
HOW MANY KHUND HAVE YOU MAIMED WITH THIS RING? "LOATHED ONE," WE CALL IT.
STOPPPP...
TODAY WILL LONG BE REMEMBERED IN THE KHUND ANNALS... SO MANY LANTERNS FELLED AT ONCE.
BUT TO STRIP THE RINGS FROM YOU AND KHO, THE TRAITOR, WILL EARN ME A SPECIAL PLACE IN OUR LORE.
SSKOOOOOMM
MORE LANTERNS.
READY THE RESTRAINTS--

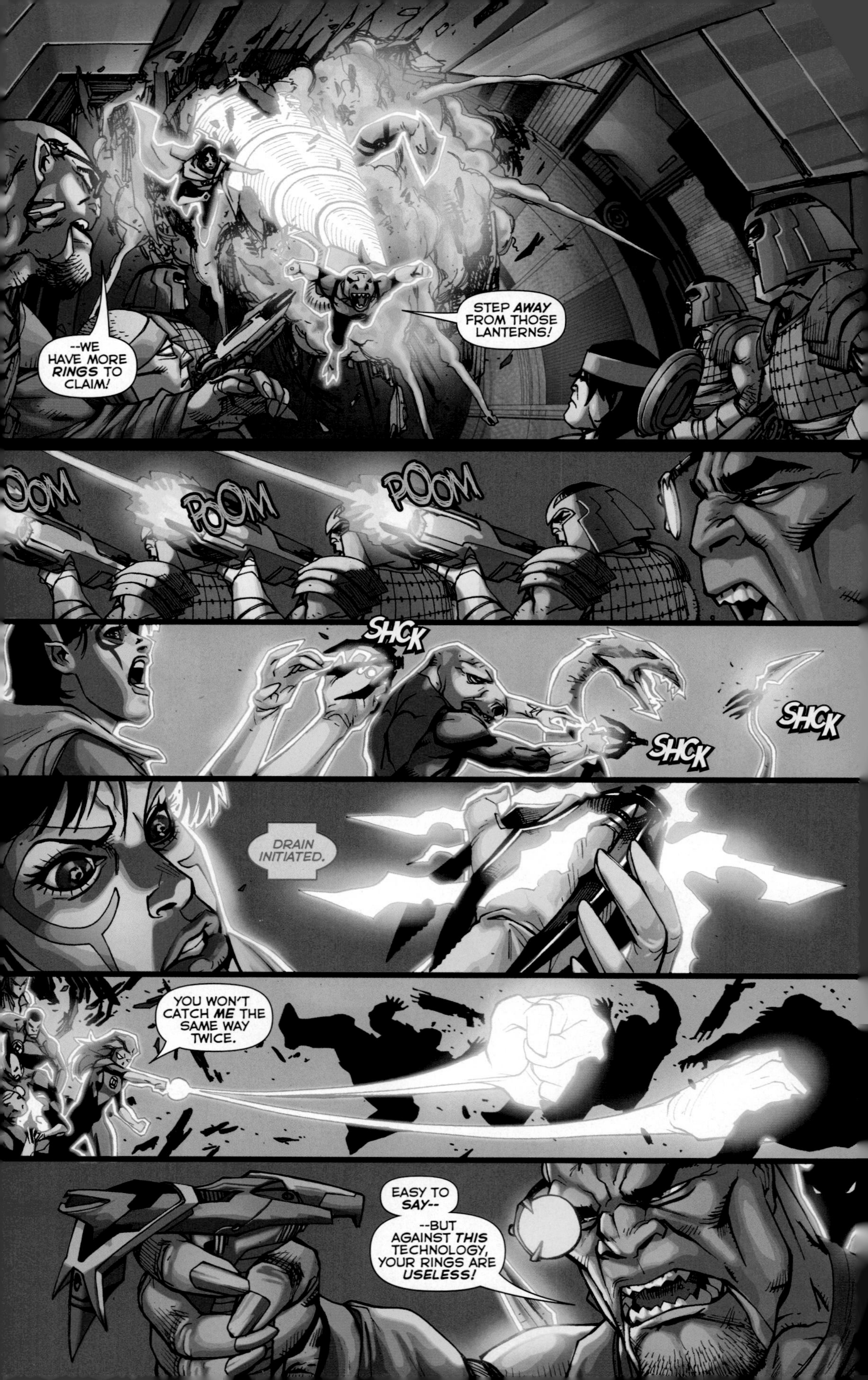
--WE HAVE MORE *RINGS* TO CLAIM!
STEP *AWAY* FROM THOSE LANTERNS!
POOM
POOM
POOM
SHCK
SHCK
SHCK
DRAIN INITIATED.
YOU WON'T CATCH *ME* THE SAME WAY TWICE.
EASY TO *SAY*--
--BUT AGAINST *THIS* TECHNOLOGY, YOUR RINGS ARE *USELESS!*

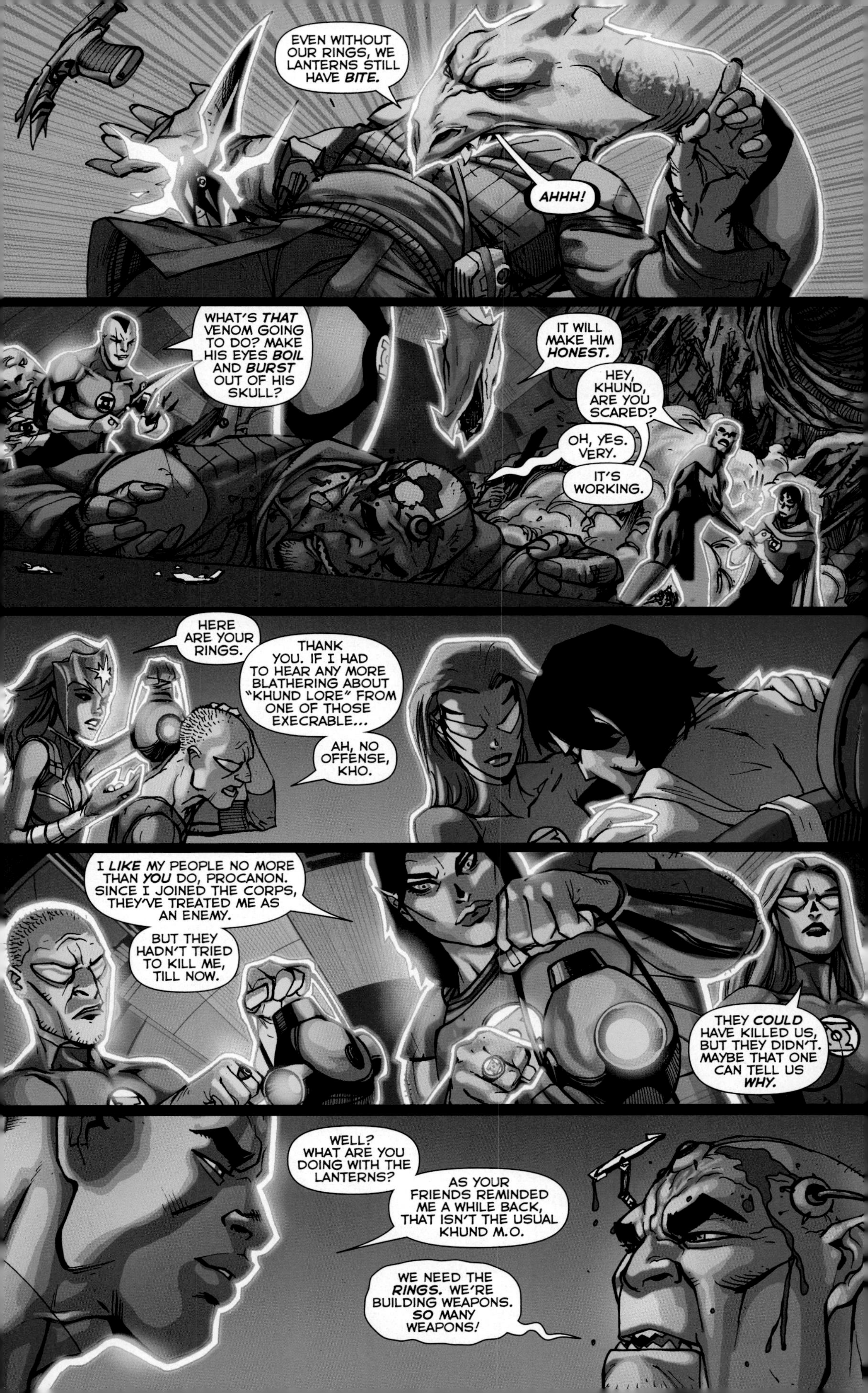
EVEN WITHOUT OUR RINGS, WE LANTERNS STILL HAVE BITE.
AHHH!
WHAT'S THAT VENOM GOING TO DO? MAKE HIS EYES BOIL AND BURST OUT OF HIS SKULL?
IT WILL MAKE HIM HONEST.
HEY, KHUND, ARE YOU SCARED?
OH, YES. VERY.
IT'S WORKING.
HERE ARE YOUR RINGS.
THANK YOU. IF I HAD TO HEAR ANY MORE BLATHERING ABOUT "KHUND LORE" FROM ONE OF THOSE EXECRABLE...
AH, NO OFFENSE, KHO.
I LIKE MY PEOPLE NO MORE THAN YOU DO, PROCANON. SINCE I JOINED THE CORPS, THEY'VE TREATED ME AS AN ENEMY.
BUT THEY HADN'T TRIED TO KILL ME, TILL NOW.
THEY COULD HAVE KILLED US, BUT THEY DIDN'T. MAYBE THAT ONE CAN TELL US WHY.
WELL? WHAT ARE YOU DOING WITH THE LANTERNS?
AS YOUR FRIENDS REMINDED ME A WHILE BACK, THAT ISN'T THE USUAL KHUND M.O.
WE NEED THE RINGS. WE'RE BUILDING WEAPONS. SO MANY WEAPONS!

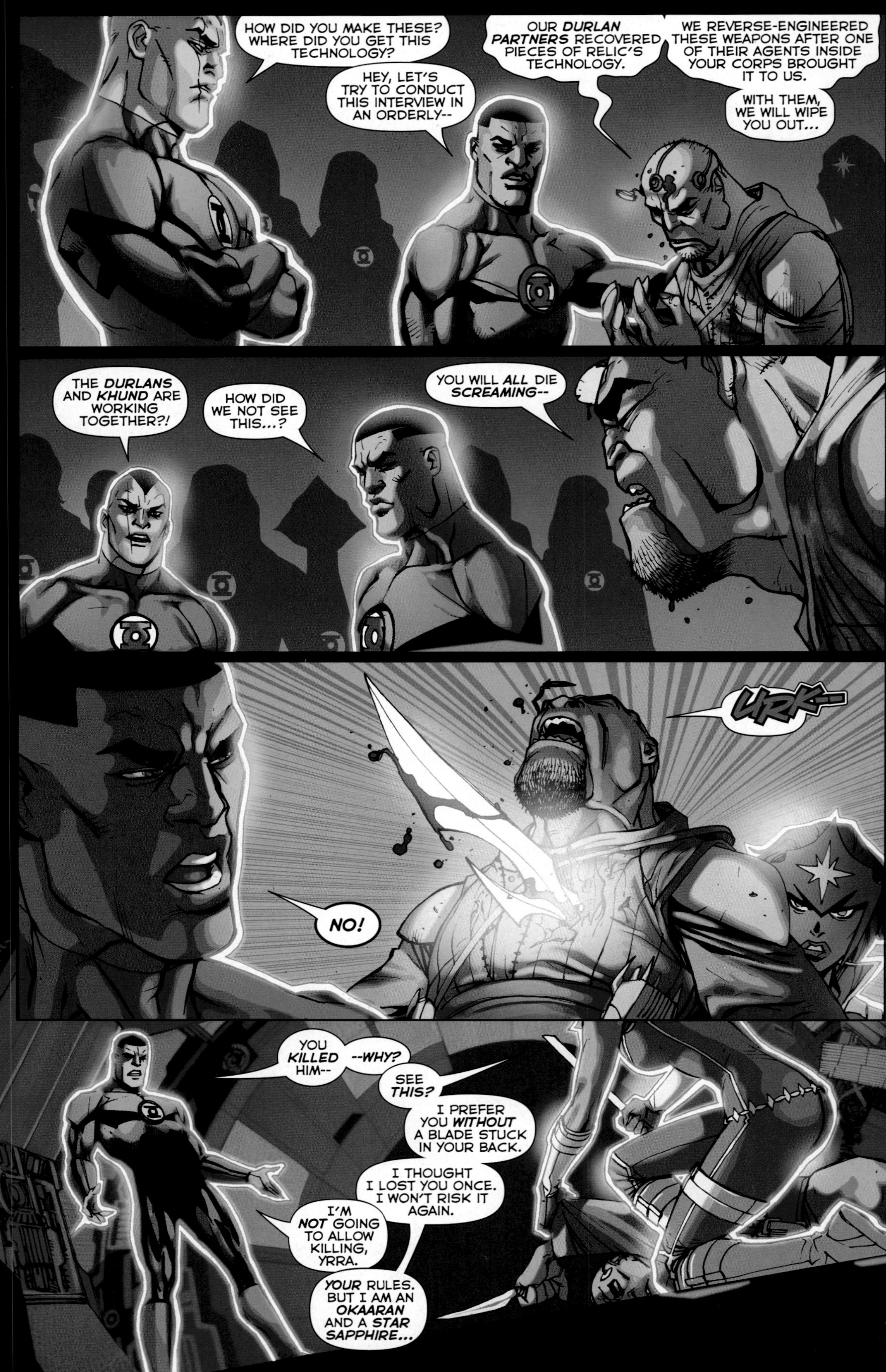
HOW DID YOU MAKE THESE? WHERE DID YOU GET THIS TECHNOLOGY?
HEY, LET'S TRY TO CONDUCT THIS INTERVIEW IN AN ORDERLY--
OUR DURLAN PARTNERS RECOVERED PIECES OF RELIC'S TECHNOLOGY.
WE REVERSE-ENGINEERED THESE WEAPONS AFTER ONE OF THEIR AGENTS INSIDE YOUR CORPS BROUGHT IT TO US.
WITH THEM, WE WILL WIPE YOU OUT...
THE DURLANS AND KHUND ARE WORKING TOGETHER?!
HOW DID WE NOT SEE THIS...?
YOU WILL ALL DIE SCREAMING--
URK--
NO!
YOU KILLED HIM--
--WHY?
SEE THIS?
I PREFER YOU WITHOUT A BLADE STUCK IN YOUR BACK.
I THOUGHT I LOST YOU ONCE. I WON'T RISK IT AGAIN.
I'M NOT GOING TO ALLOW KILLING, YRRA.
YOUR RULES. BUT I AM AN OKAARAN AND A STAR SAPPHIRE...

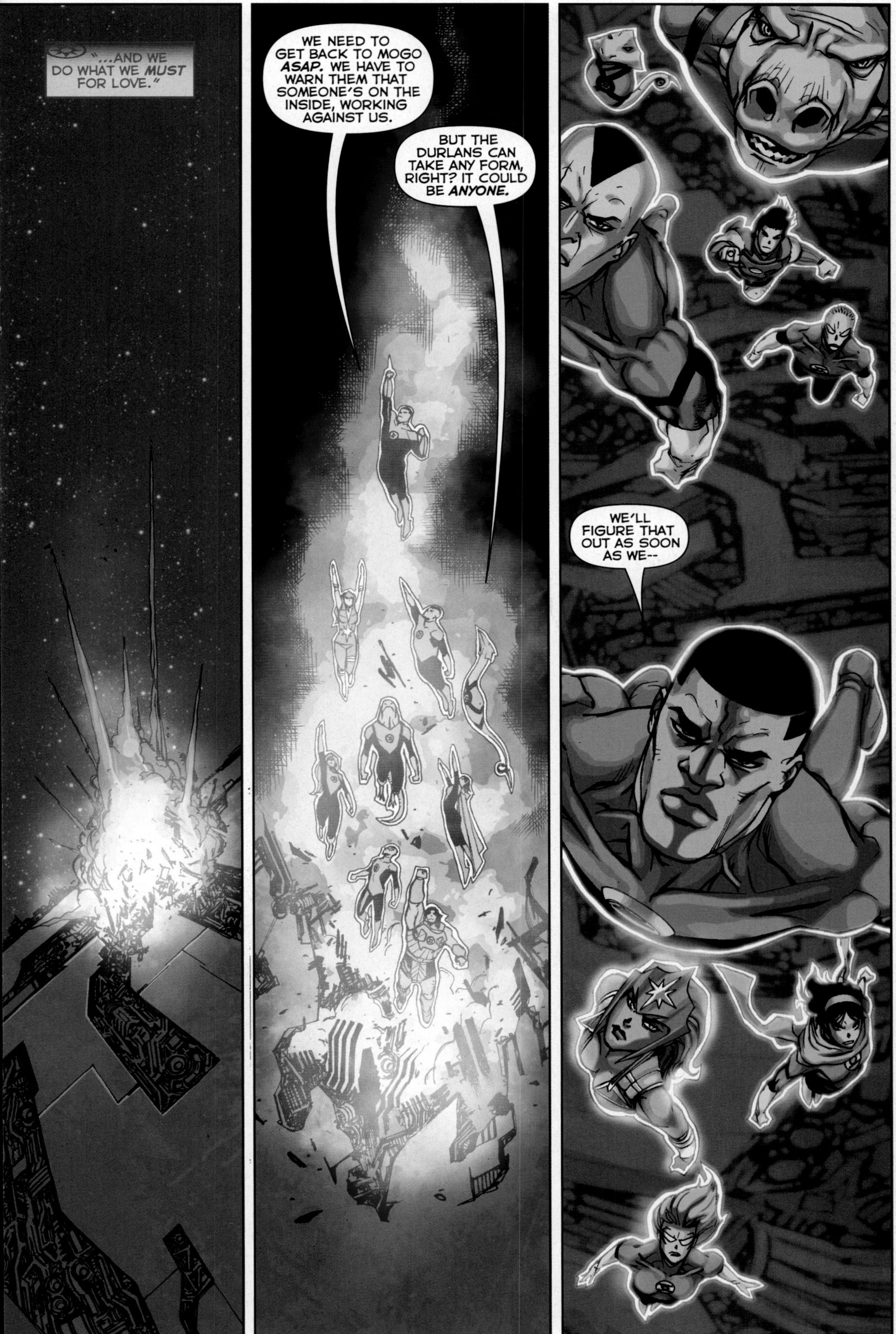
"...AND WE DO WHAT WE MUST FOR LOVE."
WE NEED TO GET BACK TO MOGO ASAP. WE HAVE TO WARN THEM THAT SOMEONE'S ON THE INSIDE, WORKING AGAINST US.
BUT THE DURLANS CAN TAKE ANY FORM, RIGHT? IT COULD BE ANYONE.
WE'LL FIGURE THAT OUT AS SOON AS WE--

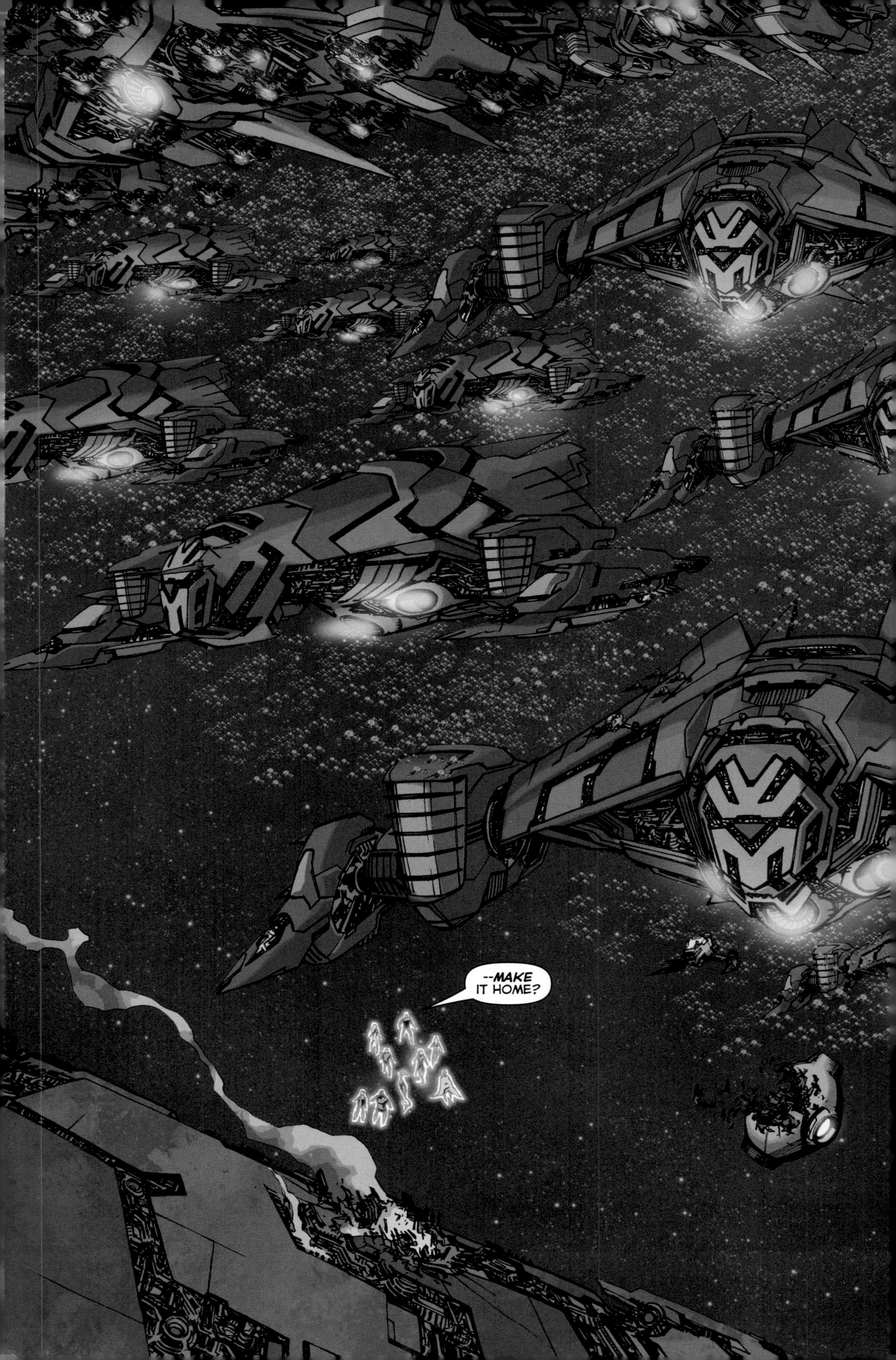
--MAKE IT HOME?